UNDERSTANDING CAREERS

SAGE was founded in 1965 by Sara Miller McCune to support the dissemination of usable knowledge by publishing innovative and high-quality research and teaching content. Today, we publish more than 750 journals, including those of more than 300 learned societies, more than 800 new books per year, and a growing range of library products including archives, data, case studies, reports, conference highlights, and video. SAGE remains majority-owned by our founder, and on her passing will become owned by a charitable trust that secures our continued independence.

Los Angeles | London | Washington DC | New Delhi | Singapore

Kerr Inkson • Nicky Dries • John Arnold

UNDERSTANDING CAREERS

second
edition

Los Angeles | London | New Delhi
Singapore | Washington DC

Los Angeles | London | New Delhi
Singapore | Washington DC

SAGE Publications Ltd
1 Oliver's Yard
55 City Road
London EC1Y 1SP

SAGE Publications Inc.
2455 Teller Road
Thousand Oaks, California 91320

SAGE Publications India Pvt Ltd
B 1/I 1 Mohan Cooperative Industrial Area
Mathura Road
New Delhi 110 044

SAGE Publications Asia-Pacific Pte Ltd
3 Church Street
#10-04 Samsung Hub
Singapore 049483

Editor: Kirsty Smy
Assistant editor: Nina Smith
Production editor: Nicola Marshall
Copyeditor: Sharon Cawood
Proofreader: Emily Ayers
Marketing manager: Alison Borg
Cover designer: Francis Kenney
Typeset by: C&M Digitals (P) Ltd, Chennai, India
Printed and bound by CPI Group (UK) Ltd,
Croydon, CR0 4YY

MIX
Paper from
responsible sources
FSC
www.fsc.org   FSC® C013604

© Kerr Inkson, Nicky Dries and John Arnold, 2015
First edition published 2007. Reprinted 2010, 2012, and 2013
This edition published 2015

Library of Congress Control Number: 2014937014

British Library Cataloguing in Publication data

A catalogue record for this book is available from the British Library

ISBN 978-1-44628-291-5
ISBN 978-1-44628-292-2 (pbk)

At SAGE we take sustainability seriously. Most of our products are printed in the UK using FSC papers and boards. When we print overseas we ensure sustainable papers are used as measured by the Egmont grading system. We undertake an annual audit to monitor our sustainability.

Contents

List of Cases

About the Authors

Kerr Inkson is an Emeritus Professor at The University of Auckland Business School, New Zealand. He has a PhD from the University of Otago. His 47-year academic career included 24 years as full professor at five New Zealand universities. An expert in management, organizational behavior and career development, Kerr has published 17 books, over 50 book chapters and 75 refereed journal articles. His most recent books are *Understanding Careers* (SAGE, 2007), *Cultural Intelligence* (co-authored with David C. Thomas, 2nd edition, Berrett-Koehler, 2009), *Career Studies* (4-volume collection, co-edited with Mark Savickas, SAGE, 2012), and *Managing Expatriates* (co-authored with Yvonne McNulty, Business Expert Press, 2013). His careers research includes interests in new forms of career, the use of metaphor in career theory and practice, and international careers. His journal credits include *Administrative Science Quarterly, Human Relations, Journal of Applied Psychology, Journal of Management Studies, Journal of Organizational Behavior, Journal of Vocational Behavior, Journal of World Business, Organizational Dynamics* and *Organization Studies*. He is a former Chair of the Careers Division, Academy of Management. He retired from employment at the end of 2012. He lives in Auckland, New Zealand.

Nicky Dries is a Research Professor at the KU Leuven, Faculty of Business and Economics (Belgium). She conducted her doctoral research on talent management and career success at the Vrije Universiteit Brussels (Belgium), during which time she was also a visiting scholar at the Vrije Universiteit Amsterdam (the Netherlands). Since then, she has been a visiting scholar at the University of Tilburg (the Netherlands), at Wirtschaftsuniversität Vienna (Austria), at Reykjavik University (Iceland), and a Fulbright scholar at Boston University School of Management (USA). Nicky has published articles in international journals in the areas of career management, human resource management, and industrial-organizational psychology, and is on the editorial board of the *Journal of Vocational Behavior, Journal of World Business* and the *European Journal of Work and Organizational Psychology*. Nicky's primary research interests are employee talent, potential, and success – and, more generally, the interplay of organizational-strategic and individual-psychological factors in shaping careers. Currently, she is the primary supervisor of four research projects on talent management, as well as a co-supervisor of the Flemish Policy Research Centre Work and Social Economy—Centre for Career Research (CCR). In addition, she is actively involved in two large-scale cross-cultural projects on contemporary careers, i.e. 5C (Consortium for the Cross-Cultural Study of Contemporary Careers) and the Career Adaptability/Life Design project.

John Arnold is Professor of Organisational Behaviour at the School of Business and Economics, Loughborough University, UK. He is a Fellow and Chartered Occupational Psychologist of the British Psychological Society. John's research, teaching and consultancy involve all areas of careers and their management from both individual and organizational perspectives. Particular interests include career choice, personal development and adjustment, work role identities and transitions (including the transition into working life), career success and failure, mid/late career issues, and the impact of career management interventions such as mentoring, development centers and succession planning. John is author or co-author of over 70 refereed journal articles, the successful textbook *Work Psychology* (FT Press, 2010; 6th edition due in 2015), and the specialist book *Managing Careers into the 21st Century* (SAGE, 1997). He is past editor of the *Journal of Occupational and Organizational Psychology*, and is currently on the editorial boards of four leading academic journals.

Foreword and Acknowledgements

This book is essentially an updating of Kerr Inkson's *Understanding Careers: The Metaphors of Working Lives*, which was published by SAGE (Thousand Oaks) in 2007: it is a 'state-of-the art' undergraduate or postgraduate text of Career Studies, suitable for use in programs concerning careers, in business schools, and in academic departments of psychology, education and counseling. In considering a second edition, SAGE recognized an opportunity to extend the book's outreach in Europe, and transferred responsibility to SAGE's office in London. For the second edition, SAGE Commissioning Editor, Kirsty Smy, worked with Kerr Inkson to develop a plan for a suitable reformulation of the book, one that would capitalize on the original edition's strengths while filling some gaps, updating the text and developing a more cosmopolitan and international feel, a greater emphasis on practice and some new pedagogical aids.

Feeling that the new edition required fresh impetus, new ideas and the potential to be extended to further editions, Kerr decided to recruit two new co-authors, and was fortunate to be joined by Nicky Dries of KU Leuven, Belgium, and John Arnold of Loughborough University in the UK. The three authors prepared a proposal for this book, which was accepted by SAGE early in 2013. The book was written in 12 months and submitted to SAGE in March 2014.

While many of the ideas and much of the text of the original book have been retained, SAGE's experience of the reception and sales of the first edition and its commissioning of reviews of that edition have guided a number of changes in both the content and form of the book. The addition of two new co-authors and our adoption of a 'mutual review' process, plus chapter-by-chapter input from SAGE's own reviewers, have enabled a wider range of perspectives to be employed.

What are the key changes? This edition maintains at its core the nine-metaphor structure developed by Kerr Inkson as the organizing framework for the first edition. However, the scope of that book has been extended by means of the introduction of a new chapter (Chapter 2) on contextual factors (e.g. economic, labor market, sociological) affecting careers, and the expansion of the 'practical' outcomes of career studies into a new 'Careers in Practice' section containing separate chapters on applications by career actors themselves, by counselors and advisors, and by organizations. The peda-gogical aids built into the book have been significantly increased. A companion website has been created. Some out-of-date material has been excised, recent work added and references updated. Recent developments in career studies have been added where appropriate. Finally, most of the career case studies from the original have been replaced by new ones, though of course instructors are welcome to use the original cases in addition for teaching purposes.

We authors believe these innovations, assisted by SAGE's rigorous 'market testing', in which every chapter has been subjected during the drafting process to multiple reviews by potential users, significantly improve the scope and applicability of the book.

There are many people who need to be acknowledged for their support in the preparation of this book.

Kerr Inkson: I named many helpers in my acknowledgements in the first edition; and those whose influence continues strongly in this edition include Gareth Morgan for the inspiration underlying the metaphor structure, the late Al Bruckner and Mark Savickas for early encouragement, Michael Arthur for ongoing mentorship, and many members of the Academy of Management Careers Division for their wonderful sup-port for my ongoing work in careers research. For this edition, many thanks to my co-authors, two of Europe's best industrial-organizational psychologists, Nicky Dries and John Arnold, for coming aboard and contributing their special expertise and hard work, to make this edition so much better than I could have created alone. I owe a special debt, too, to my good friend Julia Richardson, a user of the first edition, who has been enthusiastic in her support and unstinting in her advice and assistance. In the writing and co-ordination of the text, Mariaelena Huambachano did a great job on the massive reference list. Lastly, my thanks to my wife Nan Inkson, who put up with this author's unsociability for many months and was always supportive and encouraging.

Nicky Dries: First of all, I want to thank Kerr Inkson for inviting me to join the author team of the second edition of *Understanding Careers*. Kerr, it has been a true honor to work with you on such a personal level. Thank you! The same goes for John Arnold, for whom I have tremendous respect and whose work has inspired me ever since I started doing research on careers. Other people in the careers field to whom I am greatly indebted are Tim Hall, Jon Briscoe and Mark Savickas. A special shout-out goes to Marijke Verbruggen, Anneleen Forrier and Ans De Vos who form the heart of the career studies field in Belgium. Many thanks to my family and friends and my current and former students, who inspire my research and writing on a daily basis, some of whom have functioned as a case study for this book. Lastly, thanks to my fiancé Jeroen whom I jokingly but lovingly refer to as 'my muse', for his unwaivering support of me and my career and for making sure that I am fed and hydrated when I am up writing all night.

John Arnold: I am very grateful to Kerr Inkson for inviting me to be a co-author of this second edition, and for tolerating the consequences of his invitation when I struggled to keep pace with him and Nicky. It has been a privilege to see this second edition taking shape, and to be able to contribute to it. Thanks to Kerr and Nicky for their great work on this book and in their many published articles which make such a major contribution to the careers field. I owe a lot to past and present colleagues and doctoral researchers, especially at Loughborough, Sheffield, and the European Network of Organizational Psychology (ENOP). Particular thanks to Laurie Cohen and Martin Gubler for their collaboration, friendship and exceptional scholarship in the careers field. But, to use a cliché, home is where the heart is. My contribution to this book is rooted in my wise, witty and diverse family: Helen, Ally, Sophie, Grace, Rhian, Mickey, Sarah, Ann, Andy, Simon, Nicky (not my co-author!) and the memory of Rev. With love and thanks to you all.

For Kerr, John, and Nicky, our support from the team at SAGE has been fantastic, particularly from commissioning editor, Kirsty Smy, who first saw the potential in the book and looked after it from start to finish, ably assisted along the way by assistant editor Nina Smith, production editor Nicola Marshall, designer Francis Kenney, marketing manager Alison Borg, copyeditor Sharon Cawood, and proofreader Emily Ayers.

In today's rapidly changing world, it seems to us that understanding careers, how they work and what we can do to make them work better, is becoming more and more vital to everyone who has a career – and that means almost everyone there is – to the organizations they work in and to society as a whole. We hope this book will make a modest but worthwhile contribution to these goals.

Kerr Inkson

Nicky Dries

John Arnold

Praise for the Book

to go about doing so. The authors recognize the complexity of career, but use Inkson's framework of career metaphors to provide ways of making sense of it without trivializing as so many books about career do. Anyone using this book to teach or to learn about careers will find it immensely useful, rewarding, and enjoyable.'

Hugh Gunz, Rotman School of Management, University of Toronto

'A masterful blend of carer theory and practice, Understanding Careers offers a wonderfully comprehensive and magnificently engaging look at work and careers in contemporary times. Kerr Inkson, Nicky Dries, and John Arnold offer in this book both the best careers scholarship for the serious career studies educator and researcher as well as the most useful career intervention strategies for career practitioners, students, and anyone interested in fostering their own career development. Packed with theory, history, case studies, and practical material, this book is a must read that will serve as an invaluable resource for years to come.'

Paul Hartung, NorthEast Ohio Medical University

'Making an excellent book even better is difficult - but the new edition of 'Understanding Careers' has done exactly that. The authors keep the highly praised core of the first edition - powerful metaphors underlying careers - and add new perspectives on context and careers in practice, leading to a must-read not only for students and researchers of careers, but also for career practitioners. Absolutely recommendable!'

Wolfgang Mayrhofer, Vienna University of Economics and Business

'A first class text combining the strengths of the earlier version with new ideas from contemporary research and practice. The new chapters on career self-management and organizational management systems are perfect additions making the book an invaluable resource for scholars, practitioners and students alike. Kudos to the authors for this excellent piece of work, and lucky us being able to benefit from their collaboration! The teaching aids offer are an excellent 'toolkit' for educators seeking to prepare students for their future careers: innovative, engaging and thought provoking.'

Julia Richardson, York University, Toronto

'In a series of fourteen highly readable chapters, Kerr Inkson and his colleagues present a metaphorical approach to careers. The result is a series of insightful and contrasting views, each informative in its own right, and together a call for further conversation. Readers will be both entertained and enlightened by this book.'

Michael B Arthur, Suffolk University, Boston, USA

'*Understanding Careers* is the essential career studies textbook for general college and university-level courses. As with the first edition, the writing is crystal clear with a highly impressive range of scholarship skilfully marshalled from a number of disciplines relevant to career studies. I have used this excellent book for several years in my teaching and find it helps students easily make sense of the career studies field by linking images with contemporary case studies and exercises. This is a superb introductory text for career development professionals and their clients. This wonderful book has revolutionised the design and content of career management programmes in schools, colleges, university and the workplace.'

Phil McCash, University of Warwick, UK

'The new edition of *Understanding Careers* beautifully captures the richness and possibilities of the career concept. Building on the nine metaphors at the heart of the first edition, Kerr Inkson, Nicky Dries and John Arnold offer a unique, interdisciplinary perspective on career as a body of knowledge, and how it is considered and enacted by individuals in the conduct of their working lives. In the wake of recent economic and social turbulence it raises important questions about those aspects of career which are being transformed, and those which endure. Peppered with diverse people and their ordinary and extraordinary experiences, it provides moving insights into the ways in which navigate these waters and the role employing organizations and others serve to guide (or obstruct) them in their way.'

Laurie Cohen, University of Nottingham

'It often seems easier to appreciate someone else's career rather than your own. Yet, our own mental model of career guides our attention and action. Drawing on multiple metaphors, the authors skilfully integrate academic research with invaluable practical advice to understand careers today. This eminently readable update of its successful predecessor will add value to career actors as well as professionals working in the careers field.'

Polly Parker, University of Queensland

About the Book and Companion Website

About the Book

The new edition of *Understanding Careers* is filled with useful learning resources to help guide your study including:

Chapter Objectives   At the opening of each chapter, bulleted lists of objectives will help focus your learning.

Stop and Consider   At relevant points throughout the chapter, this feature encourages you to reflect on what you have learnt and apply the ideas in the book to the real world, particularly to your own career.

Career Case Studies   Over 50 career case studies throughout the book, most of them new, highlight real life scenarios that will help you to relate career theory to practice, with guidance analysis by the authors.

Key Points   Bulleted lists of key points at the end of each chapter will consolidate your learning.

General Questions   End of chapter questions encourage thought and reflection on your own experiences or others' careers and are ideal for discussion or revision.

'Live Case Study' Questions   In the Introduction to their book, the authors invite you to undertake your own case study of a friend or relative's career and to apply the end of chapter 'Live Case Study' questions to your case.

Additional Resources   End of chapter links to self-assessment resources, recommended further reading and online resources encourage you to explore key ideas further, for a deeper understanding.

Companion Website Walkthrough

Understanding Careers is also supported by a wealth of online resources. Visit **study.sagepub.com/understandingcareers** to access the following:

For students

Multiple choice quizzes per chapter for revision
Web links from the book, to encourage further exploration
Detailed analysis of careers as shown in the Oscar-winning film *All about Eve*

For instructors

PowerPoint slides to accompany each chapter
A comprehensive **Instructors Manual**, including additional in-class activities designed for each chapter
Over 20 **additional career case studies,** with author commentaries

Introduction

Four Career Problems

Stephan, 18, will soon graduate from high school, and has been offered places in several good universities, but he is undecided not only on which offer to accept, but also on whether to specialize in computer science (which he is good at but finds boring) or engineering (which he loves but which seems, at present, to offer inferior career opportunities). Moreover, Stephan's father, who owns a successful business, is pressing him to work for a year or two in the business 'to get some practical experience' before he goes to university. What should Stephan do?

Marie, 28, is a successful advertising account manager. She was recruited by her current agency when she graduated seven years ago. Her employer has looked after her well, but the agency is not at the forefront of the market and she is thinking of moving on, at least sending her portfolio to a top agency and asking for an interview. But perhaps it would be better not to take risks with her career. Maybe she could find more challenging opportunities in her current agency if she waited for them, or even shared the problem with her manager. Should she 'go for it' or not?

(Continued)

(Continued)

Emma, 33, a successful corporate manager, is married to Nick, 35, a high school music teacher. They want to start a family, but they both love their work and don't want to give it up. Both are anxious to 'get to the top'. Emma earns a higher salary than Nick, and they have developed a lifestyle which depends on her high income and bonuses. How can they meet both their family objectives and their work aims?

Ramon, 48, is a mechanical engineer. For the past 25 years, he has worked as engineer and, later, manager for the same company. Now the company has been taken over and Ramon has been laid off. He has been given a 'pay-off' equivalent to a year's salary. He realizes that his fortunes were very much tied to the company and that his engineering know-how is out of date. Could he have seen this coming? Should he have left the company sooner? He feels he is 'on the scrap-heap' and wonders how to make a fresh start. Is it worth spending his pay-off on going back to school and re-training to acquire more relevant skills?

The vignettes above are over-simplified but real. In all of them, there is a fundamental problem to solve. The problems are all related to employment and work, and originated in decisions the people concerned took in the past. These people have to make new decisions that are likely to have major long-term repercussions. In short, these decisions are all about *careers*.

For most of us, our careers are at the forefront of our attention. They provide our daily bread, our sense of identity, our means of achievement. Along with family relations and (for some) religious observance, they are what we judge our lives by. They determine our happiness, self-esteem, self-fulfilment and mental health.

Many people work directly or indirectly in the area of careers. Teachers and educators prepare students for their careers. Career advisors and counselors provide information and guidance aimed at helping clients to have successful careers. Organizational managers try to get employees' long-term career commitment, and keep their skills and energy within the organization. Most of all, ordinary people try to develop their own careers to satisfy their diverse needs for financial, social and psychological benefits. All these can therefore benefit from understanding careers.

The aim of this book is to provide a framework of ideas to assist you to understand how careers work. No doubt you are reading the book in connection with an academic program you are completing relating to careers. We hope you will also be able to apply at least some of the book to understand more, not just about careers in general, but also about your own career and the careers of people you know. Perhaps the book will even enable you to improve your decision making about your career, and thereby enhance your career satisfaction and success.

Careers can be looked at in many different ways. In this book, these different views are represented as *metaphors* – for example, the career as a journey, the career as a resource, and the career as a story. Each view has something to contribute to our overall understanding of careers.

The structure of the book is simple. Part 1, 'Background to Career Studies', contains Chapter 1, in which we introduce career studies and show how metaphors can be used to understand careers; and Chapter 2, in which we review the all-important context of economic, social and other factors within which careers are enacted, and which vitally influences them.

Part 2, 'Images of Career', contains nine chapters, each of them based around a single metaphor for career – an image which provides a unique understanding of how careers work: the career as an inheritance, as a cycle, as action, as fit, as a journey, as roles, as relationships, as a resource and as a story. These chapters cover a very wide range of theory and information about careers, including material from sociology, psychology, social psychology, education, and management studies.

In Part 3, 'Careers in Practice', we draw out some lessons from our understanding of careers for careers practice. Careers are influenced by many people – the individual experiencing the career, plus their family, friends, managers, and often professional career counselors. Readers of this book may in due course not only seek to develop and manage their own careers, but also to assist others, such as their friends, their work subordinates and their children. Chapter 12 is about managing one's own career, Chapter 13 about counseling others on their careers, and Chapter 14 about organizational practices relating to careers, for example through human resource management.

How to Use This Book

In writing the book, we assume that most readers will be reading it as part of a course of study, and that it will support the efforts of the tutor. (If this is not the case, don't worry; the book will still work for you!) We have therefore provided some features which should help to integrate the book into your other learning.

Chapter Objectives

At the opening of each chapter, a bulleted list of objectives will help focus your learning.

Stop and Consider

At relevant points throughout the chapter, we will ask you to stop reading for a moment and consider the application of the ideas in the book in the 'real world' you live in, particularly your own career. We believe that doing this will bring you academic and possibly career benefits, especially if you write down your answers.

Career Case Studies

You will find several of these per chapter, over 50 cases in all, providing hard information about specific real careers as a means of illustrating the theoretical content. Many of these cases are followed by a brief analysis and explanation to show how the case illustrates particular career principles or theory. This reinforces our view that to understand how careers work, you need constantly to think about real careers. Indeed, if you're more interested in the hard reality of careers than in theories, you could start your studies by looking at the 'List of Cases' at the beginning of this book, flicking over to some cases that interest you, and start to find out about careers by reading about some real ones, and our interpretations of how they work.

Key Points

Bulleted list of key points at the end of each chapter will consolidate your learning.

General Questions

Study questions at the end of each chapter of the book will ask you to try to use the content to explain things about your career or others' careers. Your tutor may prescribe some of these questions in assignments, but even if they don't, these are ideal for discussion or revision. If you don't think you have a career yet, consider your experiences as a student as part of your career.

'Live Career Case' Study Questions

In order to apply theory on a chapter-by-chapter basis to a single case, consider commencing the exercise indicated below *now*, and continue with it on a week-by-week basis as you read the book or as your course proceeds. Application to a real case will help you understand the theoretical material in the book and get a feel for actual careers.

Find a friend or relative (parents are ideal) aged at least 30 years old who would be willing to talk with you, in confidence and at length, from time to time about their career. Alternatively, if you are a mature person with a career or part of a career – at least ten years – already behind you, you might like to 'interrogate' yourself by reflecting on your own career. The idea is to write the person's career up as a kind of case study or mini-biography, and then, as you read the different chapters of the book, seek to apply the end-of-chapter questions to this case.

The first thing to do is to get your case person's trust and ensure they are willing to give you information, not just about the various jobs they held in their career (the 'objective' career), but also their thoughts and feelings about it, such as their reasons for changing jobs and their aspirations at different times (the 'subjective' career).

This is not an exercise you need to fear. We have had hundreds of students do this, usually with a parent, and universally they report that people *like* talking about their careers, and that both parties enjoy the experience. If you are like some of our students, you may even come to experience a new and more positive understanding of the person and a closer relationship with them.

When you interview the person, keep records of what they say and write these up as a case, checking with your case participant for accuracy. Start by getting a basic outline of their career, chronologically, with dates, and write it up. (The case of 'Max' in Chapter 1 is a role-model example.) As you go through the various chapters of the book, consider the live career case study questions at the end of each chapter and re-interview the person as you need to – often, a brief 5-minute question-and-answer session will be enough. If you are conscientious about this, by the time you finish the book you should have a fine understanding of at least one career.

Good luck!

Additional Resources

For those who wish to take their reading and research beyond this book, we have provided further learning resources at the end of each chapter. These include:

- five or six key readings per chapter: these are mainly academic papers available on the web, with a few books added. With limited time available, you should scan these intelligently rather than trying to read them in full
- (for most but not all chapters) web references you may find of interest
- (for most but not all chapters) self-assessment instruments available in the literature, which enable you to make some career-relevant assessments of yourself.

Part 1
Background to Career Studies

Career and Metaphor

1

The objectives of this chapter are:

- to become aware of the importance of career in your life and some of the key issues relating to your and others' careers
- to become aware of some of the characteristics of careers, the history of career studies and different disciplinary approaches to understanding careers
- to gain an appreciation for the use of metaphor as a tool to understand and develop careers and the set of specific metaphors for career on which this book is based
- to consider a single career as a case study, and see how the use of different metaphors can help us to improve our understanding of that career and other careers.

CASE STUDY

Contrasting Experiences of Career

Maria, Ultrasound technician: I work at a private obstetrics/gynaecology clinic in a big hospital. I do obstetric scans and pelvic exams. I love it! That is just as well,

(Continued)

(Continued)

as the money is OK but I could probably have done better in the commercial world. I love the doctors, the other technicians, the teamwork, the way everyone trusts my expertise, and of course the patients, and the excitement of a new life coming in to being. It's a great job, and with more experience, new technology and promotion through the ranks, I want to turn it into a great career – though of course if I have children it could change all that.

Jan, Pharmacist: I'm a qualified pharmacist in a retail store, and I'm not sure I can stand it for much longer. The junkies, the abusers, the pleading for drugs – that's bad enough, but where I work there's jealousy, exploitation and backstabbing from my paranoid boss. Of course, I could walk out any time, but the money is good and there aren't many opportunities around in my field. And there's a mortgage to pay off and a family that's counting on me. If I'd known when I was at school what I know now, I'd have made some very different choices. Maybe when the kids are grown up I can take some time out and try something else, but for the time being I'm stuck with a career I hate.

We call Jan and Maria *career actors*: that is, they are individuals experiencing their own careers and taking actions which affect those careers. Everyone who is preparing for, or already in, a career is potentially a career actor, though they also have other, often related roles, such as employee, parent and friend (see Chapter 8). Thus, 'career actor' is not just about people who are pursuing a theatrical career: we are nearly all career actors. The term will be used frequently in this book.

In these stories, Maria is very happy in her work (and life) and looks forward to progressing into an equally productive and happy career, while Jan is very unhappy in his and recognizes that previous bad choices may have long-term consequences. None of this is meant to imply that a career as an ultrasound technician is better than a career as a retail pharmacist. Some pharmacists are probably as happy and fulfilled as Maria, and some ultrasound technicians as miserable as Jan. Rather, the two stories illustrate the extremes of career satisfaction and dissatisfaction, of fulfilment versus being stuck in an intolerable rut. Their stories also indicate that career, although largely defined in this book by experiences of employment and work, is intimately connected with the non-work parts of people's lives.

What caused Jan's misfortune? Was pharmacy really such a bad choice for him? Could he have avoided the fix he finds himself in by taking action at an earlier stage? Is it simply the organization he is in that is the problem? If he could leave this organization, could he turn the situation around? Or should he make a major career change? How? And to what?

As for Maria, she seems happy and fulfilled for now, but will it last? Will the doctors she works with continue to trust her and give her the autonomy she values? Will her pay and status always be enough for her? Will she secure the promotions she hopes for? Should she be thinking ahead, planning and preparing for even better jobs in the future?

And what about you? If you already have a career, is it more like Maria's or more like Jan's? If it is like Maria's, what can you do to make sure it stays that way? If it is more like Jan's, how can you change it? If your career hasn't started yet, what can you do now to ensure that in 10 years' time you will feel more like Maria than like Jan? Studying careers and developing good career self-management based on what you learn may provide important practical skills.

The Importance of Careers

Over the past few decades, careers – defined here as 'the evolving sequence of a person's work experiences over time' (Arthur et al., 1989: 8) – have been the subject of extensive research. Here are just some of the ways that your career may affect your well-being and the kinds of action you can take in response:

- Your career is likely to be one of the most important features of your life. It will probably occupy roughly half your waking hours for 40 years or more. It will substantially determine your financial position, your status in society, your contribution to society, your general happiness, your feelings of self-fulfilment and the judgments others make of you. Your career is therefore to be taken seriously.
- You differ from others in your personal makeup, such as background, abilities and interests. Your career should ideally be congruent with your makeup. To find congruence, you need to know yourself well, have a good idea of what jobs are available, and be sensitive to changes in either yourself or the situations in which you live.
- You will age and mature. As you do so, your energies and priorities will change. At some times in your life, you may be interested in exploring the world; at other times, you'll want to make a major change or chase career success; and at still others, you'll simply want to protect your energy, health and lifestyle. At some stages, there are likely to be significant pressures on your career due to family commitments. Your career needs to be responsive to these changes.
- Careers involve many decisions and choices. You may make a choice with negative consequences you don't anticipate. You may like your job now but hate it later. You may find yourself unable to progress to a higher level. You may be offered an unexpected opportunity. You may have to choose between money and job satisfaction. You may be laid off. But if you look ahead intelligently before committing

yourself, perhaps you can anticipate and change such circumstances or adapt to them. Career planning can help you safeguard your future.

- Your home, family and leisure lives intimately affect, and are affected by, your career. Many commentators suggest that there needs to be a balance between the demands of your work career and your commitment to family and non-work pursuits. Imbalance may be damaging to both parts of your life. You need to monitor your priorities and your actions and communicate with your family and others about these matters.

Stop and Consider

Think about your career so far. If you don't think you have a career yet, think ahead to the kind of career you expect or hope for. Re-read the five paragraphs above, which are about, respectively, the *importance, congruence, development, planning* and *balance* of your career, and think about how they might relate to you. Write down any thoughts that come into your mind in relation to each one. Keep your notes for future consideration. Get into the habit of thinking about the ideas in this book in relation to *you.*

These are the kinds of practical issues that career studies deals with. By understanding how careers work, you can empower yourself to improve your career. Academic researchers have expounded relevant knowledge. Educators, counselors and managers have developed good practices for assisting career actors. This knowledge and practice is reported in this book.

Defining *Career*

What does the word *career* mean? As Moore et al. (2007) point out, 'career' in the sense of a sequence of events relating to an individual's ongoing working life did not reach the dictionaries until well into the 20th century. In earlier times, career was a mark of privilege. In 19th-century England, for example, the notion of career, involving a long-term vocation, or progression through a series of work-related roles, was applied only to men entering the military, law, medicine or the Church. The democratic concept of career as a long-term chronological sequence of paid work experiences of the majority of the population was unconsidered. Some might have a *trade* or an *occupation*, such as carpenter, maid, cook or accounts clerk. Most people thought in terms of *having a job, making a living* or *being employed*: they sold their labor and their skills for the best price they could get.

Some definitions of career have suggested that a career is more than just a sequence of jobs. For example:

> (Careers are) occupations that are characterised by inter-related training and work experiences, in which a person moves upward through a series of positions that require greater mastery and responsibility, and that provide increasing financial return. (Perlmutter and Hall, 1992: 384)

This definition appears to confuse 'career' with 'occupation', and to make vertical advancement (promotion) a precondition for having a career. Likewise, Leach and Chakiris (1988: 52) say:

> Careers flow from jobs... a job need not lead anywhere; it is just something a person gets paid for. Careers, on the other hand, are continuous behavioural episodes, leading to a path or ladder that ends, optimally, in some sort of career capstone experience.

In this view, if you have a series of odd jobs all your working life, that is hardly a career: These authors are suggesting that the idea of 'pattern' is essential to a career.

We take a wider view. First, we recognize that many, if not most, careers tend to move across different occupations (as well as different organizations). We also believe that even in the 'odd job' example, there may be patterns below the surface of 'a series of odd jobs' which are not necessarily immediately apparent, and that, in any case, 'pattern', while often desirable, is not essential to a career, and that anyone who works in employment or self-employment at some stage in their life has a career. Consider this:

'Tell Me about Your Career', by Kerr Inkson

Due to my interest in careers, as part of both my research and my social life I often say to people, 'Tell me about your career' (see, for example, Arthur et al., 1999). As well as being a surprisingly productive research method, this question is a great conversation starter – more demanding than 'What do you do for a living?', but less intrusive than 'Tell me about your religion/politics/finances/personal relationships/sex life'. Career is a personal topic, but not an intimate one. People *like* talking about their careers. It enables them to choose an interesting framing of

(Continued)

(Continued)

their history and to tell stories, rather than, as with 'what do you do?', sticking to the often mundane realities of the present. The notion of career creates that sense of *chronology* and *sequence* and *story* that differentiates career studies from other aspects of occupational psychology and organizational behavior. It also enables the researcher or questioner to understand what the word 'career' means to the answerer of the question.

But first, I find, one has to push past the superficial denials: 'I don't have a career, I'm just a housewife'; 'I don't have a career, I have an orchard'; or, most common of all, 'Oh, you don't want to talk to me – my career is kind of strange'. It turns out that in the way many people think, and talk, about career, the term denotes something rather orderly and linear: an occupational career or an organizational career. Many people consider as prototypical those existent but surprisingly uncommon forms of career: the perfectly progressive professional career and the one-company organizational career. They compare those 'ideal' forms with the sheer *messiness* of their own life histories and decide that the term 'career' is not the right one to describe these experiences. They conclude that somehow, even though their working lives may have worked out all right, they have failed to go about it in the right way and have therefore not had real careers.

The truth is that there *is* no right way. Most people at some stage, and often for long stretches of time, go through processes of what Super (1957) called 'floundering'. Many careers are knocked periodically off-track, and sometimes on-track, by error, unexpected obstacle or opportunity, contextual change, chance and whim. Such careers flow blithely across the boundaries of occupation, organization, geographical location, industry and status within which they are supposed to be conducted. Most careers, in other words, are *non*-linear (and therefore fascinating!).

Source: Inkson (2014), quoted with permission of the American Psychological Association.

This wider view did, in the later 20th century, achieve some kind of currency, and nowadays the term is much more common. Websites listing employment vacancies often advertise not *jobs* but *career opportunities*, apparently promising the chance of changing the rest of one's life for the better. In short, the notion of 'career' has become very popular.

Here is one definition of *career*: 'the evolving sequence of a person's work experiences over time' (Arthur et al., 1989: 8). This definition has important implications:

- Based on this definition, each person has only one career. If someone says, 'I've had three different careers', they probably mean they have worked in three different occupations or industries, but their experiences are all part of the same career.

The definition above directs attention to the transitions between different work experiences, and presents the career as a single developing experience rather than a series of isolated events.

- The phrase *evolving sequence* denotes that a career is not a momentary thing. It involves continuity and change. To understand a career, we need to look at what came before each experience and how the past relates to the present. We may even want to try to project our understanding into the future, for example in career planning. Careers are cumulative.

- The phrase *work experiences* focuses on employment but does not confine careers to paid work. Activities outside employment involve experiences that are relevant to one's career. For example, parenting at home may provide important career skills. A hobby such as wood-carving or mountaineering may become the basis of a full-time career. There is constant interplay between our career and other parts of our life.

- The term *experiences* also brings up the question 'what kind of experiences?' Objective experiences that are external and verifiable, such as job title and salary? Or subjective experiences, internal to the person in the career, such as career ambitions, job satisfaction or dissatisfaction, emotions about career progress and decision-making processes guiding career moves? The answer is both. The notion of 'experience' can be used to cover both the formal roles that a career actor occupies (the objective career) and the internal experiences of the career actor in terms of motivation, satisfaction, etc. (the subjective career).

- The term *over time* implies longevity. A career potentially lasts a lifetime.

The above points summarize what a career is, but don't necessarily tell us what a career is *for*, particularly for the individual experiencing it. Here, the concept of *career success* is important. Career actors are generally encouraged to pursue career success, but what career success consists of – for example, 'getting to the top' versus feeling an ongoing sense of satisfaction in one's career – depends both on the way society and its institutions define success, and on career actors' career goals. We explore career success further in Chapter 5.

A Brief History of Career Studies

This book has its basis in 150 or so years of academic thought, theory and empirical study. By theorising about careers and gathering data, we can better understand how they work. Sociology, psychology, educational studies, anthropology, economics, political studies and other disciplines can all assist us to build a new, more specialized discipline – career studies – to integrate this diverse information. It is instructive to understand how the study of careers has developed over time. For those interested, Moore et al. (2007) provide an excellent history of career theory and research, and Savickas (2008) that of career guidance and counseling.

Sociological approaches to careers

Early consideration of careers was affected by 19th and early 20th-century sociologists who believed that efficiency in work organizations was best served by specialization, requiring individuals to develop and utilize precise skills (Durkheim, 1893/1964), with obvious consequent effects on their ongoing working lives, such as the development of specialized trades and professions with codified forms of training and membership. Weber's (1920/1947) conception of rational organization, or bureaucracy, as the dominant form of 20th-century institution, also promised the creation, within organizations, of career systems that would direct employees through organizational pathways and, potentially, organizational careers.

Studies of careers were pioneered in the USA between the 1930s and the 1960s by the Chicago School of Sociology (Barley, 1989), which adopted the term 'career' as an individual's entire life history and focused on formal roles and 'career scripts' that were based on the expectations of society and enacted by individuals in their careers. In this view, careers were conduits between institutions and individual action, and could be used to study the constitution of society. The Chicago theorists also acknowledged or reinforced some of the central propositions on which today's career studies are based: everyone has a career; careers are not necessarily confined to work roles; careers are not necessarily vertical in direction; and careers involve subjective as well as objective elements. The Chicago School's studies of occupational groups such as managers, teachers and hospital physicians showed the potential of ethnographic study to provide knowledge and understanding of career dynamics.

Sociology continues to contribute to career studies. Careers are constrained by wider factors such as social class, gender, ethnicity and education, and may represent social structure rather than individual action (e.g. Blau and Duncan, 1967; Mayrhofer et al., 2004; McLeod et al., 2009). If this is true, individuals may make a limited difference to their own careers, which are rather thrust upon them by context and circumstance (see Chapters 2 and 3).

Psychological approaches to careers

In parallel with the developing interest of sociologists in careers, psychologists interested in the adaptation of individuals to their jobs have developed a 'vocational' psychology focused on individuals and their career decisions.

The term 'vocation' has a special place in career studies. What is a 'vocation'? Literally, based on the Latin root of the word, it is a 'calling', and in the Christian religion it often has connotations of a calling from God, for example, to be a minister or priest or teacher. But in the careers context, both 'vocation' and 'calling' can be wider, meaning that the person feels an external or internal compulsion that guides career decisions (Dik & Duffy, 2009). More broadly, a vocation, whether or not experienced as a 'calling', can be an occupation that a person trains for, takes up and stays in.

The term 'vocation' also has connotations of long-term adherence. The premier academic journal in career studies is the *Journal of Vocational Behavior*.

This tradition of career studies has a clear practical focus, with an objective of assisting career actors to make good career decisions, particularly in choice of job and occupation, so as to provide maximum benefit for both themselves and for society.

Savickas and Baker (2005) trace the antecedents of vocational psychology back to 19th-century events such as the founding of the YMCA (Young Men's Christian Association) in Boston in 1851. In 1909, Frank Parsons published the first systematic book in the area, *Choosing a Vocation*. Parsons advocated that people should understand themselves, understand the requirements and conditions of different lines of work, and use 'true reasoning' (logic) to find a match between the two. This philosophy is the basis of the fit-the-person-to-the-job, or trait-and-factor, approach to careers, which remains critical to the careers guidance field (see Chapter 6). Over the years, psychologists have made great strides in the measurement of career-relevant human characteristics, such as abilities, aptitudes, personality, values and interests.

After the Second World War, research and practice based on the 'fit' idea blossomed, focusing particularly on initial choice of occupation. For example, Roe (1956) theorized that motivational and personality factors developed in childhood predisposed the choice of particular occupations. In Dawis and Lofquist's (1984) work adjustment theory, career actors' abilities and values were compared with patterns of work in different occupations to predict their 'satisfaction and satisfactoriness' and enable a cost/benefit analysis, resulting in optimal choice of occupation. Holland's (1959, 1997) theoretical and psychometric analysis of career actors' vocational interests and the corresponding profiles of different occupations provided the basis of career practice for many practitioners. Such efforts were premised on the view that each career actor has a relatively stable set of personal traits, and should therefore find – if necessary with professional assistance – the kind of work that best utilizes those traits, and should stick to it long-term. Careers guidance based on such assessments continues to thrive today, and we consider its efficacy further in Chapters 6 and 13.

Some psychologists, however, took a wider perspective, developing theories based on the view that there is more to careers than initial choices, because careers are lifelong developmental processes (Ginzberg et al., 1951). In *The Psychology of Careers*, Super (1957) sought to go beyond static 'fit' theories, and consider in addition how individuals develop and change throughout their lives and what implications such changes might have for their careers. Levinson's *The Seasons of a Man's Life* (Levinson et al., 1978) portrayed careers as chronologies that, as individuals changed over time and entered into new phases of their lives, could be predicted with the inevitability of the seasons. We focus on the relationship of careers to adult development in Chapter 4.

Another tack was taken by theorists who emphasized that careers result from career actors' own actions, particularly the processes of decision making and adjustment through which they plan and implement their careers. Key theories were those of Krumboltz (1979) on career as a form of social learning; Peterson et al. (1991) on cognitive information-processing theory; and Lent et al. (2002) on the social cognitive theory of career decision making. These theories, together with 'fit' and developmental theories, form the basis of individually oriented career development theory and – along with theories of counseling – of modern career counseling practice (Athanasou & Van Esbroeck, 2008; Hartung et al., 2014). We discuss theories of action in Chapter 5, and career counseling in Chapter 13.

Organizational approaches to careers

In the 1970s, business school academics began to study careers, perceiving them as being a concern for both the career aspirant and their employing organization (e.g. Hall, 1976). The notion of using careers to 'match individual and organizational needs' (Schein, 1978) in practices such as personnel selection (based on the same 'fit' model as vocational psychology), staff development, performance appraisal and promotion policies, promised benefits for both parties. Authors such as Hall (1976) and Schein (1978) recognized the symbiotic long-term interdependence of career actors and organizations. In a kind of human resource management of careers (Baruch and Peiperl, 2000), organizations began to develop more sophisticated systems to manage their members' career development for mutual benefit (see Chapters 10 and 14).

More recently, the restructuring and layoffs prevalent in many organizations have removed some of the mutual loyalty and common interest between career actors and their organizations. Interest has grown in 'boundaryless' careers (Arthur & Rousseau, 1996), where individuals move between organizations, creating major skills displacement and labor turnover problems for these organizations to solve. This approach also focuses on career journeys – the directions, routes and pathways that careers typically follow. The ways in which professional workers with sought-after skills, such as those in science and IT, develop their careers, has become a major topic in research (e.g. Duberley et al., 2006a; Joseph et al., 2012).

All of these theories, both sociological and psychological, are based, however, on the philosophical position of logical positivism – that is, on notions of empirical evidence, testability and logical proof. An alternative, which since about 1990 has gained a strong following in career studies, is the notion of *constructivism* or *social constructionism*, which holds that people construct their own realities, including their own realities about their careers. If that is correct, then career studies is about individuals' understanding of their own careers (Young & Collin, 2004). For example, Savickas (2012a) outlines a 'life design' counseling program whereby career actor and counselor examine the various 'narratives', or stories, that the career actor has used to construct their career so far. They then collaborate to create a new narrative that will enable the actor to confront current career challenges and build a better future.

Career Studies: Separate Realities

Some of these different perspectives of career have proceeded relatively independently. In particular, the career development and 'fit' views of the career guidance movement, the social structure view of the sociologists, and the career management view of employers and business schools have to some extent ignored each other.

- The career development movement tends to view the career as a set of personal, psychologically based issues. Indeed, vocational psychology has developed as a speciality within applied psychology (Savickas, 2004; Savickas & Baker, 2005). The movement tends to understand well the processes of career decision making, such as how initial career choices by high school and college graduates are made. But it does not consider so extensively the context of careers – for example, institutional discrimination, the labor market, and formal organizations – or the long-term patterns that careers typically follow. In terms of practice, it recommends interventions by skilled counselors in career actors' decision-making processes, feedback and guidance, and the empowerment of clients (career actors) to make good choices. Its client base is the career counseling and guidance profession, and, indirectly, career actors.

- The sociological view is strongly influenced by evidence of the influence that context and social structure, such as economic cycles, political domination, social class, education, and gender, have over careers. It pays less attention to individual differences and individual action. In terms of practice, it often recommends policy and legislative interventions designed to alter the contextual conditions in which careers are enacted, and thereby changes the career opportunities available. For example, changed legislation concerning education, remuneration or taxation may reduce inequalities and improve the career opportunities and outcomes of minorities or underprivileged groups. Lobbying or radical action may also be recommended. The client base of this view is opinion leaders, advocates and policy makers in areas such as employment law, labor market policy, economic development and minority rights.

- The career management view emphasizes the role of organizations and their management of human resources. In terms of practice, it favors interventions by management to offer employees career pathways and development opportunities for mutual benefit. But it tends to underestimate both the limiting effects of the wider context and the extent of individuals' responsibility for, and control over, their own careers. Latterly, however, recognising the inherent inter-organizational mobility of many careers, it too has favored the empowerment of career actors, particularly the highly skilled, to be proactive and mobile in seeking career satisfaction and success, and new forms of human resource management that recognize and seek to capitalize on this mobility (e.g. Inkson & King, 2011).

The result of these differences of emphasis is that there are seemingly three separate research literatures on the topic. This book takes a more eclectic view. For a full understanding of careers, these different 'worldviews' of the topic have much to offer each other, and they all have much to offer the student of careers. In the belief that students, whether of sociology, psychology, education, counseling, or business, deserve a broader view of the topic, we include all of the viewpoints in this book. Recently, there have been new conceptualizations of careers as part of much wider social systems, in a systems theory approach (Patton & McMahon, 2006).

The Use of Metaphor

Each of the worldviews discussed previously generates its own images of the career actor. The sociological view elicits pictures of a tiny person, perhaps a 'pawn', controlled and overwhelmed by massive forces beyond their control. The psychological view, in contrast, invites us to see an autonomous fighter, a 'hero' or 'heroine' in a difficult environment, struggling to find satisfaction and success in their decisions and actions. The business view is of a 'busy bee' working with others in a mutual endeavour and progressing happily along career pathways thoughtfully provided by a supportive employer.

Such notions, very common in career thinking, are metaphors. They represent a natural human tendency to render complex abstract phenomena understandable by making them concrete, and as far as possible human, in our minds. Metaphorical thinking is common in all human thinking and all discourse (Ortony, 1993). And, because metaphorical thinking is particularly common in relation to careers and potentially expands our understanding, a series of career metaphors frames this book.

A metaphor is a figure of speech in which a point is made about one thing by substituting something else that demonstrates a particular quality of the first in a dramatic way. Thus, instead of saying, 'the soldier was strong and ferocious', we might say, 'the soldier was a lion'. The term *lion* embodies an extreme form of strength and ferocity and has a dramatic impact that the terms *strong* and *ferocious* lack. The metaphor also enables us to summarize complex qualities using a single word. But it ignores the fact that lions typically spend most of their time resting or sleeping: metaphors are usually selective in the ideas they draw attention to.

Using metaphors has benefits and disadvantages. Metaphors often provide compelling images that sum up phenomena wonderfully, much as 'a single picture is worth a thousand words'. Metaphors also encourage creativity and help us see things in new ways.

On the other hand, metaphors may be used to induce us to see things that aren't there and to force other views into the background. Philosopher John Locke railed against metaphor as 'the artificial and figurative application of words ... for nothing else but to insinuate wrong ideas, move passions, and thereby mislead the judgment' (cited in Chia, 1996: 134). For example, watch for metaphors in TV commercials: the house as a lifestyle, the bed as a magic carpet, the consumer as a superhero, and so on. Advertisers use metaphors to persuade. In considering metaphors, retain some skepticism, seek evidence to support the metaphor, and recognize that every metaphor has its limitations.

In 1986, Gareth Morgan made a landmark contribution to organization studies when he published *Images of Organization*, a wonderful book that used the method of multiple metaphor to analyze organizations in terms of key metaphors, such as 'machine', 'organism', 'culture', 'brain' and 'political system'. We all know organizations that have those characteristics. For example, when an organization is described as a machine, we picture mechanical moving parts, and see it as efficient, rational, and inflexible.

Morgan argued that different metaphors can be applied to any organization. Each metaphor reveals a special truth about the organization and about organizations in general. Because organizations are complex, no metaphor on its own tells the whole truth. But between them, a range of metaphors can provide a reasonably complete picture. Of course, with a wide range of metaphors available, users of metaphors – including the authors of this book – make their own choices of metaphor, to emphasize the features they consider important.

Career Metaphors

If Morgan is right, then presumably we can use metaphor to illuminate our understanding of careers. What career metaphors can we generate?

The use of metaphor to describe careers is common (Inkson & Amundson, 2002). We have heard people describe their careers, for example, as 'a roller coaster ride', 'a car stuck in the sand', 'the family's fuel tank', 'a house of cards', 'a hall of crazy mirrors', 'a straight line' and 'an LSD trip'. These images often go far beyond the most detailed résumé in conveying the overall career and the person's feelings about it.

Metaphors can also be used to advance thinking about careers. Mignot (2004) shows how the process of 'metaphorization' – the conscious creation and development by individual career actors of their own metaphors – can be used, for example, in career counseling, to assist creative career development (McMahon, 2007).

Career metaphors generated by ordinary people, employing organizations and the mass media also work their way into our consciousness. Consider the commonplace 'career path', 'career ladder', 'career plateau', 'fast track', 'glass ceiling', 'milestone' and 'turning point'. All represent the commonest career metaphor of all – the career as a journey.

Other frequent metaphors are 'playing the game', 'office politics', 'left on the bench', 'open door', 'square peg in a round hole' and 'story of my life'. Academics have added metaphors such as 'career anchors' (Schein, 1993), 'career tournament'

(Rosenbaum & Miller, 1996), 'career climbing frame' (Gunz, 1989) and 'career craft' (Poehnell & Amundson, 2002). The terms 'portfolio career' (Handy, 1989) and 'boundaryless career' (Arthur & Rousseau, 1996) are also metaphors. In a study of graduate employees in a large British company, El-Sawad (2005) categorized the metaphors they used to describe their career experience under eight headings: journeys (e.g. 'career ladder'), competition (e.g. 'rat race'), horticulture (e.g. 'corporate mushroom'), imprisonment (e.g. 'life sentence'), military (e.g. 'fighting battles'), school-like surveillance (e.g. 'someone looking over my shoulder'), Wild West (e.g. 'watch your back') and nautical (e.g. 'treading water'). Hall and Chandler (2005) drew attention to the special dynamics that exist when a career is perceived as a *calling* – work one is called to do by some higher force. And Bright and Pryor (2005) focused on the sheer unpredictability of careers by invoking the metaphor of careers as 'chaos'. The same authors also encourage career actors and counselors to be aware of the career as a 'game' – and to develop game-playing approaches to career decision making (Pryor & Bright, 2009).

All of these metaphors express their own point of view about careers. All have something to say to us. All have the potential to make us think about things in ways we may not have thought previously.

Stop and Consider

Write down the names of a few people you know who have careers. For each one, try to think of at least one metaphor which seems to summarize what that career is like. If you like, use the lists in the last couple of pages to help you.

This book looks at careers through successive metaphorical lenses by using a number of key, archetypal metaphors. Most established research and theory about careers can also be grouped and discussed under these metaphorical headings (Inkson, 2004):

- *inheritances* – predetermined outcomes passed on from our background and our parents
- *cycles* – identifiable stages through which each of us must inevitably progress
- *actions* of our own, through which we impose our will on the world
- *fit*, as in 'square pegs fitting in square holes' – career slots into which each of us must fit
- *journeys*, as indicated earlier
- *roles* acted out in a theater of life

- *relationships* arising from interactions with others, and from social networks
- *resources* that organizations use as inputs to their own purposes
- *stories* about our lives, which we tell ourselves and other people.

Each of these metaphors represents a truth about careers, but none provides the whole truth. Each represents a particular way of thinking about careers. Taken together, they may provide a wide understanding of careers. In the main section of this book (Chapters 3–11), each of the nine metaphors is explained and examined in detail. After reading these chapters, you should have a more complete, balanced and integrated understanding of careers.

As a starting point, read the following detailed account of a real career. It is a long and complex case, so take your time, read it carefully and, if necessary, re-read it. We subsequently analyze this career in terms of the nine metaphors.

Applying Metaphors to Careers: A Case Study

CASE STUDY

From Drop-out to Entrepreneur

Max came from a family with strong church connections. He lived in a major European city, in which he was destined to spend most of his career. While at school he worked part time for a local supermarket. Disliking school, he left at age 16 without qualifications and secured a full-time job as a stock assistant in a supermarket. Soon afterwards, however, he suffered serious injuries in a car accident and had to give up this job. After his recovery, he was undecided about what career direction to take, but a friend had turned down the offer of a job as a shop salesman in an auto parts company, and Max was able to obtain the unwanted job. The business owner, who became Max's mentor, was, in Max's words, a 'fantastic salesman' from whom Max 'learned how to sell things, and loved it'.

He stayed in the auto parts job for about two years, picking up good sales skills and industry knowledge. Then a customer who knew him through church circles and admired the quality of his service offered him a job in SalesCo, the auction company that he worked in, assisting the auctioning of insurance company

(Continued)

(Continued)

write-off cars. Max loved the job. He quickly learned how to be an auctioneer – an unusual accomplishment for a 19-year-old. He went to a drama therapist to assist with his breathing and speaking.

Over the next few years, Max moved through different departments at SalesCo, not through any company development plan for him, but fortuitously as he was chosen due to his hard work and reliability to fill positions left vacant when other staff moved on. He acquired a range of new skills, particularly interpersonal skills, and a better appreciation of the whole business. When his department was merged with another, he gained more responsibility. Eventually, still in his early 20s, he was offered his first management position as a team leader, and stayed in it for five years. He also became an accomplished basketball player.

At this point, Max developed a yearning to travel overseas. He quit his job and went abroad with a SalesCo colleague who shared his passion for basketball, which he wanted to play in other countries. His travels took him to the USA, where a girlfriend's father was involved with a motor racing team, and he started 'helping as a race mechanic ... Well, more like the tyre guy, and the cleaner, and the truck driver and everything else'. To Max, traveling – driving the team truck around the USA and Canada – was a great experience, especially the parties, the celebrities and the girls, but when the race season ended, he was out of work and went home.

Back home, Max was hoping to be able to go back to the USA for the next race car season, and did not want to commit to anything long term. So to tide him over he got a job as a ski-field ticket checker: 'a great way of learning how to ski, for free!' Then, interested in Japan as a possible destination, he enrolled for a three-month course in Japanese – his first period of study since leaving school. But as soon as he had finished the course, the race car team in the USA called on him to work for them again, and he headed offshore. But he had not appreciated the legal requirements for immigration to the USA, and ended up falling foul of the US immigration authorities, having his visa revoked and being declared persona non grata in the USA. 'I was young and dumb ... but I knew I could always go back to my home city and there'd be a job for me, because of my skills'. Moreover, on this trip Max had met his future wife, Kelly, in Canada, and stayed on there to test his new relationship.

By now, Max was thinking about marriage and the need to give it a secure base. So he returned to his home city, called SalesCo and was immediately offered a job: 'a step backwards in terms of my career, but I just wanted a job; I knew the people, liked the environment'. Six months later, Kelly flew over to visit him. During her visit, he invited her to watch him in action as an auctioneer, then proposed to her as part of the auction, in front of several hundred auction customers, a TV station Max had invited and her favourite VW convertible model which was decked out in balloons for the occasion. Kelly accepted and they drove away from the auction in the convertible.

Kelly had completed an education degree with a view to becoming a primary teacher. Which country to live in? His or hers? At that time there were few jobs in Canada for new teachers, whereas Max had a secure job, so they decided on Max's country.

Back at SalesCo, Max was quickly promoted to a position as a team leader, then, due to SalesCo's growth, a branch manager, a position which he stayed in for another seven years. It was very successful, and Max became highly regarded within the company: 'a sort of corporate superstar.' Meantime, Kelly had had her foreign qualifications accredited and (with assistance from a friend in the church network) obtained a good teaching job, which she kept for six years until she and Max had their first child and she withdrew from the workforce.

At this point, SalesCo, now very successful, became a publicly listed company with its own capital, was cash-rich and looking for new ventures to invest in. Due to the CEO having an old friend in Montreal who was willing to be a business partner, it was decided to launch a business there: SalesCo North America. With his continuing business success and his Canadian wife and experience, Max was an obvious choice to lead the new business and headed to his new city with his 3-year-old daughter and Kelly, now pregnant with their second child. But the business was an absolute failure and within a year it was merged with a Canadian auction company, which saw no need to retain its SalesCo managers, including Max, and laid them off. In his mid-30s, for the first time in his life, Max found himself 'nobody in Nowhereville'.

Back in his home country, Max retained goodwill at SalesCo and was able to fly home and continue on full salary. But he soon found himself stuck in a lower-level job, too low to justify his salary; and his relationship with the CEO, who blamed him for the Montreal debacle, was fatally flawed. Perceiving that notwithstanding his 17 years' service to SalesCo it was time for him to move on, Max put together a résumé and started to look for other positions. He had a lot of experience in car 're-marketing' (after use, for example, in a rental fleet), and good networks. A job came up as purchasing manager at AutoLease, a car-leasing company he had dealt with in the past. He was appointed, and within a year promoted to area manager in his home city. The new job made Max again a

(Continued)

(Continued)

manager, responsible for leading a team and accountable for profit. At about this time, his third child was born.

By now, the global financial crisis of 2008 had reared its ugly head. His new company's owners decided to sell AutoLease because it did not fit the overall corporate structure and focus. Max and his CEO decided to try to buy the company in a management buy-out, but their bid was unsuccessful. They were able instead to get agreement to 'run out the lease book' of 4,000 motor vehicles – waiting for the cars' contracts to expire and then selling them. The process was to take place over a three-year term. Max's three-year fixed contract was, he says, 'the best thing that ever happened to me, in terms of, for the first time in my life, being able to stop and smell the coffee, not having the pressures to grow a business, all I was doing was running it down'. The 'running down' process eventually took four years.

The process was financially very successful, and being vital to it Max was able to make a lot of money in bonuses. Due to the reduction in his workload, he was also able, despite having no undergraduate degree, to gain acceptance into an Executive MBA (Master of Business Administration) degree program at a local university – a 'huge blessing', he says – for which he was able to study during working hours.

By now, Max was 'fed up of the corporate environment', and he began to wonder if it was the right time to start his own business: something he had not previously countenanced because of his mortgage and other debts, because he had always felt comfortable in corporate jobs with assured salaries and cars, and because, he says, 'I am risk-averse'.

But, at the end of the wind-down, Max started to look at business plan options. Capitalizing on a research project which he had completed in his MBA, he decided to start an auto-broking business, and did so. Eighteen months later, when we interviewed Max for this book, the business had been successful far beyond his expectations, doing a 1.5 million euro turnover – 'about six times as much as I expected' – in the first year. A long-standing former business relationship with a rental car company accounts for over 50 percent of his business as he 're-markets' their cars. He also got Kelly involved, on the office side of the business. But he still has internal arguments about 'corporate career' versus 'own business', and feels under stress, overworking, denying himself holidays, and managing growth without assistance. He knows he could still do a good job in the corporate world, and wonders if he should sell his now-successful business or continue to try to build it.

Stop and Consider

Re-read Max's case and, as you go, write down a series of *themes* for his career, e.g. industries, occupations, changes, patterns, plus any you yourself perceive. Then read our analysis below and compare it with what you have written.

Understanding Max's Career

The Context of Max's Career

First, note that Max's career does not take place in a vacuum. It takes place in a *context*: a specific European country, mostly in one city; a specific industry relating to automobiles, automobile dealing, leasing, selling and auctioneering. These provide a stable context for Max's career but other factors constantly change, affecting it. A legislative control on migration to the USA destroys his dream of a career in the motor racing industry. His own industry has its own cycles of growth and retrenchment. His employing organizations change and develop, and this provides both opportunities and threats to his career: for example, the opportunity of the Canadian experiment followed by the threat posed by its failure. Later, the global financial crisis and AutoLease's changing strategy likewise impose changes on his career. In our careers, we cannot divorce ourselves from what is going on *out there*. The political, economic, social and organizational settings in which we live our careers constantly provide new opportunities and impose new constraints. Career actors therefore need to pay attention not only to what they want, but also to what is going on around them and therefore what is possible in their careers. In Chapter 2, we will look specifically at career contexts.

Max's Career as an Inheritance

Inheritances are career resources (and sometimes handicaps) that come into our careers from the past – for example, our innate abilities and personality, gender, social background and education. We 'inherit' these characteristics from our parents and elsewhere. Max's career used an inheritance of above-average intelligence and some special aptitudes, such as verbal and persuasive skills, which were partly built into his genetic makeup and which may also have been developed through his upbringing and education. On the other hand, he brought no special qualifications into his career. Notwithstanding his current self-employed status, he recognizes his inbuilt risk aversion and need for security, and only went 'out on his own' when he had plenty of savings. From his church background, Max probably gained strong ethics of service and hard work, while his male gender and white ethnicity probably played a part in the types of jobs he pursued and obtained, including his brief spell in motor racing. All careers are affected, for good or ill, by such legacies. The inheritance metaphor, dealt with in detail in Chapter 3, involves the things people bring to their careers that cannot easily be changed.

Max's Career as a Cycle

A cycle is a succession of events or phenomena completed in a period of time. The cycle most frequently used as a metaphor for human lives is the seasons, and in Max's career we can discern classic career seasons, such as growth, exploration, establishment and maintenance (Super, 1957). There was growth in Max's childhood and education, and exploration – though largely limited to a single industry – in his early movements through the supermarket and the various different functions of SalesCo. At one point, referring to his escapades in trying to pursue motor racing in the USA, Max refers to himself as 'young and dumb'; nowadays, in the possible summertime of his career, he moves more cautiously and invokes business plans and study to inform and guide his progress. We can also see shorter cycles in Max's career – for example, cycles within specific jobs, of novelty, action, progress and disillusion. Lastly, his family cycle, from dependent son, to independent adult, through courtship and dual-career marriage, to responsibility for child rearing, create additional rhythms and constraints. What will the 'autumn' and 'winter' of Max's career look like? Are these rhythms inevitable? By looking at the cycles typically affecting careers (in Chapter 4), we can find out.

Max's Career as Action

Whereas inheritance and cycle emphasize patterns imposed on Max's career, action emphasizes his personal efforts, so that Max creates his career through his own actions based on his own planning and decision making. Max made short-term plans. He worked hard constantly through his career and made a point of learning what he could from each job. As his career proceeded, he did not decide exactly what job he would have in five years' time, but he focused on a single industry, gathered information, determined what he enjoyed and was talented at, developed new skills, chose general directions and seized unexpected opportunities (the initial auto parts sales job, the Canadian venture). He built on his strengths and extended into new areas. He remained rational in his career decisions. In large measure, and notwithstanding the force of his inheritance and the cycles on his career, he constructed that career. Chapter 5 presents more information about action, self-expression and the way career choices are made.

Max's Career as Fit

In the common 'square peg in a round hole' metaphor, career actors are pegs who should have a good fit with their holes, or careers. Max was constantly aware of the extent of his fit and tried to improve it. He described 'trading' as what he enjoyed and was best at. His recognition that he had a 'risk averse' personality' – thrown off track temporarily in his auto racing and skiing period – kept him, until recently, in secure, corporate, salaried jobs. Then he made himself self-employed (to fit growing needs for autonomy) and worked from home. Neither the peg nor the hole stayed the same shape for long. Max developed new ambitions and skills, and grew himself, for example, though postgraduate study. His industry and the structure of the companies he worked in changed, and his jobs were redefined, restructured and, on one occasion, eliminated. How can career actors assess their changing values, interests and capabilities, and those of the context, and always find a good fit? We look at these issues in Chapter 6.

Max's Career as a Journey

'Journey' is the most common career metaphor of all. Journeys imply mobility, getting to a new place. Compared with many career actors, Max has not been especially mobile in his career. He has stuck largely to one industry, one city and (for a long time) one organization. But he has been mobile between roles within his organization and industry, and has taken his career twice to other countries. Moreover, he has climbed in status throughout his career, crossed a number of boundaries (particularly when moving from non-managerial to managerial positions), and moved latterly from being an employee to being self-employed. Max's journey is unique, but by thinking about it we can develop insights into the mobility aspects of career. Did Max's journey have a destination, and, if so, what was it? How clear was it? Was getting to where he was headed more or less important than enjoying the experience as he went? What are the implications of the trend towards careers becoming, more and more, *boundary-crossing* and *international* journeys? All these are significant issues and will be discussed in Chapter 7.

Max's Career as Roles

As Max's interests, skills and self-image changed over time, so did his work roles – shelf-stocker, salesman, auctioneer, race mechanic, vehicle buyer, area manager, and so on. To a large extent, these roles were defined not by Max but by his employing organizations and bosses. But as he went, he tried to put his own interpretation and imprint on them. People seldom do exactly and only what is in their job description. Also, the roles changed – for example, at one stage AutoLease's actions changed his job from area manager to downsizing contractor. Max also occupied different roles in his changing home life. His wife's career moves into, out of, and then back into different employment roles, some of them connected to his own, also affected his career. Even his role as a basketball player affected his career. Each of his roles was defined by sets of expectations that others – his parents, his employers, his family – had of him. In this sense, his career was like a theatrical performance, with others co-authoring the script with him. But Max's performance also included his own expression of himself. Careers involve multiple roles and changing expectations. In Chapter 8, we discuss these and related issues.

Max's Career as Relationships

Max's career was constantly mediated not just by what he knew, but also by *who* he knew. He got his first sales job through a friend. He got his first job in SalesCo, the key employer in his career, through a church contact, and it was his church network that later helped Kelly to get her first job in her new country. By the time he went to the USA, he had built a formidable set of contacts both in SalesCo and throughout his industry. Even those who didn't know him well knew his reputation, so that Max could always be confident that in his home city he would be able to get a job. Later, he was even able to refer to himself as a 'corporate superstar'. He pursued the business opportunity in Canada because of his boss's friendship in Montreal, but later had to leave his job back in Europe because his relationship with the same boss had deteriorated. Lastly, when he finally started his own business, half its revenue came through an important contact he had made earlier in his career. Max had wonderful networks and knew how to work them. The network element of careers is discussed in more detail in Chapter 9.

Max's Career as a Resource

Both Max and his employers used his career to achieve their objectives. His qualifications, experience and expertise created a resource that his employers combined with their other resources to create products and services. For example, early on in his career SalesCo capitalized on his abilities by rotating him through different roles, enabling him to learn new facets of the business. His career was a resource for the organization, but his experience at the organization also became a resource for his career. Each was investing in the other and looking for a payoff in terms of added resources. The resource metaphor focuses on the developing capability that every career has to contribute to a wider cause and the way that employers, as well as employees, facilitate such development. This metaphor is further explored in Chapter 10.

Max's Career as a Story

Max's career history, outlined earlier, is a faithful reproduction of what Max told us. But it is not the only story one could tell about Max's career. Would Max tell the same story in a job application? For example, what would he say about his experience of being denied entry to the USA, or of leading a disastrous business failure in Canada? Did he tell the same early-career story 20 years ago, and will he tell the same story again in 20 years' time? Would his family members, friends, colleagues and employers tell the same story about him? What story would the CEO who first championed him but then fell out with him tell? There is no single true story of any career, particularly if the stories include subjective as well as objective elements. There is nothing necessarily dishonest about multiple stories: they simply indicate subjective biases, memory lapses and the different purposes of the stories. Careers may be no more or less than the stories we tell about them – often compelling stories in which the career actor is a hero. Such stories help us to understand who we are and what our lives are about. They provide us with the logic to explain the past and give us direction for the future. They help us to maintain our self-esteem. If we know how career stories work, we can tell our own and interpret those of others. The world of career stories is explored in Chapter 11.

Conclusion

We have shown nine different views of Max's career. It is as if each metaphor provides a different lens to view the same phenomenon. Through each lens, we see different things. Each view appears to be valid and there is some overlap between them, but each metaphor generates its own unique insights. The discipline of thinking about careers in terms of each of the nine metaphors is a rigorous one but one that we believe will pay off over time in terms of your general understanding of careers and your specific understanding of your own career. In the ten chapters that follow, we explain what we can learn about careers by considering career contexts, then using each of the metaphors.

Key Points in this Chapter

- Careers are important sources of human satisfaction and fulfilment, or the reverse. Key issues are congruence with one's makeup, personal change, family matters and decision making.
- A definition of *career* is 'the evolving sequence of a person's work experiences over time'.
- The field of career studies has evolved over time from its original, psychological trait-and-factor and human development theories to include a range of approaches from sociology, social psychology and management studies.

(Continued)

(Continued)

- Careers are often described by metaphors, such as the 'pathway' metaphor or the 'square peg in a round hole' metaphor. Multiple metaphor is a way of expressing a range of viewpoints about careers to increase understanding.
- The career metaphors considered in this book are 'inheritance', 'cycle', 'action', 'fit', 'journey', 'roles', 'relationships', 'resource' and 'stories'.

Questions from this Chapter

General Questions

1. Outline three career decisions or problems that you or people you know currently face.
2. How would you advise Jan (see start of chapter) to solve the career problem he currently faces?
3. Which of the various theories in career studies seems to you to have the most relevance to your career and today's careers in general? Why?
4. Use metaphor to describe one or more authority figures you know (e.g. managers, tutors, instructors). What is the meaning you are trying to convey with the metaphors? How well do the metaphors fit?
5. Read the story of Max's career. Outline some principles you think Max used in managing it. Which of the metaphors do you think best describes his career, and why?

'Live Career Case' Study Questions

1. Ask your career actor to provide, and explain, metaphors for their career.
2. Think about the nine key metaphors outlined in the chapter in relation to your case career. Which seem to offer the most in terms of understanding the career? Why? If necessary, discuss them with the case career actor.

Additional Resources

Recommended Further Reading

Duberley, J., Cohen, L. and Mallon, M. (2006) 'Constructing scientific careers: Change, continuity and context', *Organization Studies*, 27(8): 1131–1151.

El-Sawad, A. (2005) 'Becoming a lifer? Unlocking career through metaphor', *Journal of Occupational and Organizational Psychology*, 78(1), 23–41.

Inkson, K. and Amundson, N. E. (2002) 'Career metaphors and their application in theory and counseling practice', *Journal of Employment Counseling*, 39(3): 98–108.

Mignot, P. (2004) 'Metaphor and "career", *Journal of Vocational Behavior*, 64(3): 455–469.

Moore, C., Gunz, H. and Hall, D. T. (2007) 'Tracing the historical roots of career theory in management and organization studies' in H. Gunz and M. Peiperl (eds.), *Handbook of Career Studies* (pp. 39–54). Thousand Oaks, CA: SAGE.

Online Resources

Find out about the use of metaphor and learn how to generate your own – see: www.mindtools.com/pages/article/newCT_93.htm and www.wikihow.com/Write-a-Metaphor

Careers in Context

Chapter Objectives

The objectives of this chapter are:

- to examine how careers are understood, and career decisions are influenced, by historical, cultural and ideological context factors
- to discuss how demographic, economic, labor market, social, organizational, technological and chance factors impact on the careers that are attainable and less attainable for people living in certain contexts at certain points in time
- to understand that individual career choices are always to some extent limited by boundaries imposed by factors outside of the individual
- to identify ways in which, as contexts change, career actors' ideas about what it means 'to have a career' can change over the course of their lives.

CASE STUDY

Left to Fate

At school, Fleur was an excellent student – intelligent, motivated and hard-working. She was good at all her school subjects, and her teachers agreed that she was one of the students most likely to succeed.

Her best subject, and the one she enjoyed most, was art. She painted landscapes and still lifes beautifully, endowing them with a unique vibrancy. Her paintings won prizes in local competitions. And she loved the process of painting, of animating the inanimate. She thought she would embark on a painting career. She persuaded her parents to convert an outhouse into her studio. Two years later, she had produced a large number of very fine paintings, but she had had little success in marketing her work: while she had succeeded in placing paintings in local art shops, customers had shown little interest, so she was bringing no money in. Her parents had split up and her mother, short of money, was beginning to say, 'When are you going to get a proper job?'

Realizing she might have to put her painting ambitions on hold, Fleur had an intense discussion with her mother about other career options. 'You're good at everything, the world's your oyster', said her mother. 'Look at your father, he's an accountant and he's done a bit of law. That's how he was able to hide our money so that I didn't get my fair share. Do accounting, and you'll always be able to handle your own money. And there's a shortage of accountants: you'll never want for a job.' Fleur had done well in accounting at school, but had not enjoyed it much. Reluctantly, she enrolled at university for a business degree with an accounting major.

Three years later, Fleur had a large student debt and a business degree, was on the way to professional accreditation, was still living at home and was able to secure a starting position as an accountant in a major company in the wine and spirits business. Her future now seemed secure, but she was not enjoying her job. Was she to be as bored as this for the next 40 years? And who, in a firm that sold alcoholic liquor, was she helping, apart from a lot of rich shareholders? She yearned to do something more fulfilling and sociable. Still, with money coming in, she was able to reduce her student debt and move into her own apartment. She continued to paint in her spare time.

Then, two years into her new life, the 2008 global financial crisis struck. Her company restructured dramatically. Fleur was laid off along with other staff, but was given the opportunity to reapply for one of the few remaining jobs in the company. But she had had enough. She decided that her layoff was a sign that accounting was not for her. She did not apply to go back into the company. She realized that she had a vocation to work in the health industry – to help sick people to become well again. After another heart-to-heart with her mother, she enrolled for a degree in physiotherapy.

Now, her student debt climbed higher than ever, but she loved her new vocation. By the second year, she was doing 'hands-on' therapy, interacting with patients. At the end of her third year, she graduated near the top of her class.

(Continued)

(Continued)

Although physiotherapy wasn't nearly as well paid as accounting had been, she knew she had made a good choice, where she would be happy. And she had met Martin, the love of her life, and moved in with him. What could go wrong now?

The answer was that she could not get a job. It was 2011, the effects of the recession were still being felt, the government was enforcing cuts across the health sector, and all employed physiotherapists were holding firmly on to their jobs. That year, there were only two new vacancies in her city, and over 50 new graduates from her university program!

All right, she thought, I'll go back into accounting, as a temporary measure. I'll wait till jobs in physiotherapy begin to flow again. But that didn't work either. Her professional qualification had expired because she had done no new training for three years, the technology had also changed in ways she felt uncomfortable with, and the financial recession was still making jobs hard to find. In the end, she had to settle for a junior, almost clerical position – better than nothing, but not what she had envisaged when she was a top student in her school. She was 30, and apart from her relationship with Martin, her life seemed to be going nowhere.

Fleur is talented and motivated. Why has her career had such a poor start? While one might criticize some of the decisions she has made, the answer is the simple word *context*. Careers do not exist in a vacuum. They exist in a context, a set of external structures and events that create opportunities and difficulties. In Fleur's case, a contextual factor called *labor market* was all-important. She wanted to be a painter but there was no market for her paintings. There might have been a market for physiotherapy at that time, but by the time she had qualified as a physiotherapist that market had almost gone. When there was a market for accountancy and she was an accountant she prospered, but that market too declined, and her *professional association* – another contextual force – had standards that disqualified her from good jobs. Much of this was attributable to the *economic system* and its cycles, from which few jobs can remain immune, and from her organization's *restructuring* which destroyed her one decent job. Changes in *technology* seem to have had an influence against her re-employment in an accounting role. Finally, middle-class *values* and *ideologies*, such as Fleur's mother's view that women should nowadays be independent and educate themselves financially, also affected Fleur's decision making.

No one can direct their career successfully without thinking about circumstances. Although books with titles such as *You Can Do Anything: Three simple steps to success for graduates* (Gibson, 2012) and *Success at Any Age: The baby boomer's (and Gen Y) guide to becoming an overnight success* (Bour, 2012) imply that success is wholly dependent on what *you* do, don't believe them. The context is always going to be a critical determinant of anyone's career.

Understanding Context

Part of understanding careers is therefore understanding the *context* of careers – past, present and future. And from a purely practical point of view, it's worth investing time and effort in learning what's going on out there that may affect your career. Not to do so is like walking across a busy street with a blindfold on. The main objective of this chapter is therefore to encourage critical reflection on the role of context in careers. And context involves many different factors:

- *Demographic factors* include the makeup of, and changes in, the population, particularly the population seeking employment, including numbers, age, gender, ethnic origin, education, skills and experience.
- *Economic factors* include the growth or decline in the economy, business confidence, international trade conditions, interest rates and other factors influencing business growth or decline, and current wage rates. The global financial crisis that started in 2008 is a pivotal example of how the economy can affect individuals' careers. According to the International Labor Organization (ILO), over 50 million people worldwide lost their jobs as a direct result of the crisis.
- *Labor market factors* affect the opportunities available to people. Some industries and occupations decline, whereas others grow dramatically. In recent years, for example, manufacturing has offered fewer jobs, whereas information systems and personal services have offered many more.
- *Social factors*, which affect people's lifestyle choices, both as consumers and as producers, include the demand for traditional and new products and services; and society's norms about entering the workforce, having a career, having more than one job, career goals, women's roles, etc.
- *Organizational factors* include business or occupational bureaucracies, the prevalence of large versus small organizations, the conditions for self-employment, organizational structures and restructuring, and trends towards temporary employment and part-time work.
- *Technological factors* include the substitution of machines for manual labor and skills, and the computerization of clerical and coordination activities. Technological advancement has the capacity to change jobs and occupations profoundly. In recent years, for example, social media have assumed a central position in many people's career tactics.
- *Chance factors* include unpredictable events such as natural disasters (e.g. the 2004 tsunami in South East Asia, the 2013 typhoon in the Philippines) or civil wars and conflicts (e.g. the events ensuing from the Arab Spring, which started in 2010, in Syria, Egypt and Tunisia, among others). Such events show us the volatile nature

of context. Clearly, being a citizen in a region gravely affected by a natural disaster or a war profoundly affects a person's working life and one may wonder whether having a career, successful or less successful, would still be considered an important issue at all. But chance factors also include small events, such as a fire at one's work, a casual meeting with an influential acquaintance, and opening a newspaper in a coffee shop and seeing an advertisement for your 'perfect job'.

At the higher-order level, the three forces of history, culture and ideology – pervasive contextual influences in every society – influence the way people think and feel about careers, e.g. 'What is normal? What is expected? What is successful?' Contextual cues have a significant influence on people's experiences of career, which in turn affect their career decisions and actions. Each of the three contextual factors discussed in this chapter (history, culture and ideology) might generate barriers and opportunities to the construction of meaning in careers, and thereby to careers themselves:

- A *historical* barrier might be the emergence of a global financial crisis, for instance, or a political 'crackdown', limiting the opportunities people have to express their personal values through conscious career choices and decisions (e.g. Valcour, 2010) – while an example of a historical opportunity is the rise of postmodernist thought, advocating that there is no 'one right way' to have a career and that people should craft their own lives according to their personal values and standards rather than to societal or organizational norms (Savickas, 2000).
- *Culture* has a major influence on the distribution of career opportunities across different groups: some cultures, for instance, do not allow women to work outside of the home; some cultures are characterized by caste systems; others by egalitarianism (Hofstede, 2001). It is well documented that different cultures promote different meanings of career success – for instance, US culture promotes 'big money' and celebrity status as indicators of having a successful life (Lucas et al., 2006; Samuel, 2012).
- *Ideologies* such as economic liberalism and the belief in free markets or, alternatively, socialism, can structure careers by structuring career actors' aspirations. Some ideologies (those grounded in a capitalist and individualist worldview) implicitly encourage and inspire people to follow their own individual dreams. Other ideologies (those that have their origins in collectively-oriented worldviews) suggest that everyone should strive to serve the greater good of society as a whole, even at the expense of their own personal goals (Lucas et al., 2006).

Field and Habitus

The French sociologist Pierre Bourdieu had a schema for understanding context that shows us the different structural constraints that apply to careers (Mayrhofer et al., 2004). Bourdieu talked about two critical concepts – field and habitus:

Fields are the social spaces in which people live and are characterized by internal complexity and hierarchy. Fields arise in education, religion, economic life and other areas in which people face structural constraints, rules, boundaries and expected practices. Fields contain institutions and individuals who occupy dominant or less dominant positions. They limit us but simultaneously challenge us to conserve the rules if we are dominant or to subvert or overcome them if we are constrained.

Habitus, according to Bourdieu, is the system of internal, personal, enduring dispositions through which we perceive the world. We acquire habitus through exposure to the social conditions around us, which we typically receive from, and share with, others in our predominant social groups, including family. Thus, we internalize external constraints and opportunities, and build and develop our habitus over time from new experiences. Habitus is the vehicle through which much of our inheritance of values, interests, ideas, motivations and social connections is incorporated.

Field and habitus are intimately related to each other. Gender provides an example. As will be shown in Chapter 3, gender is the source of many constraints, rules and norms in different career fields (Corsun & Costen, 2001). A woman seeking to become a firefighter or commando, for example, will, in the field, face formal and informal processes and barriers tending to keep her out of these occupations or relegating her to junior positions. These barriers may include discouragement from family and others, aptitude or endurance tests oriented to male standards of physical capability, biased interviews, special tests of character, and ridicule and scorn from other fire-fighters, managers and others (Burke, 2001; Hicks Stiehm, 1996; Morgan, 2003). At the same time, her habitus, informed by a lifetime of indoctrination from family, school, community, popular media and the like, may be giving her messages that she should 'stay away'. The outcome is the product of the two sets of forces. When we look at careers in that way, we understand that careers are not merely the product of individual willpower, abilities or motivation, but are partly structured by strong contextual forces.

History and Contextual Change

Over the last two decades, phenomena such as economic globalization, organizational restructuring (e.g. mergers, horizontal and vertical integrations within and between organizations, downsizing) and the growth of services have drastically altered the face of careers. Below, we discuss how historical forces such as the shift to a post-industrial knowledge society, labor market evolutions and changing values have impacted on careers over time, and might still be impacting on your career today.

The evolution of the global economy – at different speeds in different parts of the world – from an agricultural economy and society to an industrial and then to a post-industrial knowledge society, has contributed strongly to the current idea of what 'a career' is (Savickas, 2000).

In most Western countries around the beginning of the 19th century, the Industrial Revolution marked the end of the *agricultural economy*, in which the dominant social institution had been the family and young people had simply inherited their careers from their parents. In those days, career success was determined by physical survival and security and the development of character (i.e. compliance to the norm of hard work and ethical behavior). The *industrial economy*, in contrast, was characterized by the appearance of large, bureaucratic organizations, and formalized trades and professions, offering careers for life. Career success, accordingly, was measured by verifiable attainments (i.e. income, position and status) relating to upward advancement on the corporate or professional ladder.

In the second half of the 20th century, Western society was transformed again, through globalization as well as through scientific and technical (r)evolutions. In the current *post-industrial economy*, characterized by widespread organizational restructuring and economic uncertainty, the hallmarks of the traditional-organizational career are said to be disappearing. The post-World War II years brought huge changes to the contextual factors affecting careers and to careers themselves. Some of the major changes are shown in Table 2.1.

Table 2.1   Recent Trends and their Effects on Careers

Nature of Change	Effect on Careers
'Welfare state', protectionist and full employment policies of many countries, 1940–1980	Considerable career security for many people
Organizations becoming larger and more complex (up to 1980)	Availability of loyalty-based 'organizational careers' providing steady advancement in large organizations
Market-oriented economic policies of many countries from 1980	Higher unemployment, exposure of careers to economic cycles
Organizations restructuring for lower costs and greater efficiencies	Layoffs, unanticipated transfers and career destabilization, 'McJobs'
Mechanization – less manual work, more service and managerial work	Changed occupational structures – move from 'physical' jobs to 'knowledge' jobs
'Ageing' society – greater longevity	People stretching their careers beyond age 65
Emancipation of women, trends to two-income households	Enlarged labor pool; changes in traditional 'male' occupations; dual-career couples
Greater affluence, more discretionary spending	Growth of industries such as luxury goods and hospitality, with new career opportunities
Professionalization of specialist occupations	Structuring and protection of professional career paths through required qualifications
Growth of information technology	New occupations, organizations and careers in IT; major changes in the work in other jobs
Globalization – multinational organizations relocating business for lowest cost	Displacement of manufacturing and some service jobs to third-world countries; beginning of global careers

The top four rows of Table 2.1 detail major economic and organizational effects on careers. The mid-20th-century fashion for full employment provided working people with some protection against economic cycles, and universal education created greater opportunities for them to become upwardly mobile. In this benign environment, organizations also changed, becoming larger and more complex. Smart companies cultivated loyal long-term workforces by offering organizational careers, with inducements such as guaranteed promotions, sophisticated training and development programs, and company pensions.

However, this changed in many countries in the 1980s, when the fashion grew for market-based economic policies and for less government protection for business. Businesses found that in a world of rapid change and cutthroat competition, they could best protect themselves by minimizing their long-term labor costs and maximizing their labor flexibility. This led, in the 1980s and 1990s, to what seemed to be massive restructuring (Bridges, 1995). Some organizations downsized and laid off many staff members. Others de-layered, removing the hierarchical ladders up which staff members advanced in their careers. Others replaced long-term employees with contractors, who had no assurance of continuing employment. Some industries, such as the film industry, increasingly organized around temporary projects rather than permanent jobs. Many careers were destabilized and the individuals concerned had to start again, developing new career skills and attitudes (Goffee & Scase, 1992). Also, reorganization of the service sector for greater efficiency created more relatively unskilled 'McJobs', where the employee is easily replaceable.

All of these devices increased companies' numerical flexibility, enabling them to reduce the core of permanent employees while increasing the number of temporary workers whose employment depended on fluctuations in business. To improve their functional flexibility, i.e. their ability to redeploy people from jobs that were no longer needed into jobs that were, companies used techniques such as multiskilling and teamwork, again affecting individuals' range of skills and thereby their careers.

In other changes, much manual work was mechanized, reducing the number of jobs available. In contrast, the demand for services grew – for example, in sales, secretarial, administrative, financial and hospitality work – creating many new career opportunities. Careers became both more skilled and more secure, and improved health and longevity lengthened them into a retirement phase. More spending was discretionary, and industries such as luxury goods and leisure grew, creating further diversity in career opportunities.

In a changing social climate, newly emancipated women returned to the workforce in increasing numbers, though usually in the traditional bastions of female employment, such as retail, secretarial, nursing and teaching work. Professional bodies and trade unions developed sophisticated means of controlling entry into occupations and progression within them and of ensuring good conditions for their members.

Another major change was the information technology revolution started by the invention of the minicomputer in the 1970s. Today's organizations do not just have information systems; they *are* information systems (Senge, 1990). The jobs and career opportunities of career actors are increasingly defined by their IT skills, and their career moves are increasingly mediated through global networks of information. Consider, for instance, the increasing use of global databases and international placement consultants ('head-hunters') to fill key positions in organizations worldwide (Faulconbridge et al., 2008).

In recent years, there has also been a massive upsurge in social networking websites such as Facebook, MySpace, LinkedIn and Twitter, causing profound changes in the way we develop our careers and others control them. Recent studies have found that over 70 percent of active LinkedIn users and over 40 percent of active Facebook users admit to using their accounts to search for additional information about applicants for jobs in their organizations, and to base decisions as to who will be invited for an interview partly on such information (Davison et al., 2011). Recruitment professionals report that they would consider any information that they could find about applicants available online, even pictures and comments made among friends. Forty percent even claim that they can deduce level of extroversion and maturity from an applicant's profile picture (Caers & Castelyns, 2011). There have also been reports of applicants not being hired because their 'Klout score' (a measure of online influence) was too low, as well as of employees being fired for criticizing their employer on Facebook (Stevenson, 2012). From this, it has become clear that online 'self-branding' is an important issue, especially for current generations who are just getting started in their careers (see also Chapter 12).

Stop and Consider

The historical trends outlined in Table 2.1 apply to the Western world more than to non-Western countries such as the rapidly developing BRIC countries (Brazil, Russia, India and China). Go online and look up information about the BRIC countries. Match the information you find to the Western trends discussed in this chapter. To what extent have the BRIC countries experienced different trends to the Western world, versus similar trends but at a different pace of development?

New forms of career

How have all of these historical changes affected careers? Theorists interested in careers have suggested a range of career-related concepts and new forms of career:

Some suggest that a career is, in essence, a series of *psychological contracts* between employer and employee, in which each has implicit expectations of, and obligations to, the other (Rousseau, 2011). Rousseau (1995) and others have suggested that due to new forms of organization that have come into being – those more flexible, temporary, dynamic and project-based – these contracts have moved from being *relational* to being *transactional* – that is, specifying a short-term exchange of benefits rather than a long-term relationship with expectations of mutual loyalty. As a result, members of the workforce, scarred by their experiences of restructuring, have become increasingly disloyal and selfish – or, to put a more positive spin on it, independent and assertive – in their career behavior, and careful organizational management of careers to take account of such career attitudes may be necessary (Gerber et al., 2012; Inkson & King, 2011).

Books with titles such as *The Career is Dead: Long live the career* (Hall & Associates, 1996) argue that traditional, hierarchical organizational careers have all but disappeared, making traditional hierarchical careers obsolete and new, shape-changing 'protean' careers (Chapter 5) normative.

In a similar manner, the effect of restructuring has been to make organizations increasingly boundaryless, and to make so-called '*boundaryless careers*' (Arthur & Rousseau, 1996, Chapter 7), in which career actors move between organizations with increasing frequency, more common. Boundaryless careerists must base their careers increasingly on portable career competencies, such as up-to-date expertise, contacts and reputation.

The growth of non-permanent forms of employment – for example, temporary work, part-time work, contract work, self-employment, work for cash payments in the black economy, and service work in the evenings, at night and on weekends – has led many workers to develop '*portfolio careers*' (Handy, 1989), in which the career actor, rather than pursuing a single, full-time job, balances a portfolio of different and changing opportunities.

The focus of many people's career objectives has moved from employment to *employability* (Fugate et al., 2004; Hogan et al., 2013). As skill requirements change, so must career actors develop new skills. Education and apprenticeship, once thought of as once-and-for-all career preparation, must now be considered parts of lifelong learning to meet ever-changing demands and to retain employability.

Stop and Consider

Do some research on the careers of at least two historical figures. How might their lives and careers have turned out if they had grown up in the current day and age? Use your imagination!

Are these moves toward transactional contracts and protean, boundaryless, portfolio careers, employability and lifelong learning, good for career actors and good for society? It is hard to say. Enterprising people probably welcome the proliferation of new opportunities, whereas those oriented to security and stability may feel threatened. Proponents of the new environment argue that the new career forms contribute to a more efficient, flexible and dynamic economy; reduce employees' dependence on their employers; and provide new opportunities for talented people from any background to reap the benefits of their expertise and adaptability (Arthur & Rousseau, 1996; Chudzikowski, 2012). Opponents deplore the new insecurity of employment and worry that, for many, boundarylessness means unemployment and marginalization (Pringle & Mallon, 2003; Sommerlund & Boutaiba, 2007), and for employing organizations loss of their heart and soul (Cappelli, 1999). The desirability of what has been termed the 'new' careers (Arthur et al., 1999) will be returned to from time to time in subsequent chapters.

Economic and labor market trends

The economic context within which careers take place is in constant flux, and that means that the nature of careers also changes over time. Labor market realities have been changing so rapidly in recent years – in great part due to the global financial crisis that started in 2008 – that, even in recent times, we can find descriptions of labor market trends that are no longer recognizable today. For example, in 2001 International Labor Organization (ILO) economist Lawrence Johnson stated: 'Ireland is the poster country for European potential … with its growing productivity and almost non-existent unemployment.' In 2013, as a result of the global financial crisis, the unemployment rate in Ireland neared 14 percent and ranked among the highest in Europe.

Consider the 2013 unemployment statistics published by Eurostat:

Some European Unemployment Statistics

Eurostat estimates that in April 2013 26.588 million men and women (around 12 percent of all working-age adults) in the European Union (EU) were unemployed, 104,000 more than a month previously, and 1,673,000 more than a year previously. Among the Member States, the lowest unemployment rates were recorded in Austria (4.9 percent), Germany (5.4 percent) and Luxembourg (5.6 percent), and the highest rates in Greece (27.0 percent), Spain (26.8 percent) and Portugal (17.8 percent). In April 2013, the youth unemployment rate was 23.5 percent, with 5.627 million EU citizens under 25 being unemployed, 100,000 more than a year previously.

Source: Eurostat (2013), at: www.epp.eurostat.ec.europa.eu/statistics_explained/index.php/Unemployment_statistics

Although many economies have been hit hard by the global financial crisis, which has reduced career opportunities for young graduates worldwide (Eurostat, 2013; Valcour, 2010), organizations around the globe are, paradoxically, struggling to fill key positions. Consultants typically refer to these scarcities in the labor market as 'the war for talent' (Michaels et al., 2001). It seems strange that youth employment can be so high while, at the same time, organizations complain that there is a lack of young talent.

Stop and Consider

Go online and look up recent unemployment statistics for your country or region. A good place to start might be the website of the International Monetary Fund (IMF). Focus specifically on the economic situation of those sectors you might be interested in pursuing a career in. What do these numbers tell you? Do they deter you from pursuing a career in that sector, country or area? Also, look up which jobs are considered shortage occupations in your country or region. Would you consider entering any of these occupations, knowing that for these jobs young graduates are in high demand?

In the USA and Western Europe, a major issue is the impending retirement of large groups of older employees, combined with the fact that fewer and fewer young people are entering the workforce. Demographic trends such as the aging of society and declining birth numbers (Calo, 2008) lie at the heart of these labor market shortages. Although today there is much youth unemployment, in the longer-term labor market economists expect to see large-scale demand–supply gaps – shortages of young employees to fill the gaps created by the mass exodus of retirement-age employees from the workforce (Sels et al., 2008).

In other parts of the world – most notably the BRIC countries, i.e. Brazil, Russia, India and China – there is an *oversupply* of young workers, but these often lack the experience or education to fill key roles (Chuai et al., 2008).

Consider, for example, the case of elite Chinese employees, sometimes referred to as 'little emperors'. Because there are so many opportunities available for young people in the Chinese labor market, they are accused of being job-hoppers and of artificially driving up their salaries and status.

China's 'Little Emperors'

In 1979, to control population growth in its cities, China implemented the one-child policy. This policy has produced a generation of young adults often called 'little

(Continued)

(Continued)

emperors'. Having grown up with the undivided attention of two parents and four grandparents, and entering a labor market with acute skill shortages, the little emperors are somewhat self-centred and hold themselves in high regard. They have high achievement aspirations, expectations of material success and a sense of entitlement. They prefer 'job hopping' through short-term contracts so that they can benefit from the personnel shortages that drive up pay and promotion opportunities, and they expect to be promoted every six months to a year. A perverse effect of their over-eagerness, however, is that they are often promoted into managerial positions too soon, before they have developed the necessary skills to be successful in them. A common result is that foreign executives have to be brought in to ensure competent succession. In addition, the little emperors resent any indication that a 'bamboo ceiling' might exist – that invisible barrier believed to prevent Chinese managers from advancing to the highest levels in multinational companies. HR professionals find that recruitment, retention and development practices must be adapted to accommodate the expectations of the little emperors. For example, in some companies, HR people create unofficial levels in the hierarchy to provide the frequent promotions these young people expect.

Source: Weldon (2010).

Generational trends

Before we discuss generational differences as historical trends affecting individual careers, let us start with a brief disclaimer. Although there is much debate in the media about generational differences, we feel obliged to point out that truly scientific evidence is inconclusive. To date, it remains unclear to what extent the differences found between generations in research (e.g. 'baby boomers' versus 'Generation X') can be attributed to generational shifts in values, or to age and career/life stage effects: for example, when Generation Y-ers (those from the youngest generation) say that they value spending time with friends and not working too much, should we attribute these opinions to generational differences or to the fact that these people are 23 years old and working in entry-level jobs (Macky et al., 2008; Yang & Guy, 2006)? Nonetheless, we have chosen to include this section on intergenerational differences because many people (not in the least recruiters) believe they, in fact, exist. In that sense, even though it may be difficult to objectively assess the extent to which the generation we belong to will determine our career, we can argue that generational differences do form an important contextual backdrop to careers, if only 'in the eye of the beholder'.

Generations are defined as 'identifiable groups that share birth years, age location, and significant life events at critical developmental stages' (Kupperschmidt, 2000: 66).

Consequently, generational cohorts, e.g. 'the younger generation', may be seen as societal subcultures whose *work values* reflect the significant cultural, political and economic developments that occurred during their pre-adult years. Work values express what people want to do, or want to have in the workplace, and prevailing values in any society or its subgroups may massively influence career aspirations (Macky et al., 2008). The pervasive social environment, created most notably by parents, peers, media and popular culture, creates common value systems among people growing up in a specific historical context, distinguishing them from those who grew up in different eras.

The assumption of generational differences in work values stems from two underlying hypotheses – socialization and scarcity:

- According to the *socialization* hypothesis, an adult's basic values reflect the socio-economic conditions of their childhood and adolescence. According to Inglehart (1997), these values normally remain relatively stable across the lifespan.
- The *scarcity* hypothesis proposes that the greatest subjective value is placed on those socio-economic factors that are in short supply during that specific generational cohort's younger years (Inglehart, 1997).

Table 2.2   Generational Differences in Work Values

Generation	Birth Year	Salient Events	Life Values	Work Values	Credo
Silent Generation	1925–1945	Great Depression World War II	Conformism Maturity Conscientiousness Thrift	Obedience Loyalty Obligation Security (Stability)	'We must pay our dues and work hard.'
Baby Boomers	1946–1964	Kennedy–King assassinations Moon landing Vietnam War 1960s' social revolution	Idealism Creativity Tolerance Freedom Self–fulfillment	Challenge Workaholism Criticism Innovativeness Advancement Materialism	'If you have it, flash it.'
Generation X	1965–1980	AIDS First oral contraceptive pills 1973 oil crisis Cold War	Individualism Skepticism Flexibility Control Fun	Free agency Learning Entrepreneurship Materialism Balance	'Whatever.'
Generation Y	1981–2001	Fall of the Berlin Wall 9/11–War on Terror MTV Internet Facebook	Collectivism Positivity Moralism Confidence Civic mindedness	Balance Passion Learning Security (not stability) Willingness to work	'Let's make this world a better place.'

Source: Dries et al. (2008).

The salient events experienced by people from each generational cohort lie, at least in part, at the heart of its identity as a collective (see Table 2.2).

- The 'Veterans' entered the workforce in the post-World War II era, when the notion of 'career' was just being forged. The increase in opportunities for advancement and the broadening of occupations to choose from appealed greatly to a generation that had grown up experiencing or hearing about the Great Depression and the Great War.
- Following this era of economic prosperity, the late 1970s and 1980s were characterized by economic recession. Organizational restructuring and downsizing caused the first cracks in the image of the lifetime career with one employer. As a result, baby boomers are often portrayed as 'free agents' in the workplace, i.e. 'radical individualists who advocate individual rights over family needs and the rights of the team or organization' (Kupperschmidt, 2000: 69).
- This trend of employees distancing themselves from organizations persisted in Generations X and Y. Because the future is unpredictable, these generations have learned not to take anything for granted. They do not count on organizations to offer them security and stability in their career; rather, they tend to seek out employers that offer challenging jobs and sufficient training for them to gain 'employability' in the job market, thus acquiring career security in lieu of job security.

Generation Y-ers, currently aged in their teens, 20s and early 30s, were raised in times of economic expansion and prosperity, but the majority of them entered, or will enter, the workforce in a time of economic uncertainty. The most defining historical events for this cohort are said to be the growth of ICT, the 24-hour media and the globalized world. They have been characterized as continuous learners, achievement oriented, proficient at multitasking, competent in and dependent on electronic technology.

Stop and Consider

Reread the table on generational work values. Do you believe generational differences are 'real'? To what extent do you recognize yourself in the descriptions? Keep in mind that, if you are from a non-Western country, the generational makeup of your reference population may be different. Make a list of your personal work values. How might these translate into specific career choices that you will need to make after graduation?

Careers and Culture

The mainstream academic literature on careers was created by scholars from the USA, the UK and other developed and industrialized nations with their own communities in mind. It therefore takes a relatively narrow view of the cultural context of careers. In Third World countries, careers are affected by factors such as authoritarian governments, primitive agricultural technology, overpopulation and underdeveloped educational systems – cultural differences are critical to careers.

What is 'culture'? It is a set of shared mental programs that condition individuals' responses to their environment. Those sharing the programs may be members of the same tribe, or the same ethnic group, or the same nation, or (as we have seen) the same generation, or the same organization. For example, a key dimension of culture is individualism versus collectivism: in an individualistic culture, people are expected to make their own way and be self-sufficient whereas in a collectivist culture tasks are shared together.

Culture can thus specify the types of career paths that are to be followed by members of a given industry, company or occupation, the kinds of motives and ambitions that are considered legitimate for pursuit of careers, and the degree of prestige that is attached to different paths. These differences influence how people feel about and approach their careers, what, if anything, 'success' means to them, and even how explicitly they experience having a career (Khapova et al., 2009). Looking at careers in other countries and cultures is important because it gives us a sense of humility and appreciation for the special, and mainly benign, conditions in which we in the industrialized world develop our careers and because, as will be demonstrated in Chapter 7, careers are increasingly international and we never know when our career will take us abroad into unfamiliar contexts.

Cultural differences

The careers literature has, generally speaking, seriously underestimated the weight of cross-cultural differences in describing and explaining career phenomena. As a result, there is an overemphasis in the literature on Western career concepts and measures, especially those developed in the USA. The projection of US values onto career actors from other parts of the world, without taking into account possible differences in their definitions of career and career success, may be problematic.

From Hofstede's (2001) seminal work on cultural differences, we can draw some preliminary inferences about how people from different countries will, generally speaking, experience and evaluate their careers (Thomas & Inkson, 2007).

- *Power distance*: the extent to which the less powerful members of organizations and institutions accept and expect that power is distributed unequally. Perceptions of high power distance may create subjective hierarchies that individuals are discouraged from seeking to ascend.
- *Uncertainty avoidance*: the extent to which a culture programmes its members to feel uncomfortable in unstructured situations. A culture high on uncertainty avoidance might have tight, secure regulations and stable structures defining career progression. Individuals might have trouble adapting to contextual change.
- *Individualism*: the extent to which the ties between individuals are loose and everyone is expected to look after themselves and their immediate family. In individualistic cultures, careers may be considered as personal projects; in collective societies, the notion of the individual career may be downplayed in favor of group projects and group organization.
- *Masculinity*: the extent to which dominant values are related to assertiveness, money, material possessions and well-defined gender roles. Masculinity encourages personal agency – action in support of oneself – in a career, whereas femininity stresses 'communion' (Marshall, 1995).
- *Long-term orientation*: the extent to which values such as frugality and perseverance are dominant. A long-term orientation might encourage career actors to show patience in relation to their career goals.

Table 2.3 provides an overview of some of the average employee value scores Hofstede uncovered in his 1967–1973 study spanning 53 countries and regions (Hofstede, 2001):

Table 2.3   Hofstede Employee Value Scores: US Scores, UK Scores, World Average and European Average

	Cultural Dimensions				
	Power Distance	**Uncertainty Avoidance**	**Individualism**	**Masculinity**	**Long-term Orientation**
	Score (Rank)	Score (Rank)	Score (Rank)	Score (Rank)	Score (Rank)
USA	40 (38)	46 (43)	91 (1)	62 (15)	29 (27)
UK	35 (43)	35 (47)	89 (3)	66 (10)	25 (28)
World average	55	64	43	50	45
European average	45	74	61	59	–

Notes: 'Scores' are average employee value scores per country. 'Rank' is based on a comparison of the scores of each country to the scores of each of the other 52 countries in the Hofstede sample.

Source: Hofstede (2001).

Table 2.3 compares US and UK scores to the world and European average for each employee value, the USA and the UK being the countries that produce the largest proportion of careers literature. It clearly illustrates that specific aspects of the US and UK contexts should not be generalized to other countries without critical reflection on possible cultural differences. While Anglo-Saxon employees tend to see the advantages of self-direction (high individualism), job-hopping (short-term orientation) and regularly changing employers and sectors (low uncertainty avoidance), European employees tend to focus more energy on achieving employment security (high uncertainty avoidance) and mutual employer–employee loyalty (lower individualism) (Dries, 2011).

Although, in general, cultural differences tend to be underestimated, they are sometimes *overestimated*, due to stereotyping, and this in turn causes further stereotyping (Dries, 2011). For instance, a typical stereotype for portraying Asian people is the Buddhist monk who renounces material success and personal gain. Furnham (2010) describes how the misconception that 'the great Oriental religions do not offer an encouraging cultural framework for the rational pursuit of economic gain' (p. 134) has led to stereotypical beliefs that Asian belief systems (somehow considered to be other-worldly) inhibit an individualist approach to career attainment, and that Asians lack a need for achievement in the sense of a 'pursuit of wealth'. The fact that India and China are among the fastest developing economies in the world seems however to imply otherwise.

Stop and Consider

On Geert Hofstede's website, http://geert-hofstede.com/, you can find descriptions for over 70 countries in their power distance, uncertainty avoidance, individualism, masculinity and long-term orientation. (For some countries, you can also find information about a sixth dimension, which is called 'indulgence versus restraint'.) Have a look at the data for cultures you are personally familiar with. Is there a lot of resemblance between your own experience of these cultures and Hofstede's conclusions about them? Do you feel critical of Hofstede's approach to culture? Why (not)?

Globalization

Globalization refers to an increase in the permeability of traditional boundaries, including physical borders such as nation-states and economies, industries and organizations, and less tangible borders such as cultural norms. This increase in permeability is the result of shifts in technological, political and economic spheres. Free trade areas have reduced traditional economic boundaries. As a consequence, culture should not be considered an entirely stable feature of societies. As social, political and economic factors change, people will adapt to their new environment by assuming more relevant behaviors. Subsequently, these new behaviors can accumulate and begin to define new cultural assumptions (Hofstede, 2001), as is demonstrated by research in rapidly developing economies.

For instance, Khapova and Korotov (2007), comparing their findings to Hofstede's original scores, found clear shifts in Russian career values. Chudzikowski et al. (2009) found that the younger respondents in their Chinese sample reported career values more similar to those of Western respondents than to those of older Chinese. Care must be applied, however, in assuming that because of globalization, values around the world are converging and becoming more Western. Data from the World Values Survey found little to no value convergence between 20 different countries over a period of 26 years (Berry et al., 2014). Overall, the available empirical evidence seems to imply that *both* universalistic tendencies across cultural contexts – often referred to as 'global culture' – and culture-specific tendencies play a role in the enactment of careers. The literature on globalization argues that rather than juxtaposing different cultural beliefs regarding career and career success, researchers should aim to understand how these beliefs were shaped, and why they persist.

Non-global careers are also affected by globalization. In modern multinational corporations seeking to capitalize on location-specific advantages, functions such as research, finance, production, sales and marketing, and administration, might all be located in different countries, thereby altering the structure of career opportunities available to local workers. The globalization of product and service markets is accompanied by a globalization of labor markets, the spread of multinational corporations across the globe, the liberalization of immigration policies relating to skilled workers, and the reduced ease and cost of international travel. Many careers are in consequence 'going global' (Dickmann & Baruch, 2011).

Careers and Ideology

Where culture provides a set of attitudes, beliefs and values about social reality that affects its members' decision making, ideology involves evaluative judgment. It causes people to conform to a certain standard of what is 'right' versus what is 'wrong'; what is 'normal' or 'good'; and what is 'possible' or 'changeable'. Ideology, which is typically disseminated through mass communication, can thus be seen as a structuring principle of society (Ogbor, 2000). It thus differs from values held at the personal level in that it refers to entire value systems more or less 'forcing' the people in them to conform for the good of the larger social order.

Societal ideologies of career

For Western cultures, particularly the USA, the dominant ideological framework affecting careers is capitalism. The most typical and well-known example of capitalist career ideology is probably the strong popular belief in the career-related values of individualism, achievement and equality of opportunity, often referred to as the 'American Dream' (Lucas et al., 2006; Samuel, 2012).

According to the American Dream, any person, even from the humblest of backgrounds, can aspire, through hard work, to increasing wealth, health and happiness. The fictional story of the rags-to-riches hero Horatio Alger, popular in the early 20th century, epitomizes this view. It has a modern counterpart in the unknown-to-famous scenarios played out on our television screens in programs such as *American Idol* and *Masterchef*. Contestants who repeat ad nauseam the success mantra 'I will win because I want it so much' ignore the roles of not only background and luck, but also talent, in career outcomes.

These stories, however, involve wishful thinking. For every rags-to-riches Horatio Alger, idolized pop star or celebrity chef, there are many wannabes who are marginalized in labor markets where there are many more aspirants than opportunities, or who find the barriers to their progress are too great to combat. Much as we might like to believe that everyone has an equal chance to succeed, the truth is that career inequality is structured in our society in many different ways, for example through gender, race and social class (Chapter 3). The belief in equality of career opportunity may be a myth that increases our degree of comfort with the reality of *in*equality of opportunity.

Another ideological framework shaping career – originating from a very different part of the world – is communism. Underlying Maoist discourse in the People's Republic of China, for instance, were the values of:

- *equality* – the belief that all people are equal, regardless of their position in society
- *devotion* – the belief that a certain sacrifice of personal needs is necessary to serve the greater good
- *nobility* – the belief that working for the sake of individual financial gain or social promotion is shameful.

Although capitalism and communism are commonly depicted as extreme opposites in terms of ideology, according to Lucas et al. (2006) they serve a similar ideological purpose.

That is, they both promote a conceptualization of career and career success that benefits the dominant socio-political system at the potential detriment of individual career actors (Van Buren, 2003). The American Dream encourages people to pursue the type of career success that is most likely to sustain the capitalist system and foster nationwide economic growth. Failure is attributed to a person not being 'good enough' or not 'wanting it enough', so that it is never the fault of the system and always the responsibility of the individual. Communist discourse during Mao's era suspended Chinese people's critical thinking, restricted their career choices and obscured the fact that their society consisted of different interest groups who were *not* all equal in power, and that there was still a divide between good jobs and bad jobs. Complaining was unheard of, however, as that would go against the value of nobility (Lucas et al., 2006).

Organizational ideologies of career

Just as societal career discourse structures people's daily lives, so too do career structures, career development practices and career 'talk' in their employing organizations. By establishing an internal labor market with more or less standardized career tracks, organizations implicitly define success and failure within their structures (Buzzanell & Goldzwig, 1991). Organizational career ideology commonly departs from spatio-temporal evaluations of success – for example, 'up' is good, 'action' is positive and 'quick movement' should be the goal (Altman, 1997). Corporate career talk is less harmless than it may seem. First of all, through socialization processes and development programs, organizations seek to cultivate desired norms and values in their members, tying them to 'appropriate identities' (Ogbor, 2000). In their early career, people's definitions of career and career success are confronted by those of their organizations, often causing them to reassess their personal belief systems and goals. Second, corporate career discourse contributes to the devaluation and obstruction of alternative models of career – notable examples being the 'mommy' track, the expert track and the stationary (flat) track (Buzzanell & Goldzwig, 1991).

Within some corporate contexts, atypical career paths such as those above are considered unsuccessful. Worse still, once one is earmarked as a 'loser', there seems to be little chance of getting back 'on track'. It rarely happens that 'late bloomers' or people who have taken time off work (for example, for maternity) catch up to colleagues with a record of continuous service. Although people tend to believe that organizational assessments of advancement potential are grounded in more or less objective performance data, the rules of the career game in such organizations distribute precious career opportunities differentially. The groups with the most power will likely integrate their personal interests into the very structure of the organization, thereby influencing its members' opinion of what a successful career should look like, and marginalizing all those who do not fit the mould. The implications reach beyond mere ideological discourse – such dynamics lie at the heart of glass ceiling effects and other discriminatory processes taking place in organizations worldwide (Ogbor, 2000).

Occupational ideologies of career

Blue-Collar Experiences of 'Career', by Nicky Dries

A few years ago, when I was setting up research into people's subjective definitions of career success, I conducted a series of telephone interviews with blue-collar workers. As nearly all studies of career success have used samples of highly skilled knowledge workers (Buzzanell & Goldzwig, 1991), I was excited at the prospect of collecting data from this under-researched but important group of workers. It quickly became apparent, however, that my original plan – to randomly call up a large number of people and ask them, 'what does career success mean to you personally?' – would not generate the data I was hoping for. Instead, my question provoked a remarkable degree of resentment in respondents. As it turned out, the vast majority of the blue-collar workers I interviewed felt they simply did not *have* a career, let alone a successful one. This finding, although somewhat consistent with earlier research into blue-collar careers (e.g. Sturges & Guest, 2004), was particularly surprising considering that the specific focus of the research was on the subjective meanings attributed to career success, *whatever these might be*. Moreover, the definition of career success commonly referred to in the contemporary literature is 'the positive psychological or work-related outcomes and achievements one has accumulated as a result of one's work experiences' (Judge et al., 1995: 486). Surely, according to this definition, workers of all types have careers, each of which can be viewed as successful in one way or another? So why could my interviewees not identify with the term 'career' at all?

From the above account, we can infer that the notion of career, somehow, evokes an image with which people may or may not identify. In fact, the way people work, and the occupation they have, will strongly determine what they (subjectively) see as a legitimate career, and what type of career is (objectively) possible for them.

In that sense, educational and occupational choices made early on in life form a 'strong context' for everything that follows in mid- and late career. For a lawyer, a typical career track is for the career actor to start as an intern, and then work their way up to becoming a partner; for a bricklayer, there are fewer opportunities for upward advancement, though such opportunities will not be as institutionalized as those faced by a lawyer; and for an artist, achieving commercial success might be viewed by their peers as 'selling out'. In addition, people's occupations determine who they will compare themselves with in assessing how successful they feel in their careers. For instance, a university professor might measure her success by considering how many publications she has compared to her peers, or at what age she got tenure, rather than by salary.

In general, the career ideology a person is most exposed to will depend on the position of their occupation in society. People from upper- and middle-class environments are encouraged to believe that they are working for a common good, that their work has meaning and that their role in life is to help other people: they are rewarded socially, economically and politically for enacting these beliefs. Lower-status employees, however, are not encouraged to think of their work in such noble terms and are not rewarded as highly. They are socialized to see work as 'just a job' and to look for self-fulfillment in other life domains (Davidson & Caddell, 1994). Furthermore, career ideologies tend to convey a message that people want to hear and believe (e.g. 'you can achieve anything you want if you truly make an effort'), highlighting exceptions rather than cases more representative of reality. Such ideologies are often ambiguous, so that multiple interpretations of the same message are possible. If the definition of success is kept vague, then there are no limits to the contribution or sacrifice individuals will feel compelled to make (Van Buren, 2003).

Stop and Consider

Go to the website of one or more organizations that might appeal to you as an employer. What do you think their career ideology is? Can you find any information online about how these organizations see careers and what types of careers are available or encouraged?

Conclusion

In this chapter, we discussed historical, cultural and ideological forces impacting on careers. A country's degree of industrialization, the state of its labor market, its vulnerability to economic crisis and the demographic makeup of its population will have a strong impact on the careers of its inhabitants, such as whether the careers they aspire to are available, and what these careers look like in terms of pay, progression rate, stability and longevity. The occupation a person is in may have a typical pathway, along which it will be easy to make career moves, while, over time, alternative pathways become less and less likely. The organization a person works for may have standard career tracks in place – especially if it is large and bureaucratic – tied to promotion criteria and pay increases.

Moreover, work values, cultural norms and ideologies such as capitalism will impact on what individuals see as a legitimate, or successful, career. Although values and norms are not as tangible as, for instance, the global financial crisis, their effects on careers can be as great. Battling against what your family, friends and the media say you should do, and following your own dreams instead, is not easy.

Key Points in this Chapter

- Careers take place in a context and are affected by demographic, economic, social, organizational and technological factors. We have framed these in terms of wider historical, cultural and ideological contextual forces.
- The concepts of field (structural) and habitus (personal) conveniently help us to understand how contextual forces constrain, support and shape individual attitudes and actions.
- Historically, many factors have changed since the 19th century, dramatically changing the nature of careers. Important recent changes are the rapid growth of IT and social media, economic liberalism causing organizational restructuring, large-scale unemployment, globalization and greater longevity.
- New concepts of career responsive to these changes are psychological contracts, protean and boundaryless careers, and a focus on employability.
- Culture – organizational as well as national and regional – impacts on careers; so too does ideology: both the capitalist American Dream and communist ideology affect careers but may also be tools of control used by elites.

Questions from this Chapter

General Questions

1. Re-read the story about Fleur's career at the beginning of this chapter. Knowing the end of the story (or, at least, the state of Fleur's career at present), what career advice would you give her if you could go back in time and meet Fleur at age 18? Would you tell her to make different choices than she did?
2. Write down at least 10 spontaneous associations you have with the term 'career'. Now examine your associations critically. To what extent are your ideas about careers determined by the historical, cultural and ideological context you grew up in?
3. Which of the various factors influencing careers detailed in Table 2.1 do you consider the most significant and why?

4. Think of all the career advice you have been given by people over the years (by parents, teachers, colleagues, fellow students, friends). Also consider career advice given to you via the media and through social media. Now that you are aware of the different contextual factors that influence how people see careers, do you feel you are better able to understand where different types of advice may be 'coming from'? Does it help you figure out what you want in your career or do you feel it confuses you?

'Live Career Case' Study Questions

1. How have the late 20th-century changes in Table 2.1 affected the career of your case person? Which have had the greatest effects?
2. What contextual factors have played the greatest role in your case person's career so far? Economic and labor market conditions? Cultural and globalization factors? Or societal, organizational and/or occupational ideologies?

Additional Resources

Recommended Further Reading

Berry, H., Guillén, M. F. and Hendi, A. S. (2014) 'Is there convergence across countries? A spatial approach', *Journal of International Business Studies*, in press.

Buzzanell, P. M. and Goldzwig, S. R. (1991). Linear and nonlinear career models: Metaphors, paradigms, and ideologies. *Management Communication Quarterly*, 4(4), 466–505.

Goffee, R. and Scase, R. (1992) 'Organizational change and the corporate career: The restructuring of managers' aspirations', *Human Relations*, 45: 363–385.

Lucas, K., Liu, M. and Buzzanell, P. M. (2006) 'No limits careers: A critical examination of career discourse in the US and China', In M. Orbe, B. J. Allen & L. A. Flores (eds.), *International and Intercultural Communication Annual*, vol. 28 (pp. 217–242). Thousand Oaks, CA: SAGE.

Mayrhofer, W., Iallatchitch, A., Meyer, M., Steyerer, J. Schiffinger, M. and Strunk, G. A. (2004) 'Going beyond the individual: Some potential contributions from a career field and habitus perspective for global career research and practice', *Journal of Management Development*, 23(9): 870–884.

Self-Assessment Resources

Assess your current position in the labor market: Wanberg, C. R., Hough, L. M., and Song, Z. (2002) 'Predictive validity of a multidisciplinary model of reemployment success', *Journal of Applied Psychology*, 87(6): 1100.

Assess your work values: Lyons, S. T., Higgins, C. A., and Duxbury, L. (2010) 'Work values: Development of a new three-dimensional structure based on confirmatory smallest space analysis', *Journal of Organizational Behavior*, 31: 969–1002.

Online Resources

Bourdieu's field theory made easy – see the YouTube video entitled 'Field theory – Pierre Bourdieu' posted by Herwin Simon: www.youtube.com/watch?v=7FXPnkwSCyE

Hofstede's work on cultural differences – see the website of the Hofstede Centre: http://geert-hofstede.com/the-hofstede-centre.html

Data on the world economy with indicators per country: website of the International Monetary Fund (www.imf.org/external/index.htm)

Part 2
Images of Career

Careers as Inheritances 3

The objectives of this chapter are:

- to examine, through an illustrative case study, how factors such as family background, parents' occupations, social class, gender, race, religion and education, may provide an individual with a career background or 'inheritance' which substantially affects their career trajectory
- to consider career as a struggle for control between inheritance and personal agency
- to understand how the specific factors of social class, social mobility, education, race, gender and family background may impinge on a person's career
- to consider how people develop career ideas in childhood.

CASE STUDY

An Inherited Career

Pieter was born in the late 1960s in Zimbabwe, then called 'Rhodesia', and educated there and in South Africa, where he attended one of the best boys' schools in Johannesburg. On leaving school, he spent over a year in a Roman Catholic seminary

(Continued)

(Continued)

commencing study for the priesthood, then came to the conclusion that he might serve God in other ways. He opted to study law – a Bachelor of Arts degree followed by a law degree – at a Johannesburg university, while working part time as a hotel waiter. He also became involved in politics, being supportive of the black community in South Africa, and was shot at and arrested by the South African police.

By the time Pieter had completed the first stage of his studies, a BA degree, and formed a relationship with Lesley, the woman who was to become his wife, he had been promoted to assistant food and beverage manager in the hotel and had decided that his hotel work interested him more than his law studies. He was able to obtain a 'fast-track' scholarship in hotel management in a Rhodesian hotel company, which was to include a period as manager of a top-line hotel, to be followed by a master's degree at an overseas university. At one stage, his hotel hosted a major international meeting attended by presidents and prime ministers from around the world, an amazing experience for a man still in his early 20s. Unfortunately, the hotel company closed down the 'fast-track' scheme before he could proceed to the master's degree in hotel management that it included, and Pieter went back to South Africa, obtaining a job as an assistant food and beverage manager in a provincial town. Lesley joined him there, working in a local cinema complex.

Next, with growing ambition not just to be a hotel manager but to become a senior manager in a hotel company, he decided to travel to the UK to complete a master's degree in international hotel management, on one of the best programs in the country. For his dissertation, he returned to South Africa and studied affirmative action in South African hotels. On completion of his degree, now married to Lesley, he was offered the job of Training Manager for the hotel chain where he had originally worked. His career continued in the Human Resource function in the hotel company, then, six years later, he emigrated to Australia and continued a successful career as a senior HR manager and then as a senior manager and CEO in a major company in the retirement village industry, one of the developed world's fastest-growing industries.

Stop and Consider

1. Pieter's career is analyzed below. Before reading this analysis, consider what aspects of Pieter's background might have been influential in determining his career choices and direction. Write them down.
2. In the same fashion, consider what aspects of your own background are influential or will probably be influential in determining your career choices and direction. Write them down.

So far, Pieter's career has been very successful, and there is no doubt that he has brought about that success in major part through hard work and good self-direction of his career. But we can better understand Pieter's career, particularly his early career, if we add some pertinent details about his family and background:

- Pieter was from a very middle-class background. One of his grandfathers, from Germany, was a lawyer; the other, from South Africa, a research chemist. Tertiary education was the norm in Pieter's family. Pieter's high school education, at one of the best schools in South Africa, gave his career a 'flying start'. As we will see later in this chapter, social class and education are closely related to occupation, and persist across generations.

- As a white male commencing his career in apartheid-dominated South Africa, Pieter had the career advantages that many white males still have in developed countries, plus the special advantages of whites in South Africa at that time, including access to managerial jobs that the majority of the population could not aspire to.

- Pieter's parents had strong religious convictions as Roman Catholics, and he was brought up as a Catholic. This no doubt influenced his early choice of the priesthood (even though it turned out to be a 'blind alley') and the sense of service and integrity in which he takes pride in his career.

- Pieter's only sibling was an older sister. After giving birth to her, his mother then had nine miscarriages before he was born, the only son of the family, seven years later. His sister married and went to live in Europe when still young, so that in his teens Pieter was virtually an only child and very much at the centre of his parents' attention. They funded his study at the expensive South African high school, his mother even selling prized family jewels to make this possible. Later, his parents funded his first year of undergraduate study. Later still, they lent him the fees for his postgraduate degree in the UK.

- Pieter's father had tertiary qualifications from Europe in hotel management, and had pursued a career in hotel management in Rhodesia and South Africa. Pieter had been around hotels throughout his childhood, and got into his initial hotel job as a waiter because it came naturally given his background. Pieter therefore launched his career in exactly the same occupation as his father had, and continued in the hospitality and other service industries throughout his career.

- When Pieter obtained his 'fast-track' scholarship and early experience of managing a top hotel, his father was a senior manager in the Rhodesian hotel company that sponsored the scheme, and indeed Pieter was the only applicant accepted for the program. The reason the company decided to close the program was that it was felt nepotism might have been involved.

- Pieter believes he gained key attributes from his parents that helped him to determine his initial career choices and perform well in his first few jobs: a service ethic, hard work, integrity, a sense of social justice and the liberal consciousness which fired his student political activities and his choice of thesis topic. He has a high IQ which he considers was also inherited from his parents. He also recognizes that from an early age they encouraged him to talk on an equal basis with adults – a practice which he now thinks made him sociable, articulate and at ease in dealing with people: an important attribute in his chosen career.

Career Inheritances versus Personal Action

Is your career: (a) something you are born with, (b) something imposed on you by external forces, or (c) something you create yourself? This is a central question in career studies. Pieter received a substantial career 'inheritance' from his background, particularly his parents – ethnicity, gender, genetic makeup including IQ, education, religious beliefs, values, even early occupational experience. Some of these were extremely important in relation to the key structural characteristics in his context – for example, the South African apartheid system that divided the population into segregated groups based on race; and the tourism industry of his country, in which he had to make his way. So, Pieter's early career can be largely understood as a product of this inheritance. Later, particularly after he left South Africa and ascended his chosen career ladder, it is likely that his own effort and self-development of his career became proportionally much more important.

To inherit means 'to take or receive (property, a right, a title, etc.) by succession or will' or 'as if by succession from a predecessor' or 'to receive (a genetic character) by the transmission of hereditary factors' (www.dictionary.com, consulted 29 May 2013). Here, we use the term to represent not just what we inherit at birth, such as our parentage, genetic makeup, sex, race and social class, but also what we bring into our careers, when we commence them, from our background and childhood, particularly our family experiences. These characteristics can provide us not only with career opportunities but also with education, ambitions, values and ideology, or can equally leave us pessimistic and unambitious about our futures. Such inheritances are often woven together to intensify their effect: for example, a child from a high-income business family may inherit not just the family business, or opportunities created by the business, but attitudes, values and motivation relating to business that are prevalent in their family – for example, the 'American Dream' (Chapter 2) – and that are likely to promote the child's attraction to self-employment or a business career.

We have little control of such inheritances. They may – as in Pieter's case – be mainly helpful, or they may alternatively seem like millstones around our necks. As in his case, they often determine how our careers will be influenced by society's structures (Chapter 2) – for example, rules or hierarchies determining how much wealth or education or family contacts we require, or what gender, age or ethnicity we need to have a real chance. By considering inheritances, it is therefore possible to predict (though not with perfect accuracy) aspects of careers in advance, such as whether a specific individual will have a professional or a manual occupation. In France, for example, the son of a wealthy, white, male lawyer educated in a 'grande ecole' (elite university) is many times more likely to become a lawyer himself than is the daughter of an uneducated North African immigrant single mother on State assistance. By the time we commence our careers, perhaps in our early 20s, we are to some extent pre-ordained to conduct them along predictable lines. After we embark on them, we continue to face various barriers and opportunities related to our inheritance.

Stop and Consider

If you are 23 or under, consider yourself in your current state of career development and thinking. If you are over 23, reflect on your situation at that time. Do/did you feel propelled towards particular kinds of career options by forces in your background, such as family, social class, education, gender or race? Make a note of the details.

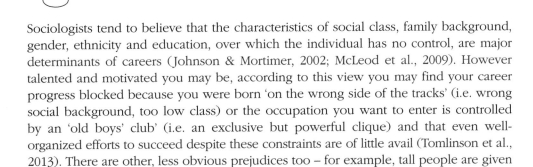

Sociologists tend to believe that the characteristics of social class, family background, gender, ethnicity and education, over which the individual has no control, are major determinants of careers (Johnson & Mortimer, 2002; McLeod et al., 2009). However talented and motivated you may be, according to this view you may find your career progress blocked because you were born 'on the wrong side of the tracks' (i.e. wrong social background, too low class) or the occupation you want to enter is controlled by an 'old boys' club' (i.e. an exclusive but powerful clique) and that even well-organized efforts to succeed despite these constraints are of little avail (Tomlinson et al., 2013). There are other, less obvious prejudices too – for example, tall people are given greater responsibility than are short people, and as a result height is statistically related to career success (Judge & Cable, 2004; Krzyzanowska & Mascie-Taylor, 2011).

The inheritance principle suggests that careers are mostly predetermined by background, and that by the time a person enters their career, at say, age 18, and possibly from birth, its direction and success are largely beyond their control. An alternative view is that in societies with high levels of freedom, rather than structures determining individual career outcomes, individuals can transcend social structures through their own energy: anyone, if talented and determined enough, can achieve the very highest career success. Indeed, the credo of the whole career development movement is to enable and empower every individual to maximize their self-fulfilment through a successful career. A term often used in career studies to express this idea of individuals acting to control their own careers is 'agency' (e.g. Smith, 2011). A central dynamic of careers is the struggle for control of the career between agency on the one hand and inheritance and structure on the other. Consider, for example, the apparent diversity of backgrounds in some of the most internationally known careers of our time – those of highly successful US politicians.

Contrasting Inheritances

The presidents and secretaries of state of the USA are among the most successful and powerful people in the world. The last two presidents (with two four-year terms of office each) and the last four secretaries have been, respectively, George W. Bush, Barak Obama, Colin Powell, Condaleeza Rice, Hilary Clinton and John Kerry. What are their backgrounds?

Note first that George W. Bush and Hilary Clinton had close relatives (Bush's father, Clinton's husband) who had themselves been presidents. Is it even conceivable that either George W. or Hilary would have gained the success they did without inheriting the family 'name'? Rice and Kerry also came from relatively privileged, educated backgrounds. On the other hand, Rice and Clinton succeeded despite being women, and Obama, Powell and Rice despite being African Americans. Powell got to the top despite the humblest of family origins as a West Indian slum child. It seems that both inheritance and agency can exert considerable influence. But demonstrations like this, with only a few cases, are not a suitable basis for drawing hard and fast conclusions about relative influence: they simply provide illustrations.

Some argue that in the current era social and organizational structures are weakening, providing greater opportunities for individual career agency (Weick, 1996). Can people empower themselves to achieve their career goals, or are their careers determined in advance by forces beyond their control?

Stop and Consider

Research the social backgrounds (e.g. parental occupations, family wealth, race, gender, education) of major politicians in your own country. Can you find examples of apparently inherited position? Can you find examples of people who seem to have come from humble backgrounds?

Consider the battle between individual action and structure in the career of Nita.

CASE STUDY

Struggling Against Inheritance

Nita came from a minority immigrant group that was discriminated against in the labor market and that generally occupied low-level jobs or was unemployed. Despite this, Nita's parents attained good jobs and middle-class status and hoped for the same for Nita. Rejecting their advice to seek formal qualifications, Nita left school at a young age and became a waitress, then a cleaner and a factory worker. While struggling to make a living in unskilled jobs, she had three children. In her late 20s, she decided to study, went to college, and, despite major privations and difficulties as she brought up her children at the same time, eventually trained as a teacher. Her work in middle-class schools enabled her to see how the education system fails people in her ethnic group, and she developed and implemented a personal mission to improve the education of her people in what she saw as a racist system.

Source: Arthur et al. (1999).

Nita's career represents a fascinating example of the struggle for personal autonomy in the face of structural and inheritance constraints. In rejecting the influence of her parents and accepting work and family status stereotypical of her gender and race, she initially allowed prevailing social structures and her corresponding inheritance of non-valued gender, ethnic and educational characteristics to determine her career. Later, through a remarkable act of willpower and ability against the odds, assisted perhaps by underlying middle-class values role-modelled by her parents, she elevated herself to unanticipated career success. But her ethnic inheritance and her experience of discrimination left their mark indelibly on the way that she conducted her long-term career as a teacher.

The career playing field, then, is not level. We are not endowed, as we start our careers, with equal resources or equal opportunity. But if we understand what we have inherited in our careers, and how that inheritance relates to the structures, opportunities and barriers inherent in the contexts we develop our careers in (Chapter 2), we may be able to take action to capitalize on those inheritances we have, and build our career resources to compensate for those we do not.

In the remaining sections of this chapter, we look at some of the main features of individual background – social class, including wealth and social status; education; gender; ethnicity; and family background – in order to explore their effects on careers.

Social Class

Social class is based on the existence, in every society, of structured inequalities in wealth, earnings, power, prestige, and access to medical care, education, housing and social welfare – which systematically favor certain groups. Social class is relevant to a discussion about careers because these differences affect a person's career opportunities.

While some might argue that in a society where merit is increasingly recognized social class is a myth or is decreasing in relevance, many sociologists agree that differences in social class continue to exist and to influence careers and other life outcomes.

Traditionally, social class is best conceptualized as a set of layers, though the distinctions between different layers, such as between 'upper working class' and 'lower middle class', may be blurred. However, there is less agreement as to how social class should be defined and measured. Karl Marx believed that class was determined largely by wealth – the ownership of property (Marx & Engels, 1848/1967). Weber (1922/1978) took the more sophisticated view that the possession of particular skills and qualifications might be as important as property wealth in determining the life chances of individuals. A third possibility is that class is based on power, but of course power may simply be a product of wealth or of skills and qualifications. All three variables tend, in fact, to be intercorrelated.

Wealth, qualifications and power clearly relate to careers. For example, the wealthy and powerful are better placed to buy their own businesses and have self-employed careers, or to pay for expensive educational courses providing qualifications and entry to more highly-paid occupations, or to be in family or social networks where good career opportunities are on offer.

In addition, occupation is linked to other markers of social class so strongly that it is often treated as a key measure of class, so that if we know what occupation a person is in, we can immediately categorize him/her in a particular stratum of society. If he/she is the main breadwinner of a family, we can even categorize the whole family in terms of social class.

Sociologists have therefore long used occupation as a proxy for social class (Goldthorpe et al., 1980; Treiman, 1977), and there is wide agreement in society about the relative status of different occupations. Faced with the occupations of secretary, truck driver, judge, high school teacher and street sweeper, most people would rank them in order of prestige: judge, high school teacher, secretary, truck driver, street sweeper. Such rankings are relatively consistent over time and across different countries. Required education and skill level are associated with occupations. Professional and managerial jobs requiring substantial education and receiving high remuneration are everywhere classified near the top, and unskilled manual jobs toward the bottom.

In the UK, for example, a commonly used classification for many years was the Erikson-Goldthorpe-Portocarero EGP system (Erikson & Goldthorpe, 1992), which ranks people according to employment status (e.g. employer, self-employed, unemployed) and occupation. More recently, work initiated by the European Union, taking the EGP as a starting point, has resulted in a more sophisticated measure – the European Socio-economic Classification (ESeC) (Rose & Harrison, 2007). The ESeC is shown in Table 3.1. It is not a definitive expression of fixed classes but an example of social classifications showing their close links to occupation and career.

Table 3.1   The ESeC Social Class Classification

Class	Description
Class 1	Larger employers, high-grade professionals, administrative and managerial populations: 'the higher salariat'
Class 2	Lower-grade professionals, administrative and managerial occupations: higher-grade technician and supervisory occupations: 'the lower salariat'
Class 3	Intermediate occupations: 'higher-grade white-collar (non-manual) workers'
Classes 4 & 5	Small employers and self-employed in non-professional occupations: 'petit-bourgeoisie or independents'
Class 6	Lower supervisory and lower technician occupations: 'higher-grade blue-collar (manual) workers'
Class 7	Lower services, sales and clerical occupations: 'lower-grade white-collar (non-manual) workers'
Class 8	Lower technical occupations: 'skilled workers'
Class 9	Routine occupations: 'semi- and unskilled workers'
Class 10	Never worked and long-term unemployed

Source: Rose & Harrison (2007).

Social classifications based on occupation, such as this one, are limited because they group people with wide income disparities in single groups, and exclude, for example, wealthy business owners who have no occupation, and people such as homemakers who are outside the labor market. For our purposes, however, it is not the detail or precision of the classification that is important, but the observable principle that income, class and career are inextricably linked. People's career choices, i.e. the type of occupation they pursue, help to fix both their income and their social class. Observation of others' occupations enables us, if we wish, to gauge roughly the class status or location on society's pecking order of each of our friends, neighbors and acquaintances. *Status anxiety* – the desire to gain self-esteem, to mark oneself as superior or at least equal to others – affects most of us (De Botton, 2004). The question often asked soon after meeting someone for the first time, 'And what do you do (for a job)?', may be an innocent conversational gambit or a means of gaining a quick estimate of the other person's status in society.

Children are assumed to belong to the same social class as their parents. Thus, a judge's child would be viewed as a person from an upper-class or upper middle-class home or from a privileged background. Such categorizations were, however, easier to apply 50 years ago, when most families were nuclear and had a sole, or main, breadwinner, the father, whose occupation was treated as a proxy for class or status. How do we classify a family in which the mother is a lawyer and the father is a janitor, or where the father is a judge but has left the family home?

In terms of career metaphors, we can treat as part of people's inheritance their social class as they prepare for, and commence, their career. Note that our concept of class includes wealth, income, education and occupation. Each of these can play a vital part in influencing the career chances of the individual.

Social mobility

All this makes it clear that the (family-determined) social class or status of an individual at the start of their career is likely to play a major part in the final level that he/she reaches. But everyday observation – for example, the account of the backgrounds of recent US presidents and secretaries of state provided earlier – tells us that it is not an all-powerful determining factor. People can be *socially mobile* – that is, they can move from one social class to another (Blau & Duncan, 1967). Such changes may be due to other aspects of their inheritance, such as the innate abilities, aptitudes and personality characteristics they inherit genetically, or to ambitions or work habits developed in childhood, or to simple good or bad luck. Here's an example:

CASE STUDY

By His Own Bootstraps

Peter's father was a wages clerk, his mother a factory worker. As a child, Peter was very interested in film and television and among his favorites were the British 1970s surreal TV comedy show *Monty Python's Flying Circus* and the film *King Kong*. He was given a small cine-camera as a gift and became obsessional about filming as a hobby. He used his camera to make a James Bond spoof and won a prize for another short film, but he left school at 16 and never attended university. He got employment as a photo engraver, living at home and saving as much of his earnings as he could to buy film equipment. Eventually, with almost a zero budget he produced a full-length 'splatter' movie, which met with success at the Cannes film festival. He began to write film scripts. At age 26, he was on his way...

'Peter' is now Sir Peter Jackson, the world-famous director of the *Lord of the Rings* and *The Hobbit* film trilogies, and the 2006 remake of *King Kong*.

Of particular importance for career studies is the notion of *intergenerational mobility* – the change of social class made by family members from one generation to the next (Smeeding et al., 2011). If social class were all-powerful, then we would expect it to be frozen across generations. For example, the children of lower middle-class parents would always remain in the lower middle class, generation after generation. The higher the level of intergenerational mobility, the lower the influence of class.

Repeated studies show that occupation, and therefore income and class, continue to be strongly dependent on parents' occupation. In the famous Oxford (UK) Mobility Study, for example, where subjects were divided into seven social classes, 46 percent of the sons of fathers in the top class had occupations in that class, whereas only 15 percent of the sons of manual workers did. Correspondingly, 57 percent of the sons of manual workers were also manual workers, and only 7 percent were in the top class (Goldthorpe et al., 1980). The stratification of society seems to persist across generations: even taking into account parents' occupations, grandparents' class origins also have a major effect (Chan & Boliver, 2013).

Stop and Consider

Research the social backgrounds of your parents, uncles and aunts, grandparents and (if possible) great grandparents. Can you see examples of social mobility (up or down)?

The situation is complicated by the changing occupational patterns and class structures of society. In most developed countries, there have been fundamental changes. Many manual jobs have been automated and restructured out of existence; new skilled occupations, particularly those connected with telecommunications, information technology, and financial, professional and personal services, have grown rapidly; larger proportions of the population have undertaken tertiary education; and the average income and level of affluence have increased. This structural mobility tends to change the class structure – or at least the proportion of people who belong in each specific class – over time. Thus, upward intergenerational mobility becomes more likely, and downward mobility less likely, as time goes by. Featherman and Hauser (1978), for example, demonstrated that half of all sons eventually moved above their fathers in social status, whereas only a sixth moved below.

On the other hand, Goldthorpe (2013: 431), author of the original Oxford study in the UK, has more recently concluded that 'the only recent change of note is that the rising rates of upward, absolute mobility of the middle decades of the last century have levelled out'. In any case, mobility varies between countries – low in Southern Europe, for example, and in the UK and the USA, but high in Scandinavian countries – and appears to be related to national spending on education (Blanden, 2013; d'Addio, 2007).

Education

Careers are mediated by education. Formal education is the normal pre-cursor to a career. Nearly all professions and trades have strict entry requirements in terms of educational qualifications. Education also punctuates many careers as career actors seek to improve their career prospects and performance by obtaining further qualifications. But access to good education and attainment within it are influenced by other aspects of inheritance, such as social class and parental wealth. Even in the first grade, children from higher socio-economic groups perform better (Entwistle & Alexander, 1993), and these early differences may become exaggerated over time as continuing differences in quality of education leave their mark (Kerckhoff, 1995). Not only one's own socioeconomic status but also that of one's fellow students may affect outcomes (Lee & Bryk, 1989).

Many other factors over which individual students have no control have been shown to affect their educational attainment and thereby their careers (Johnson & Mortimer, 2002). In tertiary education, variations in college resources and reputation, teaching quality and the presentation of specific disciplines continue to add to, subtract from or change the inheritance that people bring to their careers.

Race

Another factor, clearly inherited and clearly affecting career opportunities, is race. Internationally, there is good evidence that immigrants to any developed country, even those with good qualifications and career backgrounds, are often mainly employed in relatively unskilled and casual positions. Employment discrimination against particular racial groups clearly exists; however, there is debate as to whether the failure of certain racial groups to advance is due mainly to their race or to their typically lower class status, which might apply whatever their race (Wilson, 1981).

To examine the kinds of effects that an adverse inheritance of class, race and education may have on a person's career, consider Lily's case.

CASE STUDY

Bettering Herself

Lily was from a dark-skinned ethnic minority whose family had always been involved in unskilled factory work. When she left school, without qualifications, her aunt got her a job in the factory where she worked, where Lily did menial chores. Lily lacked confidence and thought she could never do much better. She married, became pregnant, left her job and was, for a period, a 'stay-at-home' housewife. Some years later, bored, she enrolled on a three-month clerical course, where her supervisor encouraged her to apply for a job as an accounts clerk in a supermarket chain. She got the job and was later able to do more courses and improve her skills. After eight years with the supermarket, her job seems secure and she enjoys it, and even speaks occasionally at meetings. But she has no plans for further improvement in her career: 'I can never see myself moving on.'

Source: Arthur et al. (1999).

On the face of it, Lily has much to commend her as a worker: She is a reliable and loyal employee for her company, meets family obligations and has done well enough after an unpromising start. External encouragement by an advisor appears to have assisted her. But her inheritance – her ethnic origins, a lack of family role models, a lack of education, a lack of self-confidence – appears to limit her career ambitions. Of course, in terms of the distinction we made in Chapter 1 between objective and subjective career success, Lily may be very satisfied, and therefore subjectively very successful, in her career.

Gender

In the case above, the limitations on Lily's career are probably exacerbated by the fact that she is a woman. Through the constitution of most societies, men can normally expect to have different career structures from women and usually greater career success.

Most of us are born unambiguously either male or female. That part of our inheritance remains with us for life and is likely to play a major part in the determination of our career paths. Biology determines that some tasks, such as the bearing and initial feeding of children, can only be performed by women. Differences in physical constitution and instinct encourage the gender segregation of tasks such as hunting and child rearing. From time immemorial, the gender segregation of work has meant that gender inheritance has a major effect on the way people live their lives, including their working lives (Wright, 1997).

The development of industrial societies established rigid patterns of gender segregation. In earlier forms of industrial society, men typically did most of the paid work, while women supported their families through unpaid domestic labor. Women could be employed as paid workers in certain occupations – for example, childcare, food preparation, low-skilled factory work, retail and domestic service, secretarial work and, for a small number of better educated women, nursing and teaching. All other work, and particularly all managerial and professional work, was done by men. When women married, they were expected, and often compelled, to devote their working hours to the unpaid work of caring for their husband and family.

A typical female career might therefore have consisted of a few years' work in a relatively junior capacity, followed by a lifetime as a 'housewife'. A few women who never married might pursue lifetime careers in paid work but could expect promotion only in exceptional cases. If social class may have set major limits on the careers of many men, the combined effects of social class and gender must have seemed like a veritable straitjacket to independent-minded women.

During the 20th century, and particularly in its second half, what has been termed a *genderquake* took place (Wolf, 1993). Manufacturing – traditionally largely staffed by men – declined, and service work – where women arguably have greater interest and skills – increased. Stimulated by the reform of electoral systems to allow women political votes, and more progressive social policies and processes, women became more interested in career success and returning to work following child rearing. Family structures became more diverse in ways that added to women's sense of independence, with more single mothers, dual-career couples and reconstituted families. People raised their material goals, such that it is often now expected, even necessitated, that women will contribute a wage to the family. Governments have often provided state benefits for single mothers caring for children at home, but they increasingly expect that when their children go to school those women will become economically independent of government support. Legislation in many countries makes paid maternity leave mandatory, enabling increasing numbers of women to continue their careers with reduced disruption through childbirth and the early months of their babies' lives. Different forms of childcare have become available to care for children and thereby enable their mothers to be in employment.

Thus, women have increasingly entered the workforce. In the UK, for example, the proportion of women of working age who are in the workforce has increased from 30 percent in 1900 to 56 percent in 1970 and over 70 percent today. In that sense, women are no longer as constrained as they once were from following a full career in full-time work.

What has changed a lot less, however, is the practice of segregating jobs, occupations and therefore careers into men's work and women's work. Men continue to occupy most of the positions of power and authority in society and enjoy much higher earnings than women.

The gender segregation of the labor market has two dimensions – horizontal and vertical (Hakim, 1979):

- *Horizontal segregation* divides work occupationally into men's jobs and women's jobs. Thus, in any developed society, we may expect more than two thirds of traveling salespeople, computer programmers, warehouse staff, police officers, medical doctors, lawyers, managers, skilled trade workers and truck drivers to be men. But we can also expect most primary school teachers, nurses, midwives, sewing machine operators, checkout operators, secretarial and clerical workers, and retail shop assistants to be women. These occupations, of course, tend to be lower paid than 'male' occupations requiring similar skill and qualifications. In some of these occupations, the dominating gender may have more than 90 percent of the jobs.
- *Vertical segregation* divides work hierarchically, into the more senior, responsible and better-paid jobs and the more junior, less responsible and worse-paid jobs. Typically, men occupy the former types of jobs, and women occupy the latter. A prevailing theme in recent commentaries on the contemporary workplace is that of a 'glass ceiling' in organizations: the glass ceiling allows women to see what goes on at the top of the organization that employs them but does not allow them

to reach such positions themselves (Cotter et al., 2001). For example, in 2014 only 24 (4.8 percent) out of 500 chief executive officers (CEOs) of the largest companies in the USA were women (Women CEOs of Fortune 500 Companies, 2013), though this was a rise of 12 from 2005. Table 3.2, adapted from a 2010 European Commission Report, shows a similar situation in Europe: individual country figures are available from the report.

Table 3.2 Percentage of Women Occupying Specific Positions in European Commission Countries, 2009

Position	% of Women in that Position
Governor of national bank	0
Members of boards of largest 500 companies	4
Nobel prize winners in science (1901–2009)	3
Nobel prize winners, non-science subjects	9
Scientists – first research grade	38
Scientists – top research grade	12
Presidents of trade unions	28

In the higher educational institutions in which many of the readers of this book are enrolled as students, the same phenomenon characterizes the careers of the academic staff: for example, in the UK in 2011, while 44 percent of academic staff were female, only 38 percent of *full-time* academic staff were female, only 28 percent of senior managers were female, only 19 percent of professors were female and only 16 percent of those paid over £50,000 per annum were female (Equality Challenge Unit, 2011).

The combination of horizontal and vertical segregation gives rise to stereotyped authority relationships: the male manager dictating to the female secretary; the male doctor being assisted by the female nurse; the male lawyer giving instructions to the female legal assistant; and the male professor delegating to the female assistant professor. RosaBeth Moss Kanter's classic book *Men and Women of the Corporation* (1977) provides evidence of the careers of both managers' secretaries and managers' wives being largely determined by the success of their bosses/husbands. Again, these barriers to occupation, even in today's liberated world, can lead to women consistently underestimating their career potential and men failing to consider particular 'female' occupations to which they may be ideally suited.

How does gender segregation arise in occupations? It is likely that both field and habitus (Chapter 2) are involved. In the field, structural differences in terms of gender segregation continue from the past, through inertia, tradition, prejudice and the conscious or unconscious desire of men to protect their relatively privileged position. From an early age, children's thinking is colored by what they see around them and incorporate into their developing habitus: the person who looks after them most at home is a woman; the person who comes home from work and provides most of the family's money is a man; their kindergarten and primary teachers are typically women; the sports stars and senior managers and police officers they see on television are typically men. However much their parents may encourage them to believe that gender doesn't make a difference or that 'girls can do anything', the evidence before their eyes tells a different story (e.g. Barak et al., 1991; Hall, 2010).

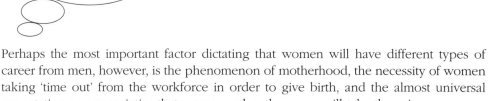

Stop and Consider

Consider your career so far, or as you see it developing in the next few years. Are there any particular barriers or opportunities you have experienced or anticipate experiencing because of your gender? If you are female, are there any actions you can take to overcome barriers, should they occur?

Perhaps the most important factor dictating that women will have different types of career from men, however, is the phenomenon of motherhood, the necessity of women taking 'time out' from the workforce in order to give birth, and the almost universal expectation across societies that women rather than men will take the primary responsibility for childcare. While some women are able to take a few weeks' maternity leave, make childcare arrangements and resume their careers almost without missing a beat, for many, the career is fatally fractured, and the return to career is likely to be part time, with considerable loss of momentum (Bertrand, 2013), though some women show remarkable resilience in being able to integrate the two roles and master both (Maher, 2013). Here's a typical case of a woman struggling with such issues.

CASE STUDY

Getting Back on the Ladder

Jeanette qualified as a high school social studies teacher and was effective and successful from the start. In her second year of teaching, she was given additional responsibilities within her department, and was regarded by the school's principal as a promotable teacher with good prospects of further advancement. When, three years after Jeanette's arrival in the school, the head teacher of social studies made it known she intended to retire at the end of the year, Jeanette seemed the ideal candidate for the job. However, she had got married in her first year at the school and was now pregnant with her first baby. Reluctantly, she took maternity leave, while the school appointed another candidate. After that, family circumstances, including a second child and relocation to a new city based on Jeanette's husband's career moves, prevented Jeanette for ten years from resuming her career. After her second child went to preschool, she was able to do some part-time teaching, but that was all. By the time she felt able to resume full-time work, ten years had gone by and she was now 35. And now, the best kind of job she could get was as a basic teacher, at the same level as when she had started her career aged 22. As for head of department jobs, these were being filled by men in their early 30s who had much more teaching experience than Jeanette and had also been able to acquire master's degrees and advanced teaching qualifications in their spare time. Jeanette finally got a coveted head of department position when she was 43, but she had lost huge traction on the career ladder.

Gender segregation and stereotyping appear to be declining but to a limited extent. There has, for example, been a huge growth in the number of women moving into management in recent years, yet the glass ceiling phenomenon means that women still appear to be constrained from reaching the highest levels and are paid less than their male counterparts (Hadas, 2013; Powell & Graves, 2003). Many more women have become entrepreneurs (Weiler & Bernasek, 2001), but just like their employed counterparts they are often restricted in what they are able to do (Bosse & Taylor, 2012). Smaller numbers of women have colonized male bastions such as engineering, science, law, the police force and the armed services. Psychologically, things are changing too. Young women are more self-confident about their careers and willing to consider a much wider range of options (Burke, 2001). Ultimately, attracting men to 'feminine' careers, such as preschool and primary teaching, may be a bigger problem (Cushman, 2005).

Sexual orientation also affects careers. Even though equal opportunities legislation supposedly protects gay and lesbian workers, they often face complex and subtle forms of discrimination and differential treatment in the workplace (Humphrey, 1999), leading to limitations on their career aspirations (Niesche, 2003). However, the relationships here are complex: for example, Peplau and Fingerhut (2004) demonstrate that lesbian women typically have higher earnings than their heterosexual female peers, possibly because of lesbians' greater need to provide for their children.

Furthermore, women from ethnic minorities suffer discrimination on at least two grounds simultaneously (Bradley & Healy, 2008). For example, in 2013 the average weekly earnings of different ethnic and gender groups in the USA were as follows:

Asian men	$1055
Asian women	$770 (73% of Asian men)
White men	$879
White women	$710 (81% of white men)
African-American men	$665
African-American women	$599 (90% of African-American men)
Latino men	$592
Latino women	$521 (88% of Latino men)

Source: www.catalyst.org/knowledge/womens-earnings-and-income

Disability

Disabled workers also form a special group who may be born with their disabilities, or carry them into their careers from childhood, or develop them during their careers and be forced to make adjustments. Again, though, it is not just a matter of disabled career actors reappraising their redefined capabilities and finding a career change to fit (Chapter 6): in addition, subtle prejudices by employers and others in society may be at play, which may only be dealt with at a higher level than the individual, as when societal education and policy change provide disabled individuals with full citizenship and economic involvement (Asaba & Jackson, 2011).

Attitudes and Ideology

Many human characteristics acquired before or during childhood are relevant to careers. Intelligence, aptitudes, personality and interests are partly genetically inherited, and partly shaped in childhood. We consider such characteristics specifically in Chapter 6. But also relevant are individual attitudes, values and ideology, which are often well-defined by the time the person commences their career (Chapter 2). Some people have specific ambitions, such as being a medical practitioner or becoming rich, or being able to support a family, or even avoiding hard work if possible. Most have values related to careers: for example, one career actor may have a strong belief in individual responsibility and independence in work, another in collective security and trade unionism. Such values are developed in family and other educational and social settings, and may crucially frame a career actor's attitudes and actions. Thus, the ideologies ingrained in societies, such as the American Dream (Chapter 2), find their counterparts in the internalized values and personal motivations that the career actor carries about.

Family

Are our careers, literally, inherited from our parents (Goodale & Hall, 1976)? Do careers run in families? Do we tend to repeat the occupations followed by our parents? Can you see any such patterns in your own family?

Parents' backgrounds, values and actions play a huge part in determining their children's career paths. As we have seen, social class is determined by parents' occupations, and determines the occupational status of many children, whose educational opportunities are often likewise determined on the basis of parents' location or wealth. Parents' status and networks can be used to buy their children influential contacts or polished manners or a good first job. Parents who own their own businesses can provide their children with good jobs in the business, give their children a share in the business, or even give the whole business to their children. Parents' money can purchase a child a business. Parents' education and their practice of superior occupations give them important knowledge, insight, values and communication skills, which they can pass on to their children. Many parents will socialize their children to aspire to university education, professional occupations or business success. Moreover, middle-class family backgrounds typically involve and provide higher aspirations, particularly for personal 'betterment' (De Angelis, 2010), than do working-class backgrounds. All these mechanisms assist children from the higher classes in their careers.

There is substantial evidence that career development commences in childhood (Watson & McMahon, 2005). Specifically, parents intervene actively in their children's career development (Young & Friesen, 1992). Consider the following case.

CASE STUDY

Family Business (by Kerr Inkson)

My grandfather, James Inkson, the youngest of 14 children of an Aberdeenshire (Scotland) crofter (small farmer), is reputed to have been a superb scholar in his youth. But the family could not afford to pay for a secondary education, so instead he went to the city (Aberdeen) and was apprenticed as a butcher. Eventually, he became a retail butcher, and in the early 20th century, he owned a shop in Aberdeen, where he would receive livestock or carcasses, butcher them on the premises, turn them into steaks or flaps or sausages, and sell them to local customers.

He had two sons, James (Jimmy) and John. Both lived over the shop as they grew up and worked in the shop or delivered meat to customers. The younger son, John (my father), was academically gifted: from an early age, his father earmarked

(Continued)

(Continued)

him for a professional occupation. The family scrimped and saved so that he could go to a local private school. He became a school teacher.

Jimmy, the elder son, had no such pretensions, and when he was 12 years old, his father apprenticed him to the butcher's trade. Jimmy spent most of his career in the shop. When Jimmy finished his apprenticeship, his father made him a paid employee. After retiring, Jimmy's father made him the manager of the shop. When his father died, Jimmy inherited the shop. Later, business declined and the shop was sold, but Jimmy continued to work as a butcher – his only real skill – for other employers until he retired. He died aged 71 of chronic bronchitis, probably contracted over the years in the cold, damp conditions in which he had spent his life's work.

Jimmy Inkson was a classic case of career inheritance from the family. His childhood socialization, pre-employment experiences and male role models were all about the butcher's trade. One wonders whether he ever considered any other kind of career and what his family would have thought if he had suggested it. In turn, he inherited his father's trade, job and business. It was truly a family career. Even his younger brother John's ascent into the professional ranks may have been triggered by his father's reaction to his own early career experience.

Such examples are common. Rupert Murdoch, the founder, Chairman and CEO of global media company News Corporation, moved in his career from journalist to editor to acquisitions manager to newspaper owner to international media tycoon. His sons, Lachlan and James Murdoch, followed in their father's footsteps to become media managers at an early age, assisted no doubt by their father's influence. Internationally renowned fashion designer Stella McCartney is the daughter of famous musician Paul McCartney of The Beatles: she is of course in a different industry from her father, but there is little doubt that his own fame and influence assisted her to establish her 'stellar' career (Inkson, 2007: 27–28).

Stop and Consider

Think about the careers of members of your own family – for example, yourself, your parents, grandparents, uncles, aunts, cousins. Consider, as far as you know it, how and why these people chose to enter the occupations and organizations in which they spent their careers. What 'family' influences, including the types of values and ideologies discussed in the previous section, can you see? If necessary, research the issue by asking family members for more information.

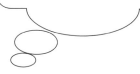

From what has already been said, it is apparent that the social class of a family can directly influence the education and types of occupation (e.g. white collar versus blue collar) pursued by its members. Parents inculcate particular values related to career aspirations and occupational choice (Johnson, 2001; Wong et al., 2011). There is evidence that the children of self-employed parents also tend to become self-employed (Mulholland, 2003). Bear in mind, though, that correlations between the occupations of parents and those of their children, although positive, tend to be modest: there is still plenty of scope for people to take up careers quite unlike those of their parents.

Childhood

We have argued that your career inheritance is not just what you inherit at birth but what you inherit at birth *plus* the modifications and additions that have taken place to your initial inheritance by the time you start your career. A 16-year-old girl's burning ambition to be a motor mechanic or a doctor may result from a complex combination of social variables (race, education, etc.) and her reflection on, and even planning for, her future. In this case, the inheritance is strong and specific before the career even starts.

During childhood, individuals begin to develop concepts relevant to career rather earlier than most people assume (Hartung et al., 2005; Porfeli & Lee, 2012). Genetic inheritance (of abilities and dispositional factors) undoubtedly plays a part in directing the child's interest towards specific occupations. Much depends on the child's exposure to, and reflections on, the world of work, which tend to move from fantasy and general considerations of the world of work ('work') toward personalized consideration of the self within a work context ('me at work') and a more realistic and mature picture of work. As indicated above, the family's social class, occupational background, values and even day-to-day conversation may be strongly influential on the child. Gender stereotypes and, later, class-based distinctions in occupational choice become apparent (Gottfredson, 2002). Socio-economic status, parental support, early experiences of paid employment, and the progressive 'ruling out' of specific occupations (Gottfredson, 2002) all play a part in creating, by adolescence, a 'vocational identity' (Porfeli & Lee, 2012). This identity is very important in framing educational and early-career choices, but needs to be flexible in the face of the increasingly uncertain context of many careers. Overall, encouragement to children to explore their own potential futures by learning about different fields of work and about careers appears to assist adult career maturity and adjustment.

Parents are very important in this process. Kohn and Schooler (1983), for example, argued that a father's occupation critically influences the work values and career ambitions of his children. Perhaps even more important than the influence of parents' occupations on their children's occupations is the link between parents' career-related

values, attitudes and interests on those developed by their children; and the intervention of parents in assisting their children to develop not only career-relevant skills and
attitudes to work, but balanced vocational identities. Parents often assume a 'de facto'
role as their adolescent (and sometimes adult) children's first career advisors (Bardick
et al., 2005). It may be that the best contribution this book can make to some of its
readers is to ask them to research and practice career-enhancing behavior appropriate
to their roles as parents: Carpenter (2008) provides a good introduction to this role.

Conclusion

Curiously, the inheritance principle, and particularly the effects of social structure,
innate characteristics, and parental influence, plays little part in most careers textbooks. It plays even less of a part in most popular books that tell us how to plan and
conduct our careers. In a society that believes in equal opportunity, it is almost as if
we don't like looking at something that implies privilege in life's chances.

Inherited characteristics often mirror the structural characteristics of the careers
contexts described in Chapter 2. Thus, the inheritance of male or female gender is
important because of contextual characteristics enhancing the careers of one group
and limiting those of others. And ideology is often a characteristic of the context, and
also of the individual career actors who act within that context.

The effects of inheritance can't be ignored, and there are plenty of people who
recognize these effects and try to redress the balance through political and social activ-
ism. The women's movement, poverty action groups, adult literacy campaigns, and
political movements aimed at redistributing wealth are all examples of attempts to
improve the career opportunities of those whose only inheritance appears to be debt
and deprivation. Many sociologists and activists believe that inequality is so deeply
embedded in society that there is little individuals can do to remove the crushing
weight of their inheritance and base their careers on agency. Fundamental, redemptive
change in society is necessary, these critics say, before careers can be truly liberated.

We take a different view. Inheritance is a significant factor affecting careers, but it
is not the only factor. Most people find that life is too short to wait for fundamental
social change to take care of their careers. Many with negative inheritances, such as
Nita in a case outlined earlier, are nevertheless able to overcome them through personal action (see Chapter 5). For all readers of this book, including those who have
not yet embarked on a career, it may be a good idea to know your inheritance, to
understand where you come from and what that means, and to look for ways to work
with the positives in your inheritance and to strive to look the negatives in the eye
and overcome them, or help your children to do so.

Many individuals are able to make fundamental, redemptive changes in their lives that
enable them to cast aside negative inheritances and enjoy fulfilling and successful careers.
It is hoped that some of the mature, midcareer readers of this book will feel that they

have already done so; if not, they are doubtless acquainted with friends who have. Some, again including Nita, go further and make it a personal mission to seek social change that can enhance the career prospects of others. In Chapter 12 of this book, we detail strategies of 'career self-management', some of which can be used by those disadvantaged by their backgrounds to try to overcome some of their difficulties. Careers are individual: individual inheritance is hugely important, but it is not all there is.

Key Points in this Chapter

- Observation of careers shows great inequalities apparently based on different forms of privilege. Each career actor takes an 'inheritance' of personal attributes, attitudes, values and opportunities into their career. These relate to the contextual factors discussed in Chapter 2 and may provide the career with a very positive or very negative dynamic.
- Structures and inheritances limiting careers are balanced by individual action or agency which may divert the career from apparently inevitable tracks, as when privileged career actors fail and those with a negative inheritance succeed despite it.
- Social class is based on differences in wealth, skills and qualifications, and power. It is inherited in careers and affects them because it is occupationally based and because it tends to persist through different generations of the same family.
- Other inherited factors affecting career opportunities are genetically-inherited personal attributes, values developed pre-career, race, education and gender. Gender segregates careers both vertically and horizontally.
- Careers and career-related opportunities, aptitudes and attitudes may be passed on in childhood, particularly in families.
- Career concepts develop and mature in childhood and adolescence, a positive process for career actors.

Questions from this Chapter

General Questions

1. In Britain, the monarchy is inherited. In the USA, the presidency is elected. But did George W. Bush, elected president 2001–2009, inherit the job from his father George Bush, president 1989–1993? Justify your answer.
2. Identify two or three well-known people you admire. Use the internet to find out more about their backgrounds. To what extent do you think they inherited their careers?

3. Do you believe career opportunities are becoming more or less affected by structural factors, such as social class, as time goes by? Justify your answer.
4. Think about your family. What aspects of your career, if any, have you inherited, or are you likely to inherit, from them?
5. Consider your own childhood and your early thinking about work and careers. What was your 'vocational identity?' What parts did fantasy, parental occupations, values and guidance, and early experiences in education, hobbies and employment have in framing it?

'Live Career Case' Study Questions

1. What are the origins of your case person in terms of social class, ethnic origin, gender, childhood experience and education? How have these affected the case person's career?
2. Has your case person ever struggled, in their career, to escape their background? Describe the process.

Additional Resources

Recommended Further Reading

Cotter, D. A., Hermsen, J. M., Ovadia, S. and Vanneman, R. (2001) 'The glass ceiling effect', *Social Forces*, 80(2): 655–681.

Goodale, J. G., and Hall, D. T. (1976) 'On inheriting a career: The influence of sex, values, and parents', *Journal of Vocational Behavior*, 8: 19–30.

Hartung, P. J., Porfeli, E. J., and Vondracek, F. W. (2005) 'Child vocational development: A review and a reconsideration', *Journal of Vocational Behavior*, 66: 385–419.

Johnson, M. K., and Mortimer, J. T. (2002) 'Career choice and development from a sociological perspective' in D. Brown & Associates (eds.), *Career Choice and Development* (4th edn, pp. 37–81). San Francisco: Jossey-Bass.

McLeod, C., O'Donohue, S., and Townley, B. (2009) 'The elephant in the room: Class and careers in British advertising agencies', *Human Relations*, 62: 1011–1038.

Self-Assessment Resources

Assess your genetic predisposition for a certain occupation: Trice, A. D. and Knapp, L. (1992). 'Relationship of children's career aspirations to parents' occupations', *The Journal of Genetic Psychology*, 153: 355–357.

Assess the origins of your career aspirations: Trice, A. D., Hughes, M. A., Odom, C., Woods, K. and McClellan, N. C. (1995) 'The origins of children's career aspirations: IV. Testing hypotheses from four theories', *The Career Development Quarterly*, 43: 307–322.

Assess your career aspirations and expectations as a child: Helwig, A. A. (2008) 'From childhood to adulthood: A fifteen-year longitudinal career development study', *The Career Development Quarterly*, 57(1): 38–50.

Assess the relationship between your childhood play experiences and your career interests: Coats, P. B. and Overman, S. J. (1992) 'Childhood play experiences of women in traditional and nontraditional professions', *Sex Roles*, 26: 261–271.

Online Resources

Why looking back at your childhood can help you find a career you love – see: www.careershift-ers.org/blog/why-looking-back-at-your-childhood-can-help-you-find-a-career-you-love

Thirteen Economic Facts about Social Mobility and the Role of Education – see: www.brookings.edu/research/reports/2013/06/13-facts-higher-educationTe laut quaesti onsero di omnis et alignimusae volupta ssimi, nimolupta ium custemp oriorio tem nobit ommos aris con num, alit rae eos provit, con exerum quatat.

Careers as Cycles

Chapter Objectives

The objectives of this chapter are:

- to consider whether contemporary careers can helpfully be described as a series of stages and, if so, what characterizes each one
- to compare and contrast some influential stage theories
- to explore how career dynamics change with increasing age, and the implications of this
- to focus on landmark moments in a career, specifically starting work, mid-career issues and retirement.

> All the world's a stage,
> And all the men and women merely players:
> They have their exits and their entrances;
> And one man in his time plays many parts,
> His acts being seven ages. At first, the infant,
> Mewling and puking in the nurse's arms.
> And then the whining school-boy, with his satchel

And shining morning face, creeping like snail
Unwillingly to school. And then the lover,
Sighing like furnace, with a woeful ballad
Made to his mistress' eyebrow. Then a soldier,
Full of strange oaths and bearded like the pard,
Jealous in honour, sudden and quick in quarrel,
Seeking the bubble reputation
Even in the cannon's mouth. And then the justice,
In fair round belly with good capon lined,

Full of wise saws and modern instances;

And so he plays his part. The sixth age shifts
Into the lean and slipper'd pantaloon,
With spectacles on nose and pouch on side,
His youthful hose, well saved, a world too wide
For his shrunk shank; and his big manly voice,
Turning again toward childish treble, pipes
And whistles in his sound. Last scene of all,
That ends this strange eventful history,

Is second childishness and mere oblivion,
Sans teeth, sans eyes, sans taste, sans everything.

From *As you Like it*, by William Shakespeare, Act II, Scene VII

Stages and Cycles

An intuitively appealing way of analyzing any phenomenon that occupies a significant amount of time is to break it up into chunks. These are often called stages, phases or cycles. Jaques's speech in *As You Like it* (above) demonstrates that this kind of thinking goes back at least 400 years. It exemplifies a number of features common to career development theories. Stages are clearly delineated and described. Each has its characteristic activities and roles. Collectively, the stages represent a sequence of physical and psychological growth followed by potency, first physical and then more intellectual, followed by loss of capability and possibly social respect. The stages start and end with helplessness, which means that collectively they form a cycle, in effect the life cycle.

On the other hand, Jaques' speech raises some questions about the application of stages to a career. Do stages arise primarily because of a person's physical change over time, or because of the roles available in a society and its expectations about who will fill them? What triggers movement from one stage to the next, and are these transitions predicable? Do stages overlap with each other? Given that Shakespeare's text is very male-oriented, how applicable are the stages to women's lives? Can recycling through stages occur?

A career cycle is, perhaps, just one facet of the broader life cycle. The age-related patterns of development and decline in our physical strength, agility, fitness and health described in Jaques' speech can affect our careers (Rholes & Simpson, 2004), as can the traditional family cycle of marriage, child bearing, child rearing and empty nest.

Age/stage theories tell us that at different periods in our lives we have particular ways of approaching our careers. With predictable sequences, career planning should become easier. We may not like everything we discover from age/stage theory, but at least it tells us what to expect. So what do the theorists say?

Donald Super: A Theory of Career Development

Donald Super (1953, 1957, 1990) was the dominant figure in career development research in the 20th century and he developed probably the most comprehensive theory. His ideas have also had a lasting impact on the practice of careers guidance (Savickas, 2002; Savickas et al., 2009).

Super and colleagues focused particularly on the characteristics and development of individuals (Savickas, 2002, 2005; Super, 1953; Super et al., 1996). Super often used the terms 'vocation' and 'vocational' (see Chapter 1), referring not just to a sense of calling and/or a deep inner need to fulfil a particular kind of work role, but, more broadly, to mean a person's career, whatever form it took. The following summary is based on Savickas (2005).

- Super's theory focuses on the individual's life course through various social roles, such as work versus family. Work roles are defined by occupations, and career patterns through occupations are influenced by both social structure and personal characteristics. People differ in vocational characteristics, such as abilities and per-sonality. Each occupation requires different personal characteristics and people seek outlets in their work for their characteristics; so that their satisfaction depends on implementing their vocational self-concept, which is based on their character-istics, their actions in relevant roles and their observation of the approval of others. This is very similar to the theories of fit discussed in Chapter 6.
- However, Super moves beyond fit by describing processes of career construc-tion in more detail. People implement their vocational self-concept through

undertaking vocational tasks and through reflection, education and role enact-ment. The self-concept changes over time but becomes increasingly stable as the individual progresses through a cycle of stages, labeled growth, exploration, establishment, maintenance and disengagement. This 'maxicycle', however, may be disrupted by 'minicycles' triggered by events such as illnesses, layoffs and job changes.

- Super and colleagues also developed the construct of *vocational maturity*, which refers to progress through the growth and exploration stages. For many years, career maturity formed the basis of much research and practice in the careers advice and education of young people (Savickas & Porfeli, 2011). More recently, the construct of *career adaptability*, or readiness to cope with current and anticipated tasks of career development, has superseded career maturity.
- Super's focus on a career (wherever it took a person) rather than an occupation (a line of work) changed the direction of career theory. His approach recognized the limiting forces of structure (Chapter 2) and inheritance (Chapter 3), and the meaning of career as a series of work roles in a wider life space that also includes other roles, such as family roles ('role' metaphor; see Chapter 8). He stressed the importance of vocational fit between individual and job ('fit' metaphor; see

Table 4.1 Key Features of Career Stages

Age	Stage	Key Features
0–14	Growth	Childhood focus on the occupational world; development of concern about future as a worker; greater personal control over career activities; ideas about how to make choices, and confidence to do so
15–24	Exploration	Learning what one might become; exploring self (e.g. interests and abilities) and the world of work and occupations in depth and making tentative matches; making occupational choices in line with one's self-concept and actualizing these choices in career behavior; developing skills, experimenting with jobs, stabilizing a job to make it secure
25–44	Establishment	Ongoing implementation of self-concept to bring about integration of self, and own values, in society; stabilizing choice within organizational and occupational parameters, adjusting the self-concept if necessary; advancement or transfer to new or higher responsibility; toward the end of the stage, reflecting on the past and the future of the career
45–64	Maintenance*	Reflecting on the career and deciding on continuation or change; if change is necessary, recycling through the previous stages; holding steady in position, maintaining performance, conserving what has been accomplished, and remaining interested; renewing and innovating where possible
65+	Disengagement	Adjusting to declining energy, decelerating, delegating to others, withdrawing, retiring, organizing a new life structure in which paid work is not central

Note: *Tentatively re-named 'management' by Savickas (2002).
Sources: Savickas (2002); Super (1957).

Chapter 6). The whole theory stresses the constructive role of the individual as builder of the career ('action' metaphor; see Chapter 5).

- The five stages of career development are summarized in Table 4.1. Essentially, said Super, the career actor is implementing a self-concept by occupying a series of work roles created by society (Chapter 8), but each stage has different goals and different developmental tasks for them to undertake.

CASE STUDY

Not Making It

Fifty-year-old Perry is thinking about his career. In the past seven years since being promoted to manager of the small claims department at the local branch of the Phoenix Insurance Company, he has been offered no further promotions. Every year, he receives a good performance evaluation from his manager, but never is it suggested that he is ready for the next step up. Perry long ago set his sights on getting to the top, but now he is beginning to wonder if he will ever make it.

This lack of promotion may not be a problem for Perry because in other ways things are going well for him. His present job is congenial, sociable and not too hard. The company seems secure. His children have grown up and left home and are doing well. He and his wife, Josie, a kindergarten teacher, have a nice house and have paid it off. They have a good social life. They go square dancing twice a week and often have friends or family visit for dinner. Perry is also active in local sports groups.

Promotion now would bring Perry more money, but it would also bring more responsibility. He would have to go on out-of-town business trips more often, and work late more often. His and Josie's social life would suffer. They might even have to move to a different city.

Perry reflects on his past hopes. When he graduated from college, he had fire in his belly. He promised Josie that nothing would stop him from becoming either a rich man or the boss of a big company by the time he was 40 years old. In his 20s, he worked enthusiastically to become self-sufficient, starting off a number of new small businesses, none of which made any money. In the end, Josie, tired of trying to bring up children while living hand to mouth, more or less forced him to take his first job with Phoenix as an insurance salesman, buy the house and settle down.

He turned out to be surprisingly good at selling and made a lot of money on commission very quickly. But after a few years, he tired of the stress of traveling and selling, and resolved instead to climb the corporate ladder. He believed he was a leader and that he could get to the top. But there were others in the company, just as talented as he was, and perhaps even more determined, who seemed to get

> all the best breaks. Gradually, he lowered his ambitions. And now, here he is, basically not caring if he never gets offered another promotion! The young Perry, he reflects, would probably feel betrayed by the middle-aged Perry's lack of ambition. But the young Perry doesn't exist any more, and the older Perry is content. Why put that contentment at risk by looking for more?

As Perry ages, his priorities change. In his 20s, he wanted to try new things (exploration) and grow rich through them. In his 30s, he wanted to get to the top of his company (establishment). In his 40s, he developed a taste for a pleasant leisure and social life and gradually lowered his career ambitions whilst ensuring that he still performed well (maintenance). As he enters his 50s, he appears to want little except continuation of the same (more maintenance). In many ways, then, Perry fits Super's career stages. But even though Perry's career pattern is a familiar one, how universal is it?

Reflections on Super's Theory

Super and his research team gathered plenty of observational data to develop and support his propositions, particularly in the Career Pattern Study, which involved 100 males in the USA who were first contacted in 1951 as 14- or 15-year-olds, and followed for 25 years. However, empirical support for the general existence of career stages appears limited, perhaps because, as Super (1985) himself noted, the proposition that discernible stages exist is hard to test scientifically (Arnold, 1997a).

Many experts feel that the use of such clearly defined stages is too rigid. It may be better to think of a career not as a series of discrete stages but as a gradual flow of development. The theory also seems to be more about the way that careers ought ideally to be or perhaps the way they were 60 years ago rather than the more erratic way they seem to be now (Chapter 2). Also, the theory appears to fit the smooth progression of men through sequences of full-time jobs more than the careers of women juggling multiple roles (Larwood & Gutek, 1987). Super acknowledged these issues. He saw the stages as more socially than biologically driven, manifested as responses to the expectations of others. This implies that if society changes, then so will expectations about what is 'normal', and therefore the stages will also change.

Savickas (2002) proposed that within the broader cycle of a person's overall career, 'a minicycle of growth, exploration, establishment, management and disengagement occurs ... each time an individual's career is destabilized by socio-economic and personal events' (2002: 156). This gives the theory greater flexibility in enabling cyclic careers to adapt to destabilizing events.

The greatest strength of Super's theory may be that it acknowledges that different stages of life bring different challenges. Although there are many exceptions, overall, people's careers do seem to be exploratory at the start and stabilize over time. Careers such as Perry's (above) are readily comprehensible as progressions through the stages suggested by Super. The theory thus provides a good retrospective explanation of many careers (Savickas, 2002).

Stop and Consider

Super originally suggested that the exploration stage took place at ages 15–24 (approximately). Read the description of this stage in Table 4.1 above. How well does it reflect your life at that age? Does the previous stage (growth) or the next one (establishment) do a better job?

Daniel Levinson: The Seasons of a Life

Another well-known protagonist of the age/stage view of careers is the psychologist Daniel Levinson, who, with colleagues, published *The Seasons of a Man's Life* (Levinson et al., 1978; see also Levinson, 1986).

The choice of 'seasons' as a metaphor for human life is significant. For Levinson, this reflected his idea that no phase of life is better or worse than any other, just different. It is easy to see parallels, in our careers, to the springtime when we sow seeds for the future, the summer of glowing success or parched failure, the fall or autumn when we harvest the fruits of the spring sowing, and the winter when our career slows down and perhaps dies.

The empirical basis for *The Seasons of a Man's Life* (Levinson et al., 1978) was a series of interviews with 40 American men, all between 35 and 45 years of age, 10 from each of four occupations: business executives, university-employed biologists, novelists and factory workers. Each man was interviewed at least five times, and the database consisted of an average of 300 pages of data per man. Levinson also studied published biographies, enabling him to get a sense of the stages of development of men beyond the age of 45 years.

On the basis of his data, Levinson divided men's lives into four stages – pre-adulthood, early adulthood, middle adulthood and late adulthood – each linked to the previous and succeeding stages by a period of transition. Adulthood is thus composed of relatively stable periods, in which the individual works at building a desired life structure, that alternate with shorter transitional periods of questioning, reappraisal and often change. Table 4.2 indicates the main characteristics ascribed by Levinson to each period up to the age of 50 years.

Table 4.2   Key Features of Life Stages

Age	Stage	Key Features
17–22 years	Early adult transition	Financial and emotional separation from parents; first attempts at adult roles
23–28 years	Entering the adult world	First stage of early adulthood; exploration of different roles while keeping options open; simultaneously trying to create a stable life structure
29–33 years	Age 30 transition	Reflection and possible redirection; reappraisal of current life structure, concern that it may soon be too late for radical change; focusing on one's Dream
34–40 years	Settling down	Last stage of early adulthood; developing a life structure that supports the Dream; finding one's niche in work, family and leisure; meeting society's expectations and timetables for career success; culminates in Becoming One's Own Man (BOOM). A period of potentially great rewards but also great demands on personal resources
41–45 years	Midlife transition	Reappraisal of life structure: 'What have I done with my life? What do I truly want?'; focused by observation of progress toward the Dream, perceptions of aging, and other changes in family; can result in personal crisis
46–50 years	Entering middle adulthood	Implementing decisions made in the midlife transition

Note: This table does not go beyond the age of 50 years because Levinson did not study men older than that age.
Source: Levinson et al. (1978).

An important element of Levinson's theory is 'the Dream', a personal view of how one wants to live one's life, and the main values that one is pursuing. The Dream is often rooted in career ambitions. It is a preoccupation of early adulthood, a period that culminates, in the late 30s, with what Levinson called the BOOM (Becoming One's Own Man) phase, in which the individual's attempts to fulfil the Dream are particularly intense. The concept is both male-oriented and a product of the optimistic post-World War II boom times.

Levinson et al.'s (1978) characterization of the early 40s as being a turbulent time has entered popular consciousness as the so-called 'midlife crisis'. Some feel they have failed to fulfil their Dream and need to change. Others have climbed career ladders but worry that they have not made a lasting contribution. Similar questions may arise concerning family relationships. Individuals may react to the crisis in radical and sometimes painful ways. Levinson, however, said that crisis was too strong a word for what many of the men in his study felt at this time of life, and there is little evidence in the research literature that the mid-life crisis is a frequent phenomenon. The case of Perry (above) demonstrates mid-life review, but not crisis.

Reflections on Levinson's Theory

Levinson et al.'s (1978) theory has the virtue of placing the work career within a cycle of wider life events, and he identified issues and tasks that most can identify with. His own Dream was to see better integration between individual development and the roles offered by society (Newton, 1994). The theory emphasizes the internal, subjective career rather than its outward manifestations. But Levinson and his colleagues may have interpreted somewhat ambiguous data to fit a specific theory, rather than making their theory flexible enough to accommodate a wide range of data. Another possibility – common to much careers research – is that both Levinson and his informants may have organized their perceptions into much neater patterns than were perhaps apparent at the time, or to the career actors studied (a process called 'retrospective sense making'; see also Chapter 11).

Levinson was adamant that the phases invariably follow one another in the correct order and at the specified ages. Particularly in an individualist culture, that might seem unrealistic. Remember, too, that the theory is based on the experiences of American men in the 1970s. Even if there were real regularities at that time, major changes which took place subsequently in the careers terrain context (Chapter 2) may have badly disrupted any such regularities. Yet, Levinson (1986) argued that the same pattern can be seen in biographies of people living in various eras.

In some ways, Levinson's theory can be seen as consistent with Super's. They both portray career actors as exploring possibilities and seeking to find their niche in the world of work, especially in early life and career. They both link stages with ages. However, Super did not see careers as alternating between transitional and stable phases, and, relative to Levinson, his view of mid-career was not about personal crisis but about maintaining one's existing position.

In the early 1980s, Levinson conducted a similar study with women, though it was not published until after his death in 1994 (Levinson, 1996). He interviewed 45 women: 15 housewives, 15 financial and corporate executives, and 15 academics. He argued that the same seasons of life could be seen in women's biographies as in men's. Nevertheless, some of the issues encountered by women were different from those typically reported by men – for example, persistent sex discrimination for the women in work, and, among housewives, limited opportunities for self-development. Still, Levinson argued that this study provided further evidence that the stages he outlined have universal applicability, even if manifested in different ways.

The fact that the theory refers primarily to what is going on within the person may make it robust against changes in the career environment. Levinson was not saying that in a stable period of building a life structure, few career transitions take place, nor that during a transitional period a person will necessarily move between jobs. In the theory, stability refers to the person having a stable purpose and goals, and transition to a time when those purposes and goals are questioned (though they may nevertheless be retained). Major events such as mass layoffs can make it more difficult to achieve personal goals, but Levinson's theory is invalidated only if it can be shown that such events fundamentally change the rhythm of people's lives.

Stop and Consider

Think about people you know. Try to identify someone who either never quite figured out who they were, or conversely someone who made quick and early choices for their adult life, based perhaps on a very clear self-concept. How have their work and lives developed since then? What, if any, have been the consequences of their developmental path?

Career Stages and 'New Careers'

Despite their influence and conceptual richness, career stage theories are nowadays rarely at the center of research studies. Why not? In Chapter 2, we noted that over the last 30 years, due to phenomena such as organizational restructuring and layoffs, international displacement of work and new information technology, employment has become much less stable for many people. The *New Careers* study conducted in the late 1990s (Arthur et al., 1999) suggested that modern careers make the notion of predictable life stages less plausible. For example, consider the career exploration and establishment of Brett, a 32-year-old plasterer.

CASE STUDY

Anarchical Exploration

Brett went to college and studied business because he thought he would learn how to get rich. Instead, he drank a lot of beer, did little work and after three years flunked out. He got a job driving a forklift in a factory and learned to do four-wheel skids and smoke pot, but he soon got bored and quit. Next, he tried being unemployed, but that was just as boring. When his parents hassled him to get a decent job, Brett bought his first suit, had a haircut and got a job as a clerk in the stock exchange. When he showed promise, his boss gave him a chance as a stock trader.

(Continued)

> *(Continued)*
>
> In the cut and thrust of trading, he found he had good bargaining skills and a strong personality, and he did well. But he also realized that the values of his industry were unacceptably materialistic: 'the business world, suit world in the inner city ... wasn't me.'
>
>   Brett was creative – for example, he played in the evenings in a professional rock group – and he took his distress out on his employers creatively, busking on a unicycle at lunchtimes, outside the stock exchange where he knew the bosses could see him. Eventually, the stock exchange experienced a major share market crash and Brett walked out.
>
>   Using informal contacts, he quickly obtained temporary work helping a friend to paint a boat. The friend was also a plasterer and next invited Brett to help him plaster a house. Brett, who had been expert as a child in building plaster-of-Paris models, knew immediately he had found his niche. The normal four-year plastering apprenticeship was unnecessary – he was already an expert. When the plasterer offered him another contract, he said no and used his selling skills to solicit plastering contracts of his own. His business prospered, and within a few years he was working only when he felt like it, subcontracting most of his work and specializing personally in ornamental plastering. He even resumed and completed his abandoned business degree in his spare time. In the evenings, his musical and dramatic work had met with success. When interviewed, he was a little bored with plastering and was beginning, at age 32, to think of going overseas in search of fortune as a performer.
>
>   *Source*: Arthur et al. (1999).

In his late teens and early 20s, Brett's method of 'exploration' was trial and error – he threw himself into whatever came up and then checked whether he liked it. Through a lucky chance, he was successful, and at the 'right' age according to Super's theory, 25, he started to establish his career in plastering. But Brett's plastering career now looks problematic, not because of the unstable external environment but because of his changing internal sense of identity. Brett appears to be about to re-enter the exploration stage.

   When Arthur et al. (1999) tried to organize their 75 career cases into a framework, they found that, despite the many cases of individuals behaving outside of type, the ideas of age/stage theory fitted rather well. They found three general kinds of behavior. First, behavior driven by the desire for exploration and novelty was labeled *fresh energy: engaging with unfamiliar situations*. Second, behavior directed at creating career momentum and establishing direction was labeled *informed direction: pursuing career pathways*. The third kind of behavior, labeled *seasoned engagement*, is where the individual is concerned with continuity. These three kinds of behavior align well with Super's exploration, establishment and maintenance, respectively, and were broadly age-related. There were, of course, spectacular exceptions, such as a nurse in her mid-50s who was fired from her job and found herself choosing between a new career in psychotherapy and another in market gardening (her final choice). Radical career change, driven by both internal and external forces, can disrupt any life cycle, as Ibarra's (2004) excellent collection of cases shows.

The Stages of Women's Careers

Both Super (1990) and Levinson et al. (1978) tended to state that their theories applied to women as well as men, and, as noted earlier, Levinson reported a second study of women (Levinson, 1996). However, studies by Ornstein and Isabella (1990) and Smart and Peterson (1994) showed little support for either the Levinson or the Super model in relation to women's careers.

Other researchers have resolutely claimed that women's careers have different dynamics from men's, for reasons to do with socialization, psychological development and the roles that men and women are expected to adopt (e.g. Gallos, 1989; Gilligan, 1982; see also Chapter 8), such as the strong tendency for women to be more involved than men in childcare (e.g. Laurijssen & Glorieux, 2013).

In the Levinson research, the main difference between women and men was the clash for women between the roles of homemaker and career woman. Professional women had similar career tasks to those of men but due to home commitments found them difficult. Work career, though important, was less central to their Dream. In general, women had a more complex and ambiguous sense of their place in the world and, hence, greater difficulty in specifying a Dream (Kittrell, 1998; Roberts & Newton, 1987). Only a few women 'had it all' – successful full-time careers and families. The others were all either single women with careers, married women with careers but no families or full-time housewives with no current career (see also Chapter 8). According to Gallos (1989), therefore, women pursue not a Dream, as envisaged by Levinson, but a *split dream* involving a balance between career and family.

O'Neil and Bilimoria (2005) interviewed 60 women in depth and proposed three career phases:

- Phase 1 is *idealistic achievement*. Here, typically in early adulthood as the woman gets her occupational career under way, the emphasis is on personal control, career satisfaction and achievement, and making a positive impact on others.
- Phase 2 is *pragmatic endurance*. This tends to coincide with child bearing and rearing, but is not confined to women who have children. It is a phase of managing multiple relationships and responsibilities, but still doing what has to be done. There is less personal control than in Phase 1, and more dissatisfaction, especially with hard-to-meet demands of organizations and managers.

- Finally, Phase 3 is *re-inventive contribution*. This is when women tend to feel more free from caring responsibilities. Although their focus is still on contributing to their organizations, families and communities, there is now a strong sense of self and a wish to express it, so that women tend to view their careers as opportunities for both learning and making a difference to others.

See if you can trace the three O'Neil and Bilmoria stages in Yasmin's career.

CASE STUDY

Growing through Pain

Yasmin grew up in Hong Kong where her father was a leading businessman and her mother a homemaker devoted to Yasmin and her two brothers. Yasmin combined sharp analytical and quantitative skills with a strong ability to relate to people. After completing undergraduate and master's degrees in business, she achieved rapid promotions in general management. She was already mixing with Hong Kong's business elite and being noticed.

At age 28, Yasmin married Lawrence, an up-and-coming publishing executive. They soon had two children together. With difficulty, and utilizing considerable paid domestic help, Yasmin was able to continue with her career. Lawrence played little part in the childcare.

Yasmin began to feel guilty about not always being available for her children. Work seemed ever-more demanding, and her (male) managers were not sympathetic to her need for work–life balance. Moving between companies didn't help. Worn out by the demands on her, and impatient at Lawrence's lack of practical support, Yasmin felt she was 'running on empty', with little opportunity for leisure or the development of relationships with family and friends. Although she remained successful at work, the personal costs were high.

Eventually, Yasmin quit paid work. This helped her relationships with Lawrence and the children, as well as her physical and mental health. However, six years later, when the children were in their teens, she wanted to go back to work. Through her earlier business contacts, she set up as a management consultant, at first taking any work she could get, but later using her growing reputation to specialize in consulting on diversity and work–life balance issues. She enjoyed helping to improve both company performance and working relationships, and she felt comfortable with leaving Lawrence and the children to manage their own lives. After all, she told herself, they are intelligent and resourceful and I'm always here to provide help and advice if they need it.

Many women in their 40s and 50s pursue career and professional accomplishment with considerable self-confidence. This tends to put men and women on opposite developmental trajectories, because whilst women are becoming more agentic men the same age may be discovering their more relational side (Brim, 1976). However, some (e.g. Gallos, 1989) would argue that women's agency is still more likely than men's to be expressed in ways which foster community and joint action, rather than individual achievement. Again, Yasmin's case reflects this.

Maxi-Stages and Mini-Cycles

One response to major deviations from stage theory is to think more flexibly about stages. Hall (2002: 118) stated that 'as (people) move in and out of various product areas, technologies, functions, organizations, and other work environments', their careers will 'increasingly become a series of "mini-stages" (or short-cycle learning stages) of exploration-trial-mastery-exit'. So, at any one time, a career actor might be in, for example, the establishment phase of the career cycle but the disengagement phase of a job or project cycle. A career actor may also, over the course of a career, work in several occupations – for example, at 50 years old they may be in the establishment phase of an occupation entered just a few years earlier. The interplay between long-, medium- and short-term cycles or stages and how they affect people's careers is frequently discussed but rarely investigated.

Hall and Foster's (1977) notion of the 'psychological success cycle' depicts how a career actor can develop a positive identity in their job through successful completion of challenging assignments. This sense of self as competent then prompts willingness to take on even more challenging work, which (hopefully) leads to further success, thus creating a virtuous circle (Hall & Chandler, 2005). This 'mini-cycle' within a job may feed through to subsequent choices of job and even occupation, so that a long-term career is shaped by an escalating sense of competence.

Super et al. (1988) recognized the need to detach career stages from ages. They developed the Adult Career Concerns Inventory, which asks people about the extent to which they feel preoccupied with each of 12 career concerns – three from each of the four stages of exploration, establishment, maintenance and disengagement. As they recognized, a career actor's concerns at any given time depend not only on where they are in their career overall, but also on mini-cycles based on the job they are in, and on non-work factors such as family commitments.

Calendar cycles, such as the farming seasons, the financial year, the school semester and the monthly sales report, often build smaller cycles into our careers, providing our working lives with texture and predictability. But they also alert us to the danger of stagnation: a 40-year career may turn out to be not 40 years of experience but one year of experience 40 times over. In practice, external events often ensure that repeated cycles involve change and learning, such as doing the same basic job cycle with more sophisticated software packages.

Age and Career

Another response to the inflexibility of stages is to avoid chopping time into chunks as stage theories do, and to instead treat it as continuous. Age effects, after all, occur gradually, whereas moving from one stage to another tends to imply a fundamental and possibly sudden change. Some psychologists have dispensed with the idea of stages and have instead studied how various attributes such as personality, ability and values change with chronological age.

Due to declining birth rates and increasing life expectancy brought about by improved health care and living conditions (Magnus, 2008), most Western countries have rapidly aging populations (see also Chapter 2). In the Organization for Economic Co-operation and Development (OECD) countries, in 2008 for each person over 65 there were on average about five people aged 20–64. By 2050, this ratio is expected to be only 1 to 2 (Nilsson, 2012), making it more and more difficult for the working population to support so many non-working elderly. Increasing efforts are therefore being made to keep older people in the workforce (e.g. OECD, 2006). Compulsory retirement ages are being increased or abolished, and the age at which retirement pensions are payable is being increased in many countries from 65 to 66 and 67 (OECD, 2007). The focus of attention in analyses of age is therefore on the latter part of the career.

Despite some negative stereotypes about older workers (Posthuma & Campion, 2009), evidence on the whole is that the job performance of older workers is as good as that of most younger workers (Ng & Feldman, 2008), depending on the nature of the work. As people age, physical work requiring strength and/or agility becomes increasingly difficult for them, and their ability to think quickly about new and/or abstract problems (so-called 'fluid' intelligence) declines (Salthouse, 2010), though for most people the decline is not severe enough during the working years to threaten their basic competence. On the other hand, 'crystallized' intelligence, which is one's store of accumulated knowledge and the capacity to use it, increases with age (Salthouse, 2010). One can often be traded off against the other to achieve good work performance (Greller & Stroh, 2004).

Older career actors tend to desire more autonomy and control at work. Their desire for a wide range of tasks may decline, but they do not lose interest in the intrinsic nature of their work (Kooij et al., 2011): they want to use their accumulated skills and knowledge. They also increasingly wish to contribute to the collective good, and value work relationships for the affirmation of their identity.

An important issue for older workers is how to avoid feeling that one has stagnated and/or failed to do anything worthwhile in life (Erikson, 1959). A key wish is often to exercise *generativity*: that is, accomplishments which make a contribution to the world, especially to subsequent generations. Generativity may combine altruistic goals with a more egocentric wish to be remembered after one has gone (Grant & Wade-Benzoni, 2009). Generativity is clearly relevant to the supervision and mentorship of others, as well as to certain kinds of leadership (Clark & Arnold, 2008). It can also manifest in a wish to uphold organizations and institutions (McAdams & de St Aubin, 1992). This causes some in mid/late career to take on roles that emphasize communication and cohesion, possibly at the expense of personal advancement. The downside of this may be resistance to change.

How, then, might work be designed for people in the latter part of their career (Kanfer & Ackerman, 2004; Truxillo et al., 2012)? For them, autonomy and control over how the job is done is probably even more critical than for younger people, but that does not mean that they should be left to their own devices. As noted above in relation to generativity, opportunities for affiliative, supportive and community-building work relationships are important. Pursuing multiple tasks simultaneously requires a lot of fluid intelligence, so a better option may be for older workers to make use of their crystallized intelligence and well-learned skills and experience within a relatively small set of tasks. Some organizations have introduced 'age-friendly' human resource management initiatives (see Chapter 14). Use of these HR techniques is however patchy (Greller & Stroh, 2004).

CASE STUDY

Back to his Roots

Wilfred is a top-quality civil engineer born in Uganda to a family that was astute enough to recognize his talents and wealthy enough to fund educational opportunities. After completing engineering degrees, he took up academic roles in European universities involving applied research and consultancy, some of which took him back to Uganda. Wilfred was successful and a good team player but by mid-career he felt stretched, taken for granted by his university and less happy than he had been. His wide variety of assignments had been exciting at first but was now becoming frustrating and tiring, especially as he had little control over which projects he was assigned to.

Some of Wilfred's work had been in water engineering, where his strongest interests and talents lay. So when he was approached to become the chief field engineer of the water supply agency for part of Uganda and to build a team of engineers to safeguard water supplies for years to come, he took the opportunity. He could use his well-established skills in solving a range of related problems, the general parameters of which he was familiar with. He was promised any additional training he needed to carry out this specific role. He also had a lot of autonomy and was able to contribute to the well-being of communities close to where he grew up, something that he found he cared a lot about.

Wilfred's case illustrates how a career actor's approach to work can change with age. What was exciting in his early career became unpleasant for him. Now he was able to sastisfy an increasing wish to use his hard-won skills in roles where he was trusted to make decisions, for purposes which contributed to the collective good.

Psychologists have studied how people can manage their own aging process and some of this research is relevant to the work setting. The Selection-Optimization-Compensation (SOC) model (Baltes & Dickson, 2001) posits that, as we get older, it becomes more important to *select* carefully a limited range of tasks to focus on, *optimize* our performance at them by maximizing our resources (which can be as simple as going to bed a bit earlier) and carefully developing skills key to task performance, and (especially important) *compensate* for our limitations by, for example, seeking out tasks that play to our strengths and delegating those that don't.

There is evidence that these are indeed good strategies for career actors to use at work as they age (Weigl et al., 2013). Still, they have their dangers. For example, compensating for limitations by neglecting parts of one's job could have negative organizational and personal consequences. More generally, it is not always possible or desirable to design work exactly as older people want it, nor to exempt older workers from the need to update and develop their skills. Although eagerness to learn new skills typically decreases with age, it seems that the capability of doing so remains sufficient. However, older workers' learning may sometimes be slower and less confident than that of younger workers (Kanfer & Ackerman, 2004).

Age-linked Phenomena in Careers

Young People

Gottfredson's (1981) theory of circumscription, compromise and self-creation is one of the most established theories of childhood career development. It describes an age-related set of stages that children pass through regarding occupational choices. Their thinking evolves from generalized perceptions based on gender and/or status associated with occupations, to matching personal with occupational characteristics, and also with the opportunities and constraints provided by the labor market. However, it has recently been argued that children start learning about the world of work earlier than previously thought, and that this affects the choices they make later in life. Their early learning is not only about their own skills and preferences, but also about adult roles and responsibilities (Schultheiss, 2008).

Erikson (1959) argued that in adolescence we face an identity crisis as we endeavor to establish a clear sense of who we are. Early choices of education or occupation may well be part of that process, and there are twin risks of 'identity diffusion' on the one hand and over-commitment to a rigid identity on the other ('foreclosure' – Marcia, 1966). In early career, we try to resolve competing desires for intimacy and independence, and again the resolution may be reflected in work-related behavior. On the one hand, a young career actor may immerse themselves deeply in the life of an organization, or on the other maintain a distance and unwillingness to commit. Each of these poles carries both rewards and risks.

Early career may be a critical period in development, a time when career actors are unusually open to major change in the way they function. Although the transition from education to work is smooth for many young people (Bauer et al., 2007), for others it is a struggle to find work of any kind, let alone work that fits their educational achievements. This is especially the case at the time of writing when there are high levels of youth unemployment in many countries (see Chapter 2). Those who are unable to access opportunities to learn, earn and contribute via their work at this stage often experience major distress, exacerbated by feeling blocked from adopting adult roles (Bjarnason & Sigurdardottir, 2003).

The personal priorities of those who successfully launch themselves into the world of work are usually a mixture of (in Super's terms) exploration and establishment. Young career actors want to look around for niches that fit them especially well (see Chapter 6), whilst also achieving worthwhile accomplishments. However, new entrants often find that their abilities are not well used. If this is the case, the 'psychological success cycle' (Hall & Foster, 1977), described earlier in this chapter cannot get started. Limited opportunity to shine also reduces the newcomer's chances in the organization's career progression 'tournament' (Rosenbaum, 1989), which in its purest form is a knock-out competition where if you lose in the first round, you are out of the running for subsequent promotions.

In addition to performing well in their work, newcomers need to learn the formal and informal rules of their workplace. Through this *organizational socialization*, the newcomer not only acquires proficiency in their job but also builds relationships and learns the history, traditions, rituals, heroes, goals, values, power structure, informal language and other norms of the organization (Bauer et al., 2007; Chao et al., 1994). In organizational socialization, carefully programmed 'institutionalized' ways of processing newcomers can be contrasted with less systematic 'individualized' methods. Newcomers tend to like the former more, but the latter may be more likely to produce innovative employees (Allen & Meyer, 1990). Recently, it has been shown that the socialization tactics used by organizations produce their results through the relationships and social embeddedness they generate for the newcomer (Allen & Shanock, 2013). However, as the case of Harry illustrates below, newcomers are not necessarily passive recipients of socialization, nor should they be. Regularly seeking information and feedback (Hays & Williams, 2011) and developing relationships with members of the organization (Korte & Lin, 2013) help the newcomer's learning and also serve to make a good impression.

CASE STUDY

Harry's First Day

My first day in the company? I'd have to say it was a bit of a disaster. After all the song and dance they had made about 'we are a people company', no one seemed to be expecting me! Eventually, a secretary saw me looking lost and showed me my office, but no one had cleared it, and I spent the first morning throwing out old files and cleaning it up. My boss found me and gave me a long lecture on the proud history of the company, how honored I should be to be a member, blah blah blah, but to me everything seemed smaller and pokier than it had looked in the brochures. Then he took me to see the CEO, supposedly a hero who had saved the company from going under, but he seemed ordinary too – he had egg on his tie and kept losing his glasses on his desk. He said to me, 'That's a most interesting shirt, Mr Peters. Red. Very flamboyant!' And he kind of glared at me. I asked someone about it later and she told me that the company standard was white or pastel-colored shirts and dark ties – the CEO thought that was what the customers liked. We had a good laugh about it and she's been a source of useful information ever since.

Midcareer Issues

According to the traditional stage theories discussed above, when career actors reach their 40s, it is usually clear whether or not the 'Dream' (Levinson et al., 1978) will be achieved. Advancement further up an organizational hierarchy is likely to be hard to obtain, and challenges to self-image may be coming from younger people both at work and at home. Some of the age-related changes described earlier in this chapter may well be apparent, and age stereotypes may affect the person's prospects. For Super, this signals a transition into the maintenance stage of holding on to what one has achieved, and for Levinson it means a fairly urgent re-appraisal of the life structure.

Those who choose to re-commit to their current life structure often have to come to terms with the *career plateau*, which occurs at the point of a career when the chances of additional hierarchical advancement or increased responsibility are very low (Feldman & Weitz, 1988). Perry, in a case study earlier in this chapter, appears to be on the plateau. It is tempting to see the career plateau as a problem, and for some people it is indeed hard to accept and adjust to (Nachbagauer & Riedl, 2002). Employing organizations may combat this by expanding job assignments and project work (see Chapter 14), mentoring (Chapter 9; Rotondo & Perrewé, 2000) or otherwise re-designing work roles to accommodate age-related changes in motives and values. Many people, however, adapt well to the plateau and accept that there are other means of fulfilment for them, such as continuing to perform their role well and taking more of an interest in their fellow workers and/or in family and leisure activities (Feldman & Weitz, 1988). Perry is an example. The employees who pose the greatest problem for the organization and for themselves are those who are 'dead wood' (Ference et al., 1977) – plateaued, dissatisfied and ineffective. These employees may need major interventions initiated by themselves, their advisors or the organization (see Chapters 12, 13 and 14).

In mid-career, some people decide to change the occupation or context in which they work, or both (Neapolitan, 1980). Often, the move is from employment into self-employment, for example when teachers and business executives abandon corporate life to start new ventures or become store owners or self-employed potters. For women especially, this may be a response to feeling undervalued or discriminated against (Mallon & Cohen, 2001). Self-employment is not necessarily liberating in all respects because usually the person has to compete for work, and not be too choosy about what work it is (Van den Born & Van Witteloostuijn, 2013). It is not always very well paid either. Still, whatever the causes of mid-career change, there is evidence that the process is a functional one for many individuals. Roborgh and Stacey (1987) studied a sample of mid-career changers in a small town and found that although most of them were worse off financially, they were also much happier with their lives than were the general population.

CASE STUDY

Long-Playing Record

Canadian musician and writer Leonard Cohen was born in 1934 and, at the time of writing, is still, at age 79, producing new material and performing in huge arenas. With his band, he gave 246 concerts worldwide between May 2008 and December 2010. What keeps him going? After all, as he says, his voice is a low growl and he can 'barely hold a tune'. One factor is robust health, though he plans to celebrate his 80th birthday by resuming smoking. Another is his need to resolve his well-publicized financial problems, arising from the alleged actions of his former manager, and the subsequent legal proceedings that consumed his retirement savings. But surely that cannot be the whole story. Cohen's music, poetry and art have always been a mixture of the reflective, spiritual, drily humorous, sexual, loving and cynical. He engages with personal, interpersonal, religious and political issues that preoccupy many of us at various points in our lives. As well as having deep meaning for his fans, it seems that his work is also important to him in making sense of life and expressing his deepest thoughts and feelings. Why retire from that?

Ending Working Life (or Not)

Some people, like Leonard Cohen, seem not to want to retire. Unusual but by no means unique was 94-year-old Ada Hostler who in 2011 was working a 45-hour week as administrator in her daughter's nursery in the UK. As she put it: 'I want to make the most out of life. You are dead a long time and don't have much time to live in comparison.' However, many people in late career have more modest aims. They seek to hold on to what they have with as few changes as possible until they can afford to retire (Arthur et al., 1999). Even at this career stage, some people seek personal growth, and this seems to have positive consequences for well-being (Clark & Arnold, 2008).

As noted earlier, many countries need people to stay in work longer in order to maintain viable economies in the face of aging populations. According to Dychtwald et al. (2004: 48), 'it's time to retire retirement'. Indeed, the meaning of retirement is not at all clear these days (Wang & Shultz, 2010). It once signified a clear-cut event where on one day a person is working and being paid, and on the next they are no longer in work or seeking it, and living on a pension. Now, however, trajectories in late career are becoming more blurred and varied. More options for part-time work are available, enabling retirement to be phased in rather than sudden (Kim & Feldman, 2000). Indeed, retirement is increasingly seen as a process and/or career stage rather than an event (Shultz & Wang, 2011). Not surprisingly, stages/phases make a return here, with Feldman and Beehr (2011) proposing three: imagining the future as retired, assessing the past and deciding the time to let go, and making the transition into retired life.

Inkson et al. (2013) identify four patterns of working in late career. *Phased retirement* is where a person gradually decreases working hours, usually staying with the same employer. *Bridge employment* involves working on a contract, part-time or temporary basis after retirement from a full-time position. This usually works out best when the bridge employment involves a type of work that is already well known to the person (Zhan et al., 2009). A third possible trajectory is *self-employment*, where older workers, perhaps with the security of a pension from previous employment, set up on their own, usually but not always doing the kind of work for which they have built up a reputation over previous years. This often requires considerable personal resources and is not for everyone (Parker & Rougier, 2007). The final notion is that of *encore careers* (Freedman, 2007). Here, the older worker uses their skills to contribute to the well-being of others, for example through voluntary work in a charitable institution, and/or develop their self-knowledge and wisdom. This is definitely not a strategy for those who seek to disengage from the world of work (Ibarra, 2004).

Most research on retirement has focused on predicting when people will retire and how well-adjusted they will be after they do. Not surprisingly, those with greater financial resources, poorer health and lower work centrality (i.e. the opposite of Leonard Cohen, above) tend to choose to retire earlier, but it seems that a large number of interacting factors make this a very individual decision (Schultz & Wang, 2011). People also often feel the need to explain and justify their decisions (see Chapter 11), so that, for example, those who retire relatively early tend to see those who carry on as lacking anything more interesting to do with their lives, whilst those who carry on sometimes position themselves as the heroic ones who are making sacrifices to keep the economy going (Nilsson, 2012).

As for how people adjust to retirement, most seem to be fairly unaffected by it, and, even if there are some initial difficulties, relatively few end up poorly adjusted (Wang et al., 2011). An exception is those who are in poor health, which may have precipitated their retirement in the first place. Poor health is a continuing burden post-retirement, though perhaps less so than if the person had remained in employment (Kim & Feldman, 2000). Material resources, feelings of autonomy or mastery about the retirement decision, timing and being married all contribute positively to post-retirement adjustment (Wang et al., 2011). Perhaps surprisingly, there is less consistent evidence that the centrality of work makes adjustment to retirement more difficult. This may be because most retired people seem to more than fill the time vacated by work with alternative pursuits, especially hobbies, family activities and staying healthy (Wong & Earl, 2009).

Conclusion

We conclude that it is helpful to consider careers as a series of stages or phases. They give us a sense of predictability and offer clues about what to expect ahead of time. The character of each stage as described by theorists gives us a language and conceptual framework to understand some of what happens to us. However, it is important not to see ourselves as the helpless victims of stages – with acts of will and favourable circumstances we can perhaps find our own sequence of experience. In any case, events (especially unexpected ones) in economies and in our personal lives may invalidate the idea of predictable stages or at least increase the variety of ways in which people experience them. It may well be helpful to apply stages to specific career episodes, such as a job, rather than to the career as a whole. An alternative to stage is age, which is a continuous variable that does not require arbitrary divisions into chunks, and there is a growing body of research about how it relates to the experience of work and career. Insights from research and theory on stages and age help us to understand how a person tackles tasks at different key moments, including when starting work, in mid-career and in retirement.

Key Points in this Chapter

- People change over time in their career attitudes and aspirations. Age/stage theories of career attempt to explain career behavior as part of a life cycle, sometimes considered akin to predictable seasons.
- Super proposed a five-stage theory in which the key stages were exploration in early career, establishment in mid-career and maintenance in late career. Levinson

(Continued)

(Continued)

proposed a life-span theory in which periods of relative stability were predictably linked with more dynamic transitions, including mid-life transition. These theories accord with many observed cases but cannot be applied universally.

- Typically, and partly due to women's greater involvement in childcare activities, the nature and timing of career tasks differs somewhat for men and women.
- With increasing age, rapid flexible thinking declines, but expertise at familiar types of problem increases. Desires to contribute to human well-being and to have autonomy in work also increase.
- These trends give insights into the development and contribution of older workers. This matters in the context of an aging population where people need to work for longer.

Questions from this Chapter

General Questions

1. Use the theories in this chapter to analyze the career of Perry in the first case. What stages and transitions can you discern?
2. Can you observe any of the stages from your own career or the careers of other people you know?
3. Compare and contrast the theories of Levinson and Super. Which (if either) do you find the more convincing, and why?
4. What are the main differences between the typical career cycles of men and women?
5. According to research on aging, in what ways might older and younger workers differ in their perceptions of what makes a good job?
6. Why is reaching a career plateau not a problem for many people who experience it?
7. What measures do you think will be most effective in encouraging older workers to stay in the workforce when they can afford to retire?

'Live Career Case' Study Questions

1. Ask your career case person to divide their career into no more than five stages, which the case person can differentiate. Do they find this possible? If so, what are the characteristics of the stages, and how well do they fit the theories presented in this chapter?

2. Ask your case person how what they want from their career, and their strategies for achieving it, have changed over the years. Compare this with the research on aging.

Additional Resources

Recommended Further Reading

Arthur, M. B., Inkson, K. and Pringle, J. K. (1999) *The New Careers: Individual action and economic change* (Chapters 4–6). Thousand Oaks, CA: SAGE.

Greller, M. M. and Stroh, L. K. (2004) 'Becoming elders not relics', *Organizational Dynamics*, 33: 202–214.

Levinson, D. J. (1986) 'A conception of adult development', *American Psychologist*, 46: 3–13.

O'Neil, D. A. and Bilimoria, D. (2005) 'Women's career development phases: Idealism, endurance and reinvention', *Career Development International*, 10: 168–189.

Savickas, M. L. and a large international team (2009) 'Life designing: A paradigm for career, construction in the 21st century', *Journal of Vocational Behavior*, 75: 239–250.

Super, D. E., Savickas, M. L. and Super, C. M. (1996) 'The life-span, life-space approach to careers', in D. Brown, L. Brooks, & Associates (eds.), *Career Choice and Development* (3rd edn, pp. 121–178). San Francisco: Jossey-Bass.

Self-Assessment Resources

Assess your 'early career' indecision: Feldman, D. C. (2003) 'The antecedents and consequences of early career indecision among young adults', *Human Resource Management Review*, 13: 499–531.

Assess your 'early career' adaptability: Vianen, A. E., Pater, I. E. and Preenen, P. T. (2009) 'Adaptable careers: Maximizing less and exploring more', *The Career Development Quarterly*, 57: 298–309.

Assess your 'early career' decision-making process: Germeijs, V. and Verschueren, K. (2007) 'High school students' career decision-making process: Consequences for choice implementation in higher education', *Journal of Vocational Behavior*, 70: 223–241.

Online Resources

Early career stage advice – see: www.forbes.com/sites/danschawbel/2013/10/17/my-10-best-pieces-of-career-advice-for-millennials/

Advice for your first-ever job – see: www.bothsidesofthetable.com/2012/12/10/some-quick-sage-advice-for-young-employees-early-in-their-careers/

Careers as Action

Chapter Objectives

The objectives of this chapter are:

- to explain what personal agency is and how it is related to career development
- to describe and evaluate five theories of career development: social learning theory of career choice, social cognitive career theory, career construction theory, contextual action theory, and protean career theory
- to help readers formulate their own personal definition of career success
- to enable readers to understand the dynamics behind career inaction and its possible consequences.

CASE STUDY

Blonde Ambition

She was born into an Italian Catholic family and grew up in middle America. She had five brothers and sisters. Her mother died when she was 5 years old, and her father, a stern disciplinarian, worked hard to bring her up. She was educated in a nunnery and at one stage wanted to be a nun. But music entered her life: first piano, then dance. At 14 years of age, she enrolled in a dance school and fell under the spell of her dance instructor. He took her to gay clubs, enabling her to see a different way of life. When she danced, people looked at her. And her dance instructor was the first man to tell her she was beautiful.

A straight-A high school graduate, she enrolled in the School of Music at the University of Michigan, but it wasn't for her, and she moved to New York, intent on succeeding in the entertainment industry. She arrived in Times Square with less than $20. She waited tables, took more dance classes, and danced in clubs, but it wasn't enough: she wanted to sing and act as well, and to be famous. To make ends meet, she modelled nude. She got a break as a backup dancer overseas, but it didn't work out, and she came back to New York.

With a boyfriend, she formed a band and got her first taste of professional singing. She formed another band. She was out in front singing, but it was sporadic: she wasn't really getting anywhere.

She tried to network – with dancers, musicians, DJs. She had an in-your-face style but could charm people. She wasn't above using her sexuality to get what she wanted. She and a new boyfriend squatted in the Music Building in Manhattan, a shrine to pop music, full of music companies. She hustled executives for a break, and eventually a woman executive offered to be her manager. The story goes that when the manager entrusted her with the care of her pet poodles, she spray-painted rude words on the poodles and took them walking on Fifth Avenue – anything for publicity.

She continued to live hand to mouth. She dyed her dark hair blonde. Then she met a club DJ, slept with him and got him to play a demo tape at his club, where she danced often and had a following in the crowd. The crowd loved the tape – loved her! The DJ hawked the tape around the record companies. A few said no, but at last she got a deal. Like his predecessors, the DJ disappeared from the scene, his job done. A record was released. She recorded a video to go with one of the songs and it went straight to the top of the dance charts. A stellar career had begun. It was 1983. She was 24 years old. For her professional name, she dropped her family surname, Ciccone. She kept her first name, Madonna.

Source: Evans (1995).

Perhaps it is no accident that one of Madonna's biggest world tours was called Blonde Ambition. Evans's (1995) colourful mini-biography of the superstar's early years is a portrayal of huge, vaulting egotism, of an individual with big career ambitions imposing herself relentlessly on the world, much of the time by sheer outrageousness, until she got what she wanted. As she said herself, 'It's a great feeling to be powerful. I've been wanting it all my life.' In her early years, Madonna was a prime example of the career as action. Her career did not just happen to her: by her own actions, she made her career happen. She produced it, directed it and starred in it. It was her own creation. Today, in 2014, Madonna is still on top of the world: Forbes magazine announced that she was the highest-earning celebrity of 2013, at 125 million dollars.

This chapter is about careers as action. Chapters 3 and 4 emphasized forces such as inherited characteristics, social structure, aging and family cycles, which exert external power over careers and limit individual action. In contrast, this chapter focuses on people exerting power to create and direct their own careers. It emphasizes that careers do not just happen to us: they are also something we *do*. We all exert some influence over our careers. The career of Madonna has been introduced not because it is an especially admirable one but because it appears to be one where her own ambitions and actions dominated, and where constraining forces, such as limited family assistance, childhood discipline and the inhospitable labor market of the entertainment industry, were conspicuously overridden. It is a career in which the career actor was unambiguously in charge. Few people have the talent, the strength of will or the selfishness to emulate Madonna, even in their own fields. But by and large, career experts consider that most of us could benefit from greater empowerment and expression of ourselves in our careers (Hansen, 2012). It therefore seems worthwhile to pay special attention to the ideas in this chapter.

Personal Agency

Agency refers to the capacity of human beings to make choices and to impose these choices on the world, which implies having some degree of control over the social relations in which one is embedded, and an ability to transform these social relations to some extent (Seeck & Parzefall, 2008). Madonna exerts agency over her career because she is exceptionally active and energetic about it and has her own ways of making things happen.

In his seminal book, Bakan (1966) identified two basic strategies for dealing with life's uncertainties and labeled them communion and agency. *Communion* is a strategy of opening oneself up to the world and other people, accepting them, adjusting to them and integrating with them. *Agency*, introduced as a key concept in the study of careers by Marshall (1989), is a strategy of dealing with the world by independent self-assertion and control. In essence, the individual imposes him- or herself on the world, rather than allowing it to dominate. In agentic career behavior, the individual takes the initiative, attempts to make progress through personal action, applies assertively for new jobs, seeks progression and attempts to take charge of their own career (Svejenova et al., 2010).

In career behavior, agency, if carried to extremes – as in the hard-driving, fast-paced, competitive way of living that stress researchers have labelled Type A behavior – can have negative consequences (including heart disease) for both the agentic person and those with whom they deal (Edwards et al., 1990), although according to recent research this effect may be less strong than is popularly believed (Hallberg et al., 2007).

There is good reason to believe that without going to extremes individuals can practice agency to improve their careers (Duberley et al., 2006a; Guo et al., 2013). For example, Boyatzis et al. (2002) considered the problem of lack of passion for one's job and noted various agentic practices, such as creating reflective structures, learning from a coach or a development program, or searching for new meaning in familiar territory, whereby people can take their own action to reawaken their passion. Employing organizations are becoming less willing to provide either the security or the automatic promotions that might enable members to have successful careers without practicing agency. A catch-cry of recent years has been that organizational careers are declining or even dead and that from now on individuals will have to look after their own careers (Duberley et al., 2006b; Hall & Associates, 1996). In other words, agency is more essential than ever for career development.

Theories of Career Decision Making

In an agency approach to careers, it is assumed that if people are empowered to take responsibility for their own careers and are provided with the information and skills to do so, then they will act on their own careers to make decisions, leading to greater career satisfaction and success. Some of the theories that appear most to emphasize personal action in careers can be grouped under the heading of *career development*. This is the term of choice used by the careers research and career counseling movements to describe their work.

The word *development* is however ambiguous: a thing can develop solely under the influence of external events or it can be developed by a human agent. In this chapter, the latter meaning is used, the career being developed actively by the individual whose career it is. A number of theorists, including Donald Super, discussed in Chapters 4 and 8, have proposed theories that stress the active role of the individual in determining their own career path. In these theories, career actions – for example, seeking a new job, working hard to achieve success or making social contacts to help one's career – are the obvious outcomes. But internal processes, such as motivation, concept formation, learning and decision making, energize and inform such career behavior and need to be understood. These theories therefore stress the importance of individual *psychology* in determining careers. In what follows, we discuss the most important career development theories, from older to newer.

Social learning theory

The social learning theory of career choice (Krumboltz, 1979; Mitchell & Krumboltz, 1996) is based on the observation that career behavior is learned behavior, which can be explained to a considerable extent by theories of learning. The theory acknowledges the influence of four factors on the career paths that individuals choose (Larson, 2012):

1. The person's *innate genetic endowment* includes race, sex, physical appearance and/or disabilities, and any special abilities (gifts and talents) they may possess (see also Chapter 3).
2. *Environmental conditions and events* include the number and nature of job opportunities, the number and nature of training and learning opportunities, social and labor law policies, union rules, technological developments and natural disasters that affect the economy (see also Chapter 2).
3. According to Krumboltz, the most important factor is *learning experiences*, in the sense of instrumental, associative and vicarious learning. In *instrumental learning*, where people are reinforced (e.g. by praise) for particular responses and punished (e.g. by ridicule) for others, the rewarded behavior tends to increase so that a child whose parents and teachers and internal psychology reward them for activities connected with biology, healing and high-level educational performance, may develop a desire to be a doctor. Another form of learning, *association*, also contributes – for example, when positive stimuli, such as enjoyable medical TV dramas are paired with more neutral stimuli, such as hospitals, possibly inducing interest in careers in the health sector. In a third type, *vicarious learning*, individuals learn through observation and imitation of others, who are career role models, for example where a doctor is the mother of a daughter who admires her (see also Chapter 8).
4. *Task approach skills* refer to the skills an individual brings to a learning task, such as expectations about performance, work habits, attitudes and thought processes. Krumboltz saw task approach skills as skills that individuals need to learn in order to define a goal, identify alternatives, gather information and take action. Furthermore, he believed that task approach skills could be taught. He defined the steps to do so in his DECIDES model (Krumboltz, 1979; Mitchell & Krumboltz, 1996).

Krumboltz's Seven-Stage DECIDES Model

The DECIDES model is the acronym of seven particular activities needed in the career decision-making process:

   D = Define the problem

   E = Establish the action plan

   C = Clarify values (by examining self-observations and worldview generalizations)

   I = Identify alternatives

D = Discover probable outcomes

E = Eliminate alternatives systematically

S = Start action.

Source: Krumboltz (1979); Mitchell & Krumboltz (1996).

Mitchell and Krumboltz (1996) stated that people make worldview generalizations about the context – for example, the generalization that opportunities in certain occupations may be limited because of sex discrimination. More directly related to occupational choice, people also make generalizations about themselves through observation of, and learning from, their day-to-day experiences (e.g. 'I'm better with machines than I am with people'), an idea apparently not far removed from Super's (1980) notion of self-concept.

These generalizations may be explicitly stated or may simply represent a person's internal awareness. They are constantly adapted as the person learns from experience, and at the same time they determine career behavior – for example, when a child with a self-observed generalization that they are good at carpentry attempts to make a piece of furniture and modifies the generalization on the basis of the observed results. Krumboltz (1994a) suggested that attraction to an occupation will be influenced, through learning, by success at tasks typical of the occupation, observation of role models being rewarded for such tasks and positive statements made about the occupation by others.

Although the social learning theory of career choice is introduced in this book as an example of agency (the career actor learns active responses, through which they can impose their will on the environment), like all learning theories it also reminds us uncomfortably that our own careers can perhaps be controlled, particularly when we are young and impressionable, by rewards and punishments administered by others. For example, a sexist teacher may say to a girl, 'You can't do that – that's a boy's job'. Krumboltz and Henderson (2002) outlined a more positive approach, in which learning theory is applied to the task of career counselors, who can focus not so much on the reinforcing of specific choice responses of their clients as on their clients' learning of such broad and useful career behaviors as self-reflection, open-mindedness and creativity in the use of unplanned career events.

Social cognitive career theory

In making career decisions, we *think* about things: about ourselves and our interests, abilities and goals; about the world of work and the various opportunities that may

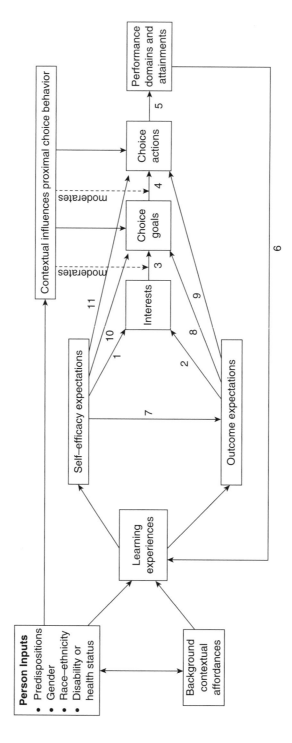

Figure 5.1 Prediction of vocational choice in social cognitive career theory

be available; and about the outcomes we may expect from putting ourselves into these situations.

Social cognitive career theory (Lent et al., 2002) is about individual thought processes in the making of career decisions, and is based on Bandura's (1986) well-known general social cognitive theory. It attempts to provide the following:

> a unifying framework for understanding the processes through which people develop vocational interests, make (and remake) occupational choices, and achieve varying levels of career success and stability ... (The theory) highlights people's capacity to direct their own vocational behavior (i.e. human agency) yet it also acknowledges the many environmental influences ... that serve to strengthen, weaken or even over-ride human agency in career development. (Lent et al., 2002: 277)

Key to understanding the theory are two central variables through which the theorists say individuals regulate their career behavior:

Self-efficacy beliefs are a person's judgments of their ability to carry out particular actions or activities. These beliefs are learned through the various learning forms outlined above in relation to social learning theory. The belief that one is competent, or potentially competent, to carry out a particular job is likely to have a big influence on a career's direction toward or away from such jobs. People who have low self-efficacy beliefs across a range of different activities may have difficulty finding career options.

Outcome expectations are a person's expectations about what will happen – what the outcomes will be – if they follow a particular course of action. Thus, a person with good artistic ability and interest might feel capable of embarking on a career as an artist but might also think that the outcome of such a choice would be financial insecurity.

Stop and Consider

Is your perceived self-efficacy high or low? Where do your self-efficacy beliefs (high or low) come from, do you think? If you need help assessing your self-efficacy, have a look at the self-assessment resources listed at the end of this chapter.

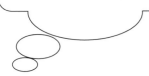

Social cognitive career theory, recently validated empirically by Conklin et al. (2013), integrates self-efficacy beliefs and outcome expectations into a complex model (see Figure 5.1) in which they act together to determine: first, the individual's broad interests (for example, having physics as a favorite school subject); second, their occupational choices, both in terms of goals (for example, to become an architect) and actions (for example, enrolling on an architecture program); and third, performance attainments in that occupation (for example, winning a bid to build a major project).

 Note that as interests lead to goals, goals lead to actions and actions lead to performance, self-efficacy and outcome expectations which continue to influence people at each stage in the process. Also, contextual variables relating to a person's career inheritance and the external environment may continue to affect the process at any stage. Below is a career case study analyzed in terms of social cognitive career theory.

CASE STUDY

Finding Her Way

Leslie attended public schools in a predominantly White suburban area. Her father was a lawyer and her mother had some college education and was active in community organizations. They were supportive of Leslie's education, and she did well, particularly in mathematics (where she gained tutoring experience) and science. But she did not get career guidance at school or from her parents and found it difficult to make choices. Unsure whether she could be successful at university, she enrolled instead for a general course including math and chemistry at her local community college, where most of her friends had also chosen to study. After a year, however, she transferred to a State university, not for educational reasons but because she had a boyfriend there.

 At college, she chose courses that kept her options open. She considered mathematics, engineering, creative writing, psychology and medicine, but her father wanted her to do business, a subject she did not like, and her mother wanted her to get a good education but assumed she would soon marry and it would not matter. She continued to vacillate. In her advanced math class, where she was the only female student, she found that the professors singled her out for her mistakes. Psychology would require extensive graduate training, which she did not feel motivated toward, and in engineering her professors told her that it was difficult to combine engineering with looking after a family. Her final decision, to major in secondary education with an emphasis on mathematics, was based on her interest and ability in math, her belief that teaching and raising a family could easily be combined and the fact that postgraduate work would not be necessary. Over the next few years, she developed an initially enjoyable and successful career in math teaching.

 Source: Swanson & Fouad (1999).

This excellent source provides information on the development of Leslie's career up to the age of 35 years and analyzes Leslie's case from six additional theoretical viewpoints, including those of Gottfredson (Chapter 3 of this book), Super (Chapter 4), Krumboltz (this chapter) and Holland (Chapter 6). Using diverse approaches to consider a single case is an excellent way of learning career theories.

Swanson and Fouad (1999) provided an analysis of this case from the standpoint of social cognitive career theory. They focused on the special influence of self-efficacy beliefs and outcome expectations on Leslie's career choices, in particular her initial choice of community college over university and, second, her deliberate avoidance of postgraduate academic work.

Swanson and Fouad (1999) pointed out how early experiences – for example, doing math tutoring while still at school – provide a basis for Leslie's feelings of self-efficacy in math and teaching but noted that she may have lacked challenging role models or encouragement at school to pursue demanding courses. A lack of belief in her ability to do challenging academic work may have caused her initial choice of the easier community college curriculum and her later avoidance of postgraduate work. At college, areas of potential self-efficacy were removed from her range of choice by others' actions, and, as a result, she was unable to see positive outcomes from pursuing advanced academic work. It is likely that she was better able to see a secure positive outcome in the familiar local community college among her friends than in the unknown setting of a university with its higher standards. Her occupational choice of math teaching combined a strong self-efficacy belief in her capabilities with an appreciation of likely positive outcomes in terms of both career success and satisfaction and later opportunities to combine career with family.

Career construction theory and 'Life Design'

In Chapter 4, we discussed some of the work of Donald Super, the age/stage element of his theories and the continuation of his work by Mark Savickas. In fact, Super's (1980) theory, although it describes stages of career development, is basically about the career as an implementation of the person's self-concept in their working life.

In most of his publications, Super (e.g. 1953, 1980) used the words *vocational development* and *career development* to refer to the study of careers in general and his theory in particular. In his recent formulation of Super's theory, Savickas (2002, 2005) calls it *career construction theory*. Thus, 'careers do not unfold: they are constructed' (Savickas, 2002: 154). Construction is a form of action. The metaphor of 'construction' and the resulting imagery of the career being put together by the actions of the person, and having physical, manufactured form – for example, a hierarchical structure or a delicate work of art – are potent.

In this theory, the process of career construction is that of developing and implementing a vocational self-concept, an image of what one is like in relation to the various possible contexts of work. We develop a self-concept through our experiences, starting in early childhood, including being aware of physical and psychological attributes, having opportunities to undertake various roles and to watch others do so, and being rewarded for particular forms of behavior. We begin to get a sense of who we might be and what kind of job we might realistically do. As we progress through childhood and adolescence, the vocational concept gradually stabilizes and provides lines of possible continuity for the career. An important concept in this respect is career maturity, which traditionally refers to a student's readiness for making occupational choices (Savickas & Porfeli, 2012). As stated in Chapter 4, career maturity is shown by the ability to master the tasks at each stage. The notion of self-concept explains how and why we can experience a satisfying career by constantly finding work that is a good fit with our developing self-concept (see Chapter 6). Thus, career construction theory embraces both the adult development approach of Chapter 4 and the vocational fit approach of Chapter 6.

Next to career maturity, an increasingly important concept is *career adaptability*, which refers to an individual's resources for coping with current and anticipated tasks, transitions and traumas in their occupational roles. Career adaptability resources are psychosocial constructs, in the sense that they are not traits possessed by an individual but rather are shaped by interactions between that individual and the context in which they function. Typically, they are deployed when an individual faces developmental vocational tasks (for example, choosing a major in college), occupational transitions (for example, being promoted to a line manager position) and work traumas (for example, mass layoffs due to bankruptcy). According to Savickas and Porfeli (2012), adaptive individuals are characterized by four 'adapt-abilities' (called the 4 Cs):

- becoming concerned about the vocational future (Concern)
- taking control of trying to prepare for one's vocational future (Control)
- displaying curiosity by exploring possible selves and future scenarios (Curiosity)
- strengthening confidence to pursue one's aspirations (Confidence).

Students who are in the process of composing their curriculum or are about to enter the labor market face a rapidly changing job market. The link between receiving specific vocational training and finding a corresponding job is weakened. Young adults therefore face great uncertainties, and many of them have to adjust their hopes and aspirations early on in their careers. Career transitions such as from school to work or from one job to another trigger a person's career adaptability, especially in times of high environmental uncertainty (Van Vianen et al., 2012).

In his most recent formulation of career construction theory, Mark Savickas and colleagues (Savickas et al., 2009) extended the theory of career construction to embrace the idea of Life Design. The notion of Life Design shows how the leading questions that have guided the career development domain have changed quite a lot over the last six decades or so, from *How do we match individuals and occupations?*

through *What are the factors, stages and processes of lifelong career development?* to *How may individuals best design their own lives in the human society in which they live?* According to Savickas:

> Individuals in the knowledge societies at the beginning of the 21st century must realize that career problems are only a piece of much broader concerns about how to live a life in a postmodern world shaped by a global economy and supported by information technology. (Savickas et al., 2009: 241)

Contextual action theory

A recent career development theory that is often used in career counseling practice is contextual action theory. Action theory, more generally, addresses the goal-directed, intentional behavior of human beings (Von Cranach & Valach, 1983). The contextual action theory of careers (Young & Valach, 2008; Young et al., 2011) proposes that the career construct that allows us to keep all the pertinent information together so we can understand the meaning of our own and others' behavior is *goal-directed human action*.

Contextual Action Theory Made Easy

Phoning your grandmother to ask for her career advice is an action. Handing in your resignation letter is an action. Applying for a job is an action. Deciding to go to a careers fair is an action. Looking outside, seeing that it's raining and deciding to stay home from the careers fair is an action. Each of these actions has a number of levels:

(1) Manifest behavior – what you actually do;
(2) Internal process – how you decide what to do and what you intend to achieve by this action; and
(3) Social meaning – how this action would be interpreted by others, for instance what goals or intentions would be inferred by someone witnessing your actions.

Source: Winter (2010).

The features of action theory are subsumed in a three-dimensional conceptual framework for the analysis of action – the perspectives that one can take on action, the levels at which action is organized and the systems of action (Young et al., 2005):

- *Perspectives on action*: three different perspectives on action can be taken – focusing on manifest (observable) behavior, focusing on (cognitive and emotional) internal processes such as thoughts and feelings, and focusing on the social meanings of an action (i.e. how the action is interpreted by oneself and others).
- *Levels of action*: actions can be hierarchically ordered from elements (specific verbal and non-verbal behaviors), to steps (movement toward a desired end-state or goal), to goals (the entire motivation behind the action process).
- *Systems of action*: actions take place at the individual level (individual action), as well as at the collective level, for example when spouses or partners develop interdependent career goals (joint action). A series of actions connected by a common goal over a delineated period of time is called a project; and a life's worth of projects adds up to what we call a career.

In contextual action theory, a career is not just to do with a sequence of jobs; it is all the accumulated things that you do to give ultimate meaning to your life. Career gives meaning to projects. Projects give meaning to actions (Young et al., 2005).

Protean Career Theory

An especially important theory related to 'career as action' is Tim Hall's (2004; Hall and Associates, 1996) concept of the protean career. In 1976, writing about managerial careers in organizations, Hall noted the tendency of organizations to want to manage members' careers for them (see Chapter 14). In contrast, Hall and colleagues stated:

> The protean career [...] focuses on achieving subjective career success through self-directed vocational behavior [...]. Individuals who hold protean career attitudes are intent upon using their own values (versus organizational values, for example) to guide their career ('values-driven') and take an independent role in managing their vocational behavior ('self-directed'). (Briscoe et al., 2006: 31)

The protean career, thus, comprises two distinct attitudes, i.e. self-directed and values-driven:

- The *self-directed* dimension refers to people displaying high career proactivity (i.e. taking initiative in improving current circumstances or creating new ones); a proactive personality (i.e. a dispositional tendency to be more proactive, meaning they behave more confidently, actively work to control their environment and seek out information); career planning (i.e. setting career goals and developing strategies for achieving those goals); and mastery orientation (i.e. an orientation toward continued task improvement or mastery, even when it is not required, associated with deep engagement and great perseverance in the face of setbacks).

- The *values-driven* dimension of the protean career refers to people with high vocational self-concept clarity (i.e. a relative degree of clarity and certainty of self-perception with respect to vocationally relevant attitudes, values, interests, needs and abilities); personal identity (i.e. a sense of self built up over time as the person embarks on and pursues projects or goals that are not thought of as those of a community, but as the property of the person – personal identity thus emphasizes a sense of individual autonomy rather than of communal involvement); behavioral integrity (i.e. the fit between a person's espoused and enacted values); and authenticity (i.e. the self-perception of behaving in keeping with one's values).

Stop and Consider

Do you think you are a protean career actor? Why (not)? Have a look at the self-assessment resources listed at the end of this chapter if you find it difficult to answer this question straightaway.

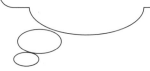

The protean career manifests a phenomenon that takes place outside structures and traditional boundaries of organizational hierarchy, professional progress or stable direction, and indeed protean career theory has been developed as an individual antithesis of organizational career management (see Chapter 14). The protean career actor takes on the role of being their own agent (Hall & Mirvis, 1996). A protean career must be considered as a lifelong series of experiences, skills, learning, transitions and identity changes that is managed by a person instead of an organization. As a career attitude, the protean career refers to one's contract with oneself, rather than with an organization (Kossek et al., 1998). Hall and Moss (1998) emphasized that in a protean career, development is not necessarily understood as formal training, retraining or upward mobility, but rather as self-directed and relational continuous learning by means of work challenges. According to Hall and Moss (1998), within the protean career the ingredients of success change from know-how to learn-how, from job security to employability, and from 'work self' to 'whole self', with psychological success as a terminal goal. Organizations are thus expected to provide challenging assignments, developmental relationships, information and other developmental resources. The following is an exemplar protean career.

A Career Built on Stubbornness

When Pilar, now 37, told one of her colleagues the story of how she ended up becoming one of the youngest professors in her department, he exclaimed 'So you're the poster child for the protean career!'

It is indeed apparent from Pilar's life story that her career has been largely self-directed. Pilar's working-class parents did not push her too much to do well in school – but much to their amazement she did quite well with minimal effort. Growing up in the Southern European education system in which (at that time) students were oriented towards secondary education purely based on their grades, even at age 12 Pilar was a stubborn one. Although her primary school teacher advised her not to pursue a degree in Latin and Greek in secondary school (because she was not a straight-A student nor did she seem to put much effort into her schoolwork), Pilar chose Latin and Greek anyway – because she believed she could do it. Again, she flew through high school with remarkable ease, hardly studying at all, achieving mostly A's but not straight A's. And again, this led one of her teachers to advise her not to pursue a university education 'because the attitude wasn't there'. Of course, Pilar didn't listen to him (being highly critical of the public education system even at age 18) – and went off to university, as the first person in her family ever to do so. Her parents pleaded with her to choose a major that would at least ensure secure employment after graduation (such as a teacher's degree), but she wanted to study archaeology, which to them seemed 'useless'.

But Pilar was determined. She went to all open days of all universities in her region, collecting information to build her case. A few months later, she was enrolled in the archaeology program at her university of choice (of course, the one her parents opposed the most, because it was furthest away and in the largest city of the country). In spite of her extremely active social life (which caused her father to tell the whole town back home that 'she will never graduate'), Pilar graduated at the top of her class, again with minimal effort. It was not that the classes were easy – it was just that she was so passionate about archaeology that it was easy for her to memorize and apply all of the theories without having to study very much. This did not go unnoticed, and one of her professors offered her a position as a doctoral researcher. This is when Pilar really started to flourish. She became passionate about research and determined to become a professor. After she had finished her PhD, however, many people told her that she shouldn't get her hopes up too high, since only around 10 percent of junior academics actually end up in a professor position. The bureaucratic system in her country dictated that an older professor had to retire first before a new one could get hired.

Never deterred by the odds, Pilar pushed through anyway. After a few years as a postdoctoral researcher, she applied for special government funding reserved for young academics with an exceptionally ambitious research program, and managed to create her own position as a professor at age 30. No one had to retire, and Pilar didn't have to teach and could spend all her time doing research, just like she wanted.

Pilar says she has learned two major lessons in her career so far, that reflect the values-driven and self-directed dimensions of the protean career:

- First, that you shouldn't listen to other people too much. Pilar realized at a relatively young age that whereas her parents put great value on conformity, employment security and minimal risk-taking behavior, she did not. Her teachers did not notice her potential because she was critical, outspoken and easily distracted, and therefore did not fit their traditional profile of a good student. Rather than internalizing the expectations important people in her environment had of her, and planning her career according to their values, Pilar figured out what her own career values were (independence, intellectual stimulation and constant challenge) and decided to do it her way, regardless of what others might think of it, and whether or not they believed she would succeed.
- Second, that you can't count on other people to 'do it for you'. Pilar says that, had she allowed her parents to assume control of her career when she was younger, she might be an office clerk or a shop assistant right now (and probably a very bored and unmotivated one at that!). In fact, her parents did succeed in convincing her brother to go into IT, a field he hated and still hates, because 'computers are the future and there will always be work'. Pilar's brother, a gifted visual artist, now expresses his creativity by designing websites and flyers for events after working hours (often for free). Every now and then, Pilar tries to sway him into going back to school and pursuing a degree in computer game design, but he believes it is too late for him as most other students who enroll have a degree in visual arts, which his parents flat out forbade him to pursue in college. The truth is that not all career advice you will receive in your life, even when it comes from respected elders, will be sound and valid. Sometimes people simply do not know what they are talking about or what is truly possible or not possible. Or, as Pilar would say, 'There's only one way to find out!'

Finally, in relation to protean careers, we might mention that metaphor was important in the genesis of the protean career idea. Proteus, according to Hall et al. (1996), was a mythical Greek sea creature who could change shape at will. As Arnold and Cohen

(2008) point out, however, the protean metaphor has sort of started to live a life of its own, away from the original myth upon which it was based. According to these authors:

> While Proteus did have the power to change shape, he only did so under moments of extreme duress: to escape capture. A far cry from freedom, growth, and self-direction, this is about mere survival. In addition, the kinds of shapes Proteus chose were scary, even at times bewitching. Their purpose was to frighten or deceive [...] the only values that appeared to drive Proteus were a malicious sense of autonomy and over-riding concern to be left alone. (2008: 14)

Career Success

In any discussion of personal agency, the following questions arise: 'What for? With what end in view?' If people are indeed seeking to exercise influence over their own careers, what goal is it that they are pursuing? In terms of career construction theory, what self-concept are they trying to express? In terms of social learning theory, what rewards do they find reinforcing? In terms of social cognitive career theory, what outcomes do they see as realistic for them? In terms of protean career theory, by what values are they driven? In terms of contextual action theory, towards which goals are they drawn? And in terms of normal human discourse, what are their career ambitions? (Gunz & Heslin, 2005).

According to Reardon et al. (2012: 73), 'Almost every college student working through a career problem or decision is really pursuing a vision of "having a successful career"'. But many people, including students, find the concept of success fuzzy, and, insofar as they can define it, each is likely to define it differently.

Traditional measures of career success relate to the objective career: status on an organization ladder, amount earned in salary, reputation in one's profession. This is also what the general public understands as success (Gunz & Heslin, 2005). The occupational hierarchies outlined in Chapter 3 carry success connotations, but within each occupation and within many organizations there are further hierarchies to be climbed.

Other definitions of success are possible. In fact, the recent careers literature talks more about *subjective* career success than about objective career success (Heslin, 2003). Subjective career success, also referred to as psychological success – 'the experience of achieving goals that are personally meaningful to the individual, rather than those set by parents, peers, an organization, or society' (Mirvis & Hall, 1994: 366) – is typically conceptualized as a multidimensional concept, encompassing a range of different meanings that people may ascribe to 'being successful'. Each individual is thus considered as likely to have their unique and personal definition of career success. Consider, for instance, the different forms of career success described by Dries et al. (2008):

- *performance*: success in terms of attaining verifiable results and meeting set goals
- *advancement*: success in terms of progressing and growing, both in terms of level and experience
- *personal development*: success in terms of reaching one's full potential through self-management of challenges and learning experiences
- *creative outlet*: success in terms of creating something innovative and extraordinary
- *financial security*: success in terms of being able to meet one's financial needs
- *job security*: success in terms of being able to meet one's employment needs
- *personal satisfaction*: success in terms of achieving personal satisfaction and happiness, both in the work domain and in the family domain
- *recognition*: success in terms of being adequately rewarded and appreciated for one's efforts and talents
- *cooperation*: success in terms of working well together with peers, superiors, subordinates and clients
- *contribution*: success in terms of contributing something to the collective (an organization or society at large), through work, in an ethical way.

Have a look at the different excerpts below, taken from three pop songs – What do these reveal about the meanings their authors hold about career success?

Beyoncé – I was here

I want to leave my footprints on the sands of time
Know there was something that meant something that I left behind
When I leave this world, I'll leave no regrets
Leave something to remember, so they won't forget
I was here
I will leave my mark so everyone will know
I was here

Travie McCoy ft. Bruno Mars – Billionaire

I want to be a billionaire so freaking bad
Buy all of the things I never had
I want to be on the cover of Forbes magazine
Smiling next to Oprah and the Queen

(Continued)

(Continued)

Oh, every time I close my eyes
I see my name in shining lights

Lady Gaga – Applause

If only fame had an IV, baby could I bear
Being away from you, I found the vein, put it in here
I live for the applause, applause, applause
Live for the way that you cheer and scream for me
The applause, applause, applause
Sources:

'I was here' performed by Beyoncé Knowles on the album '4' (Columbia, 2011), written by Diane Warren, and produced by Ryan Tedder, Brent Kutzle, Kuk Harrell and Beyoncé Knowles.

'Billionaire' performed by Travie McCoy featuring guest vocals by Bruno Mars on the album 'Lazarus' (Fueled by Ramen, 2010), written by Travie McCoy, Bruno Mars, Ari Levine and Philip Lawrence, and produced by The Smeezingtons.

'Applause' performed by Lady Gaga on the album 'ARTPOP' (Interscope, 2013), written by Stefani Germanotta, Paul 'DJ White Shadow' Blair, Dino Zisis, Nick Monson, Martin Bresso, Nicolas Mercier, Julien Arias and William Grigahcine, and produced by Lady Gaga, Paul 'DJ White Shadow' Blair, Dino Zisis and Nick Monson.

If we can draw inferences about Beyoncé's, Travie and Bruno's, and Gaga's definitions of career success from their lyrics, we would say that Beyoncé wants to contribute something to society ('leave something to remember'; 'leave my mark'), in part through her creations as an artist ('something that meant something that I [will leave] behind'), but also be recognized for it ('so they won't forget [her]'; 'so everyone will know'); that Travie and Bruno are mainly concerned with achieving (ample) financial wealth ('be a billionaire') and advancing themselves, mostly in the socio-economic sense ('buy all of the things I never had') in a visible way, which implies public recognition of their status ('be on the cover of Forbes magazine'; 'my name in shining lights'); and for Lady Gaga it's all about recognition ('I live for the applause'; 'I live for the way you cheer and scream for me'), although there is also a strong cooperation dimension to her song ('[I can't] bear being away from you [her fans]').

According to Heslin (2003) and Gunz and Heslin (2005), when people evaluate which aspects of career success are more versus less important to them and to what extent these are fulfilled, they do not just consider their own situation – they also look at the career attainments of 'reference groups' (see also Chapter 8) surrounding them in order to gauge how they themselves are doing. Self-referent criteria of career success, such as 'Am I meeting my earning potential?' and 'Am I performing well in my job?', are thus complemented by *other*-referent criteria of career success, such as 'How am I doing in terms of salary compared to the people I graduated college with?' and 'Am I performing better than my colleague Diane?' (Gunz & Heslin, 2005; Heslin, 2003).

Career success and satisfaction are not the same as job success and satisfaction, which can be momentary. One of the defining characteristics of the career is its continuity over a long period. Reardon et.al. (2012) suggested that it is probably best to 'think of the career as a journey, a path, a process, rather than a destination or prize' (p. 73). Career success in this view is determined not just by where the career gets to but also by satisfaction and feelings of self-efficacy along the way. At the same time, the person may deliberately make sacrifices of success and satisfaction in the short term to create opportunities for long-term career benefit – for example, when someone enrols in a long, arduous program of study or takes a relatively low-level job in the knowledge that it will provide long-term opportunities to meet their career goals.

Stop and Consider

Look back at the lyrics in this chapter. Which of these songs reflects your subjective meaning of career success best? Or is there another song you would like to adopt as your 'career theme music'? Which song and why? What part of the lyrics speaks to you, specifically? Could you draft a personal statement of career success based on it?

Career Inaction

To conclude this chapter, we offer a brief discussion of the relatively new concept of career inaction, a term coined by Belgian careers researcher Marijke Verbruggen (2013). Verbruggen suggests that although most of the career development literature is about decision making followed by action, inaction is actually more prevalent in the working population, as indicated, for example, by the number of people who complain about their jobs on a daily basis without ever looking for employment elsewhere. She defines career inaction as either deciding not to do something or failing to act on one's decisions. Importantly, both meanings of inaction refer to situations where people make a decision which is followed by the absence of action or change (Verbruggen, 2013).

First of all, inaction follows a *decision* – a situation in which a person had a choice between different alternatives. In that way, inaction differs from situations where people did not do or change something simply because there was no other option or because they did not see or were not aware of such an option. Consider the case of José, who for many years now has distinctly disliked his job as a high school teacher. He complains about it to his family and friends on a daily basis, in great detail too. When they suggest to him, however, that he take a sabbatical to try something else for a year – an option available to him in his country's education system – rather than looking into it, he always sighs and says he'll 'stick it out' until his retirement (ten years from now).

Second, since inaction relates to decisions, it concerns situations where people have sufficient *control* to choose between the available alternatives. Thus, inaction differs from situations where someone is forced to do nothing or where the individual has no immediate power to change something. This element of agency, which is inherent to inaction, makes it different from related concepts such as unmet expectations. In José's case, it is clear that he has the power to change his current situation, if he would choose to do so – it's more that he cannot find the courage, or the energy, to make a change. José soothes his conscience by saying to himself that 'all jobs are disappointing in one way or another – if it wasn't this nonsense, it would be some other nonsense'.

Third, inaction concerns decisions which are followed by a lack of action or change. Since people have a natural focus on action, action is generally more *salient* than is inaction. This explains why people's reactions to inaction tend to intensify over time, whereas their reactions to action typically weaken when time passes. As for José, he is finding it increasingly difficult to simply count down the days to retirement – after almost ten years of dragging himself to work, he has now resorted to calling in sick for extended periods of time on a regular basis with the help of his cousin, who is a medical doctor. He is finding, however, that going back after periods of sick leave is becoming more and more daunting each time.

Career inaction is believed to be related to life regrets: research indicates that career steps not taken are a major source of regret (Roese & Summerville, 2005) and can cause 'inaction inertia' (Tykocinski et al., 1995), where people who have bypassed an initial attractive opportunity are less likely to act on a further opportunity even if it is an objectively attractive one (Verbruggen, 2013). Or to put it simply: inaction spurs further inaction. Inaction inertia may be relevant to understanding certain career phenomena. For instance, it might help explain why people get stuck in a career they dislike (Ibarra, 2002), why they end up in long-term unemployment even after getting several job offers, or why career goals are not acted on and remain a distant dream (Verbruggen & Sels, 2010).

Stop and Consider

What are the barriers standing between you and the career of your dreams? Can you take action to remove these barriers? Make a list of regrets you might experience in the future if you do not at least try.

Conclusion

Despite the career predictabilities brought about by career inheritances and social structure (Chapter 3), and by patterned sequences of human development and aging (Chapter 4), much of our career behavior and success depends on our own actions. Understanding human psychology, particularly concepts such as motivation, learning, cognition, intention, decision making and self-efficacy, and applying them to careers, provides a basis for us to increase our agency and control over our careers. Proactive career behavior and the practices of self-direction and adaptability around clear identity and values, as in the protean career ideal, enable understanding to be put into action. Practices of goal setting and career management (Chapter 12) can assist.

Key Points in this Chapter

Careers result not just from social structure and natural human cycles but also from deliberate action taken by the person concerned. The term *agency* represents the idea that people are agents determining their own careers.

Various career development theories indicate the processes underlying career action. Social learning theory shows how people learn career behavior in social settings. Social cognitive career theory indicates the psychological processes that people go through when making their career decisions and choices. Career construction theory presents career behavior as being based on the implementation of the individual's changing self-concept. Contextual action theory focuses on the inherently goal-directed nature of human behavior. Finally, the protean career combines adaptability, self-direction and values and is a good model for career self-management in contemporary conditions.

Career success is a criterion for career action, but success can be defined in many different ways, reflecting both the objective and the subjective sides of career.

Contrary to what the career development literature might have us believe, career inaction actually occurs more frequently than action, and can lead to major life regrets.

Questions from this Chapter

General Questions

1. Consider the careers of well-known people. Find out more about them on the internet if you need to. To what extent do you think they have succeeded because of their personal actions? Which actions?

2. Identify someone you know (in person, in your broader social circle or from the media) as your role model in terms of career. Make a list of the ways in which they have made their career happen through personal action. If the person is famous, read their biography. If they are in your social environment, ask them to tell you how they got where they are today. What can you learn from your role model?

3. Visualize the career outcomes you would like to achieve in the long term. For instance, you could make a mood board of clippings, words, mantras and images to hang in your room.

'Live Career Case' Study Questions

1. Evaluate your case person's career against the criteria for the protean career.

2. Ask your case person to pick a song (or several songs) where the lyrics reflect their personal definition of career success. Listen to the song together (or read the lyrics) and reflect on your case person's definition of success, and how far along they are in achieving success according to that definition.

3. Ask your case person about their biggest regrets in their career so far. Are they related to inaction? If so, what motivated the inaction? Ask your case person to describe what might have been different in their situation today had they not chosen to take that course of inaction.

Additional Resources

Recommended Further Reading

Dries, N., Pepermans, R. and Carlier, O. (2008) 'Career success: Constructing a multidimensional model', *Journal of Vocational Behavior*, 73: 254–267.

Forrier, A., Sels, L. and Stynen, D. (2009) 'Career mobility at the intersection between agent and structure: A conceptual model', *Journal of Occupational and Organizational Psychology*, 82: 739–759.

Hall, D. T. (2004) 'The protean career: A quarter-century journey', *Journal of Vocational Behavior*, 65: 1–13.

Ibarra, H. (2002) 'How to stay stuck in the wrong career', *Harvard Business Review*, 80: 40–48.

Lent, R. W. and Brown, S. D. (2002) 'Social cognitive career theory and adult career development'. in S. G. Niles (ed.), *Adult Career Development: Concepts, issues and practices* (3rd edn, pp. 77–97). Tulsa, OK: National Career Development Association.

Svejenova, S., Vives, L. and Alvarez, J. L. (2010) 'At the crossroads of agency and communion: Defining the shared career', *Journal of Organizational Behavior*, 31: 707–725.

Self-Assessment Resources

Assess your self-efficacy beliefs: Chen, G., Gully, S. M. and Eden, D. (2001) 'Validation of a new general self-efficacy scale', *Organizational Research Methods*, 4(1): 62–83.

Assess your career adaptability: Savickas, M. L. and Porfeli, E. J. (2012) 'Career Adapt-Abilities Scale: Construction, reliability, and measurement equivalence across 13 countries', *Journal of Vocational Behavior*, 80(3): 661–673.

Assess how 'protean' and 'boundaryless' your career attitudes are: Briscoe, J.P., Hall, D.T. and DeMuth, R.L.F. (2006) 'Protean and boundaryless careers: An empirical exploration', *Journal of Vocational Behavior*, 69(1): 30–47.

Assess your career competencies: Francis-Smythe, J., Haase, S., Thomas, E. and Steele, C. (2013) 'Development and validation of the Career Competencies Indicator (CCI)', *Journal of Career Assessment*, 21(2): 227–248.

Online Resources

Need help making career decisions? See the 'career advice' section at: www.prospects.ac.uk

Career advice from Reid Hoffman, the co-founder and chairman of LinkedIn – 'The start-up of you' book and free companion website is available at: www.thestartupofyou.com/start/

Careers as Fit

6

Chapter Objectives

The objectives of this chapter are:

- to consider the concept of fit between person and work environment, and which aspects of each are important in the fitting process
- to describe and evaluate three theories of fit, and the practical tools they have produced to help people find jobs and careers that suit them
- to place these theories in the broader context of person–environment fit research
- to identify ways in which the fit between person and job or career can change over time, and how this happens
- to examine how career decisions are made on the basis of fit.

CASE STUDY

A Match Made in Heaven

Philip is not academically or intellectually gifted. He has no qualifications beyond a high school education, but he is practical and good with his hands. He loves constructing and repairing things. He is also sociable, has good interpersonal skills and enjoys meeting people. Since his conversion to the Christian religion a few years ago, he has developed strong altruistic values and a desire to express his faith in his work. He has also cast aside his previous materialistic values. Lastly, he is not very literate, hates routine and has a real antipathy to filling in forms and doing other administrative work. What job can he find that simultaneously requires manual and social abilities and religious and altruistic interests, but not administrative work?

Philip found just the job! He was appointed to a manager/caretaker position at a camp facility that specializes in catering for small conventions and retreats organized by Christian church groups. He and his wife, Martha, and small son Jonathan live on the premises in a small chalet, provided rent-free by the camp organization. Philip loves it. There is plenty of manual work to be done in developing the facility and keeping it smart and well maintained. Hosting the client groups requires ongoing interaction with pleasant people who share his religious views. True, the job is poorly paid, but then he doesn't care about that any more. After all, it is God's work he is doing.

But what of the administrative side? The job requires supplies to be ordered, bookings to be confirmed, space allocations to be planned and recorded, letters to be written, financial records to be kept. Here, too, Philip has found a solution. Martha shares Philip's religious beliefs, has a background in office administration and enjoys that kind of work. So Philip delegates all the administrative work to her, which she does unpaid on a part-time basis while also looking after Jonathan. The camp owners don't mind, as long as the work gets done. In fact, they get two employees who are committed to the goals of the camp for the price of one. As for Philip, he feels both he and Martha have indeed found the 'perfect fit'.

In expressing his satisfaction with his job, Philip is reflecting a career ideal that most of us can identify with: that however complex and demanding we may be in our expectations of work, somewhere out there is a role that fits like a glove, requiring exactly the abilities and personality that we have, and offering exactly the rewards and satisfaction that we want, in a context that is consistent with our own values. The obverse – not fitting – is represented by the common metaphor 'you can't fit a square peg in a round hole', with its imagery of 'pegs' (people) walking around a field full of 'holes' (jobs) looking for one that is a good fit. Extending the notion to careers, we have to recognize that over time the pegs are likely to change in size and shape (Chapter 4) and so are the holes (Chapter 2). How far then can we apply the 'fit' metaphor to careers?

The 'Fit' Approach to Careers

Recall from Chapter 1 that in 1909 Frank Parsons published *Choosing a Vocation*, the first-ever book on career choice and guidance. The term *vocation* implied that careers should be defined by occupations. Parsons wanted to ensure that people made good choices of occupation, i.e. choices with a good fit between personal and occupational characteristics. In its essentials, Parsons's formulation is still the philosophy of much career guidance today.

The advent of the internet has given new opportunities for the selling of the 'fit' metaphor by those who think they can help us find the perfect fit. Consider the following case.

Searching for a Fit

Here is an excerpt from a website called FindaCareer4U*:

'Can I really find a career for me?

'Asking "can I find a career that's for me?" is one of the most important questions you will ever ask. If you find the right career, then you will be satisfied, successful and maybe even rich for many years to come.

'There are many things to consider when looking for a career, including your abilities, personality, aspirations and values. The key question is whether you will find it satisfying.

'This is where our career test can help. It is based on unique research to identify the best job for you. It uses a sophisticated method to match you with a long list of careers.

'You can get a free online report on your personality type, which can help you in your career. There is also the option of a low-cost detailed report which will help you see why the careers we suggest are good for you...

'Start the Career test now!'

....

*To avoid seeming to endorse any particular website or service provider, the name of the site and some minor details of its approach have been changed.

Using this type of advertising, FindaCareer4U offers an immediate assessment of your individual characteristics and a systematic way of measuring your degree of fit to different careers. All you have to do is complete the online questionnaire. FindaCareer4U's computer systems will score it automatically.

If you were searching for a new career direction, do you think that FindaCareer4U might be able to help? Would you go immediately to your computer and send FindaCareer4U money? If so, read the rest of this chapter first: there may be strengths in what FindaCareer4U and similar websites offer, but there are weaknesses, too.

FindaCareer4U's publicity information implies the following:

- People are different. They have different characteristics. Therefore, they are suited to different occupations.
- Like people, each occupation has its own profile – characteristics that indicate what kind of person is suited to it.
- Through its process of assessment, FindaCareer4U is able to measure accurately people's individual characteristics that are relevant to their occupational choices.
- FindaCareer4U can use the information from the assessments it makes of different people to advise them of their suitability for different occupations.

Thus, FindaCareer4U claims to establish a degree of congruence between each person and various career choices. Find a good fit, according to the website and the metaphor, and you will have a happy and successful career. That seems logical. How could it be wrong?

On the other hand, as usual, the situation is more complicated than it might seem. The fit metaphor has many hidden complications and assumptions. For example, the characteristics of both career actors and occupations can change over time. While the idea of fit does not rule this out, it does assume that they are fairly stable over significant periods. If they are unstable, it will not be worth finding a fit because the fit will soon be gone.

Now, let us take a closer look at the different forms of matching that might be important (see Table 6.1). Which aspect(s) of the career actor should be taken into account? He or she may seek sociability at work (personality – extraversion), or have a wish to help disadvantaged people (values – altruism) or to work with sea creatures (interests – marine biology) or to do work requiring precise movement (skills – dexterity). Some of the characteristics in Table 6.1 emphasize what a good fit Philip enjoys in the opening case study of this chapter. His personality (sociable), values (Christian, non-materialistic), skills and abilities (practical), interests (making and fixing things, talking to people) and personal circumstances (having living accommodation; being married to someone who is willing and able to pick up the parts of the job he does not like) all mean that he is indeed ideally suited to the job.

Some characteristics represent what the career actor is *able* to do (e.g. skills and abilities), others what they *want* to do (e.g. values and interests), but these aspects of individuality will tend to go together, so that people are often – though not always (Anthoney & Armstrong, 2010) – interested in what they are good at.

We can also ask what aspect of the person's work environment matters most. For example, is the key objective for a teacher simply to be a teacher (occupation), the culture of the chosen school (organization), the relationships with other teachers (group) or the characteristics, such as autonomy in lesson planning, of the role they occupy (job)? While most applications of the fit metaphor, such as FindaCareer4U, focus on matching people to occupations or jobs, the second column of Table 6.1 indicates other possible contextual variables.

Table 6.1 Fitting What with What?

Characteristics of the Person	Characteristics of the Work Environment
Personality: a person's general tendencies to behave, think or feel in certain ways	Occupation: the line of work (professional or otherwise) the person is in
Values: what a person considers important and valuable in its own right	Organization: the size, characteristics and culture of the organization(s) in which the work takes place and/or which employs the person
Skills: capabilities to accomplish specific tasks at a high level of proficiency	Group: the other people who work in close proximity and/or co-operation with the person day to day, including the boss
Abilities: general capability in a broad area of endeavor	Job: the characteristics, demands and constraints of the work tasks the person undertakes day by day
Interests: the specific activities or tasks a person enjoys doing	Rewards: what rewards are available and what the person has to do to obtain them
Personal Circumstances: the aspects of a person's life situation which facilitate or constrain his or her choices at any given time	Working Conditions: the physical and contractual conditions in which the work takes place
Social Class: the social status of the person's family of origin and/or current attributes (e.g. educational qualifications)	Status: the hierarchical position in society associated with the occupation, organization and job
Fitness for Work: a person's physical and mental strength and resilience	Labor Market: the kinds of occupations, jobs and organizations that are available

Notwithstanding the common focus on *occupational* fit, some argue that fitting the organization is equally important. The Attraction-Selection-Attrition (ASA) model (De Cooman & Dries, 2012; Schneider, 1987) proposes that career actors are *attracted* to, and *selected* by, organizations because of the fit of their values and interests with those inherent in the organization and its culture. Those who do not fit will leave the organization (*attrition*).

Stop and Consider

Consider a job you hold or have held in the past, or, if you have had few jobs, a school or university course you have taken. Overall, how good is/was the fit between you and your work environment? Give your answer on a 0–5 scale, where 0 means terrible fit, and 5 means perfect fit.

Now, consider carefully why you gave this answer. Using Table 6.1 to help you, identify the aspects of fit that are/were good and not so good. Which aspects of fit matter(ed) most to you, and why?

Traits and their Measurement

Fitting people to jobs and fitting jobs to people are two traditions at the core of work psychology (Arnold et al., 2010). The theories, tools and ways of thinking that have been developed form the basis of many people-management activities, including personnel selection, training, motivation and the design of work tasks, environments and equipment. The fitting-people-to-jobs tradition requires good description and measurement of both personal and contextual characteristics (job, occupation, organization, etc.), but the emphasis in career counseling (Chapter 13) has always been more on assessing people than on assessing contexts. The development of measures of human attributes has been a huge research area for a century, and more recently also a thriving industry because career actors and organizations will often pay for effective tests and questionnaires that enable them to find a good fit.

Starting in the USA and Europe, clear possibilities began to be seen for using a range of assessment devices to gather information about the traits of young people who were unsure about their career choices, and using these as the basis for offering them advice. The distinction between abilities (what the individual is capable of) and values, needs or interests (what the individual wants to do) was recognized early. The first tests of general intelligence – commonly known nowadays as IQ (Intelligence Quotient) tests – appeared early in the 20th century (Binet, 1911), and the first assessment device for vocational interests, the Strong Vocational Interest Blank, in 1927.

The approach came to be known as trait-and-factor theory (see Chapter 1) because of its focus on different human traits and its use of the statistical technique known as factor analysis to discover constructs or traits by analyzing the statistical associations contained in mass test and questionnaire data (Betz et al., 1989). To some extent, the career counseling movement was driven not just by the wish to assist people to make good career decisions but also by the possibilities inherent in a burgeoning technology of paper-and-pencil measures of human traits.

In considering such psychometric (meaning, measuring the psyche) instruments, we need to distinguish between *tests* and *questionnaires* or *inventories*. Abilities tend to be measured by tests, where the career actor is striving to do their best, with the implication that the test involves 'correct' solutions or answers, i.e. those that demonstrate presence of the ability in question, and that a high score is 'good'. With personality factors, interests and values, questionnaires and inventories are used, often asking the career actor to choose between different options, with no implication that any option is 'right' or better than any other option. Thus, one answer may tend to demonstrate suitability for a particular occupation while an alternative answer suggests suitability for a different occupation.

Counselors and managers using psychometric instruments, and even career actors completing them, need to understand that such measurements have considerable limitations. Psychological characteristics are often nebulous and hard to isolate, so that psychometric assessment is an inexact science, and the resultant 'scores', while often better than guesses or even than estimates based on observation or informal questioning, need to be treated with caution. Good devices are those developed by expert psychologists, and pre-tested with large samples to provide estimates of validity (to show that the instrument measures what it is intended to measure) and reliability (to show that the instrument will give similar results with the same individuals on different occasions). Even good devices will, however, be liable to considerable error in particular cases. Also, the counselor or manager using the device, whose job it is to interpret the results, should be thoroughly familiar with its construction and objectives, the meaning of the results it provides, their relationships with other variables and their relevance to the occupations under consideration. Lastly, in modern counseling, measures are used not to dictate or even recommend to clients that 'your scores show that X is the occupation for you', but rather to provide information to career actors so that they can apply 'true reasoning' (Parsons, 1909; see Chapter 1) and arrive at their own career decisions (see Chapter 13).

Measures of key individual characteristics – abilities, personality, values and interests – are also available online, sometimes free of charge, for personal use in 'career self-management' (Chapter 12). It is often informative to complete such self-assessments. Websites for some of these are provided elsewhere in this chapter. In the areas of abilities and personality, you should be particularly careful to check the validity of any tests or inventories on offer.

Some career-related measures have been painstakingly developed and improved over many years, validated through well-constructed research and used extensively and with good effect by professional career counselors (Crites & Taber, 2002). These instruments are generally quantitative, measuring individual behavior against predetermined constructs, though recently there has been growing interest in the use of qualitative methods (McMahon & Patton, 2002; see also Chapter 13).

Other measures have been relatively casually developed by people with no particular qualifications or insight to do so. Many devices sold on the internet or through the popular media may be of this type. If you seek career-related assessments to assist your own decision making, you should always ask questions about these instruments' origins, the extensiveness of their use in the past and their validity as demonstrated by good research.

Abilities

Much of the impetus for career assessment came from the work of early psychologists, such as James Cattell (1890), Alfred Binet (1911) and Charles Spearman (1923), who developed the first intelligence tests to determine students' fitness for various forms of education. World War II saw the massive application of the 'fit' metaphor and trait-and-factor theory in the mass testing of millions of military personnel in order to assign them efficiently to suitable tasks (e.g. Stewart, 1947). After the war, the same kind of thinking was applied to personnel selection in large organizations.

Abilities range from general intelligence – the famous 'g' factor, which is thought to underlie all other human abilities (Spearman, 1923) – to special aptitudes, such as numerical and mechanical ability, and specific skills, such as mastery of a foreign language or a particular software program, or typing speed. Tests of abilities are inherently controversial due to concerns that they are culturally biased against certain groups (Casillas & Robbins, 2005), and in the USA their use in personnel selection is limited by law to situations where good correlations with job performance can be demonstrated. Over a range of different occupations, these relationships have been shown to be moderate to high (Hunter, 1986; Schmidt, 2002).

Many employing organizations and recruitment agencies use techniques such as aptitude and skill tests, manual dexterity tests, work simulations, in-basket tests, assessed group discussions and assessment centers to assess ability to do a job (see Chapter 14). The accuracy of such measures may be affected by factors such as the anxiety of candidates, but tests are part of the careers landscape and career actors seeking new jobs should be prepared for them.

Personality

The broadest type of disposition is *personality*: 'an individual's unique constellation of behavioral traits' (Weiten, 2001: 486). Personality theory assumes a degree of consistency in our behavior – that is, we carry traits such as extroversion or adaptability with us so that they influence our behavior, including career behavior, in different situations. Nowadays, there is considerable expert consensus that much personality variation between people can be attributed to five identifiable traits – the 'Big Five': extroversion, neuroticism, openness to experience, agreeableness and conscientiousness (McCrae & Costa, 2003), which can be measured using a questionnaire called the NEO Personality Inventory (Costa & McCrae, 1992).

Another much-used personality inventory is the Myers-Briggs Type Indicator (MBTI) (Myers et al., 1985), which measures people on four dimensions: introversion versus extroversion; sensing versus intuition; thinking versus feeling; and judging versus perceiving. Taken together, the four dimensions enable people to be classified into 16 different personality types.

We can easily see how some personality characteristics might be related to fit with specific occupations. For example, extroversion might have a good fit with people jobs, such as teaching or selling. Conscientiousness might be better for jobs involving analysis and organizing, such as computer programming or inventory control. However, personality characteristics are often so broadly conceptualized that only low correlations with occupational fit are likely (Crites & Taber, 2002). Personality measures may say more about the style people bring to their work than about the kind of work they should do.

Values

Values represent abstract outcomes that individuals seek. For example, The Values Scale (Super & Nevill, 1985; Zytowski, 1994) divides ten values into three general types: Service Orientation, Teamwork and Influence form the 'Working with Others' type; Creativity, Independence, Excitement and Career Development fall into the 'Self-Expression' type; and the 'Extrinsic Rewards' type consists of Financial Rewards, Prestige and Security. The potential to affect career behavior is clear: a Service Orientation person may seek work as a relatively poorly paid teacher or social worker, whereas a Financial Rewards person may make salary a major job criterion. Values thus provide much of the motivation for career-related actions.

Interests

Interests are more specific than values. They are about what we like and dislike, what we choose to spend our time doing, and are often expressed in hobbies and non-employment environments. Concrete examples of interests are camping or playing video games (rather specific) and active outdoor activity or using computers (rather general). Interests are derived from a range of sources (e.g. values, family, social class, education; see Chapter 3) and, like abilities, they develop and become more specific over time. Vocational interests can be measured by, for example, the Kuder (Kuder & Findley, 1966) Occupational Interest Survey (www.kuder.com), the Holland (1979) Self-Directed Search (see below) and the Strong Interest Inventory (www.cpp.com). In career counseling, such interests are more commonly assessed than values.

Self-Assessment

If good matching matters, then in our career decision-making choices we need an accurate self-concept, or at least one which is plausible to ourselves and people who know us. If we are self-deluded, we are unlikely to be able to match ourselves effectively to work contexts. But how accurate are self-assessments? Studies comparing self-assessments of abilities and interests with independent assessments suggest that although we tend to overestimate ourselves, there is reasonable agreement (Mabe and West, 1982; Miller, 2007). Our self-assessments of specific skills and interests, such as word processing, may be more accurate than those of broad traits, such as general intelligence or agreeableness.

Self-estimates are subject to a number of biases. An example is gender: girls and women tend to under-estimate their mathematical ability relative to boys and men, whilst the reverse tends to happen for verbal ability. Such biases affect the educational and occupational choices made by males and females (Correll, 2001). In Holland's SDS (see below), there is a section where people are asked to estimate their abilities in different areas, relative to people their own age. The authors have seen university students of both genders with good grades in mathematics up to age 16 rate themselves as below average, despite objectively being in the top 20 percent of the population. This may be because they are comparing themselves with other students, many of whom are on science, engineering and mathematics courses.

However, for effective career decision making, abilities and interests are not the only elements which often need to be assessed. Others include knowledge of the world of work, decisiveness, self-efficacy, decision-making styles, handling pressure from others (e.g. parents) who think they know what's best for us, and recognition of situational constraints such as family circumstances. Measures have been developed for many of these factors, potentially affecting career decision making (Brown & Rector, 2008; Krumboltz, 1991; Taylor & Betz, 1983). Interventions to help people find a good fit with an occupation have been developed (Gati & Amir, 2010) and focus mainly on the accurate evaluation and optimal use of information in decision making. The 'rational' approach of specifying and giving weightings to the pros and cons of each option is not necessarily superior to a more intuitive 'gut feel' style (Phillips, 1997). This is not because intuition is a substitute for information. It is a different, less conscious way of processing it.

Assessing Jobs and Occupations

The other side of assessment concerns the 'holes' in our 'pegs in holes' metaphor – the jobs and occupations that career actors try to fit into. These can be analyzed to determine what combination of activities, interests, values, skills and abilities they require or benefit from. People working in an occupation can be surveyed to see whether they exhibit specific profiles. Research on the validation of vocational tests led Tracey and Hopkins (2003: 178) to state that 'interests and abilities … have a high level of correspondence with occupational choice', but not all research shows that a good fit produces good outcomes.

An excellent resource available from the US Department of Labor, at www.onet-center.org, is the set of information packages and self-completion inventories known as O*NET. O*NET enables you to match yourself to as many as 20,000 different occupations and provides information about tasks, skills required, salaries, long-term prospects and a host of other things. Thus, O*NET seeks to move beyond the assessment of job seekers to enable those job seekers, and other interested parties, such as employers, human resource managers, educators and career counselors, to consider how the 'pegs' match with the various 'holes' available. The European Union offers ESCO (see https://ec.europa.eu/esco/home) which stands (approximately) for European Skills, Competences, Qualifications and Occupations, and offers a detailed breakdown of different jobs and the competencies they involve. At present, though, ESCO is not as easy as O*NET to use as a matching tool by individuals seeking the right job for them.

However, as Table 6.1 reminds us, occupation is not the only basis for determining fit between person and career. Within the same general occupation, there are major differences in type of work, such as the many specialties within medicine, which may suit different profiles. There are also major differences between organizations, such as size, location, financial health, facilities, organizational culture and social life. There are differences between jobs within the same occupation, such as variety of tasks, physical setting and levels of responsibility, stress and independence.

Also, there is the labor market to consider (see Chapter 2). However congruent your characteristics may be with your chosen occupation, someone has to want to hire you. Many would-be dancers, athletes, entertainers, private eyes, politicians, astronauts and the like have strong interests, abilities and qualifications relevant to these lines of work, but often they cannot break in because there are too many able people chasing too few opportunities. Fortunately, much labor market information is available on the internet and elsewhere about areas of shortage and of oversupply, and prospects for expansion in the years ahead (Reardon et al., 2012; Chapter 12).

The Theory of Work Adjustment

An important application of the 'fit' metaphor is called the theory of work adjustment (TWA) (Dawis & Lofquist, 1984) and (in a more general form) person–environment correspondence (PEC) theory (Dawis, 2002). This theory goes back to the 1950s and is thought to be a highly effective general theory (Eggerth, 2008; Hesketh & Griffin, 2005).

The theory has both a structural and a dynamic element. The structural element is shown in Figure 6.1.

The TWA theory proposes that a career actor's adjustment to their work environment is a product of (1) the satisfaction they gain from the environment, and (2) the satisfactoriness of their behavior within that environment. Satisfaction is determined by 'reinforcers' offered by the environment that meet the career actor's values. Satisfactoriness (similar to 'job performance') depends on the person's abilities and their willingness to use them to behave in ways expected by key players in the environment (e.g. managers).

When satisfaction and satisfactoriness are both present, there is correspondence, which both parties seek to maintain. When satisfaction and/or satisfactoriness are insufficient, there is discorrespondence, which one or both parties may seek to eliminate so that correspondence is restored. Who takes action, what action they take and when they take it depend on the adjustment styles of person and environment. For example, some people and environments are tolerant of some discorrespondence (called 'flexibility' in the theory), whereas others are not. A person might try to change the environment to meet their needs better (active adjustment; see also 'Job crafting' below) or change the relative importance of different needs (reactive adjustment), which is often easier (Eggerth, 2008). If all attempts at increasing correspondence fail,

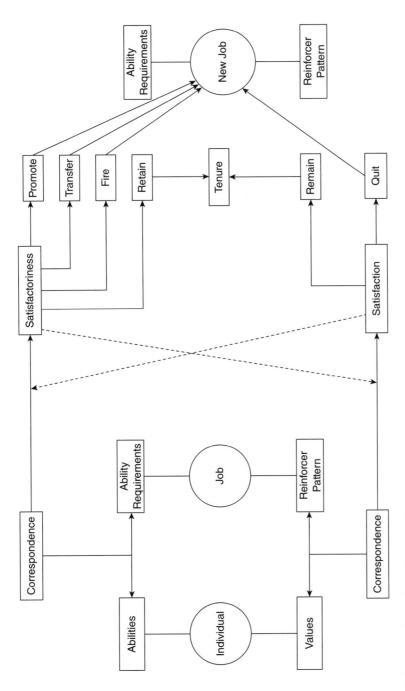

Figure 6.1   Prediction of work adjustment

Copyright © Dawis and Lofquist (1984)
Reprinted with permission of John Wiley & Sons, Inc.

then the person will leave the environment or the environment will eject the person. Because organizations have an interest in their employees' satisfactoriness, and employees seek maximum satisfaction, ensuring close correspondences is presumed to be functional for both.

High or moderate satisfactoriness or satisfaction, or both, normally lead to the individual remaining in the job. But high satisfactoriness can lead to promotion, low satisfactoriness to being fired, and either to transfer. Low satisfaction can lead to quitting. All these outcomes mean that the cycle recommences, with the individual seeking to find a new correspondence between their abilities and values and a new job.

Suzanne's case (below) is an example of active adjustment to discorrespondence.

CASE STUDY

Making Adjustments

Suzanne was a graduate biological scientist with several years' experience in a company offering technical consultancy to the food industry. Her job was to develop product inspection programs according to US Food and Drug Administration (FDA) requirements, and to work with clients to ensure that the applications met their needs. Suzanne, technically competent and interested in the software, was also somewhat extroverted. Her day-to-day work as a laboratory scientist without much contact with other people made her envious of the company's sales and service people, who spent time 'on the road', dealing with clients. She felt she was missing out on 'people' experience and failing to develop as a person. She feared she might eventually find herself consigned permanently to boring technical roles, unable to access the networks that might eventually lead to promotion or transfer to a managerial position.

Without telling her employer, Suzanne applied for sales and client liaison positions with other companies in her industry. However, her skills were very specialized and she had no other relevant experience, so she was offered no jobs. What should she do? Try to train herself in new skills? But why should she? Apart from the routines of her job, she really liked working for her current employer – a good company, with understanding bosses, in a convenient location, with generous pay.

So Suzanne went to her manager and talked the problem over with him. The manager was sympathetic: he had been concerned about Suzanne's apparent isolation and lack of self-confidence, and didn't want to lose a good employee. Eventually, they agreed to redefine her role so that she took over part of the client liaison work for some of the applications she was developing; and to appoint a new graduate to assist Suzanne and others on the technical side. So Suzanne now had a fresh job description. Six months on, Suzanne's job satisfaction and sense of self-efficacy have dramatically increased due to the redefinition of her work, and she has increased her performance and value to the organization. Her new job is a much better fit.

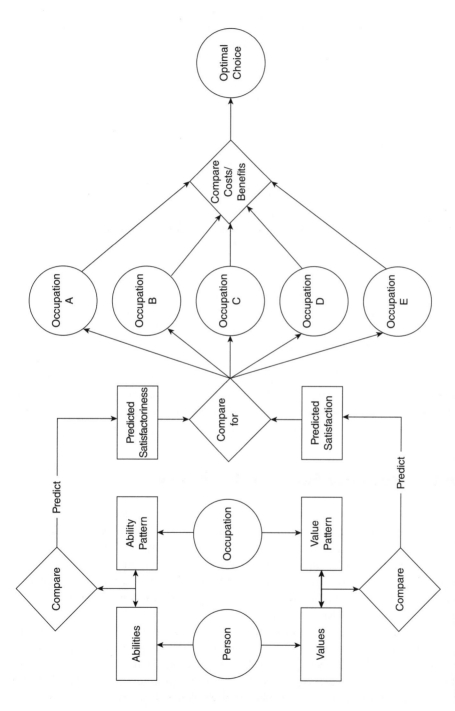

Figure 6.2   Using the theory of work adjustments in career choice

In this example, the conflict was mainly between Suzanne's values and the organization's reinforcement patterns. With the help of her manager, she was able to make an appropriate active adjustment that brought the job into correspondence with her values. Employers as well as employees can help to ensure good fit (Chapter 14).

The original TWA treated the job as the environment. Other work-related roles, such as retirement, have also been considered in the context of TWA (Hesketh et al., 2011). More radically, the development of TWA into person–environment correspondence theory (PEC) recognized that environment can be understood in a number of ways other than the job, including occupation, organization, culture and co-workers (Dawis, 2002). PEC can therefore provide a framework for understanding occupational choice. This process is shown in Figure 6.2 (Dawis, 1996).

In this process, the correspondence is between person and occupation. The idea of occupation implies that even though every job is unique, jobs in the same occupation are sufficiently similar to enable us to identify an occupational profile of ability requirements and reinforcement pattern. Individuals can also be assessed to see if they are congruent with this profile. This comparison enables the prediction of satisfactoriness and satisfaction. Thus, career actors can compare themselves with different occupations, compare the costs and benefits in satisfactoriness/satisfaction terms and make the optimal choice. Organizations or employment consultants can apply similar principles to their personnel selection, choosing applicants who have a close correspondence with the occupations and jobs available.

In common with many adherents of the 'fit' metaphor, Dawis and Lofquist (1984) were strong on measurement and used validated standard instruments to assess career actors' abilities, values, reinforcement patterns, satisfactoriness and satisfaction. These have enabled systematic tests of the work adjustment theory to be developed, with results moderately favorable to the theory (Dawis & Lofquist, 1984: Rounds et al., 1987).

John Holland: Vocational Personality Theory

Over many years, American researcher and former career counselor John Holland (1973, 1985, 1997) developed an influential conceptual scheme for classifying individuals and occupations according to 'vocational personality'. Holland's scheme is based on a huge volume of research conducted from the 1950s onwards, in which he remained involved until close to his death in 2008. It has provided not just an important theory of occupational fit but also a series of assessment devices and practical techniques to assist career actors in finding a good fit.

Holland's system identifies six 'pure types' of 'vocational personality'. Occupational environments are classified using the same typology. Career actors and occupations are then measured to ascertain the extent to which they resemble each of the six pure types. For a detailed description of each type, interested readers are referred to Holland's own work and to commentaries on it (e.g. Nauta, 2010; Spokane & Cruza-Guet, 2005).

The hexagon shown in Figure 6.3 represents a space around which the different types are arranged. This means that, in a sense, different types are considered opposites: Realistic is the opposite of Social, Investigative the opposite of Enterprising, and Artistic the opposite of Conventional. Individuals high on a particular type are also likely to be above average on adjacent types – for example, those strongest on the Artistic dimension may also have relatively high scores on Social and Investigative.

Figure 6.3   Holland's RIASEC Hexagon

An individual's correspondence with each of the six types can be measured using an instrument called the Self-Directed Search (SDS). The SDS asks questions about occupations you think you might like, activities you enjoy or dislike, self-estimates of competence in specific and general activities, and even your occupational daydreams.

When the questionnaire is scored, it provides you with an indication of the three types for which you score highest, each indicated by its first letter. For example, SEA would indicate that the individual's strongest area is Social, followed in order by Enterprising and Artistic. Full information about the SDS and a range of related assessment products is available in Holland and Messer (2013).

The SDS can also be accessed for a fee (US$9.95 at the time of writing) on the internet (www.self-directed-search.com). A free brief RIASEC questionnaire based on the work of Armstrong et al. (2008) can be found at http://personality-testing.info/tests/RIASEC.php. You will be fed back your three-letter code but the site does not have the extensive linkage to occupations that the SDS website offers.

Holland and other researchers administered his inventory to many people from a range of occupations, and computed, for each occupation, a profile that represented the best fit. Because this was an impossibly huge task to carry out for all occupations, job analysis information was used to classify many more occupations, and an assessment

Table 6.2   Holland Types for Some Common Occupations

CSI	Accountant	EIS	Lawyer
CSR	Accounts Clerk	ESR	Warehouse Manager
AES	Actor	ESC	Sales Manager
ASI	Artist	SEC	Human Resource Manager
AIR	Architect	ISE	Medical Doctor (General)
CSE	Bank Teller	ASI	Musician
SAE	Career Counselor	ISE	Nurse, community
RCE	Carpenter	SIR	Nurse, midwife
CES	Checkout Cashier	ISE	Optometrist
REA	Chef	RIE	Pilot, commercial
IRC	Computer Programmer	SER	Police Officer
CSE	Data Entry Operator	IES	Psychologist, organizational
RAC	Dental Technician	SIA	Psychologist, clinical
EAR	DJ	CSE	Receptionist
RIE	Engineer, automotive	ESA	Salesperson
IRE	Engineer, chemical	SCR	Shop assistant
EIC	Engineer, production	SEA	Social Worker, psychiatric
RIS	Farmer	ASE	Teacher, art
ASR	Fashion Designer	SEC	Teacher, kindergarten
ESR	Funeral Director	SAE	Teacher, secondary school
SER	Hair Stylist	CSE	Travel Agent
SEC	Homemaker	RIS	Welder
AEI	Journalist	ISE	X-ray Technologist

instrument, the Position Classification Inventory (Gottfredson & Holland, 1991), was developed. The *Occupations Finder* included with the SDS provides more than 1,000 occupations grouped under their RIASEC codes and required level of education. The *Dictionary of Holland Occupational Codes* (Gottfredson & Holland, 1996) provides three-letter RIASEC codes for more than 12,000 occupations. If you complete the SDS, you are encouraged to think about occupations with profiles close to your own. The purpose of comparing personal and occupational profiles is not to prescribe what occupations career actors should enter, but to provide them with a framework for thinking about fit, and additional information about their characteristics.

Table 6.2 shows the Holland codes for a number of occupations. Different occupations really are for different kinds of people. Also, some occupations have broad scope and therefore need to be broken down into different sub-types. For example, the skills and personalities typical of tax accountants (who analyze numerical data) are likely to differ from those of auditors or chartered accountancy partners (who sell services). The codes for different kinds of manager, engineer, nurse and teacher are different. Even in the small number of occupations listed, there are plenty of duplicate codes. For example, homemaker, human resource manager and kindergarten teacher are all SEC. Probably most kindergarten teachers would not want to be human resource managers and vice versa, so the three-letter code does not capture everything about people's preferences.

Holland and his colleagues demystified the psychometric assessment process and made validated assessments accessible to ordinary people. Because most career actors have a reasonably good idea of which occupations might suit them, the SDS is usually reassuring, but also gives new ideas for potential occupations. Only if SDS results are puzzling or contradict one's long-held beliefs need a counselor be consulted.

If the theory is correct, then people who are working in congruent occupations ought to experience more career satisfaction, more success and greater stability of employment than those whose types are incongruent with their work. Also, people who are in occupations with a poor fit to their vocational personality should presumably move over time into something more congruent. Is this what happens?

The answer is complex. Many reviews of Holland's theory seem understandably in awe of his achievements and therefore possibly less critical than they might otherwise have been (e.g. Gottfredson, 1999). Some reviews of research suggest that there is a moderate relationship between congruence and outcome variables such as career satisfaction (Spokane et al., 2000; Tsabari et al., 2005), and that people are often able to increase their congruence by adjusting their interests or by moving to a different occupation (Donohue, 2006). However, the effect of congruence on outcomes seems to be less than one might hope from a theory that aims to be the basis of effective careers guidance (Tranberg et al., 1993). Even though the theory is an important and valuable one, it has some obvious potential limitations (Arnold, 2004; Tracey & Rounds, 1996):

- As already noted, the occupation is only one part of a person's working environment, so fit with other things such as the specific job may matter more. The exact nature of a job as (for example) a human resource manager may vary depending on the exact duties (payroll? industrial relations? training and development?) and on organizational factors such as the boss and the organization's mission and culture.
- The three-letter code does not use all the information in a person's SDS scores. For example, a career actor may have very low scores on two types and seek to avoid work in those two areas. Their three-letter code will suggest only a few of the occupations they might find congenial.
- Researchers (e.g. Darcy & Tracey, 2007; Yang et al., 2005) have questioned the regular hexagon configuration of the six types, whether six is the correct number of types and how well they replicate across cultures.
- Holland's measures may not adequately take into account career actors' values as opposed to their interests.
- Especially in more skilled occupations, career actors often have some scope to shape their duties to fit their profile (see, for example, Suzanne in the case study above). We discuss this 'job crafting' below.

CASE STUDY

Trying to Find a Fit

Angela grew up in Sydney, Australia. Her parents ran a succession of moderately successful small businesses. They were ambitious for Angela, but it seemed to her that although she desperately wanted to please them, she never could. She tried hard at dancing, for which she had some talent, and at age 13 went to a ballet school which her parents struggled to afford. In this and her subsequent college-based performing arts training, she was an adequate student but did not excel. In order to earn much-needed money while at college, she was a 'dresser' on some major shows. This required some artistic talent but mainly good organization and quick action in getting the actors ready between scenes. She also picked up a few conventional academic qualifications.

In order to get a foothold in showbusiness, Angela took a contract for a dance tour of South-east Asia and whilst on this tour she was 'swept off her feet' by the man who became her husband. She went to live with her new partner in China and they had two children. Angela trained as a teacher of English as a foreign language and was successful and in demand. But her marriage came to an unpleasant end, and she returned to Sydney with the children. For a time, they lived on very little, yet because of her resourcefulness in living simply and buying cheaply, they had an adequate quality of life. As the children became more independent, Angela trained as a fitness instructor, studied for advanced instructor qualifications and, due to her interpersonal skills and her knowledge of the human body acquired on her courses, built up a large and loyal clientele. However, after about eight years she tired of the demands of clients, the administration of her business and the difficulty in earning a good income. At the time of writing, she is working as a shop assistant while she considers her future, which she thinks may involve training as a geriatric nurse.

Angela's career shows the often partial and evolving nature of fit. She would probably score highly on Artistic and Social, with Enterprising, Investigative and Realistic not far behind. Investigative probably increased as she re-discovered her academic abilities and scientific interest in the human body. Artistic is decreasing as she moves further from the performing arts and frees herself from a desire to please her parents. Nevertheless, the Enterprising (small business) environment she grew up in appears to have left its mark (inheritance metaphor, Chapter 3). It is likely that many occupations will feel like a moderately good fit for her, but none will be compelling enough to stay for a lifetime. Dancing reflects Artistic and Realistic, theatre dressing Artistic and probably Enterprising, teaching English as a foreign language is primarily Social with a bit of Artistic and Enterprising, self-employed fitness instructor is Enterprising, Social and Investigative and/or Realistic, and geriatric nursing is primarily Social, Investigative and Realistic. As with Philip in our opening case study, the thing you shouldn't ask Angela to do is Conventional tasks such as administration.

Edgar Schein: Career Anchors

In his book *Career Dynamics: Matching individual and organizational needs*, Schein (1978) first put forward a conceptual scheme based on 'career anchors'. Schein subsequently (1996: 80) explained the notion of anchor as follows:

A person's career anchor is his or her self-concept, consisting of (1) self-perceived talents and abilities, (2) basic values, and most important, (3) the evolved sense of motives and needs as they pertain to the career. Career anchors evolve only as one gains occupational and life experience. However, once ... formed, it functions as a stabilizing force, an anchor, and can be thought of as the values and motives that the person will not give up if forced to make a choice. Most of us are not aware of our career anchors until we are forced to make choices ... yet it is important to become aware of them so that we can choose wisely when choices have to be made.

Schein proposed that each career actor develops just one dominant anchor, and that this remains dominant, apparently impervious to changes in their life and the labor market. A summary of the anchors is shown in Table 6.3.

Table 6.3   Schein's Career Anchors

Career Anchor	Summary of Characteristics	Reward Valued
Technical/Functional Competence	Use of skills in specific work; focus on specialist work rather than management	Recognition for skills
Managerial Competence	Orientation to management of others, including accountability and interpersonal competence	Promotion, responsibility
Autonomy/ Independence	Freedom from organizational rules, control over one's own work	Increased autonomy
Security/Stability	Feeling that it is possible to continue in the same or a very similar job without having to move on	Recognition for loyalty
Entrepreneurial Creativity	Creating new organizations, products or services; achievement of something worthwhile; being prominent	Income, profitability of organization
Service/Dedication to a Cause*	Doing work that meets personal values (e.g. service to others)	Helping others, influencing organizational mission
Pure Challenge*	Achieving results against the odds, solving difficult problems	Novel or challenging work
Lifestyle*	Integrating work demands with other demands (e.g. family responsibilities), balancing expenditure of time	Job flexibility (e.g. flexi-time, parental leave)

Note: *These three anchors were not in Schein's (1978) original five-anchor schema but were added in a later revision (Schein, 1985).

Although Schein portrays anchors as an amalgam of motives, abilities, needs and values, it has been pointed out that the anchors reflect different types of characteristics (Wils et al., 2010). Managerial competence, technical/functional competence and entrepreneurial creativity seem mainly to reflect a person's abilities. The job security, geographical stability, lifestyle and autonomy/independence anchors are based mostly on needs for structuring work to fit personal preferences. The service/dedication and pure challenge anchors reflect a person's values.

Anchors refer to the person. They do not translate directly into work environments. Being the marketing director of a charity might fit well with service/dedication to a cause, but equally it could fit with managerial competence, technical/functional competence or any of the other anchors. Also, according to Schein (1996), managerial competence is the dominant anchor for only about half of middle and senior managers. Does this mean anchors are not useful for matching? No, but the matching needs to be done 'locally', taking into account the organizational context, the particular job and any opportunities for the job-holder to 'craft' the job as they wish.

Schein's (1978) interest in organizational fit suggested that good matching could be facilitated by organizational management, where systems of employee development, transfer, promotion and rewards could take anchors into account. This is not about occupations: instead, it shows how organizational arrangements for individual employees can be tailored to their anchors, regardless of occupation.

Like Holland, Schein (1985) developed a questionnaire – the Career Orientation Inventory (COI) – to measure and research individuals' anchors (see www.careeranchorsonline.com). However, the research conducted on career anchors lacks both the volume and the rigor of that on Holland's types. It has nevertheless proved popular in some research areas, for example on the careers of IT workers (e.g. Chang et al., 2010). Most tests of the structure of the COI suggest that Schein's anchors are valid concepts, separable from each other (Danziger et al., 2008). The COI is also widely used in career development workshops, and Schein (1993) developed a self-help workbook for individuals.

The career anchor concept has been criticized on a number of grounds. Schein's notion of 'one dominant anchor per person' has been challenged. Rodrigues et al. (2013) have summarized the main critiques and also offered an alternative approach, arguing for the concept of career orientation, which is relatively stable but more open than anchors to change in the light of experience or new circumstances. Also, they demonstrate that some of the pharmacists they studied clearly had a secondary orientation that was less dominant than their main one, but still influential, especially if expression of the dominant orientation was blocked.

CASE STUDY

Running His Life

Sebastian Coe has had a varied and very successful career. From humble beginnings in Sheffield, England, he became 1500-metres gold medallist and 800-metres silver medallist in both the 1980 and 1984 Olympics. Later, he went into politics in the UK, and became a Member of Parliament, rising to hold some junior governmental and senior Conservative party positions. Then in 2005, he headed up the UK's successful bid to stage the 2012 Olympics in London, and for the next seven years was head of the Olympic and Paralympics organizing operation. The preparation was managed very skilfully, the events ran well and a legacy of increased public engagement with sport will most likely be achieved.

The authors of this book do not have access to Sebastian Coe's scores on the COI, but we can use the anchors framework to make some intelligent guesses about the driving force behind his extraordinary achievements in diverse occupational fields. Two anchors seem likely candidates: Pure Challenge and Service/Dedication. Clearly, his recent work has required a lot of Managerial Competence, but perhaps for him this is merely a set of skills to achieve his most valued goals. The final words of his autobiography *Running My Life* might suggest Pure Challenge is the key: 'although my children consider me ancient, I'm still only in my mid-50s. And while I may no longer hope to run faster, jump higher or be stronger, there's still a lot I want to do with my life. I'm not ready to slow down yet' (Coe, 2012: 457).

Stop and Consider

Think of someone you admire and whose work and career you know about: for example, a sports star or music performer, a writer, a business person, a television personality. Consider which career anchors might be the key ones anchoring their careers. If you want to, try this with more than one person and write down the evidence for your choices. Try the same with people you know, for example your bosses or teachers. Try the same, with the same people, using the Holland system. This is an interesting way to learn the material.

Job Crafting

The case of Suzanne earlier in this chapter shows how people can take action to develop their careers by improving the fit between self and job. Although Dawis (theory of work adjustment) and Holland (theory of vocational personality) are best known for their theories of matching, they also discussed how, over time, people and jobs may become more aligned. In this tradition, Wrzesniewski and Dutton (2001) have written about how people 'craft' their jobs, crafting being defined as 'the physical and cognitive changes individuals make in the task or relational boundaries of their work' (2001: 179). Crafting can include changing the form or number of tasks in the job, changing how one views the job and/or changing who one relates to and how one does so. Thus, a career actor, rather than choosing a job or occupation to fit their characteristics, can try to alter the characteristics of the job for a better fit.

Jobs vary in their opportunities for crafting, and people vary in their perception and taking of those opportunities. The possibility of job crafting depends partly on the supervisor's co-operation with the job-holder, and that co-operation depends partly on the person's job performance (Clegg & Spencer, 2007). And it is not only the job that changes. As a person does different things, or the same things differently, over time their sense of identity and attitude to work also change. Therefore, people's satisfaction and satisfactoriness (Dawis's theory) and congruence (Holland's theory) can change over time.

Stop and Consider

Consider a job or university course you are, or have been, involved in. To the extent that it did not suit you, did you try to improve the fit? If not, why not? If so, what did you do and how successful were you? Try to explain your success, or lack of it.

Person–Environment Fit: The Bigger Picture

As stated earlier, the notion of fit is a broad one. It can refer to different aspects of the person (abilities, interests, etc.) and of the environment (occupation, organization, job, etc.). In addition, fit can be construed as *supplementary* or *complementary* (Cable & Edwards, 2004). Supplementary fit is when the person and environment are similar, offering each other 'more of the same', though of course if an occupation or organization contains people of only a certain kind, it is unlikely to be innovative. Complementary fit is where the person offers something the environment needs but does not have, and/or vice versa. Here, person and environment can be thought of as two jigsaw pieces, different in shape but fitting together perfectly. The two types of fit are not mutually exclusive.

A great deal of research has examined person–environment fit in the context of work, considering not only person–organization or person–job fit, but also person–group and person–supervisor fit. Kristof-Brown et al. (2005) conducted a meta-analysis of this enormous literature, and discovered that both person–organization (P–O) fit and person–job (P–J) fit were strongly related to satisfaction, commitment to the organization and intention to stay in current employment. P–J fit was moderately related to job performance, and P–O fit less so, though P–O fit was a reasonable predictor of 'good citizen' organizational behaviors. Person–supervisor fit was important in some respects, but person–group fit less so. In general, P–O and P–J fit are more strongly related to outcomes like job satisfaction than, for example, congruence measures derived from Holland's instruments. That might mean job or organization are a more useful way of classifying a work environment than occupation.

Conclusion

The use of the 'fit' metaphor in theory and practice is based on a simple, common-sense view of life: most of us have been in jobs or courses that we felt 'fit' or 'didn't fit' us. The metaphor reflects the undeniable diversity of people and jobs and attempts to systematize it, thereby enabling the development of an impressive technology for measuring people and occupations, so that individuals and their advisors can make well-informed decisions. It has stood the test of time well: Parsons's initial 1909 formulation – 'understand yourself, understand the world of work, use "true reasoning" to find a match', or something close to it – still underpins the underlying system of beliefs of many experts on careers.

Against these strengths, we must set some undoubted weaknesses. The characteristics of humans and of work contexts are difficult to measure. The typical application of the metaphor seems to suggest that occupations are homogeneous, but within occupations jobs may vary greatly, and both occupations and jobs may change substantially over time. The metaphor may lead to the stereotyping of individuals, jobs or occupations as having particular characteristics permanently, and consequently stifle innovation and adaptability. It may also imply that career actors are helpless to shape their job to make it a better fit. Nevertheless, if these deficiencies are recognized and compensated for, the 'fit' metaphor, as a cornerstone of understanding and improving careers, continues to prove its worth.

Key Points in this Chapter

- A common approach to careers is to ensure that there is a good fit between people and the work they do. This can be done by assessing people, assessing work and logically matching them.
- Work adjustment theory suggests that if there is congruence between workers' abilities and values on the one hand, and their occupations' requirements and rewards on the other, their satisfaction and performance increase, and that people change jobs to achieve greater congruence.
- John Holland's theory is based on six types of vocational personality such that an individual's pattern can be matched against a large database of occupations using the Self-Directed Search (SDS) questionnaire.
- Schein's theory of career anchors uses a typology of eight clusters of values, interests and abilities. These anchors reflect what a person most cares about in their work, regardless of job or occupation.
- Assessments of career actors' abilities, personality, values and interests provide a structure of key traits and enable accurate professional measurement.

- Assessing the nature of jobs and occupations is also important. Holland's theory connects assessments of people with occupations, but in general job analysis techniques are underdeveloped, making it hard to translate self-knowledge into effective occupational choices.
- The fit of individual to organization or job, as well as to occupation, is important.

Questions from this Chapter

General Questions

1. Find at least one website offering a service of personal assessment and information on suitable careers. As far as you are able to judge, how worthwhile and professional a service does it offer? Use the information in this chapter to help you make a judgment.
2. Consider the three theories put forward by Dawis, Holland and Schein. What do you see as the main similarities among them, and the main differences? Which do you consider most helpful in improving your understanding of careers, and why?
3. Consider the reasons why a person's estimation of their abilities might be inaccurate (or, if you prefer, different from the estimations of people close to them). Consider how much this might apply to you, and whether it has any dangers for your career decisions.
4. Think of an occupation that you don't know much about but that interests you. Gather information about the occupation – for example, read job advertisements, research the job on the internet, find out about related educational programs and talk to people who do that job. Prepare a specification of the traits required by that occupation and assess its fit with your own traits.

'Live Career Case' Study Questions

1. Ask your career case person about the fit of some of their jobs. Were there times when the fit seemed poor? How did the person resolve the issue? What can you learn from this?
2. Discuss Holland's six dimensions with your case person. Try to estimate your case person's profile. If you can afford the money and time, have the person complete the SDS online. What did you, and your case person, learn from this activity?

Additional Resources

Recommended Further Reading

Dawis, R. V. (2002) 'Person–environment correspondence theory', in D. Brown and Associates (eds.), *Career Choice and Development* (4th edn, pp. 427–464). San Francisco: Jossey-Bass.

Gottfredson, G. D. (1999) 'John L. Holland's contributions to vocational psychology: A review and an assessment', *Journal of Vocational Behavior*, 55: 74–85.

Holland, J. L. (1997) *Making Vocational Choices: A theory of vocational personalities and work environments* (2nd edn). Odessa, FL: Psychological Assessment Resources.

Schein, E. H. (1996) 'Career anchors revisited: Implications for career development in the 21st century', *The Academy of Management Executive*, 10(4): 80–88.

Schmidt, F. L. (2002) 'The role of general cognitive ability and job performance: Why there cannot be a debate', *Human Performance*, 15: 187–210.

Wrzesniewski, A., and Dutton, J. E. (2001) 'Crafting a job: Revisioning employees as active crafters of their work', *Academy of Management Review*, 26:179–201.

Self-Assessment Resources

Assess the role of fit in your job search: Cable, D. M. and Judge, T. A. (1996) 'Person–organization fit, job choice decisions, and organizational entry', *Organizational Behavior and Human Decision Processes*, 67(3): 294–311.

Assess your ideal organizational culture profile: O'Reilly, C. A., Chatman, J. and Caldwell, D. F. (1991) 'People and organizational culture: A profile comparison approach to assessing person–organization fit', *Academy of Management Journal*, 34(3): 487–516.

Assess how you would come across in a job interview: Cable, D. M. and Judge, T. A. (1997) 'Interviewers' perceptions of person–organization fit and organizational selection decisions' *Journal of Applied Psychology*, 82(4): 546.

Online Resources

Learn about the importance of realistic job previews in assessing fit with a potential employer – see: http://en.wikipedia.org/wiki/Realistic_job_preview and rtc.umn.edu/docs/rjp.pdf

Would being a cabin crew member at easyJet be a good fit for you? Assess your fit with easyJet at: http://careers.easyjet.com/try-before-you-fly/

Careers as Journeys

7

Chapter Objectives

The objectives of this chapter are:

- to consider careers from the perspective of the most common career metaphor of all – the journey – including such journey characteristics as destination, direction, ascent and routes
- to examine the implications of different *types* of career journey, particularly occupational careers and organizational careers, and the idea that careers can usefully be divided into journey 'types'
- to critically assess the popular theory that career journeys are increasingly 'boundaryless', and to consider how career journeys are disrupted by marginalization and interruption
- to consider the growing internationalization of careers.

CASE STUDY

Moving Out, Moving On

David did not shine academically at school, and when he left at age 16, he decided not to pursue academic qualifications any further. He took his parents'

(Continued)

(Continued)

advice – 'learn a trade, secure your future' – and got himself taken on as an apprentice electrician at a local factory. He proved to be good at what he did and gained his qualification in minimum time. He also liked the security that full-time employment gave him, and within a few years he was able to marry his girlfriend, buy a new home and start a family. His employer valued his services, paid for him to obtain advanced qualifications at a local college and promoted him to a supervisory position. It seemed David's career was 'on track'.

But when David was in his late 30s, with 20 years' service in the company, he began to realize that he had become rather discontented with his work, which seemed to be more and more of the same: more a job than a career. He found himself thinking, 'Is this all I'll ever be?' Then his company was taken over by a large multinational, which first replaced most of the managers that David had worked with for many years, and then began to downsize. Eventually, David was told he was to be laid off, but was offered the opportunity to apply for an electrician position in the new structure. 'Don't worry', said his manager. 'We can't afford to do without your experience – you'll get the job.'

But David had realized that even if that happened, manufacturing in his location was on the slide and his employment would from now on be very precarious. Why apply for a job that he probably wouldn't enjoy, working for people he didn't respect, in a dying industry? He talked it over with his wife, and in the end took a redundancy payment without even applying for the job.

David was quickly able to get a new job, as an electrician in a tertiary college in his city, helping to maintain the college's equipment. He worked with other tradesmen, particularly engineers, who were employed in the college as teachers of technological subjects. These men spoke warmly about the fulfilment they got out of using education to spread their skills, and David began to feel he had missed his vocation. So, after a year in the job, and with his redundancy payment still intact and his wife earning a salary, he enrolled in the college as a student, to train as a teacher.

From the very first day, David loved his new life. He loved learning new subjects and teaching in new environments. After initial training, he enrolled for a degree in social science by distance learning and eventually qualified to teach social studies as well as technology. He became a useful all-round teacher at a local high school. But there was a problem: David did not handle children well and found he had a problem with anger when provoked. After a few years of enjoying his job less and less, and receiving two disciplinary warnings from the school authorities concerning minor violence against pupils, he again decided to move on.

David had always spent much of his spare time working as a volunteer in local charities, and through this and his various jobs he was well connected in his town. Because of this and other skills, he has gained employment as a business development manager for a local centre which helps blind and disabled people. His job is to look for sponsorship, business support and funding to supplement the centre's government funding. The job suits him because of his sociability, and he no longer has to deal with children.

David is happy again. His only regret is that he didn't discover 'white collar' work earlier in his career. He realizes that early on in his career he tended to over-value security and to do what others suggested. His youngest son, aged 16, wants to leave school and learn how to invent video games. David privately thinks this is a pipe dream, but is careful not to 'lecture' his son on what he should do. Life, he says, is a journey: 'and my son's life is his journey, not mine'.

If David's career is indeed a journey, what are its characteristics? First, it has been a journey without a stable *destination*. David started off as an electrician, then became a teacher and is now a business development manager. His journey has had short-term destinations along the way, but like most middle-aged people he would now say, 'If you had told me when I started where I would end up, I wouldn't have believed you!' Of course, his journey is not yet complete, and it is perhaps unlikely that when he finally retires he will still have the same job as he has now.

Second, at different stages of the journey, David has had different degrees of *control* over his direction and speed. His parents seem to have set his early direction. When he became an electrician, his organization assumed more control. But when he decided to leave, he took control of his own career and since then he has been more 'in charge'.

Third, David's journey has, after 20 years of being linear, become *non-linear*. It has had major changes in direction and has crossed important organizational and occupational boundaries. The skills required for the journey have changed in emphasis, from technical to social. In this respect, David's career is probably typical rather than atypical. While a few careers, nowadays, remain linear, the vast majority are non-linear.

Different Journey Metaphors

The first recorded meaning of the word *career* was 'race course' and 'the charge of a horse, in a tournament or battle'. This provides a sense of progress along a course, so that people tend to think of careers in terms of progression and journeys.

The 'journey' metaphor is common. We have found that if people are asked for metaphors that describe their careers, more than 50 percent of them will, like David in our opening case, nominate some kind of journey. But they tend to say more than just 'journey': usually their metaphors indicate what kind of a journey it is. For example:

- a train journey
- a hard road
- a roller-coaster ride
- an expedition; a safari
- flying
- stuck; trying to get out of a swamp
- like white-water rafting.

We also use 'journey' metaphors in everyday talk about careers. Sometimes these metaphors tell us the type of route: career *path*, career *ladder*, fast *track*. Sometimes they talk about the destination: What *direction* do you want to take? Where do you want to *get to*? They might describe the destination as getting to *the top*, new *territory*, fresh *fields*. Sometimes they describe what the journey is like: *climbing* the mountain, on the *escalator*, job *hunting*, job *hopping*, *bailing* out, *cruising*, facing a *brick wall*.

These are powerful, evocative images. They tell us what a person's career journey is like. They enable us to identify instantly with the person's experience. The differences make each journey unique. Each one can be evaluated in terms of its destination or aimlessness; its trajectory and route – upward, downward, sideways, winding, random; and its purpose – for example, exploration, the experience of 'getting there', enjoyment along the way.

Society and organizations often create intended career pathways for individual career actors: for example, a career guided by the standards of a profession and its institutions in terms of required qualifications, standards of practice, advancement through professional ranks, etc., or an organizational career in which the career actor and an employing organization plan an ascending career route through increasing expertise and progressively more responsible jobs. Such paths provide clarity and security, and some security-conscious career travelers are constantly looking for clear predetermined pathways. But because of the dynamism and change in the economic and organizational terrain through which they nowadays journey, and because some simply don't like such paths, much career travel nowadays has to take place along improvised or personal pathways.

Stop and Consider

Consider your career, or the careers of people you know, in terms of predetermined or personal 'improvised' career paths. Which have their careers mainly followed? Has the type of path changed during their careers?

Destination

Career travelers are often expected to have a sense of destination, or at least of direction. Children are asked, 'What are you going to be when you grow up?' They and their parents are often encouraged to think about their futures and to set, or collaborate on, career goals (Dietrich & Salmela-Aro, 2013). This kind of thinking implies that career journeys should always be moving toward a destination, even if that destination changes over time.

One favored destination is 'the top'. Teenagers with strong career ambitions are more likely, as adults, to have high career status attainment (Ashby & Schoon, 2010). In occupational careers, for example, career actors tend to conceptualize occupations in terms of status hierarchies. Some look for ways to enter superior occupations, and then try to gain higher responsibility and better paying positions within them. A further powerful dynamic for upward mobility may be created by the motivation to lead (Kark & van Dijk, 2007). Organizations' hierarchies of salary, status and authority provide clear cues to the expected direction of a career. We are encouraged to be interested in our own and others' movement up, sideways or down (Altman, 1997). Society's expectation – at least in developed countries – is that the route should never take us downwards.

But a problem with upward career paths is that organizations tend to be the wrong shape to accommodate them. If everyone at the bottom wants to be the CEO, most of them are going to be disappointed. Further, some people, particularly blue-collar workers, explicitly reject the idea of promotion, or upward mobility, as a mark of career success, and instead pay attention to other monetary, psychological and social attainments (Hennequin, 2007).

There are many other potential destinations that career actors can head in. As discussed in Chapter 5, some direct their careers towards satisfaction more than progress and others, like Perry (Chapter 4), value lifestyle more. Shepard (1984), in a memorable journey metaphor, talked about the 'path with a heart', a journey towards fulfilling values such as social service, the creation of beauty or balance. The notion of 'career anchors' (Schein, 1993; see Chapter 6) indicates further alternatives including entre-preneurial creativity, security–stability and autonomy–independence. Many career actors simply want to get better or more expert at what they do, while others look for projects that are exciting in the short term. Women's careers can be drawn, for long periods of their lives, down the 'mommy track' (Buzzanell & Goldzwig, 1991) of child rearing.

Further, a career destination can be very long term, and the route a career actor follows to get there may be circuitous. Consider this case:

CASE STUDY

Clear Destination, Winding Route

Helga graduated with a Bachelor's degree in film studies and an intense desire to create documentary films or television programs. During her studies, she had also taken time out to qualify as a chef and acquire some work experience in that role.

She quickly identified the XBC organization, one of the world's biggest and best-known broadcasters and makers of documentary films, as her 'target' organi-zation, and secured a job as a sous-chef in XBC's staff restaurant. After two years of getting to know the organization, she resigned, bought a computer and trained herself in the basics of the main software programs that XBC used. Next, she got herself taken on as a 'temp' (temporary office worker) by an agency that filled XBC's short-term vacancies, covered for staff absences, etc. As a temp, she com-pleted many short-term secretarial/clerical assignments in finance, publicity, human resources, etc., but eventually she got a week's assignment in a creative department that produced historical documentaries. Helga quickly made herself indispensible to the department, so that every time they needed a temp they asked for her. After about a year, she was appointed as a production coordinator, doing the administration, but not the creative work, on documentary projects: not what she wanted, but a step in the right direction.

In her production coordinator role, Helga had an exciting life, traveling the world in connection with various documentaries. She learned the crafts of docu-mentary making from her colleagues, broadening beyond history and always seek-ing projects from which she would learn. This enabled her to climb in the XBC hierarchy, always moving towards the more creative roles. After two years as a production coordinator, she moved into the role of researcher, then later to assis-tant producer and, finally, in her late 30s, to full producer.

Along the way, Helga survived three major restructurings by XBC in which many of her colleagues lost their jobs. But the length, depth and variety of her experience in the broadcasting industry is such that she is confident that should she be laid off or choose to leave XBC, she will easily find good alternative employment. Meantime, while she continues to enjoy 'hands-on' television production, she is beginning to think about moving towards a more strategic or managerial role at XBC.

Helga recognized that immediate access to her 'dream job' was impossible, so she improvised. By starting her career journey 'at the bottom', using an organizational route to reach an occupational goal, keeping her destination in clear focus, and along the way acquiring additional broadcasting industry skills, Helga was able to fulfil her career dream, as well as creating a secure future and alternative onward career paths.

Note that Helga's career goals, so clear for so long, are changing: as Chapter 5 shows, this is likely to be true over the period of any career actor's life. So while career journeys often have short-term destinations within them, these destinations change and vary as the career progresses. And, as Robert Louis Stevenson (1907) long ago pointed out, a journey may be less a means to getting somewhere and more about enjoying the process: 'I travel not to go anywhere, but to go. I travel for travel's sake.'

Trajectory and Route

Topography describes the features and configuration of structures, such as hills, valleys, plains and buildings. Career journeys take place through distinctive topography – social, industry, organizational and occupational structures that create career opportunities and barriers (Chapter 2). The journey through the topography results from individual action (Chapter 5).

In seeking to persuade us that action and structure – traveler and topography – are equally important and interdependent, Gunz (1989) replaced the familiar metaphor of the 'career ladder' with that of the 'career climbing frame'. A climbing frame allows for different types of career moves. Climbers can choose their own movements. They are not necessarily trying to reach the top – they can go up, sideways or down. Frames may change over time or even suddenly disappear. Most intriguing of all, as people clamber on the climbing frame, they become part of it and change it, renewing the structure as they go.

This is one of the wonderful things about career journeys: they are recursive. As we clamber over climbing frames and pass through landscapes, we change them, altering organizational structures, becoming facilitators of, or obstructions to, others' careers, not just following pathways but creating them for others to follow.

Stop and Consider

Can you see any sort of 'career ladder' or 'climbing frame' ahead of you? What is it like? How will you negotiate it? What can you do to prepare? Will you change it as you climb it or climb on it?

Types of Career Journey

How can we make sense of the wide range of types of journey observable in people's careers? One way is to look at real career journeys, their typical patterns and routes. Can we discern any main types of career?

A feature of many career journeys is that they are restricted to established pathways within clear boundaries: boundaries help to remind us in our careers who we are, and where we are 'at home'. Two common types of journey are the occupational career, for example a medical career; and the organizational career, for instance a career with IBM.

Kanter (1989) distinguished three major career patterns, each driven by its own logic of career opportunity:

- In *professional* careers – careers defined by professional occupations – there is a logic of acquisition of socially valued knowledge and expertise within professional boundaries, which again enables the key career rewards to be accessed.
- In *bureaucratic* careers – Kanter's term for organizational careers – there is a logic of advancement, or status, in a single organization, through which major career opportunities – in earnings, responsibility, power and challenge – can be accessed.
- In *entrepreneurial* careers – a new type – there is a logic of growth, as the individual grows territory, or adds value, beneath her or him. An entrepreneurial career is characteristic of the ambitious owner-managers of small businesses but is not confined to them. The principles of the entrepreneurial career can be used, according to Kanter, in any job setting.
- In this typology, Kanter (1989) focused on higher-level careers. Those in mass occupations such as sales, customer service, and clerical and manual work, tend to be neglected. Also, many careers either move between the types at different stages or do not conform to any of them. For example, Driver (1979) talked about *spiral* careers, in which the individual moves from area to related area on a cyclic basis; and *transitory* careers, in which the individual moves from job to job with no particular pattern. But probably relatively few careers can be assigned completely to a single type. Nevertheless, in essence, Kanter defined some key routes for career journeys.

Occupational Careers

Occupations differ from each other in social status, in market value and in exclusiveness (Chapter 2). Many occupations – for example, professions such as medicine, law and teaching – are restricted, in terms of entry, to those who have acquired specialist qualifications and training and are accredited by a licensing authority. In such occupations, there are strong professional associations that guard the interests and reputation of the profession to ensure that jobs are confined to qualified people, that standards are high, that numbers in the occupation do not grow too quickly and that those in the occupation remain loyal to it. Other occupations, for example sales, computer programming and management, are less restrictive, though those seeking to make progress to positions of higher responsibility may well find later that credentials are helpful.

An occupational career journey takes place along a route that can involve much geographical and inter-organizational mobility. A sense of progress is denoted by the kind of work being done, which typically retains its occupational focus but becomes progressively more responsible or more specialized. These journeys therefore have something of the effect of traveling along deep valleys: travelers may find a valley congenial and make good progress along it, but if they change their minds, it is difficult to go back or climb into another valley.

This provides incentives to career actors to remain loyal to their occupations. The Dutch have a saying – 'schoenmaker, blijf bij je leest' (shoemaker, stick to your last). Consider the case of Greta.

CASE STUDY

Sticking to the Last

Greta, age 40, is a supervising radiographer – that is, she is qualified and skilled in the production and interpretation of images of the interior of the body created through radiation technology. She works in a large hospital, managing and practicing in a unit specialising in neuroradiology.

Greta comes from a medical family: her father was an ear, nose and throat specialist, her mother a physiotherapist and many of her other relations work in medical fields. At school, Greta was good at science, with a special liking for biology, especially working with microscopes. A friend's uncle was a radiographer and that enabled her to make a few visits, with her friend, to his work and to learn about what he did. Greta was instantly captivated, and so, against her parents' advice – they thought she could 'do better', for example train as a doctor – she

(Continued)

(Continued)

went directly from school into a bachelors' degree program in medical science and followed this with training as a radiographer. From there, she obtained a job immediately in a local hospital. Since then, she has found her skills in high demand, and has moved between a number of hospitals and private clinics. Because of her husband's career, she has moved to different regions twice, and she has also had spells of maternity leave and part-time work as she looked after her family needs. But her qualifications and experience have meant she has always found new jobs, and flexible hours, easy to get.

From the beginning, Greta has loved her profession. She has always found – and still finds – the biological images that she works with 'beautiful', and she even considers that the skilled production of images of the interior of the body has an artistic side, as well as being grounded in very rigorous science. In the 20 years since she started, Greta has seen massive new developments in her field: for example, ultrasound scanning, 3D imaging, functional imaging such as watching the brain work and magnetic resonance imaging (MRI). All these developments require her to continuously upgrade her skills, but they also create novelty and variety in her day-to-day work. She is active in professional affairs, takes courses in new technology, attends conferences and is proud of the breadth and depth of her personal knowledge. She also counts many radiographers and other work colleagues among her personal friends.

Greta also has good interpersonal and managerial skills, and her boss has recently suggested she could move to a more senior position: that would mean more responsibility and more money, but less direct radiography. Greta is reluctant to make the move. With 20 or more years still to go before she retires, she honestly can't imagine herself doing anything else.

Greta's career has been focused on a single occupation. Unlike many career actors, including some radiographers, she found it early and has 'stuck to the last' ever since. Yet, she has gained several different types of experience within the occupation, has advanced in responsibility through organizational hierarchies, and has been able to move between work and home, between different organizations and between geographical locations to fit her family requirements. Her occupation has become the anchor point of a mobile career.

Another issue demonstrated by Greta's career is the ongoing obsolescence and revitalisation of her knowledge base. A degree or basic training, or both, provides a basic skill set to commence a career journey. But as the career actor progresses, some of these skills become outdated and new developments require their replacement with new knowledge, particularly if he or she seeks upward career progress.

Some occupations disappear altogether due to technological change. Barrel makers were long ago replaced by mass-production operators in factories making containers, typesetters by software workers. Checkout operator positions are, as we write, being decimated by scanning machines. Thirty years ago, occupations such as computer programmer, web designer, software engineer, motorcycle courier, one-on-one fitness coach, life coach and laser surgeon hardly existed; now they are commonplace, creating opportunities to commence or move into quite new occupations.

Organizational Careers

Much interest has centred on organizational careers – career journeys that take place within the boundaries of a single, usually large, organization. Probably few career actors nowadays have complete organizational careers, i.e. only ever work for a single organization. But many will have *partial* organizational careers, where for a period of 5, 10 or 20 years they stay loyal to a single organization and find that organization very involved (through organizational actions such as promotion, transfer and layoff) in their career progression.

As indicated in Chapter 2, organizational careers are a logical by-product of the hierarchical and bureaucratic structures that were predominant in organizations for much of the 20th century and are still rather prevalent today. By encouraging and controlling its employees' careers, an organization can cultivate the special expertise it utilizes, fill vacancies through promotion and retain a stable, loyal workforce. Organizational careers are therefore determined to a considerable extent not by individuals but by organizations, as a means of recruiting, retaining and developing the overall human resource on which their profitability or achievement of other goals is based.

Organizations develop career systems (Weber, 1920/1947) through which the individual can progress to higher levels of status, responsibility and salary, while retaining high security of employment. The potential career rewards are substantial but tend to be delayed so that the individual can only qualify for them (e.g. a full pension) by restricting their career journey to one within the organization. This leads to the danger of overspecialization – that is, a person may become highly expert and valuable in certain work of the organization, but this specialist organizational expertise may not be relevant elsewhere. Considerable co-dependency between the individual and the organization may result.

Organizational careers can be encouraged and supported, particularly in large organizations, by appropriate practices of Human Resource Management (HRM). The organization can provide, for example, training, development, job rotation and performance appraisal in order to assist the career actor to acquire relevant skills and promotion. Such policies provide clear career pathways within the organization, and remuneration, fringe benefits and pension provisions to increase long-term commitment to the organization. We provide more detail of such practices in Chapter 14.

The idea of an organizational career sometimes conjures up 'Big Brother' images of a gigantic and powerful corporation directing and controlling its members' careers for its own benefit, with scant regard for their own goals and concerns. While there may sometimes be truth in this stereotype, organizational careers may also provide opportunities for employees to plot their own routes to career destinations. Helga's career in broadcasting, described earlier in this chapter, is an example of a career actor utilizing organizational career systems for personal – or, rather, mutual – benefit.

As Helga's case shows, however, the tendency of today's organizations to amalgamate, restructure and downsize (Chapter 2) has made organizational careers increasingly problematic (McCann et al., 2010). Many organizations spent the 1950s to the 1970s building structures suitable for traditional organizational careers. However, they found in the 1980s and 1990s that under more competitive business conditions such arrangements could not be maintained. Organizational career journeys are most sustainable long term if the organization is either stable or expanding in an orderly manner.

In many organizations and countries, the disruption to the workforce caused by restructuring has fractured the careers of many employees, left promises of long-term employment in ruins and reduced the level of employer–employee trust – an essential factor in organizational careers (Van Buren, 2003). In 'journey' terms, employees' career paths were bulldozed out of existence. In consequence, they had to pick themselves up and start a quite different journey. Overall, although some people continue to have successful organizational careers (Clarke, 2013; Gunz et al., 2002), and in some countries and companies 'the firm's career management practices still mark the careers of employees [and] serve as benchmarks for making sense of career' (Dany, 2003: 821), it is apparent that total reliance on a single job or organization for continuation of one's entire career journey may be increasingly problematic.

Boundaryless Careers

Occupational and organizational careers have in common the notion of *boundaries* within which careers are conducted. The terrain in which career journeys are traveled – the 'field' (Chapter 2) – has lots of boundaries: even within occupations and organizations, there are, for example, status and specialization boundaries for career actors to cross. And, in addition to organizational and occupational boundaries, there are job, industry, employment status (e.g. employed versus self-employed), geographical and international boundaries, not to mention the boundary between work and home. In the 1990s, new forms of career journey began to be talked about: careers that crossed boundaries rather than being confined by them and which therefore provided greater mobility and flexibility than either of the 'traditional' career forms.

This revolution in career concepts has been well summarized as follows:

In the 1990s observers noticed a radical shift in organizations' structure and processes in response to the environmental changes of increased competition, globalisation and improved technologies. New organizational strategies, policies and practices emerged which profoundly affected the expectations and career behavior of individuals. The challenge to traditional views of career unsettled the seemingly perfect and constructive relationship between organizations and careers. Individuals were tasked with taking charge and assuming personal responsibility for their careers and their employment settings and new career theories such as the boundaryless career … emerged to explain new phenomena. (EGOS, 2008)

A *boundaryless career* – which might more accurately be called a boundary-*crossing* career (Chen et al., 2011a; Sullivan, 1999) – is one that is not confined to a single employment setting but takes place in a number of settings through the individual's crossing of boundaries and associated barriers (Arthur & Rousseau, 1996). As the 'field' (Chapter 2) becomes less stable and clear, career boundaries become more permeable and career actors become more able and willing, in their career journeys, to cross them. An important element of the boundaryless career is the implicit responsibility it places on people for their own career choices and career development.

Arthur and Rousseau (1996) stated, in particular, that the boundaryless career is 'the opposite of the organizational career' (p. 5) – that is, it is *inter*-organizational. But it may cross other boundaries as well and is clearly predicated on a boundaryless attitude by the person concerned. Boundaryless careers therefore have a subjective as well as an objective side (Briscoe et al., 2006). People in boundaryless careers have career goals, expertise and networks that go beyond their current employer, and they can therefore build their careers across a range of settings. Examples include research and development careers in the semiconductor industry of Silicon Valley (Saxenian, 1996) and creative careers in the film industry (Jones, 1996), with a basis in temporary and 'project' structures, to which boundaryless careers seem especially well suited.

Proponents of boundaryless careers argue that this career form has come, relatively suddenly, to dominate the careers landscape. Thus, 'managers and professionals are switching jobs at an ever-increasing pace' (Forret & Sullivan, 2002: 245), 'boundaryless careers have become predominant' (Banai & Harry, 2004: 98) and we now live in 'the era of boundaryless careers' (Eby et al., 2003: 689). In addition, boundaryless careers are often portrayed as desirable, with images of talented men and women, liberated from the crushing constraints of organizational life, moving freely and autonomously between exciting opportunities for them to develop ever-more interesting and prosperous careers.

The boundaryless career type provides us with a model of career development that appears to have some advantages over traditional occupational or organizational models. In a changing environment, it encourages mobility, flexibility, the development of currently valued knowledge and the taking of responsibility for one's own career. And there is evidence that it is associated with career success and marketability, both inside and outside the organization (Eby et al., 2003). Boundaryless careers theory and research have therefore responded well to recent contextual changes (Chapter 2) and have countered a preoccupation with 'organizational' careers. The focus, in boundary-less careers, on individual agency in careers has provided an important counter to the common characterization of organizational members as inert 'human resources' (Inkson, 2008). In an authoritative review of career studies, Sullivan and Baruch (2009) therefore advocate major extensions to boundaryless careers research.

Nevertheless, the authors of this book are among many who have been critical of contemporary boundaryless careers writing (Arnold & Cohen, 2008; Inkson, 2006; Inkson et al., 2012). For example, the concept is not well defined (Feldman & Ng, 2007). In particular, boundaryless career proponents focus almost exclusively on the crossing of boundaries between organizations, but it is not clear why these boundaries should be considered more important than, say, occupational, industry or geographi-cal boundaries (Inkson, 2006).

Have careers suddenly switched, as boundaryless career proponents suggest, from being mainly organizational to being mainly boundaryless? Are boundaryless careers now, as the quotes above suggest, predominant? Official statistics indicate that the average organizational tenure in Western countries is about ten years (Rodrigues & Guest, 2010), while in the USA, over half of all men ending their career had been with their current employer for over 20 years (Stevens, 2005). More recent figures published by the OECD (2013) confirm that the majority of workers in OECD countries remain in their jobs for over 10 years. These studies found little change in statistics in recent times. There isn't much evidence there of a sudden change to boundaryless careers. There is, however, substantial evidence that in Western countries young career actors, in stark contrast to the middle-aged, change organizations on average every two years or so (OECD, 2013). Many careers therefore seem to start out boundaryless and become progressively more stable.

In addition, a number of studies have indicated that even in professional occupations where one might expect boundaryless careers to be multiplying, there are substantial groups of workers who, for whatever reason, have been able to maintain their commit-ments to specific organizations over long periods (e.g. Arnold et al., 2006; Donnelly, 2008; Duberley & Cohen, 2009; Ituma & Simpson, 2009). Finally, comparing the job transitions, in Austria, of two groups of MBA graduates, from the 1970s and 1990s respectively, Chudzikowski (2012) found only modest changes towards the kind of inter-organizational mobility characteristic of boundaryless careers, and concluded that career mobility within organizations was still predominant and had much to commend it in terms of career progress. Vinkenburg and Weber (2012: 592) have concluded from a review of studies of the career mobility of managers that 'upward mobility is still the norm'.

Another criticism of the boundaryless career is that in focusing primarily on indi-vidual agency determinants of career, it neglects potential contextual influences. 'The emphasis on "free agency" can discredit a legitimate role for institutions' (Arthur, 2008: 173). Zeitz et al. (2008) suggested that the individualism bias in the boundaryless career model causes underestimation of the institutional resources (e.g. career counseling, socioeconomic support, skill certification, labor market assistance) on which boundaryless career actors must call.

Stop and Consider

Outline the benefits and the drawbacks of organizational and occupational careers, and boundaryless careers. Which of these forms is most attractive to you, and why?

International Careers

Careers are becoming more international. Consider the career of Joanna Grabowski, aged 33.

CASE STUDY

Itchy Feet

Joanna was born in Poland, but her parents moved to Germany when she was 9. Through her childhood, adolescence and university studies, she was able to travel extensively as a tourist. She visited many countries and developed a keen desire to live in different places.

Joanna was educated at the University of Bochum, in Germany, where she gained a BA degree in Political Science and English, and also studied Slavic languages (Polish and Czech). She was able to obtain a scholarship to study for six months within her degree at the University of Missouri in Kansas City, USA. She then, 'just to be able to be abroad', studied for a two-year master's degree at Aaarhus University in Denmark, choosing Aaarhus because she was able to complete her studies in English (though she also learned Danish at the time). Throughout her studies, Joanna part-supported herself by obtaining casual administrative work with local employers.

(Continued)

(Continued)

At the end of Joanna's studies, she went to visit her sister, who had moved to Chicago, and worked for several months there in an administrative position in a local law firm. She then obtained a temporary position – which lasted nine months – with the Goethe Institute in Los Angeles. She also applied for an overseas position with the German Chamber of Industry and Commerce, which had offices all round the world. She missed out on a position in her first-choice country, Canada, but was offered one in her second choice, New Zealand, and traveled there at the age of 29.

She worked for the Chamber in Auckland on a six-month contract and also found a second job working on a project for the Austrian Trade Commissioner. When her contracts were finished, she found work with a local consulting company on a specific project for the Defence Forces, also supporting her boss's wife on another contract. When these projects were completed, she spent two months working as a nanny for two Auckland families. Then, still enjoying living in New Zealand and finding the beaches and relaxed lifestyle a positive contrast with Germany, she sought a more secure position and obtained one as an administrator at The University of Auckland Business School.

Having decided to serve the five-year qualifying period for New Zealand residency, Joanna has stuck with her present job for three years, and has been in her present country for four. She describes her present situation as like 'living in a warm nest'. But there is still a lot of the world to see, and she is still intrigued by the possibility, once her New Zealand residency is obtained, of living and working in Canada. She also recognizes that for all her travel, and her excellent skills in administration, organization and computer systems, and the five languages she speaks fluently, she has been doing the same level of work for a number of years – perhaps a penalty for her mobility – and may need to set higher ambitions.

Joanna's career has so far been driven by an intense desire to 'see the world'. While she might have done better in terms of conventional measures of career success to have stayed in Germany and sought to climb a conventional occupational or organizational career ladder, she has decided that for at least her early career, traveling and experiencing life abroad are more important. She has good qualifications and portable and versatile skills, and will most likely be able to find a job wherever she chooses.

More and more, today's career actors from developed countries have both the wish, and the opportunity, to be able to pursue careers across countries other than their own. Some commentators (Cerdin & Le Pagneux, 2010; Suutari & Taka, 2004) indeed argue that it has become a necessity to add a new career anchor – 'internationalism' – to those described by Schein (1993; Chapter 6). How has this come about?

In the process of globalization, conventional organizational forms are giving way to strategic alliances with other firms, affecting the career locations of millions of people (Thomas, 2002). New multinational companies retain control and disseminate expertise by transferring employees to subsidiaries in foreign settings (McNulty & Inkson, 2013). Countries solve labor shortages and build their reservoirs of talent and expertise by opening their borders to immigrants with suitable backgrounds, creating 'brain drains' of talent journeying toward better opportunities (e.g. Beine & Docquier, 2001). Political refugees seek a better life abroad. Young people from developed countries seek new cultural experiences involving employment (Inkson & Myers, 2003). Business travel multiplies. Increasingly, career journeys take us across international boundaries. Increasingly, careers are global (Thomas et al., 2005) and national boundaries become matters of indifference to global career travelers (Dickmann & Baruch, 2011).

International career journeys involve three types of travel: permanent migration, expatriate assignments (EAs) and self-initiated experiences (SiEs).

Permanent migrants travel overseas with the intention of settling in a new country. Frequently, they encounter cultural difference, discrimination, lack of recognition of their qualifications and career disruption because their skills go unrecognized in their new country (Mahroum, 2000). Acculturation processes are necessary to enable them to adapt to their new situation (Berry, 2001). Not all migrants remain in the country to which they first migrate.

EAs are organized by multinational organizations as a means of managing far-flung subsidiaries and developing their staff internationally (Farndale et al., 2010). This type of travel is mainly restricted to the professional and managerial staff of large multinationals, but is nonetheless mushrooming (Brookfield, 2012). The large research literature on EAs, as opposed to that on SiEs, tends to see them as an exercise in career management by the organization rather than career self-development by the expatriate (Collings et al., 2011).

SiEs are working experiences abroad initiated by the individual, usually for purposes of broadening cultural experiences rather than for career advancement, although SiEs may nevertheless have career benefits (Doherty et al., 2013; Inkson et al., 1997; Varma et al., 2011). More generally, many professional people initiate employment overseas as part of their normal career development (Suutari & Brewster, 2000; Vance, 2005).

There are signs that these three types are becoming increasingly indistinguishable from each other. For example, there are increasing indications that even those going overseas on EAs, ostensibly in the service of their multinational employers, are largely driven by their own, personal, career goals (SiEs), which are likely in due course to induce them to move beyond the current organization (Altman & Baruch, 2012; Dickmann & Doherty, 2008) McNulty & Inkson, 2013). Increasingly, international career travelers come to see themselves as global citizens or citizens of the world, who have no firm national identity and will pursue their lives and careers wherever the best opportunities are in terms of their priorities. They do so in pursuit of a range of goals – economic security, political freedom, a certain lifestyle, cultural betterment, career improvement and prospects for family members (Carr et al., 2005).

A career skill or resource relevant to all who pursue international careers is *cultural intelligence* – the ability to be sensitive to, and to respond to, the vast cultural differences that exist between the many countries and societies that one may encounter around the world. Cultural intelligence requires skills of observation and sensititvity, respect for others who are different, and adaptability to respond appropriately to cultural difference. Early and Ang (2003) and Thomas and Inkson (2009) provide guides to cultural intelligence.

Marginal Careers

The boundaryless career concept has been criticized as being mostly advantageous for those also privileged in traditional career settings (i.e. highly motivated, highly skilled white-collar employees) (Buzzanell & Goldzwig, 1991; Van Buren, 2003). Accounts of boundaryless careers provide images of talented people, liberated from organizational constraints and insecurities, moving autonomously between exciting opportunities for further career development. Thus, boundaryless career actors are perceived to be 'mobile, self-determined, employer independent, and free of hierarchy … free agents who are able to seamlessly connect with work in multiple contexts' (Harrison, 2006: 20).

This 'glamorous' side of boundaryless careers may however divert attention from the deprivation and marginalization of a large section of the workforce – those with low status in terms of background, gender and skills. These people may seem boundaryless, or at least highly mobile between jobs and organizations, but they may be bound instead by the crushing structural constraints mentioned in Chapter 2.

By making individuals totally responsible for their careers and by applying market forces logic at the level of the individual, boundaryless careers theory and discourse arguably assist those with skills in demand only at the expense of those on the margins of the workforce (Pringle & Mallon, 2003). This may also have hidden penalties for organizations, as employees adopt a consumerist career mentality, reducing organizations to tools merely there to help equip them with the resources they need to develop their personal projects and inter-organizational careers (Inkson, 2008).

Many people whose careers appear boundaryless travel on the margins of employment, apparently unable to get a secure enough footing to make much progress on their journey. If you are a female doing occasional sewing work on contract, with minimum job security, at minimum wage, for whichever local company needs it at the time to fulfil a short-term order, it may be little consolation to know that you have a boundaryless career. Marginal journeys are typically experienced by such groups as low-level workers in the catering industry, seasonal workers such as fruit pickers and the long-term unemployed.

Thus, although the careers literature tends to promote the universality and the benefits of boundaryless careers, its discourse has also been said to serve the needs of the present-day 'ruthless economy' in that it enables organizations to be rid more elegantly of as many permanent workers (and their associated costs) as needed (Van Buren, 2003). It appears that while the original goal of boundaryless career theory was to free career actors from the dogmas of the traditional organizational career, it has created, or at least promoted, new, neo-liberal ideological dogmas instead (Roper et al., 2010).

Stop and Consider

How do you respond to the issue of marginal careers? Who should do what about them?

Knowledge Journeys

Few people nowadays have full-blown occupational or organizational careers, or careers that are constantly boundaryless or marginal. Most have mixed careers – career journeys linked together in a series of episodes such that we cannot describe them as being of any single type. A career typically involves periods of years or even decades with an occupational or organizational focus, as well as times in flight from, or attraction to, particular organizations, occupations, roles, industries and locations, followed by consequent boundary-crossing as the career actor moves on. How do we explain such changes? Career studies should not just be about career types, but also about the multiplicity of processes, including, for example, boundary construction, boundary acceptance, boundary celebration, boundary defence and boundary shifting, that take place, along with boundary crossing, at one time or another in most careers (Inkson et al., 2012). Career studies is currently dominated too much by stereotypes and slogans, and we need to consider every career as both more complex and more unique than these stereotypes make them seem.

One way of thinking about career journeys is the notion of a 'knowledge journey', in which what is important is not the places traveled but the knowledge acquired in traveling. In a memorable metaphor, Bird (1996) described careers as repositories of knowledge, with much of the knowledge being tacit (Polanyi, 1966), experience based and internalized. Career journeys can thus create a key resource for individuals as they progress, a resource that can be exploited by their employers or by the individuals themselves. Perhaps a good traveler will always ask the questions, at each possible stage along the way, 'What will I learn from this and how valuable will the knowledge be?

What unique combination of competencies is my journey giving me?' Here, acquiring knowledge that will ensure not so much short-term employment but long-term 'employability' (Hogan et al., 2013) may be key.

Modern societies are mobile, and if there are key principles that provide careers with their patterns, they may be more subtle than the observable ideas of occupational and organizational membership. Elements in our personal makeup, such as our values or career anchors (Chapter 6), may give us the stability that we need in a rapidly changing scene, but also allow us plenty of scope in our expression of them. Increasingly, as we show in Chapter 10, the 'journey' metaphor may be superseded by the metaphor of career as a repository of personal knowledge capital, with our journeying being only a means to the accumulation of such resources to ensure, in the long term, happy and productive careers.

Journey Interruptions

Some career actors pursue successful careers for a time, then find themselves 'on the scrapheap' through redundancy or illness. Given current and likely future levels of unemployment, and the continuing restructuring of the workforce towards insecure forms of employment, it is likely that many of the readers of this book will at some point in their careers find themselves in the situation of desperately wishing to continue those careers when there is no work available for them. This is where career journeys often come, not just to a standstill, but to a crisis, as society's prejudices about the unemployed sap the morale of career travelers. In journey terms, it is like being thrown off your train at a station where, although there are trains traveling in all directions, all of them are full up, other passengers and even the station's staff seem hostile and there is no indication of whether your delay will be for a few days, a few weeks, a few years or the rest of your life. The following is the account of Jeremy Messenger, an unemployed man from the UK.

CASE STUDY

Counting for Nothing

I have now lived through 683 days of redundancy, each one against my embattled will. Like 26 million people across the EU, I long, desperately, to fall asleep with the contentment and exhaustion of a full and productive day.

My time is spent writing application after application, repeating the same information in different words. A wearisome and unproductive task: it is rare to receive an acknowledgment, let alone an invite to interview. I lead a life without achievement. In fact, my life is quite the opposite: a life waiting to begin again – a waste.

Finding myself unemployed, I am no longer immune to the aggressive and hateful propaganda that is pitched against people in my situation. Regardless of our employment histories and efforts to find work, we are labelled scroungers and treated with contempt. Many people treat me with an air of superiority while others, some friends and relatives included, doubt me.

The job centre and my work program provider (WPP) have become significant in my life, yet I only attend the former fortnightly and the latter monthly to prove, in both cases, that I am searching for work. It hangs over me daily that if I make a mistake, I stand to lose the £111.45 a week that my partner and I rely on to survive. I have now reached a point where I wonder what the purpose of the job centre and WPPs is.

The pitch is that these places are here to help jobseekers. For example, my WPP calls their advisers 'tutors'. These tutors lead mandatory group workshops, covering material such as communication, motivation and personal hygiene. We are treated as though we have never been employed or lived in the outside world. In reality, we are an educated bunch and many were previously highly paid professionals – a very different picture of the unemployed to the one most often projected.

Being 'redundant' (a word that both the job centre and WPP avoid but imply; for example, I've been told that 'unemployed you're no good to man nor fowl'), I provide no function or meaning in the world because I do not perform a role for someone else, I do not produce profit. Even voluntary work does not shake this idea – paid work is key. Those that employ us define who we are.

Likewise, the role of the job centre and WPPs is to impose a hierarchy. And they achieve this with efficiency. During short and intermittent meetings with jobseekers, they check that the person's time has been used in a particular way, they belittle and bully, backed up with threats of hunger and homelessness. The unemployed are left blind to their own potentials and the potential of the world.

Source: excerpt from an article by Jeremy Messenger, *The Guardian*, 9 January 2013, at: www.theguardian.co.uk/commentisfree/2013/jan/09/redundancy-life-wasted-threat. Published by permission of Jeremy Messenger and *The Guardian*.

Although there are ways of preparing oneself for redundancy that facilitate re-starting a career (Gardiner et al., 2009), such catastrophes may be unavoidable.

Conclusion

If our careers are indeed journeys, we all need to give some thought to what sort of journey they are likely to be, whether that is what we truly want and how we can best prepare to travel. The 'journey' metaphor enables us to tease out some characteristics of many careers in terms of the routes traveled and to show some main types. But overall, we are left with the impression of immense variety in the routes that individual people choose, or are forced, to follow.

It seems that much of the terrain over which career journeys must be traveled is rough, uncertain and unexplored. Under such circumstances, much travel must be improvisational. Success is defined not just by the outcome of 'getting there', but also by the experience and knowledge gained from travel.

Industrial society had industrial careers, organizational society had organizational careers, professionalization encouraged professional careers, and these careers provided stability and development to both the employees who lived them and to the institutions that sponsored them. Post-industrial society will have post-industrial careers, and the career actors will travel them:

> The life of men and women of our time is very much like that of tourists-through-time: they cannot and will not decide in advance what places they will visit and what the sequence of stations will be; what they know for sure is that they will keep on the move, never sure whether the place they have reached is their final destination (Bauman, 1995: 268–269).

In the world of the new careers, no job is a permanent home for world-weary travelers or even a long-term guest house for visitors. These images are too static for the new realities. If the word *journey* implies destination, then perhaps careers are not journeys at all. Perhaps they are, purely and simply, travel.

Key Points in this Chapter

- People commonly use the metaphor of 'journey' to describe their career, but there are many different kinds of journey, in terms of destination, speed, ground covered, and so on.
- Notions of destination (e.g. 'getting to the top'), topography (e.g. gradients and barriers) and career maps may usefully be applied to career journeys.
- Careers may be classified into different types. Occupational careers take place within occupational boundaries but must be revitalized by appropriate knowledge. Organizational careers usually involve upward movement but are sometimes put at risk by restructuring.
- Boundaryless careers involve the crossing of occupational, organizational, industry, work–home and other boundaries. They are attractive to those in possession of scarce skills who are prepared to be mobile.
- Some careers, particularly of the unskilled, are marginal because they are based on casual, occasional and otherwise insecure work.

- An increasing trend, driven by globalization, overseas assignment, self-initiated travel and permanent migration, is for career journeys to cross international boundaries.
- Most people follow careers that, looked at in their totality, are not of any one type but involve elements from all types, and in which the knowledge acquired on the journey may be more important than the places visited.

Questions from this Chapter

General Questions

1. Which is more important to you in your career – the destinations you reach or the experiences you have in getting there? Can you justify your answer?
2. Find out about the careers of some members of the prior generations of your family. In terms of the various types of career described in this chapter, what types did these relatives have?
3. Are you aware of career boundaries that you experience now or may experience in the future? If so, what are they and how strong do they feel? How do you feel about crossing them?
4. If you believed that in pursuing a career journey, acquiring knowledge was the most important consideration, how would this affect the route that you might travel?

'Live Career Case' Study Questions

1. Consider your case study career as a journey. To what extent does it show the characteristics of predetermined pathways, destination and direction, knowledge expeditions and movement into management? Were there maps? Can you describe some of the terrain and topography traveled through or any climbing frames involved?
2. Consider the various types of career boundaries listed in this chapter. Which ones did your case person cross and which did they stay inside? With the benefit of hindsight, how does your case person feel about these boundaries now?

Additional Resources

Recommended Further Reading

Arnold, J. and Cohen, L. (2008) 'The psychology of careers in industrial-organizational settings: A critical but appreciative analysis', in G. P. Hodgkinson and J. K. Ford (eds.), *International Review of Industrial-Organizational Psychology*, 23: 1–44.
Clarke, M. (2013) 'The organizational career: Not dead but in need of redefinition', *International Journal of Human Resource Management*, 24: 684–703.

Feldman, D. C. and Ng, T. W. H. (2007) 'Careers, mobility, embeddedness and success', *Journal of Management*, 33: 350–377.

Inkson, K., Gunz, H., Ganesh, S. and Roper, J. (2012) 'Boundaryless careers: Bringing back boundaries', *Organization Studies*, 33: 323–340.

Vance, C. M. (2005) 'The quest for building global competence: A taxonomy of self-initiating career path strategies for gaining business experience abroad', *Journal of World Business*, 40(4): 374–385.

Self-Assessment Resources

Assess your cultural intelligence: Ang, S., Van Dyne, L., Koh, C., Ng, K. Y., Templer, K. J., Tay, C. and Chandrasekar, N. A. (2007) 'Cultural intelligence: Its measurement and effects on cultural judgment and decision making, cultural adaptation and task performance', *Management and Organization Review*, 3(3): 335–371.

Assess your motivation to lead: Chan, K. Y. and Drasgow, F. (2001) 'Toward a theory of individual differences and leadership: Understanding the motivation to lead', *Journal of Applied Psychology*, 86(3): 481.

Assess your willingness to accept mobility opportunities: Noe, R. A. and Barber, A. E. (1993) Willingness to accept mobility opportunities: Destination makes a difference', *Journal of Organizational Behavior*, 14(2): 159–175.

Assess your propensity for entrepreneurship: Carter, N. M., Gartner, W. B., Shaver, K. G. and Gatewood, E. J. (2003) 'The career reasons of nascent entrepreneurs', *Journal of Business Venturing*, 18(1): 13–39.

Online Resources

On the sense and nonsense of following your passion – see the YouTube video entitled 'Follow your passion is wrong: Cal Newport speaks at World Domination Summit 2012', posted by Dennis Decoene: www.youtube.com/watch?v=LUQjAAwsKR8

Do you view your career as a journey or a destination? See: http://blog.learningbyshipping.com/2013/03/28/defining-your-career-path-journey-or-destination/ (includes a link to a survey at the end)

Your career journey (a series of self-assessments) – see: https://careers.asbgroup.co.nz/career-journey/intro;jsessionid=87C7F869EF9EA88E9DC5B14F3A2DD6DB

Careers as Roles

8

Chapter Objectives

The objectives of this chapter are:

- to consider careers as a series of transitions between roles, both inside and outside of the work domain
- to describe a model of four stages people typically go through during role transitions
- to consider the different levels of identity that affect the roles people experience throughout their careers: personal identity, social identity and, more specifically, the potential self, the ideal self, the feared self, the ought-to-self, the reflected best-self and the alternative self
- to introduce the subject of reference groups and role models in relation to careers
- to understand the different potential sources of role conflict, for instance imbalances between work and private life, and to list some of the individual and organizational strategies through which role conflict can be resolved.

CASE STUDY

More than Meets the Eye

Actress, film director, screenwriter, model, human rights activist, breast cancer awareness spokesperson, wife, mother of six. It appears there is more to Angelina Jolie than meets the eye.

Born in Los Angeles, California, as the daughter of two actors (Jon Voight and Marcheline Bertrand), Jolie's choice to pursue an acting career was perhaps not so surprising, but some of her other life choices were. In her youth, she was mostly known for her antics, such as wearing the blood of her then-husband Billy Bob Thornton in a bottle around her neck and giving interviews about how much she loved her brother that were so 'weird' that the media made inappropriate remarks about their bond. In recent years, however, she has become one of the most respected people in Hollywood, and a role model to many. One of the most notable things about Angelina Jolie is the number of roles she seems to juggle in her life and career.

In her acting career, Jolie has mostly played female action heroes – most famously, the video-game character Lara Croft – due to her 'dark' and 'tough' image, which made it difficult for her to land female lead roles in her early career. Her on-camera roles are in stark contrast, however, to the non-acting roles she plays.

In 2002, after traveling to Cambodia for humanitarian work and while she was still married to Billy Bob Thornton, Jolie adopted her first child, a boy, Maddox – only to find herself a single mother three months later. In 2005, she met Brad Pitt on the set of their movie *Mr and Mrs Smith*. Soon after, Jolie and Pitt adopted a second child and Pitt also adopted Maddox. Between 2005 and 2008, they adopted one more child, and Jolie gave birth to a daughter and to a pair of twins. With their six children, Jolie and Pitt form one of the largest famous families in Hollywood. In interviews, they often gush about their family and say that family is the most important thing in life.

In addition to being an actress, the partner of one of the most famous actors in the world, and a mother of six children, Jolie has recently got into screenwriting and directing. Outside of her acting, however, she is best known for her humanitarian work. For more than a decade, Jolie has been a UNHCR (United Nations High Commissioner for Refugees) Goodwill Ambassador, and in 2012 she was promoted to be a Special Envoy to High Commissioner António Guterres, a role that involves diplomatic responsibilities. In 2003, she wrote a book and produced a documentary about the horrors she witnessed in refugee camps around the world. She is an important donor to charities.

In 2013, Angelina Jolie published an op-ed in the New York Times stating that she had undergone a double mastectomy to prevent cancer, the disease that killed both her mother and her grandmother. Promptly, TIME put her on their cover, reporting that her decision to have a preventive mastectomy had had a noticeable and immediate influence on thousands of women worldwide faced by similar difficult medical choices. They dubbed Jolie's impact on breast cancer awareness 'the Angelina effect'. Dr. Anne McTiernan, director of the Prevention Center at the Fred Hutchinson Cancer Research Center, has been quoted as saying: 'There's been a ripple effect globally. I've traveled to the Philippines and China and Vietnam and it's all over. I saw vendors promoting cancer genetic testing at an oncology meeting in China and they had big pictures of Angelina Jolie in their booths. Before, I would introduce the concept of genetic testing and counseling and the importance of family history but now, they're generating it. People get it.'

Today, Jolie is one of the best-known celebrities in the world. In a 2006 survey in 42 countries, Jolie, together with Pitt, was found to be the favorite celebrity endorser of brands and products worldwide. She was the face of St John and Shiseido from 2006 to 2008, and in 2011 had an endorsement deal with Louis Vuitton, reportedly worth $10 million, a record for a single advertising campaign. She has been among the Time 100 – a list of the most influential people in the world. Forbes named her Hollywood's highest-paid actress in 2009, 2011 and 2013, with estimated annual earnings of $27–$33 million, and in 2009 she topped the magazine's Celebrity 100, which is a ranking of the world's most powerful celebrities.

Careers such as Angelina Jolie's fill us with awe. How can one woman excel at so many things? One way of understanding Jolie's career is to see it as a set of different roles. According to the *Concise Oxford Dictionary* (Stevenson & Waite, 2011), a *role* is:

1. 'A person's or thing's characteristic or expected function'; or
2. 'An actor's part in a play, film, etc.'.

In terms of the first of these definitions, Jolie plays a wide range of roles, some consecutively, others simultaneously. In terms of the second definition, she is indeed a professional actress, and within her acting career she has played hundreds of discrete roles. She appears to move from role to role effortlessly yet without abandoning her key values: in this sense, her career is protean (see Chapter 5).

Several aspects of Jolie's case however warrant critical reflection. On the one hand, her life is by no means comparable to that of the average person. Being a wealthy superstar, she has a team of people surrounding her to support her both in her work (e.g. a booking agent, a manager, a team of accountants, an acting coach) and her non-work roles (e.g. a team of nannies, a cook, a personal trainer, a driver). On the other hand, Jolie is just one woman. Even with all the extra support she has available, she appears to be more multiply committed than most. Without a doubt, this creates stresses and strains on her relationship, her family and herself. (The tabloids periodically report on the 'separation' between Jolie and Pitt due to their never-at-home lifestyles.) It might even be argued that her decision to have a double mastectomy and talk about it publicly may have been even harder for her than for others less wealthy, due to its potentially large impact on her identity, both in her own perception and that of others, as a 'sexy actress'.

Jolie's life contains one of the great riddles of career: role versus self – playing a part versus being oneself. On the one hand, Jolie's actions are dictated by the life roles and acting roles in which she finds herself. When she is on camera, for example, she might bring a personal interpretation to her role, but basically, like any actor, she has to say the words that the writer has written and follow the instructions that the director has provided. When she is being a wife, a mother, a daughter or a human rights advocate, others expect her to behave in ways appropriate to those diverse roles. Yet Jolie is a unique human being with specific physical features, abilities, dispositions, attitudes and interests. Whatever role she is playing, she applies herself and her own values and dispositions consistently to her life, always knowing who she is and maintaining a steely determination and ideals of self-sufficiency. In short, no matter what role she is playing, she remains herself – Angelina Jolie.

All of us, to some extent, in life and in career, face the problem of remaining ourselves while discharging roles to the satisfaction of others. Careers demand that we play multiple roles, which are not always compatible with each other and which may threaten our sense of who we are.

Roles and Society

As mentioned in Chapter 1, an early model of the social framing of careers through social roles, identity and associated mechanisms came from a group of scholars at the University of Chicago, School of Sociology, working in association with Everett Hughes (1937, 1958). An excellent review of the work of this group is provided by Barley (1989).

In 1937, Hughes wrote:

> A career consists, objectively, of a series of statuses and clearly defined offices ... Careers in our society are thought very much in terms of jobs, for these are the characteristic and crucial connections of the individual with the institutional structure. But the career is by no means exhausted in a series of business and professional achievements. There are other points at which one's life touches the social order. (p. 413)

The idea of 'statuses and clearly defined offices' indicates the importance of roles in this view of careers. The work of the Chicago School embedded the notion of career in a range of theories also concerned with self and identity (individual-level constructs) and with organizations and institutions (collective constructs), with role providing a key link. In noting that careers extend beyond the work sphere and that it is possible, for example, to talk about the 'career' of a hospital patient (Roth, 1963), these sociologists were perhaps ahead of their time.

To a considerable extent, roles are representations of the social structures and institutions referred to in Chapter 2. They bring us face to face with the reality that organizations, groups and other individuals have an interest in our careers and express that interest by trying to define our roles for us. Many jobs are defined, for example, by formal job descriptions, standard rules and procedures, organization charts, authority relationships and the like, so that a career, looked at from that perspective, could be regarded as little more than a sequence of formal roles defined for career actors by the organizations they work in. In practice, as we shall see, career actors normally put their own stamp on the jobs they do.

We need to recognize the following facts:

- Each job involves multiple roles, and these change over time.
- Our roles are defined by us, by others, by the organizations in which we work and by the social institutions in which our careers are embedded.
- The work career is affected by non-work roles.
- Maintaining and developing our identity through this plethora of roles and role changes are major career tasks.

Roles and Identity

Identity represents one's sense of individuality and personality – who one is. It is important because it provides values and gives a sense of direction. Defining who we are enables us to ascribe new meanings to our lives: for example, 'I am a medical student', 'I am a doctor', 'I am a heart surgeon' and also 'I am a totally honest person', 'I am a go-getter', 'I am a Muslim'. Regardless of what job descriptions and company norms say, most individuals inject their own identity into the situation by 'being themselves' to a greater or lesser extent, and by taking on roles in which they can express that identity, such as leader, joker, workaholic or, indeed, greaser, dictator or petty bureaucrat.

Many career theories include a concept such as identity to represent the basis for individuals to choose and enact their roles. For example, Super's (1990) career development theory (Chapter 4) talks about career as the implementation of a self-concept, and Ibarra and Barbulescu (2010) discuss how people convey who they are to others using 'narrative identity work' – i.e. social efforts to craft stories about themselves that feed into how they want to be perceived. Hall (2002) referred to the *career sub-identity* as a component of a broader identity and regarded this identity as 'an internal compass ... in the midst of all the turbulence' (p. 32). In Chapter 11, we develop the idea that identity is a key element in the stories we tell about our careers.

We derive our identity partly from the roles we enact, but correspondingly those roles are often chosen on the basis of identity and provide the opportunity for further identity development.

Possible Selves and the 'Reflected Best Self'

People often find it quite difficult to come up with a personal statement of who they are and what they stand for. The literature on identity offers some insights into how one might go about dissecting one's identity, in relation both to career and to life in general. One starting point might be to describe yourself (preferably in writing) from different angles, called 'possible selves' in the literature, making the descriptions as vivid as possible!

- Potential self: What type of person do you think you might become?
- Ideal self: What type of person would you most like to become?
- Feared self: What type of person are you afraid of becoming?
- Ought-to-self: What type of person do you feel you should become because of pressures or expectations in your environment?
- Alternative self: What type of person could you have been today if certain things had happened differently in the past?

Another approach is to conduct an investigation into yourself based on input from others, resulting in a 'reflected best-self-portrait' (RBS). In the RBS exercise, you ask 10 to 20 people who know you well professionally and/or personally to send you some input on the following questions: '(a) Please describe me in two words; (b) What are two of my personal strengths? How do you see those manifesting in my life? (c) What two personal challenges, weaknesses or pieces of advice would you like to give me? If applicable, how do you see those manifesting in my life?' After collecting the data, try to assemble a portrait of yourself, preferably in writing, building on the common themes and tensions you see in the data. If you want, you can send this back out to the people who provided the input as a way of 'validating' your findings about yourself!

Source: Markus & Nurius (1986); Obodaru (2012); Plimmer & Schmidt (2007); Roberts et al. (2005).

Social Identity

Identity theory proposes that identity develops through taking up certain roles, developing within these roles and fulfilling the expectations that accompany them.

Identification with a role and the expectations it carries demands interaction with others to enable us to understand the role's expectations fully and to enable us to make corrections when we do not fulfil them. Note that although identity is individual, it is often derived from reference groups that provide rules, role models and even a language for understanding it. Thus, identity and role can become very close to each other. Faced with a role change or career change – for example, the opportunity of writing and directing her own films – Angelina Jolie would have to consider whether this new role would be compatible with her actress-humanitarian identity and either decline the role, seek to change the role in line with her identity, alter her identity to suit the role or live with the incongruence of the two. Many career decisions represent triumphs of identity over role, notably when someone leaves a job because the duties required by the role are incompatible with the person's core values.

An important tension is that between the need to be distinctive and the need to belong to a group. It is generally assumed that *personal identity* fuels individual agency and with that it possibly also activates group- or role-based sub-identities, while *social identity* creates structural constraints on behavior (Grote & Hall, 2013).

This discussion of identity and role echoes some of the considerations in the 'fit' metaphor (Chapter 6). Having to practice role behavior that is inconsistent with one's identity results in stress. An example is the expectation of 'emotional labor' by employees in personal services, such as air cabin crew or call centre personnel, who have to consistently smile and maintain cordial relationships with customers, even though, for all sorts of reasons – some of them personal, some of them related to how they are treated by customers – they may be feeling miserable (Nath, 2011; Wegge et al., 2010; Williams, 2003). In extreme cases, individuals become so preoccupied with their roles that they lose their true identity, for example undercover agents who have trouble reconciling their 'true self' with their undercover persona (Girodo et al., 2002), rogue Wall Street traders who have 'lost themselves' in their pursuit of big money (Krawiec, 2000) or workaholics who have neglected their families and other aspects of their non-work lives (Snir & Harpaz, 2012).

Career Reference Groups

Lawrence (2011) defines a career reference group as 'the set of people an individual perceives as belonging to his or her work environment that defines the social world of work in which he or she engages, including people with whom the individual does and does not communicate and those with whom awareness is the only connection' (p. 266).

According to Grote and Hall (2013), your career reference group will probably consist of three types of people:

1. People you know and interact with directly (such as parents, teachers, colleagues, friends);
2. People you know of, with whom you do not interact personally (such as famous people, role models); and
3. Abstract social categories (such as 'artists', 'successful women').

Your career reference group will probably serve three distinct functions: (a) a *normative* function: offering standards concerning how you should think, feel and act; (b) a *comparative* function: identifying you with certain roles and people and distancing you from the opposite roles and people (e.g. 'being a teacher means being different from students but similar to other teachers'); and (c) a *supportive* function: receiving advice, encouragement or inspiration from your reference group.

Stop and Consider

Map your own personal career reference group on paper or digitally. Who is part of your reference group? Put yourself in the middle of the page and draw three boxes connected to you for the three types of people that might be part of your reference group (those interacted with, those known about, abstract categories of people). Now, enter specific names and categories into the boxes. Which of the three functions of reference groups (normative, comparative, supportive) are associated with which people? To what extent do they have an influence on your career? What roles or identities are they steering you towards or away from?

Role Transitions

If we approach careers as sequences of roles, then an important feature of careers is the process of role transition: 'the psychological (and, where relevant, physical) movement between roles, including disengagement from one role (role exit) and engagement in another (role entry)' (Ashforth et al., 2000: 472). Because new roles require new skills, behaviors, attitudes and interactions, they may produce fundamental changes in an individual's self-concept (Ibarra, 1999). Examples are: entering one's first job, moving between education and employment, being promoted, being laid off, leaving voluntarily to move to another organization, retiring. Work-role transitions also include changes within a present role, where, for example, new duties are added or the nature of the role is altered by reorganization or technology. Most career actors use role transitions as marking points and they often feel life-changing and stressful.

It is difficult to generalize about work-role transitions because the term includes so many different types of change. As seen in Chapter 7, transitions may be made within the current organization or to a new one, at the current level or to a new one, within the current occupation or function or to a new one, or to a new industry or geographical location or even country. Ashforth et al. (2000) describe role transitions as boundary-crossing activities.

Perhaps the most important characteristic of role transitions is whether the change is deliberately sought by the individual or is inadvertent due to some (positive or negative) external circumstance – for example, being promoted, being laid off, fired, demoted or transferred, getting offered a new and exciting project or changing role due to an accident or illness. Alternatively, job changes may be actively sought by individuals as a means of escaping a disliked role, finding more challenging work, changing career direction, gaining higher status or rewards, or addressing family circumstances (Nicholson & West, 1988).

Nicholson (1984) outlines a four-stage process that individuals typically go through in making their transitions. The four stages are preparation, encounter, adjustment and stabilization.

Preparation

In preparation, the change is expected and the career actor seeks to be ready for it. Part of this process is saying goodbye to the role one is leaving, a process often involving the severing of familiar routines and personal ties, which may cause something close to grief (Adams et al., 1976). In terms of looking ahead, expectations – possibly influenced by the 'sales pitch' of a new employer or boss – may be unrealistically optimistic. The onus is on both individual and organization to maximize prior information about each other.

Encounter

This is the initial experience of a new role, in which the career actor encounters and comes to terms with new requirements and expectations. Employers often provide a range of information to assist newcomers – for example, technical information concerning the role, management expectations and organizational norms, as well as feedback on the newcomer's initial performance and behavior (Klein & Weaver, 2000). Sophisticated organizations often employ strong orientation programs, in which the new employee is indoctrinated not only into their own job but also into being a knowledgeable and committed member of the new organization. The range of ways in which individuals learn their new roles and how those new roles fit their new organizations are diverse and include both organization-managed and informal, individual components (Van Maanen & Schein, 1979). Through a combination of formal induction/orientation and informal feedback, people learn what is expected, even if they do not necessarily like it. This process is called socialization and it is an important source of assistance to individuals in their personal career development (De Vos et al., 2003).

Adjustment

In this phase, the individual adapts their behavior and perhaps even identity to accommodate the new role or attempts to enact or alter the role in such a way as to accommodate their own identity and motivation (McArdle et al., 2007). While the term *adjustment* has connotations of emotional well-being, there may be difficulties in store if the individual slips too easily into a role, does not question or change it in any way and continues to remain similarly adjusted forever. Eventually, such a person might be regarded as moribund, to the detriment of both person and organization. There is evidence that strong socialization practices by the organization encourage acceptance of, and commitment to, the organization, but may limit innovative behavior (Ashforth & Saks, 1996). In contrast, the possibility of the individual adjusting the role rather than adjusting *to* the role reminds us that roles are not always fixed and that individuals acting with autonomy may escape potential enslavement by roles (see 'Job crafting' in Chapter 6).

Stabilization

In this phase, the adjustment becomes stable – the individual is in balance with the organization. However, there are many forces that may disturb this state: individual boredom, stagnation or poor performance and organizational change. This stage, of course, may never be reached. Indeed, many of today's employees may well feel that they are so bedevilled by changes to organizational structure and technology that their role never stays stable long enough for them to adjust, let alone stabilize.

Stop and Consider

Identify the different stages of role transition in relation to a transition you have experienced (for instance, from high school to college). How effectively do you think you handled the transition?

The conditions of technological and structural change in today's organizations make role transitions frequent and substantial, even for long-standing employees. For those pursuing boundaryless careers (Chapter 7), major role transitions become part of their lives and are often found to be enjoyable and energizing. It may be that the personality characteristic of flexibility or adaptability is becoming ever-more critical in careers as the sources of transition increase (Ebberwein et al., 2004).

Role Expectations and Role Models

In the definition of *role* provided earlier – 'a person's characteristic or expected function' – the word *function* reminds us that when we discharge a role it is for a purpose, while *expected* tells us that the purpose may be defined by the expectations of others (Dierdorff & Morgeson, 2007). If we were to divide a career into the jobs of which it is composed, each job would have a purpose or function, and many would also have a formal job description. Roles provide guidance as to how to conduct our careers but they also create difficulties. We may not be able, or want, to do the job in the way prescribed or expected by others. Different people involved with our job, such as our boss, colleagues, subordinates, co-workers and customers, and perhaps even family and friends, may have their own, often contradictory, ideas of how we should do the job.

Compounding the problem is the fact that a job is only one of the many roles that job-holders have: other roles, such as parent, partner, relation, spouse, consumer, hobbyist, church member, holder of a second job, and so forth, all provide their own expected behavior, which again may conflict with the job role. There is also the problem of role change – taking up and learning new roles, adapting to roles as they change and relinquishing roles.

One way of understanding roles is to use two subsidiary concepts: role set and role expectations – terms used by Katz and Kahn (1978). A *role set* is a set of other people who attempt to define parts of the role of a *focal person*. For example, if the focal person is an office manager, the role set may consist of the focal person's subordinates, secretary, direct boss, spouse, the manager of an adjacent department and perhaps one or two major customers. Each member of the role set has *role expectations* regarding how the focal person will discharge their role, and communicates these expectations directly and indirectly. From this, the focal person receives a perception of what the required role behavior is and complies or resists in their behavior.

Role expectations are often conveyed through role modelling, which refers to a psychological process in which cognitive skills and patterns of behavior are compared between a 'model' and an observing individual. We tend to model our behavior on that of others who we are attracted to, either because we perceive them as similar or desirable in terms of behavior, goals and status, or as helpful to us in learning new tasks, skills and norms (Gibson, 2004a).

We look for role models because they offer clues as to what role expectations are held, and because having a role model might help us figure out who we are and who we want to become. Typically, we will identify different role models for different aspects of our lives. We might also 'pick and choose' aspects of different role models to combine these into one ideal notion of the type of person we want to become within one specific domain. For instance: 'I want to be a successful athlete like Tiger Woods, but I also want to be a loyal husband and father like my own dad'. Some basis of similarity between a person and their role model is required in order to be able to identify with the role model (e.g. being a woman, coming from a working-class background, being alumni from the same school), but there also needs to be a discrepancy between both parties so as to ensure that the role model is 'aspirational'. Finally, it is also possible for a person to identify negative role models. This type of role model makes us aware of who we don't want to become and how we don't want to act in our lives and our careers. Typically, arrogant bosses, workaholics, frauds and leaders who have fallen from grace serve as negative role models (Gibson, 2004a).

Stop and Consider

Can you identify at least one positive and one negative role model for your career? Who are they? How are they similar to you and how are they different? What qualities of your positive role model do you find inspiring? What qualities of your negative role model do you find off-putting?

Role Conflict

The role expectations of members of a role set lead to various complications for a role member. The expectations may not be clearly defined, leading to role ambiguity. They may conflict with the focal person's personal values, leading to person–role conflict. The expectations of various members of the role set may be different and incompatible, leading to intra-role conflict. Two different roles held by the same person, for example, job-holder and family member, or avid football fan and project leader of an all-consuming project, may get in the way of each other, leading to inter-role conflict. Finally, the sum total of expectations inherent in a particular role may be more than the focal person can handle, leading to role overload. Such difficulties can cause significant stress (Perrewé et al., 2004). Eva's case is an example:

C A S E   S T U D Y

Between a Rock and a Hard Place

Eva is the supervisor of a small department in a 'rag trade' clothing factory. She supervises seven women machinists and performs some machining herself. For years, she has found herself mediating between her subordinate machinists and her boss, Mr Smit, over the role of the machinists. The machinists find their work hard and boring. Several of them are extroverts, and they discharge their energy by gossiping, joking, horse playing and sometimes singing. Mr Smit is a strict disciplinarian who believes that his employees should work every minute of every paid hour and maintain a quiet, productive atmosphere in the factory.

Eva constantly feels as if she has been put 'between a rock and a hard place'. Mr Smit constantly reminds her that it is her job to ensure that the machinists meet his standards. The machinists remind her that she is one of them – she was a machinist herself for 15 years – and that she should stand up for them in the face of Mr Smit's unreasonable expectations. Eva tries to reason with each side, tactfully requesting each try to compromise its attitude a little, but she feels under stress.

Recently, Mr Smit has asked her to institute disciplinary action against the noisiest woman, who is also an old friend of Eva's – action that could lead to the woman's eventual dismissal. Eva recognizes that he has a good case: her friend's behavior has often gone over the top, including occasional instances of drinking on the job. But, on the other hand, what Mr Smit is suggesting is directly contrary to her own value of loyalty to one's friends. This has put Eva under real stress – she doesn't know what to do.

When she confides in her husband, Derek, about the problem, however, he is very clear about what she should do. 'I know you've been preoccupied with this', he says. 'You haven't been sleeping properly. You're not any fun with the family the way you used to be. Frankly, you don't need it. In fact, you don't need the job. You have two choices. One is to tell Smit you don't want to be supervisor any more. It simply isn't worth the extra money. Tell him you want to go back on the factory floor as a machinist. The other is to walk away. Find another job. Find one where *you* are in charge of your own life.'

In the above case, Eva's career may undergo an important change due to a mixture of intra-role conflict (different messages from different role senders), person–role conflict (Eva's values vs. what she is expected to do) and inter-role conflict (Eva as a supervisor vs. Eva as a family member). Her predicament comes about not just because of pressures put on her by those around her but also by fundamental characteristics of her social situation, such as the level of authority possessed by her boss and societal definitions of what roles such as supervisor and friend entail.

Eva's husband recognizes that people can become imprisoned by their roles and advises her to engineer her own liberation. In so doing, he is echoing a frequent criticism of role theory and the consequences of institutions, organizations and individuals defining other people's roles:

> One of the most objectionable aspects of role theory is that it assumes that all people must adjust to society. There is no historical vision of a society which changes to fulfil people's needs. Role in society is taken to be analogous to roles in a play. Details of how a dramatic role is to be played are indicated by writer, producer, the stage setting and other actors; and the words are written down and actions prescribed. The actor merely conforms to expectations ... it is sometimes even asserted that an individual is no more than the sum of the roles s/he plays: Mary, for example, is mother, daughter, wife, and housewife. Apart from that, Mary as a thinking, feeling being with potential for development, does not exist. (Sargent, 1994: 84)

Sargent (1994) was arguing chiefly against prescriptive roles being used, with the implication that there is only one way to conduct them, and by powerful institutions to impose their will on individuals. And it is certainly true that much of what we do in our career roles is prescribed in detail. Fortunately, the concept of personal identity, discussed earlier – which can be considered the intrapersonal counterpart of role – enables us to take a more balanced view.

Work–Life Balance

Work–life balance is an issue more relevant than ever for career actors now that we have entered a 24-hour economy and smartphone devices have created a reality where all of us are in constant contact with colleagues (Greenblatt, 2002; Sturges & Guest, 2004). The phrase *work–life balance* reminds us that each of us has other life roles in addition to our work role.

Super (1992) used the metaphor and visual stimulus of a life–career rainbow (Figure 8.1) to illustrate the multiple work and network roles occupied by each individual over their life span.

The rainbow diagram includes the following elements:

- the internal, personal determinants of career behavior, such as attitudes, aptitudes and interests
- external determinants, such as social structure, employment practices and family
- the five life stages in Super's age/stage theory (see also Chapter 4), paralleling age changes
- eight roles that tend to operate in the individual's life and that become active and inactive at different ages so that many are simultaneously active for much of life: child, student, leisurite (e.g. hobbyist, sports player, volunteer worker), citizen, worker, spouse, homemaker and parent.

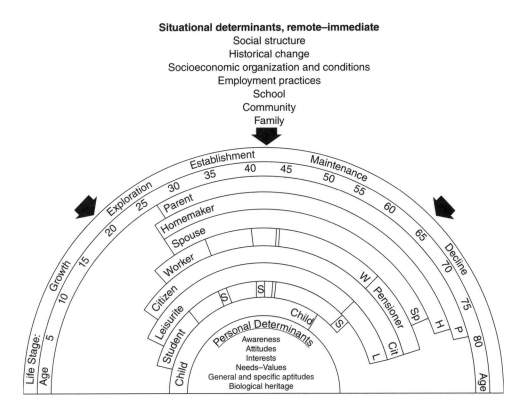

Figure 8.1   Super's Life/Career Rainbow

Chief among these other roles are family roles, such as son, daughter, brother or sister, spouse or partner, parent, grandparent and caregiver. To many people, their family roles as partners and parents are particularly important, perhaps even more so than their work roles. Indeed, the chief point of work roles for some may be the opportunity they give to provide money for the well-being of the family. Although much of the focus on work–life balance has been on the competing demands of work and family, the real problem for many people may be that early in their careers the pursuit of career success (Chapter 5) draws them into the habit of working harder and for longer hours than is good for them (Sturges & Guest, 2004).

An unfortunate feature of the phrase *work–life balance* is its apparent implication that work is not part of life but rather something separate from life, perhaps even something opposed to life, something akin to being dead. In reality, work is very much a part of life and many people gain immense liveliness and pleasure through their work. *Work–nonwork balance*, or possibly *work–family balance*, is a better alternative.

Nevertheless, it is true that there is, for most people, a problem of balancing the demands of work roles with non-work roles, particularly family roles. For example, a woman's contract of employment may state that she is expected to work from 9 a.m. to 5 p.m., Monday through Friday. But if she receives a phone message at work at 10 a.m. on Tuesday stating that her 12-year-old son was injured in an accident, was taken to hospital and is asking for Mum, she knows which takes priority. In this type of situation, the work role is normally compromised in favor of the family role.

Historically, this problem was solved in nuclear families by having one adult member, usually the man, take on the breadwinning work role, while the woman stayed at home and discharged all the roles relating to the family. The wholesale entry of most women into the workforce (Chapter 2) did away with that solution, spread both women and men much more thinly in relation to their family responsibilities and created a major problem, especially for women, of competing devotions (Blair-Loy, 2003).

Work–family role incompatibility

Greenhaus and Beutell (1985) developed a model of the problem of work–family role incompatibility that is still very current. In this model, role expectations from the work domain and the family domain conflict with each other in three areas:

1. In respect to *time*, many jobs nowadays require irregular hours. For example, an employee may work late to clear a backlog, take work home, attend evening or weekend meetings, work irregular shifts or be on call 24 hours a day. All of these conditions can interfere with normal family time, and the problem is exacerbated if the family is large; if family members are infants, very young children or frequently sick; and if other adult family members also have jobs.
2. In respect to *strain*, we have already seen how work-role conflicts, such as role overload and ambiguity, can provide their own stresses, even without the complicating factor of family responsibilities. In the family too, various factors such as family size, children's behavior problems and lack of spousal support, can likewise be stressful. Under these circumstances, it is hard not to take work-related stress home to the family and family-related stress to work and as a result fail to discharge either role satisfactorily.
3. *Behavior*, such as competitive or aggressive actions or strong control of emotions – which may be part and parcel of the work role – may be inappropriate in the family role, just as family behavior such as warmth and affection may not sit well in the work role.

These conflicts are moderated by *role salience*. For some family members, often men, work roles may have higher salience; for others, often women, family roles have higher salience, and these predispositions provide guidance as to how to solve the problems (Noor, 2004). In practice, this often means that when family demands are high, women modify their work arrangements to 'be there' for their family. In the case of the woman quoted below, note how she finally decides to build her career around her family's needs, rather than vice versa.

Opting Out

'After I had put a number of years into the job, I looked at my husband – worn down from travel, working hard on weekends – and I said, "Something's gotta give". So it was me. How long were we going to go on like that? My husband had needs, my children were saying they needed me more, my parents needed someone to take them to the doctor's appointments they made, my brother's marriage ended in divorce ... there was so much going on that I could not do the 9 to 5 anymore. So I gave up the big job where I wasn't going anywhere fast anyway and became a copy editor and now work from home, make my own hours, and work when I can'.

Source: Interview quote reported by Mainiero & Sullivan (2005: 111).

Women – and some men – with families constantly juggle aspects of their hours and type and location of work to ensure they meet their family commitments (Milkie & Peltola, 1999). For example, some husband–wife duos work different shifts so that one can always be home with the family, or try to arrange shortened hours of work so that they can drive their children to and from school or nursery. Part-time work is often preferred, particularly by women, because of the additional time it releases for family commitments (Gottlieb et al., 1998). Another solution is to telework or start a home-based business (Hilbrecht et al., 2008) so that young children always have a parent with them. Of course, all these options typically mean, as demonstrated by the 'opting out' quote, that the person is compromising their career opportunities to serve a higher priority. Some may be good for the family but may put a strain on the parents' relationship. And although nowadays 'reverse role' patterns exist (especially in Northern European countries such as Sweden and Denmark), women continue to take primary responsibility for childcare and housework, in addition to their career roles (Friedman & Greenhaus, 2001).

Stop and Consider

Consider whether your life is balanced between work (or education) roles and other roles. What could you and others do to help you achieve a better balance?

Balance in Women's Careers

Work–life balance is an issue mainly affecting women's careers. The limitation of family on career is compounded for women during pregnancy and their children's early years, when women often feel that the energy required by their family roles is so great that they cannot consider taking even a part-time job at the same time. As discussed elsewhere in this book, women's careers as a result tend to be more interrupted, less linear and (by objective measures of career success, such as salary and status) less successful than men's. Women may of course continue to acquire career-relevant skills through their work in managing the home and through voluntary activities, such as play centre and Red Cross, but such skills tend to be undervalued by employers. The overall effect is one of severely limiting women's work careers.

Kaleidoscope careers

Although individuals differ hugely in their 'natural' balance of work and non-work, many could probably find a better balance than they currently have. The practice of downshifting (Ghazi & Jones, 2004) – deliberately seeking a new, less demanding work role or reducing the role one has to achieve a better quality of life – is attracting increasing interest. Mainiero and Sullivan (2005) drew attention to the 'opt-out revolution' of women who deliberately choose not to aspire to conventional career success. These women, the authors claim, develop 'kaleidoscopic careers' and 'shift the pattern of their careers by rotating different aspects in their lives to arrange their roles and relationships in new ways' (p. 106).

Mainiero and Sullivan's Kaleidoscope Career Model (KCM) incorporates three key parameters that shift over a typical professional woman's career: authenticity ('can I be myself in the midst of all this and still be authentic?'), balance ('if I make this career decision, can I balance the parts of my life well so that there can be a coherent whole?') and challenge ('will I be sufficiently challenged if I accept this career option?'). They then move on to posit that these three parameters combine in different ways throughout a woman's life, depending on the unique pattern of her career.

Mainiero and Sullivan identified two main career patterns. *Alpha pattern careers* start with a desire for challenge, but later a desire for authenticity and finally a desire for balance become more significant. *Beta pattern careers* also start with a desire for challenge, then a desire for balance, and finally a desire for authenticity is more significant. They found that Alpha patterns were more often associated with men and Beta patterns with women. A 'typical female career', then, would look something like this:

- In *early career*, one predominant life/career pattern for women is to be concerned with goal achievement and challenge in their careers. Issues of balance and authenticity may be present, but stay in the background while the woman pursues her career interests.
- In *mid-career*, women must typically cope with issues of balance and family/relational demands – these issues thus move to the forefront. Women also wish for challenge and authenticity at this point, but these issues take on a secondary role, and compromises are made in favor of balance issues.
- In *late career*, women have typically been 'freed' from balance issues, and issues of authenticity move to the forefront. Women may also be concerned with challenge and remain concerned about balance, but their pattern of priorities (their 'kaleidoscope') will typically shift.

Source: Mainiero & Sullivan (2005).

Although work–life balance is usually seen as a problem faced by women, let us not forget that men too often face work–life balance issues, particularly in relation to the expectations attached to their primary breadwinner role. As women increasingly extend their activities across workplaces, there are signs that men too are taking more of an interest in their non-work roles, particularly as family members (Perrone et al., 2009).

Stop and Consider

Do you recognize the 'typical' model of a woman's career described above? Do the women in your life (and possibly yourself) comply with the kaleidoscope type of career model? Do you feel they should, or not? Why?

Family-friendly policies

A key factor moderating career versus family issues is the existence, or not, of family-friendly policies by employers, who may assist parents to reduce the negative impact of competing family roles on their careers by making suitable arrangements (Chou & Cheung, 2013). This is not just a matter of being understanding and providing some latitude in cases of family emergency. It also includes formal procedures for maternity and other leave without financial or career penalty; flexible working hours; opportunities for part-time, job-sharing or contract options; and the provision of childcare facilities at the place of work. Such policies are not just the responsibility of employing organizations but also need to be encouraged by a supportive state framework of policies, laws and regulations (Hantrais & Ackers, 2005).

Indeed, some argue that if organizations are to capitalize on the new diverse workforce of female as well as male professionals, they must redesign organizational processes to take account of these workers' dual roles (Bailyn, 1993). Although some employers may say that it is not their function to cater to the family arrangements of employees against their own financial interests, there is increasing evidence that such arrangements enable the retention of good employees and the maintenance of staff morale and thereby have indirect bottom-line benefits (Lambert, 2000; Perry-Smith & Blum, 2000). As a result, flexible work arrangements such as flexible hours and being allowed to work from home are increasingly common.

Although in the broader work–nonwork arena work–family balance is the main area of concern, we should not forget that work roles (and therefore careers) can also become unbalanced in relation to other activities (Schein, 1996). Organizations seek to maximize their employees' commitment and have become better at arranging work conditions, corporate norms and work and career incentives so as to encourage commitment. Many people work long hours and the phenomenon of workaholism – addiction to one's job, even to the extent of risking one's health – is well known (McMillan & O'Driscoll, 2004). This possibility may be exacerbated by management pressures for individual and organizational performance (White et al., 2003).

Finally, the trend to greater flexibility in working arrangements changes the dynamics of work–life balance (De Bruin & Dupuis, 2004), frequently freeing up more time for family commitments, vacations, tertiary study, hobbies, voluntary work and home-based small businesses or business start-ups (Inkson et al., 2001; Peel & Inkson, 2004). For example, although temping – working temporarily with different employers through an agency – has rightly been criticized for its tendency to spread insecurity and marginalize workers (Hardy & Walker, 2003), enterprising workers with skills in demand can use the flexibility and freedom entailed in temping to become 'lifestyle' temps, with a good, self-chosen balance between paid work and other activities (Alach & Inkson, 2004).

Dual-Career Couples

A special case of work–family conflict is that of the dual-career couple: two people in a loving and usually cohabiting relationship who are also conducting their own separate careers, which may come into conflict not only with non-work roles but also with each other, for example, if one seeks to transfer to a new work location. How does a relationship survive when the career ambitions and behaviors of its partners become incompatible (Friedman & Greenhaus, 2001)?

Dual-career couples typically face many of the problems of work–life balance, particularly if they also have children. However, there is no evidence that the children of working women suffer unduly compared with the children of non-working women (Wills & Brauer, 2012). But other problems may surface, such as career competition and jealousy between partners, and issues of role identity for men who seek to be providers or women who cherish their role as nurturers.

Keeping a relationship healthy under such circumstances requires open communication between partners, support for each other's career, recognition that the two careers function interactively within a wider family system and the conscious development of mutually agreed strategies for dealing with the issues. Each partner can adjust their role expectations of the other, redefine their own role or try to work differently to accommodate the wider demands of the two-career situation (Bures et al., 2011).

Role Innovation

Formal roles in organizations do not need to be accepted exactly as they are. Role innovation (Aime et al., 2011; Schein, 1971) and job crafting (Wrzesniewski & Dutton, 2001; see also Chapter 6) imply that individuals can, literally, carve out a role for themselves in their work by adding things to the role that are not in their job description or that they can change in desired directions. Schein (1971) distinguished between custodians, who do their jobs according to traditional job descriptions and do not innovate; content innovators, who accept the purpose of the role but change the detail of how it is done; and *role innovators*, who change the whole nature of their role. Sienna's case is an example of role innovation.

CASE STUDY

Flying High

Sienna, bored with high school, left at age 16. With good typing skills and a pleasant personality, she secured a job as a typist in an advertising agency. As one of the most junior people in the organization, her role was very limited: she was expected to stick to the information-recording tasks in her job description and to take orders from most of the professional staff in the agency. However, she took an active interest in the content of what she was typing, in the interactions of other staff and in the overall business of the agency. She quickly became fascinated: advertising was wonderful! She also realized that sometimes she could see things more clearly than some of her superiors could.

(Continued)

(Continued)

Sienna began to speak up, as tactfully as she could, in executive and account meetings at which she was taking the minutes. Initially, the professional and managerial staff members were surprised to hear her voice, and on one occasion her direct superior advised her to remember that speaking up was not her job. Using the latitude her job description allowed, she made friends with the other staff, joined them for lunch and talked informally with them about her ideas. In her spare time, she read books about advertising and studied other agencies' campaigns. Gradually, her contributions became accepted and then encouraged. The professional staff began to see her almost as one of them.

Within a year, it was clear that she was wasted as a typist. Her boss brought her to the attention of the CEO, who appointed her to a position as media planner, with time off to pursue a relevant educational qualification – thus commenced Sienna's rapid rise to senior positions in the industry. Sometimes, a job description need be a constraint only if the person lets it.

Sienna's movement in the organization is based on the idea of 'job crafting' (Chapter 6) – changing one's work activities to achieve a better fit with one's abilities, interests and personality, which in Sienna's case were fitted for more responsible roles than her typist's job allowed. Her transformation appears to be to both her own advantage and that of her employing organization. But as she sought to innovate there was some initial uneasiness in the organization as to whether that was appropriate. Much depends on the organization's tolerance of people who go outside their formal role and its encouragement of creativity (Hammond et al., 2011). At the extreme is a story of a new employee in an especially open-minded organization who came to work on his first day and asked his supervisor what his job was. 'Walk around and find something useful to do', said the supervisor. 'I'll come and look for you in a couple of weeks' (Manz & Sims, 1991).

Role innovation may be built around learning opportunities. One concept is the *self-designed apprenticeship* (Arthur et al., 1999). In a formal apprenticeship, the new learner sacrifices higher earnings by accepting a low pay rate, mundane work and a subservient role; and learns skills from skilled practitioners or teachers until they are also qualified and skilled. In the self-designed apprenticeship, the same principles apply, except the apprentice designs the curriculum and chooses the teachers, and there is not necessarily a formal qualification. Here is a brief case.

CASE STUDY

Growing New Opportunities

Albert, a young unemployed engineer, offered to work as a bartender for no pay for two weeks in return for being taught bar skills. When the two weeks was up, he had made himself indispensable and was offered a full-time job. A year later, he obtained a good engineering-based job but continued with bar work in the evenings and was promoted to night manager. He banks his night earnings and is considering investing his savings to become part-owner of a bar.

Source: Arthur et al. (1999).

Conclusion

When roles are expressed in an abstract form, such as a job description, they can sound curiously lifeless and can make even the most interesting jobs seem dull. It is when we start exploring the complexities of informal role expectations and roles, the expectations of 'role senders' and reference groups, the congruence or conflict of role with identity or with non-work roles, and the endless possibilities of role innovation and role transition, that we understand how role analysis can reflect much of the dynamism associated with modern careers. Reflecting on the roles we have had, the roles we have now, and the roles we seek in the future, and on how these roles were defined and changed, and by whom, is an exercise well worth doing.

Key Points in this Chapter

- A career can be considered as a succession of work roles. Individuals have many other roles (e.g. son or daughter, parent, consumer, friend). These may overlap or conflict with work roles.
- Identity is a personal recognition of who one is and is often expressed in one's roles. People can find identity in occupations, job titles and social roles such as leader.
- Role transitions, such as moving from one job to another, are an important part of the career process, and involve stages of preparation, encounter, adjustment and stabilization.
- The coexistence of competing work and non-work roles can lead to problems of work–life balance or work–family balance, which may need to be dealt with by forms of adjustment, including career adjustment, by the individual. In dual-career couples, mutual adjustment to each other's career roles may be necessary.
- Individuals may modify their roles through role innovation.

Questions from this Chapter

General Questions

1. Think about two or three people you know well and investigate their life histories and lifestyle. What different roles do (and did) they occupy, and how have they fit these roles into their lives?
2. Compose a reflected best-self-portrait. What did you learn about yourself that you didn't already know? In what roles are you likely to thrive? What roles are likely to be less suitable for you, considering the strengths and weaknesses your informants attributed to you?
3. Define, and give an example of, each of the following: role, career reference group, role transition, role set, role expectations, inter-role conflict, role model.
4. Why is work–life balance an issue about roles? What are the main work–life balance issues facing women at different points in their careers? Illustrate using friends and family as examples.
5. Think of one or more of your current roles. What are the role expectations and how much scope is there for going outside them? In what ways have you role innovated or could you role innovate?

'Live Career Case' Study Questions

1. What have been the main non-work roles of your case person? How have these complemented or conflicted with the case person's work roles and how have they affected the case person's career? Have they ever been in a role that 'really wasn't them'? How did that play out in the end?
2. How does the career case person identify him or herself? How do these identities fit with each other and which is most central? How has the case person's identity changed over time?
3. Ask your case person to describe an important role transition and an example of role innovation during their career. Are you able to identify the different stages of role transition? What did you learn about role innovation from the example?

Additional Resources

Recommended Further Reading

Ashforth, B. E., Kreiner, G. E. and Fugate, M. (2000) 'All in a day's work: Boundaries and micro role transitions', *Academy of Management Review*, 25: 472–491.
Gibson, D. E. (2004) 'Role models in career development: New directions for theory and research', *Journal of Vocational Behavior*, 65: 134–156.

Grote, G. and Hall, D.T. (2013) 'Reference groups: A missing link in career studies', *Journal of Vocational Behavior*, 83: 265–279.

Ibarra, H. (1999) 'Provisional selves: Experimenting with image and identity in professional adaptation', *Administrative Science Quarterly*, 44(4): 764–791.

Lambert, S. J. (2000) 'Added benefits: The link between work–life benefits and organizational citizenship behavior', *Academy of Management Journal*, 43(5): 801–813.

Snir, R. and Harpaz, I. (2012) 'Beyond workaholism: Towards a general model of heavy work investment', *Human Resource Management Review*, 22(3): 232–243.

Self-Assessment Resources

Assess your propensity for workaholism: Mudrack, P. E. and Naughton, T. J. (2001) 'The assessment of workaholism as behavioral tendencies: Scale development and preliminary empirical testing', *International Journal of Stress Management*, 8(2): 93–111.

Assess your school–life balance: Law, D. W. (2007) 'Exhaustion in university students and the effect of coursework involvement', *Journal of American College Health*, 55(4): 239–245.

Assess your 'best self': Roberts, L.M., Dutton, J.E., Spreitzer, G., Heaphy, E.D. and Quinn, R.E. (2005) 'Composing the reflected best-self portrait: Building pathways for becoming extraordinary in work organizations', *Academy of Management Review*, 30(4): 712–736.

Online Resources

A reflection on social identity – see the TEDTalk entitled 'Embracing otherness, embracing myself' by Thandie Newton at: www.ted.com/talks/thandie_newton_embracing_otherness_embracing_myself.html

Role models for women's careers – a website containing inspirational role model videos for women for a large number of occupations can be found at: www.careergirls.org

OECD data on work–life balance – see the OECD 'better life index' website at: www.oecdbetterlifeindex.org/topics/work-life-balance/

Careers as Relationships

9

Chapter Objectives

The objectives of this chapter are:

- to consider careers as ongoing and developing sets of relationships with other people
- to consider the different levels of intensity and complexity in relationships affecting careers, including social encounters and impression management, relationships, networks and communities
- to understand some of the characteristics of social networks, including their basis in interactions, the possibility of active 'networking' to create and sustain them, their mirroring of social structure, and their continuity, reciprocity, enhancement of reputation and serendipity
- to show how the following concepts can help us to understand how careers work and can help us to develop better careers: social capital, concentrated versus diverse networks, individualist versus collectivist cultures
- to introduce the subject of mentorship in relation to careers
- to reinforce that although the complexity of careers and the differences between different career settings mean that it is hard to establish principles of social relationships that will be effective for all careers, nevertheless social activity mediates all careers in some way.

CASE STUDY

It pays to advertise

Peter Cullinane (his real name) grew up in Wellington, New Zealand, and was educated at a convent school. His best subject was English and he was excellent at conversation, debating and writing, but had no idea what career to follow. Despite having qualifications to enter university, he did not do so. Instead, he secured a junior position at a small local advertising agency: the first step in what was to become a very successful career in advertising.

Within a year of starting, Peter was an 18-year-old account executive with the agency. Within a year after that, he had been recruited to the local office of one of the world's premier agencies, Ogilvie and Mather, where, by proactively pleading for a big job, he held the account of a major local client, the New Zealand Air Force. He worked hard and was successful, but, by age 22, he was 'burned out' and decided to resign his job and take a year of 'time out' overseas, where he did only manual work.

On his return to New Zealand, Peter quickly obtained an account manager job at McKay King, another local agency. Soon, he became the manager of the Wellington office of the agency and acquired his own financial stake in the business, which grew dramatically for ten years before being acquired by the major international agency Saatchi and Saatchi. Saatchi and Saatchi kept Peter on after the takeover as CEO of its New Zealand operation, to which he later added responsibility for the Australian part of the business.

In 1997, another New Zealander, Kevin Roberts, was appointed as CEO of the entire Saatchi and Saatchi organization, based in New York. Roberts immediately appointed Peter as Chief Operating Officer, and Peter flew with his family to New York to take up what promised to be an increasingly international career. Between 1997 and 2001, with responsibilities all around the globe, Peter did a massive amount of traveling. But in 2001, triggered in part by his family being in New York at the time of the 9/11 disaster, Peter found himself asking the question, 'What am I doing here?' Being unable to provide a satisfactory answer, he flew back to New Zealand.

There, with three business partners, he quickly formed Assignment, a new advertising and communications agency modelled on the best practices Peter and the others had experienced in their careers. Again, the business grew rapidly and was eventually able to be sold to STW, an Australian-based organization, which kept Peter on as CEO and put him on its Board. Most recently, he has been involved

(Continued)

(Continued)

in new ventures with Antipodes, a high-end bottled-water company, and Lewis Road Creamery, in the high-end butter market. He has also compensated for the lack of tertiary education in his early career by completing an Executive MBA at The University of Auckland.

These are the bald facts of Peter's career. What accounts for his high level of success?

Peter recognizes that his creativity and unusual skills with language – in his own words, 'being able to make a huge leap in thinking and then express it in a way that seems rational' – are very important. So too is his motivation: he constantly seeks to extend himself through new challenges, his pursuit of an MBA being a case in point, and he has always been an extremely hard worker. But when you look below the surface of Peter's career, the other thing that stands out is the importance of *relationships, networks* and *reputation*. Consider this additional information:

1. Peter has never applied for any job. He has obtained all his jobs through personal contacts, mostly because others have been aware of his reputation and/ or impressed by the quality of his work, and have offered him unsolicited jobs.
2. His first job as an office boy was offered to him by the agency's CEO, who was a friend of his family. That single contact has led to Peter spending virtually his entire career to date in the advertising industry.
3. Early in his career, he attended a meeting at which a number of Ogilvie and Mather executives were also present, one of whom offered him a lift in his high-powered sports car. The conversation in the car led to an interview at Ogilvie and Mather, and his next job. There, his boss offered excellent mentorship.
4. While he was abroad early in his career, a friend he knew at McKay King wrote to him about opportunities there. That resulted in his job there and the opportunity to work with Terry King, one of the 'family' owners of the business, to build an organization impressive enough to be bought by one of the world's premier agencies. The working relationship with King was key to his success at this time.
5. While at Saatchi and Saatchi, Peter was on an international global management board, which was eventually the group that recruited Kevin Roberts as CEO. Kevin, a fellow New Zealander, promptly recruited his compatriot Peter as COO, and Peter went to work in New York.
6. Peter's return to New Zealand was triggered not only by 9/11, but also by a breakdown in his relationship with his boss, Kevin Roberts: relationships can make your career, but break it too.

7. Back in New Zealand, Peter had dinner with a friend from his McKay King days, Kim Thorpe, who had also become part of the Saatchi and Saatchi empire but had stayed in New Zealand. Peter says, 'I can remember his wife Bronwen saying to me, "Whatever you want to do, Kim will want to do it too", and I thought "we should do it together"'. The two of them approached two other friends from the Saatchi and Saatchi network, and started Assignment, their new agency.

8. Peter's career has been assisted by his involvement in organizational and industry networks that have constantly helped him to increase his expertise and become aware of new opportunities.

9. Here's a part of Peter's personal and business philosophy: 'The most important thing you can earn is respect ... I'm sociable because I want to be able to attract and to work with the best in the business, and for them to be equally attracted to want to work with me, and you don't do that by being grumpy ... You create serendipity, so that people just want to help and open doors ... and another thing is reciprocity – always give before you ask.'

Careers and Networks

In the Western world, we tend to view careers as individual projects resulting in individual rewards and achievements (Grey, 1994). But as Peter's career shows, careers are also *social*: they are mediated, mentored, made and sometimes marred by contacts, networks, partnerships and reputation, in the communities – groups, organizations, professions, industries and others – in which they are enacted. Peter gained all his positions through being noticed by other key people, and advanced in his career by working, and developing relationships, with them. It is not just a matter of using networks to help find good jobs, but also using networks within those jobs to advance in skills, 'insider' knowledge and reputation. For example, recent research in Peter's industry tells us:

> Creatives learn their craft by becoming immersed in the multiple, inter-related communities that constitute the advertising world during the demanding 'pre-peripheral' and 'peripheral' stages of their career. Learning through immersion continues throughout the journey from the periphery to the centre, since creatives participate in a competitive, tight-knit creative community, actively engaged in social networking and constantly monitoring each other's creative output. Creatives' legitimacy (and power) is earned by winning peer regard for their work. (McLeod et al., 2011: 114)

Careers thus need relationships not just for assisting mobility, but also for knowledge acquisition. They are also assisted by reputation.

Furthermore, careers are frequently *interdependent*. In the case above, the careers of Terry King, Kevin Roberts, Kim Thorpe and probably others not only affected

Peter's career for a period but were also affected by it. Svejenova et al. (2010: 707) define shared careers as 'the co-evolving sequence of work collaboration and jointly pursued career opportunities by two or more career actors'. These include business partnerships, informal complementary partnerships between, for example, creative people and administrative people, and mentor–apprentice relationships, ongoing or fleeting collaborations. In some cases, the career liaison is temporary, but is powerful in framing the futures of the career actors: an example is the celebrated Steve Jobs–Steve Wozniak collaboration that also created the Apple company in the late 1970s. In others, careers may be symbiotically entwined on a lifelong basis, as in the partnership of Rolling Stones musicians Mick Jagger and Keith Richards.

More generally, if we think back over our careers, what we often see is not just a succession of jobs but also a succession of people with whom we worked, people who gave us opportunities, people who made a big difference, for good or bad, in our careers: bosses, mentors, colleagues, subordinates, work groups, committees, clients, professional associates. We live our careers through relationships with others. Careers are social.

At the same time, sociability works in different ways in different occupations and industries. A career may be conducted, for example, in a service industry where relationships and reputation with clients is important; or a family business where family networks are critical; or a profession where wide-ranging professional networks and reputation are the route to advancement; or a close-knit formal organization that values loyalty and commitment to the firm and others within it; or a project-to-project industry such as film-making where career actors utilize relationships and personal reputation in order to find their way into fresh projects. In each of these cases, the rules of the relationships game will be different.

Stop and Consider

Consider an occupation, organization, department, industry or project that you know a bit about, and the career development of those involved, possibly including yourself. In those settings, how important is networking to career success? What particular kinds of contacts, relationships or networks seem to be the most important and how do they work?

Collectivism

While relationships probably mediate all careers, their influence differs between different societies. Hofstede (1980) noted that one of the key cultural factors differentiating societies was individualism–collectivism (see Chapter 2) and that the individualism characteristic of North America and north-western Europe is extreme. In individualistic societies, the career is often considered to be basically an *individual project*, for which the career actor takes personal responsibility (Grey, 1994). Others may be involved in assisting the career actor to reach their goals, but their involvement is more likely to be engineered in support of the career, rather than the career developing as a by-product of relationships.

In many contrasting, collective societies – for example, in Asia, Africa and South America – collectivism is powerful, meaning that individuals view aspects of behavior, including career behavior, from the perspective of groups, including the family, of which the individual is a member (Thomas & Inkson, 2007). Granrose and Chua (1996), in their careful analysis of global boundaryless careers in Chinese family businesses, showed how careers may be viewed from a quite different perspective – that is, as the property of the family or wider kin group. Such groups provide career opportunities and resources to all family members, so it makes more sense in these cases to consider family career systems rather than individual careers.

Chinese careers, for example, often involve the concept of *guanxi* – a system of mutual obligations and favors between individual members of a collective, such as a family, a local community or an organization, where each individual feels a moral obligation to meet others' requests for assistance. This can result, for example, in favoring those in *guanxi* relationships with the offer of a job, further contacts, skills, advice, hospitality or financial support, all of which can benefit the recipient's career, sometimes at the expense of others who lack *guanxi* relationships. *Guanxi* networks are often complex and extensive, spanning geographical boundaries and enduring over long periods of time. Failure to honour a *guanxi* obligation can result in terrible loss of face, making this a powerful influence in career-affecting decisions. Even ordinary workers may use *guanxi* to influence their supervisors and assist their careers (Wei et al., 2010). On the other hand, relying on *guanxi* for career success may limit one's choice of jobs, job satisfaction and personal agency in pursuing one's career (Song & Werbel, 2007). Also, the adoption, in large organizations, of transparent, standardized systems of selection for finding the best candidate tends to reduce the influence of *guanxi* (Huang, 2008).

Even in Western societies, many career actors experience close, collective relationships as the basis of their careers. A familiar career stereotype is the 'mom-and-pop' business run by a husband and wife: a grocery store, perhaps, or a garage where one partner fixes the cars and the other does the administration. Generation-to-generation family businesses enmesh careers irretrievably into family relationships, making it difficult to consider the career other than as one facet of a series of developing personal relationships. In another form, a pair or group of colleagues may have a business idea that they can work on together and may form their own company, binding their careers together, at least temporarily.

Nepotism – the practice of favoring family members over outsiders, such as in appointments to jobs – is controversial. In many cultures – for example, in Arab nations

(Sidani & Thornberry, 2013) and developing countries (Kragh, 2012) – nepotism is deeply embedded. Notwithstanding the exceptions noted earlier, Western societies adhere more to an ethic of merit-based appointment where jobs should go to those best qualified to do them.

Yet, even in the West, nepotistic acts are common. For example, a family farm is often passed on to the eldest son of the retiring farmer, regardless of whether he has the skills and motivation to emulate his father. A long-service employee may likewise secure from her employing company an apprenticeship for her son or daughter without submitting a formal application. In most jurisdictions, such acts are not illegal, but they are sometimes frowned upon, and often resented by those who lack powerful family connections. But some commentators, such as Bellow (2004), argue that the entrenched nature of nepotism is no bad thing, since it appears deeply embedded in human anthropology, part of a cycle of bonding which potentially provides society with a source of stability and integration.

Levels of Relationship

One way to understand social influences on careers is to think about four different levels of social relationships potentially affecting careers:

- At the lowest level, we have *encounters*, in which meetings of individuals, some deliberate, others occurring by chance, enable them to influence each other and sometimes collaborate to mutual benefit, usually in the short term. For example, two strangers meet at a party and discover that one of them is looking for a job and the other knows of a suitable opportunity in her firm.
- At the next level, encounters solidify into *relationships* so that the individuals develop a longer term association, enabling them to influence each other and collaborate on a repeated or ongoing basis. For example, a young career actor approaches a senior person for advice, and over time that person becomes a trusted mentor, offering the career actor ongoing guidance and opportunities.
- At a higher level still, relationships are combined into complex *networks*, in which, for example, A is being mentored by B, who in turn is a friend of C, D and E, who in turn are employed by F, who has important information concerning relevant career opportunities, etc.
- Beyond this, networks may be part of informal and formal *communities*, so that one member of a community can gain advantage from, or give advantage to, another member they have never met. Extended families, professional associations, colleges, churches, social service organizations such as Rotary, and work organizations can all serve as career communities (Parker et al., 2004). Recently, social

networks such as Facebook and LinkedIn have begun to assume more and more importance in this respect.

Interpersonal Influence

The social side of career development depends in part on *interpersonal influence*. It is of little value for a career actor to talk to lots of people at parties, or to recruiters at employment agencies, if he or she consistently makes a bad impression on them. Relationships start with, and are defined by, interactions. Consider, in the case below, the plots of two films about characters who develop careers in stockbroking on Wall Street.

CASE STUDY

Breaking the Ice

Wall Street (1987), director: Oliver Stone

Tired of his life as a low-level Wall Street stockbroker, Bud Fox, played by the young Charlie Sheen, decides to try to break into the big time and become a major, and successful, player on the market. To do so, he figures he needs the patronage of Gordon Gecko (Michael Douglas), a highly successful broker. The problem he faces is that everyone wants Gecko's time and attention. Gecko is protected in his office by a personal assistant (PA) and sees people only by appointment. How can Bud get even a few minutes of Gecko's time? And if he does, how can he persuade Gecko to take him on as a protégé?

Bud first researches Gecko. Studying the great man in gossip columns, he finds that Gecko has a penchant for a particular rare brand of Cuban cigars. He also discovers Gecko's birthday, and purchases a box of the cigars, wrapping them as a birthday gift. In the days leading up to the birthday, he constantly calls Gecko's PA, flattering and sweet-talking her on the telephone. On the day of the birthday, he turns up at Gecko's office with the cigars and tells the PA he is only willing to give the gift if he is allowed to deliver it personally. He is kept in the waiting room for hours, but eventually the PA grudgingly grants him five minutes in Gecko's presence – five minutes to sell himself! But being in Gecko's office is a nightmare: the phone rings every few moments with more deals that Gecko must attend to. Bud has gone in with carefully considered stock tips he thinks may interest Gecko, but Gecko dismisses them out of hand: 'Tell me something I don't know!' But, in

(Continued)

(Continued)

the end, Bud at last says something of interest to Gecko, and a passing acquaintanceship becomes a relationship and, indeed, a mentorship.

The Wolf of Wall Street **(2013), director: Martin Scorsese**

Donnie Azoff (played by Jonah Hill) has a low-paid, going-nowhere job as a furniture salesman. In a bar, Donnie notices up-and-coming stock salesman Jordan Belfort (Leonardo de Caprio), who is smartly dressed and has his gleaming Jaguar car parked outside. Donnie sits down with Jordan, admires his expensive car and asks him how much money he makes. After some prevarication, Jordan tells him he made $72,000 the previous month. Donnie demands proof, and Jordan shows him his pay check. In that case, says Donnie, I'm coming to work for *you*. He immediately calls his boss and tells him he's quitting the furniture job to go into the stock business. Jordan is a little taken aback, but can't help admiring Donnie's decisiveness, ambition and willingness to take risks. Donnie becomes Jordan's loyal assistant, a career path that is to take him with Jordan into a life of both fabulous wealth and eventual imprisonment.

In the first of these scenes, Bud uses a number of techniques for influencing others. Such techniques include researching them beforehand to find out their interests, flattering them, communicating positive expectations, using confident body language, maintaining eye contact, listening, asking questions, name-dropping (e.g. 'I'm a friend of your associate Julie'), negotiating desired outcomes and reinforcing them when they act in ways helpful to you (Owen, 2012).

In the second story, Donnie too is seeking to impress the other party, and both he and Bud perceive that allying themselves in a relationship with a powerful sponsor is an effective route to career success. In both these stories, they initiate the relationships mainly because of self-interest: they seek only their own career advancement. This contrasts with many other situations where interpersonal relationships, including family relationships, are developed for reasons of sociability, friendship, mutual interests and love, but can also have far-reaching effects on the careers of those involved.

Impression Management

Much of this networking behavior is a goal-directed conscious or unconscious process in which people attempt to influence the perceptions of other people about a person, object or event; they do so by regulating and controlling information in social interaction

(Leary & Kowalski, 1990). Sosik and Jung (2003) distinguish five different impression management strategies:

- *Ingratiation* or 'getting people to like you'. For example, you might take an interest in your colleagues' personal lives, or give them compliments, with the main purpose of showing them that you are a nice person.
- *Self-promotion* or 'telling people how good you are'. For example, you might talk proudly about past accomplishments to make your colleagues aware of your talents or qualifications.
- *Intimidation* or 'making people believe you are powerful or dangerous'. For example, you might speak forcefully to get your way in group assignments.
- *Exemplification* or 'convincing people that you work really hard'. For example, you might arrive first at the office and/or leave last so that your colleagues will see you as dedicated.
- *Supplication* or 'getting people to sympathise with you'. For example, you might act like you know less than you do so that your colleagues will help you out.

Impression management, designed as it is to promote image as much as reality, is open to abuse and even untruth – for example, when people claim they left their company voluntarily when they were really fired, or when they forge references. Weiss and Feldman (2006) found that lying was common in job interviews, and was more likely in extroverts than in introverts. Bratton and Kacmar (2004: 291) noted that unacceptable impression management is likely to be used in *extreme careerism*, defined as 'the propensity to pursue career advancement through any positive or negative non-performance-based activity that is deemed necessary'. On the other hand, candidates deserve the opportunity to present themselves at their best, and indeed such self-presentation can become a self-fulfilling prophecy by enhancing work performance (Eden, 1991). Each individual has their own standard in terms of the tactics used in career self-promotion.

Social Networks

In a classic study by Granovetter (1974), 56 percent of a sample of American professional, technical and managerial workers reported that they had found their current jobs by means of personal contacts, compared with 19 percent who found jobs by formal means, 19 percent who applied directly to the employer and 7 percent who found jobs in miscellaneous other ways. Furthermore, those who found their jobs through personal contacts were on the whole more satisfied with them and were earning higher salaries.

A more recent study, again in the USA, found even more striking results (www.quintcareers.com/getting_jobs.html). In the sample reported in this study, only 5 percent of employees had found their jobs by answering ads in newspapers and the like; 48 percent had found them through personal contacts and referrals, 24 percent by calling the employer directly ('cold-calling') and 23 percent through some form of intermediary employment agency. A third study, by Forbes (2010), suggested that in 2010, while internet bulletin boards and postings were gaining ground as a means of finding employment, networking remained easily the best way to find a job, accounting for over 40 percent of placements. The results of these and many other studies appear to bear out the old dictum that, in finding a job, what counts is not 'what you know' but 'who you know'.

Although networking to access jobs is well known, this is not the only career-related function that networks perform. Networks – particularly networks of like-minded people, such as those in the same organization, occupation and industry – can provide reassurance, support, motivation and knowledge relevant to the individual's career development. The academic literature recognizes the value of networking techniques to assist careers (Cross & Parker, 2004; Greenbank, 2011). For example, an Australian study suggested that women seeking to access senior management and board positions, even if they could overcome the common resistance to the employment of women at these levels (Chapter 3), were unlikely to succeed unless they were seen to have valuable business contacts (Sheridan, 2002). Here, bias against women was a career barrier, but networking was a way to overcome it.

Network connections can come into being as a by-product of people's natural sociability and the non-work-related as well as the work-related circles in which they move. For example, a career actor might discuss a problem with a friend and the friend might say, 'Oh, my next-door neighbor went through a similar experience and might be able to help you.' People who network naturally because of their sociability and interest in others may unintentionally build a major resource for their careers. Others develop career-relevant networks purposely by taking advantage of day-to-day encounters. Consider the account of Sarah, a recently unemployed journalist, and her networking activities at a party given by her friend Craig, also a journalist.

CASE STUDY

Partying for Profit

When Craig invited me to his party I jumped at the chance because I knew there would be some very influential people there. When I got there, I was nice to Craig and asked him to introduce me to a few people. First, he introduced me to his friend Dorinda, who is an assistant editor of *The Press*. We exchanged a few pleasantries, but there's no point beating around the bush, so after a few minutes I explained my situation and asked her point-blank if *The Press* had any vacancies. It didn't work. I don't know what I did wrong, but she couldn't back off fast enough. She was like 'nothing at the moment' and almost 'how can you be so rude as to ask?' I know when I'm beat, but people like that can be really useful in the long term, so I listened sympathetically while she raved on about her attempts to get *The Press* to change its editorial policies, and I must have sounded like I really cared because at the end she said, 'We might have a freelance job or two. Can you call me next week?' and gave me her card. Well, that was a good start. Then I saw Jacko Jacobsen, one of my tutors at journalism school. I hadn't seen him for years, so I grabbed another drink and had a yarn with him, catching up on the old crowd. Jacko knows everyone who is anyone in feature journalism and he genuinely seems to want to help his students. He said that right now he didn't think there were many openings in the city but that if I were willing to go out of town he could think of some publications that seemed to be growing quickly. He said, 'Send me your résumé and portfolio, and I'll make some calls.' But then he tried to make a date with me, and when I said I was already in a relationship, he was, sort of, 'you might have told me!' That really worried me. Maybe he's only interested in what he can get. Anyway, he was a bit drunk by this stage, so I said I'd call him next week and moved on. I spent the rest of the evening talking to some people in one of the big PR companies. PR is not my cup of tea, but I've learned to take an interest in all sorts of people and to always get their cards and always write some notes about them when I get home. After all, you never know when someone like that is going to come in useful, do you?

Note how Sarah seeks to advance her career by using established relationships to build new ones. Although she may seem somewhat calculating and self-serving in her social interactions, her networking activities are based on her appreciation of the realities of job seeking and job finding. She is sociable and willing to approach those who may be able to help, showing that extroversion can help and shyness can hinder career-enhancing relationships (Greenbank, 2011). Thus, she spreads the responsibility for her career beyond herself and brings others in to help her.

Developing interpersonal relationships through networking is considered to be an important career competency (Forret & Dougherty, 2004; Rastetter & Cornelis, 2012), enabling the career actor not only to solve immediate career issues such as finding a new job, but also to safeguard long-term employability. According to Forret and Dougherty (2001), five types of networking behavior may be identified: maintaining contacts, socializing, engaging in professional activities, participating in community, and increasing internal (organizational) visibility. Thus, examples of networking behavior might include sending Christmas cards, going to social events, attending meetings of one's professional association, doing charitable work with others and getting to know work colleagues better.

There are plenty of self-help books on how to network (e.g. Baber and Waymon, 2007; Darling, 2003). It can be a complex process. Darling (2003), for example, wrote about network planning, inventories of networks, network evaluation, network accessories (business cards, cell phones, etc.), networking locations, conversation guidelines, network etiquette, handshakes, VIP meetings, follow-up for contacts, and so on. Social networking sites such as Facebook and LinkedIn add even more complexity.

In a thoroughgoing networking approach, networking becomes much more for career actors than simply taking advantage of their contacts. Rather, networking becomes an important career self-management strategy, as systematic and thought through as a business plan (see Chapter 12). But not everyone is comfortable with such a calculative approach. Some may decide that obsessive socializing in pursuit of career opportunities is not something they want to do. However, in light of some of the studies cited above, pushing the development of relationships, even if it takes courage and sometimes the ability to withstand rejection, may be a worthwhile way not just to get jobs but to extend one's networks for long-term benefit.

Networks have additional characteristics:

- *Social structure.* Networks can be influenced by individual action but do not come about solely because of personal agency and sociability. To a large extent, larger structural forces, such as those discussed in Chapter 2, dictate networks. The contacts we make are often constrained by things such as the organization we are in; the level we are at; our circle of other employees, clients and suppliers; the industry; the geographical location; our social class, gender, education, sexual orientation and race (Chapter 3); and our family and social connections. Breaking into new networks may require considerable effort, risk-taking and luck.
- *Continuity.* Networking is continuous. Although networking techniques can be mobilized quickly to solve a specific problem, in most networking the contacts and relationships are built over a long period so that when help is needed there are lots of potentially useful contacts the career actor can call.
- *Reciprocity.* As noted by Peter Cullinane in the opening case in this chapter, networks are reciprocal. That is, network members put energy into the network as well as take energy out, and members also offer help to others as well as seeking help from them (Deckop et al., 2003; Gouldner, 1960). In the case of Sarah above, if she continues to be interested in contacts only for the assistance they might give her rather than for anything she might do for them, she runs the risk of appearing selfish and manipulative (which may be true), and may find it harder to access network resources. Of course, lower status networkers usually have less to offer than their senior counterparts, so giving back may have to be extended over a long period, though, conversely, experienced senior networkers may be rewarded by 'drawing out' unexpected wisdom and assistance from their protégés.
- *Reputation.* Networks function not just through direct interactions between people but also on the basis of reputation – what is believed about particular people by others, including those who have never met them (Chan et al., 2008). Employers and corporate recruiters with good networks know who may be available on the job

market and what their strengths and weaknesses may be (Finlay & Coverdill, 2000). In some occupations and project networks, for example in IT (Hu et al., 2012), art (Beckert & Rossel, 2013) and even cyber-crime (Decary-Hetu & Dupont, 2013), reputation appears to be a key prerequisite for career advancement. But reputation is a function not just of the real person but also of their subjective and sometimes self-interested evaluations and publications (including résumés, Facebook pages, twitters and tweets) and those of other network members, which can cause reputations to be misleading.

- *Serendipity* (having desirable things happen, apparently by accident). Networks often provide spectacular examples of 'planned happenstance' (Mitchell et al., 1999; see Chapter 5), where career actors are able to take advantage of chance meetings and transform them serendipitously into career development opportunities: for example, someone you are introduced to in the street by a mutual friend happens to know of a great career opportunity for you. Social and community life present many such unplanned events. The happenstance is planned in the sense that every contact we make may later become a new opportunity. We can't plan how particular contacts may be useful to us, but we can plan to behave socially to make lots of contacts and/or to be selective in the relationships we choose to develop: serendipitous good fortune is more likely for those whose networks are extensive and relevant, and whose relationships are cordial.

Social Capital

A term that is used with increasing frequency to emphasize the importance of networks in careers (and elsewhere) is *social capital* (e.g. Adler and Kwon, 2002; Mouw, 2003; Zhang et al., 2010). Put simply, a career actor's social capital is the resources they are able to access through their networks. The notion of *capital* – 'wealth owned by a person or organization or invested, lent, or borrowed' (Allen, 1990: 207) – emphasizes the idea, which will be pursued more completely in Chapter 10, that each of us possesses different amounts and types of career capital, which we are able to invest, if we wish, in our own career development. Studies from different societies suggest that the accumulation of social capital significantly improves career success (O'Brien et al., 2011; Pezzoni et al., 2012; Zhang et al., 2010).

Social capital is an important part of career capital that can only be accessed through contacts. Social capital also enables us to build other forms of career capital, such as motivational energy, knowledge and skills. However, Mouw (2003: 868) suggested that 'much of the effect of social capital in the existing literature reflects the tendency for similar people to become friends rather than a causal effect of friends' characteristics on labour market outcomes'. In other words, some of the apparent effects of social capital on career development may simply be a reflection of social structural variables, as detailed in Chapter 2.

Social capital also provides a potential asset for employers, who may hire new workers not just for the skills they possess but also for their social connections: investing in the social capital of employees may bring a firm significant economic returns (Kiessling & Simsek, 2011). Companies seek to build their social capital by developing contacts with agencies and individuals who can undertake special projects for them, source new customers or new employees, or broker relationships leading to joint ventures (Jones, 2002). Such activities provide opportunities for career actors to receive worhwhile career invitations by moving actively in the right circles, increasing their social capital as they go.

Stop and Consider

Consider your current social networks, listing or diagramming them, if necessary, as sources of social capital directly relevant to your present or future career. Is your amount of such social capital small, moderate or large? How might you increase it?

Career Communities

Wenger (1998) and Brown and Duguid (1991) introduced the term *communities of practice* to refer to groups of practitioners in a particular trade, skill or profession, who grow together through their sharing of knowledge and experience. Career actors often find themselves drawn into such communities, enabling them to build relationships, share skills and engage in shared activities and enterprise. Such communities may exist in a virtual form, through online discussion groups. Communities of practice can affect careers both by sharing ideas and norms about career development in the setting in question, and by providing attraction and adhesion to the community (McLeod et al., 2011; Raz, 2007).

Parker et al. (2004) used the term *career communities* to describe member-defined communities from which people draw career support. Career communities can be developed in an industry, an occupation, a region, an interest group (e.g. a charity), a project, a set of alumni, an informal support group, a family, an organization, a department or a work group. Churches, sports clubs and hobby organizations can all function as career communities, even though this is not their primary purpose. Career communities typically involve the shared development, by members, of meanings and priorities for working life that will assist them to make sense of their careers and undertake new learning related to their careers. Each community in which an individual shares career-related knowledge is likely to generate its own norms about how to conduct one's career (Gibbons, 2004). Many individuals occupy positions in more than one network or community simultaneously, and this can lead to conflict and ambivalence as to appropriate career direction.

Concentrated and Diverse Networks

Networks and communities vary not just in focus but also in power, density and relevance. Some networks are immensely powerful in terms of potential benefit to one's career, whereas others are weak. A young person whose main career community is their family, and whose family members are largely unemployed or in low-status jobs, may be hindered more than helped by the network.

Regarding density, a *dense network* is one where many of the contacts are also contacts of each other – for example, an organizational network where everybody knows each other – whereas a *sparse network* contains a wider range of contacts with little overlap. Granovetter's (1974) concept of, and research on, 'the strength of weak ties' suggests, surprisingly, that people with many weak ties are more successful in accessing jobs through these contacts than are people with only strong ties to an immediate group. Weak ties put people in touch with others who are socially distant, thereby creating new opportunities to progress in one's career by moving outside of one's habitual networks. People who are 'weak ties' typically have their own strong ties. Weak-tie relationships thus provide 'a crucial bridge between two densely knit clumps of close friends' (Granovetter, 1982: 106) and as such are important in the flow of information among groups. Weak ties assist career actors to access information about jobs, and find them (Raider & Burt, 1996), and also enable marginalized groups such as contract workers to develop new networks in which careers are more strongly linked and mutually supported (Antcliff et al., 2007).

Much depends on the heterogeneity of network contacts: familiar, high-density networks that are limited (e.g. to one's family or one's employing organization) may, however comfortable and supportive they seem, be bad for one's career. Consider the network limitations of Clyde in the following case.

CASE STUDY

A Driving Ambition

Clyde is 28. His career so far has been totally in the transportation industry. Clyde's grandfather was a truck driver. His father is a truck driver who has won prizes in

(Continued)

(Continued)

truck-driving competitions. His uncles and his sister are also truck drivers. Clyde knew from an early age that what he wanted to do when he grew up was to drive trucks.

Clyde has had five jobs, all in transportation companies. The first, when he was too young to have a license to drive trucks, was as a truck loader. His last four jobs have all been truck-driving jobs, the first two of them arranged for Clyde by his father, in companies he worked for, the others gained by Clyde through his own expertise and reputation. In his last job, Clyde drove a high-quality truck and won a major truck competition, but his employer was bought out by a larger company. Clyde was kept on the staff, but he found things had changed and the personal treatment was gone: 'at the end of the day you were just a number.' A friend at another company got him an interview there and he was offered a job immediately. Clyde says all good drivers get their jobs by word of mouth. He is proud of his expertise and his value as an expert role model and informal trainer of other drivers.

Clyde's involvement with truck driving and truck drivers extends far beyond the sphere of work. His and his family's lives revolve around the trucking industry. Most of his friends are drivers. He and his wife go to parties with other drivers and their wives. They go to truck shows, where Clyde wins prizes. He has helped several of his friends to get jobs at his company. His pre-school daughters play with toy trucks.

In looking to the future, Clyde says he may eventually give up driving. The nights away from home don't suit family life. But he will remain in the industry, and perhaps, '... move into the office: every now and then I help the office with dispatching. But I wouldn't want to be a dispatcher, I would rather be a fleet manager.'
Source: Arthur et al. (1999: 138).

In this case, Clyde's career networks are exceptionally important. They constitute a career community that both supports and envelopes his career. Every job he has had was gained by means of personal contacts and recommendations. He has begun to reciprocate, feeding his growing expertise back into the network and helping others. Clyde's communities – family, occupational, social and organizational – overlap in a dense network, with few apparent connections with any other industries, occupations or wider opportunities. He has a strong sense of building his career in an industry he knows well and loves. But his eggs are very much in a single (transportation industry) basket, and he apparently has few 'weak ties' elsewhere to assist him should anything go wrong. His career community nourishes him and gives his life meaning and direction. It will continue to be a huge asset in his developing career – as long as he continues to want to stay within the trucking and transportation industry. Should he wish, or be forced, to move into a new field, the same network could turn out to be of little assistance. But what other social capital does Clyde have?

This type of analysis suggests that the most helpful types of career networks may be wide and diverse, rather than tight and focused. This is especially true in current times, when all sorts of social institutions – families, companies, jobs – are becoming more fragmented and uncertain and less able to be trusted to provide a secure, long-term future. According to Higgins (2001), the greater the diversity of a person's network, the more job offers they will receive during a job search and the greater the likelihood of changing careers.

Although networking within one's organization is related to career success in that setting (Bozionelos, 2003), building networks only within one's employing organization, and relying on only those contacts to ensure a successful organizational career, may be a risky strategy. Some organizations stress the value of internal organizational networks, and use the metaphor of 'family' to encourage their employees to see the company as a warm, nurturing, sociable place where a lifelong commitment by the employee will be reciprocated in a worthwhile career (Casey, 1999). In becoming ideal, loyal 'family' members, employees, particularly those who are located close to the 'core' of the organization, may cut themselves off from other contacts. Those in regular communication with suppliers, clients, customers and associated organizations may be able to develop more diverse contacts.

Fields such as film-making (Jones, 1996), television (Tempest et al., 2004) and biotechnology (Casper & Murray, 2005) nowadays have fluid industry structures, collaborative as well as competitive relationships between firms, geographical proximity in 'industry regions' or 'business parks', and work organized in finite projects rather than permanent employment. These characteristics are reflected in dynamic new patterns of career in which industry networks are vital.

Mentorship

While career-relevant relationships may come from any part of an individual's work life and social life, career actors have especially important relationships with *mentors*. A mentor is a trusted advisor or confidante on whom another person (sometimes called the 'mentee' or 'protégé') relies for advice and support. In the context of careers, a mentor is normally understood as being an older, more experienced person who is able, on the basis of that experience, to provide help to a younger career actor in developing their career through its early stages. Mentoring is a key topic in career studies (Ragins & Kram, 2007), and there is good evidence of overall beneficial effects of mentoring on careers (Aryee & Chay, 1994; Chun et al., 2012; Kammeyer-Mueller and Judge, 2008), including benefits to mentors as well as protégés. Mentors can become co-learners with their protégés, particularly in situations where the rules of the game have changed since the mentors were younger (Hall, 2002), and can learn new skills or attitudes from their protégés (Ghosh and Reio, 2013).

What does a mentor do? Kram (1985) described two functions, which she labeled *career* and *psychosocial*. Career functions are instrumental and directly related to career development: for example, offering advice as to career direction, coaching for a job interview, introducing to a new business contact. Psychosocial functions are about background support and affirmation of the protégé's worth. In combination, the two facets of mentoring can provide support for individual career development that takes it beyond career problem solving and makes it a potentially rich and supportive development process.

A mentor familiar with a protégé's current occupation or organization can facilitate their rapid learning of work methods, norms and strategies for overcoming barriers. Influential mentors can make a difference in the jobs the protégé is able to obtain or the projects the protégé is assigned to. Empathetic mentors can act as confidantes, sounding boards and counselors to the protégé about work and career issues. Mentors who are not the direct boss of the protégé can provide independent and confidential advice on how to deal with current issues. Mentors may act as role models.

Many people in the exploration and establishment phases of their careers (Chapter 4) want, and can benefit from, the counsel of those who have been through the process in their time. For example, when in a study by Dupuis et al. (2005), young people (aged 15–34) were asked who had influenced them most in their employment choices and how they had influenced them, the most common responses were that the influential people had given encouragement, support and advice; had modeled behavior (particularly through their own work); and had provided information, inspiration and further contacts of their own. Additionally, in some cases, they had 'hassled' the individual into showing greater career energy – for example, parents saying 'get a proper job or move out' – or changing direction. As the young people's careers advanced, the identity of the mentors tended to change: initially parents had considerable significance, later teachers, and later still employers, supervisors and colleagues at work.

Informal mentoring tends to occur naturally due to a relationship between the mentor and the protégé – for example, when parents act as career mentors to their own children or when a senior manager finds a young staff member likeable and promising and takes the employee under their wing. Formal mentoring – which can include computer-mediated e-mentoring (Headlam-Wells et al., 2006) – is arranged by institutions, such as universities, business organizations and professional bodies, to assist the development of their junior members by assigning them to senior members and providing a formal basis for mentoring activities. Activities may include formal pairing of mentors and protégés, regular meetings following specific formats and training in how to benefit from mentorship (Cranwell-Ward et al., 2004). Career counseling (covered in detail in Chapter 13) can be regarded as a form of mentoring or can be developed from mentoring, but often relates to immediate assistance to a protégé to resolve a specific issue, such as choice of educational program, poor work performance or response to layoff, at a particular time in the career, so that a longer-term relationship need not be developed.

The advantages of career mentoring are so apparent that many organizations have developed formal schemes to ensure that mentorship is provided – at least for their elite, young professional groups – within the ambit of the company on a regular and regulated basis, with senior managers assigned as mentors (Klasen and Clutterbuck, 2002). The US company Proctor and Gamble (2012: 18), for example, reports that it sees mentoring as part of every manager's responsibility, that over 60 percent of employees report that they have a trusted advisor in the company and that its program includes mentoring that is 'reverse', cross-cultural, cross-generational, cross-disciplinary and across time zones.

However, not every manager necessarily has the attributes best suited to mentoring (Van Emmerik et al., 2005) and organizations may have to be careful when setting up mentor–protégé partnerships (Armstrong et al., 2002). The effects of mentorship are affected less by whether it is formal or informal than by the quality of the relationship between mentor and protégé (Ragins et al., 2000), though of course voluntary informal mentoring often has a built-in advantage because it is embedded in a good relationship.

In addition, the concept of mentorship can be widened beyond the notion of a one-to-one relationship between an older mentor and a younger protégé. For example, in considering the mentorship experiences of a sample of women in the entertainment industry, Ensher et al. (2002) reported that many relied on their peers rather than on senior people for support. Many people like talking with others about their careers and find that good ideas, advice and support do not need to come from an 'older head' or a trained counselor. Indeed, Bosley et al. (2009) developed the idea of career shapers – typically co-workers and other contacts of a career actor, who act on a day-to-day basis as career advisers, informants, gatekeepers and intermediaries, and assist actors in their development of their career aspirations, enactment and self-concept. While anyone may come to be a career shaper, people such as line managers, human resources staff and professional careers advisers may, as further described in Chapters 13 and 14, be among them.

Developing the idea of mentorship further, Higgins and Kram (2001) reconceptualized the notion of mentoring as a *developmental network* involving inputs from not just one or two mentors but a range of sources, which may change over time and have more significance for long-term career success than will a relationship with a primary mentor, and which may provide benefits to all participants (Dobrow et al., 2012), so that the hierarchical mentor–protégé notion is replaced by one with more equal partners. In thinking about mentoring in this way, these authors extend our thinking from career-relevant relationships to career-relevant networks. But networks may affect careers in ways other than by being 'developmental', most noticeably when they assist career actors to find jobs.

How valuable and effective is mentoring? This is hard to determine, because so many different variables are involved: mentoring may be formal or informal, regular or sporadic, career-focused or socially-focused. Mentors and protégés may be male or female, high-status or low-status, highly trained or untrained. The value of mentoring in any specific situation is therefore hard to predict: Tharenou (2005), for example, found in a study in Australia that career mentoring increased protégés' advancement, but more for women than for men, whereas psychosocial support *reduced* women's advancement, and that female mentors had the strongest effects in helping and hindering their protégé's advancement. Dougherty et al. (2013) noted that the seniority of mentors positively affected the subsequent earnings of both male and female employees. Multiple mentors in diverse networks may be even better and may be consciously sought by the individual (De Janasz et al., 2003). Overall, though, while the research on mentoring generally suggests that it has positive effects, it has to be admitted that the detail of the research literature paints a confusing picture.

Stop and Consider

1. Considering your career so far, including your education, can you identify any mentors or 'career shapers' who assisted you? How did they do so? Was it effective? What, if anything, did they get in return from the mentoring relationship?
2. Do you know of any formal or semi-formal mentoring programs at your work, at your college or elsewhere? From what you know, do these seem helpful?

Conclusion

In Western societies, the career is conceptualized as being essentially an individual project for which each person is personally responsible. Yet the evidence in this chapter makes it clear that in practice it is impossible to separate any career from the social contexts in which it is conducted. Family, education, position in the social structure (Chapter 3), non-work roles (Chapter 8), as well as employing organizations, all provide us with contacts and network connections that can crucially affect our careers. In other societies organized on a more collective basis, the effects may be even stronger. Thus, notwithstanding the personal efforts that career actors can make to build the right networks, to some extent our relationships are predetermined and we cannot change them.

It therefore behooves career actors, and those interested in the careers of others, to pay close attention to their network of relationships and contacts. However, the issue of how far to go in cultivating relationships solely for the purpose of personal career benefit (rather than occasionally using relationships developed for other reasons) is a delicate one for each individual to resolve in their own way.

Key Points in this Chapter

- Careers are powerfully facilitated and mediated by work relationships and social connections, even for people such as film directors, where the career seems highly individualistic.
- Career transitions are frequently mediated by personal networks, making networking a key career attribute or skill.
- Networking may be done spontaneously or deliberately for career purposes. Effective networking needs to be done continuously and reciprocally. Reputation can be enhanced through networks.
- Social capital consists of the resources we are able to access through our contacts.
- Careers may be enhanced through participation in career communities, based, for example, on educational, occupational or organizational networks where career-related issues are discussed.
- For career development, networks involving diverse 'weak ties' may have advantages over those with more narrowly focused 'strong ties', such as those in close-knit organizations.
- Techniques of impression management can be used to enhance interpersonal influence – particularly for career advancement – but raise issues of personal ethics.
- Mentorship is a form of career-related social connection between more experienced mentors and younger protégés seeking career development. Sometimes mentorship is formally organized.

Questions from this Chapter

General Questions

1. Make a list, or draw a diagram, of your own major social connections – for example, family, friends, tutors, employers and work colleagues. Which ones, if any, have had, or are likely to have, the most influence on your career? How diverse do you think your networks are?
2. What do you think of the techniques used by Bud Fox and Sarah in the case studies in this chapter to advance their careers? Would you do the same?
3. How good do you think you are at networking? Is this of concern to you? What could you do to improve your networks and networking skills?
4. Have you had, or do you have, any mentors? How much have they helped you?
5. Have you observed other people using impression management techniques to try to influence others? What techniques did they use? Do you think this is effective?
6. Are you a member of any groups – career communities – that discuss careers? How helpful is this? If you wanted to get some advice on your career, whom would you go to?

'Live Career Case' Study Questions

1. Ask your case person to list the other people who were most influential in their career and indicate the nature of the relationships and their effects.

2. Ask your case person to indicate other people whose careers they affected and describe how these careers were affected.

3. Describe the concepts of impression management and mentorship to the case person and ask whether these played any part in the person's career.

Additional Resources

Recommended Further Reading

Adler, P. A. and Kwon, S. (2002) 'Social capital: Prospect for a new concept', *Academy of Management Review*, 27: 17–40.

Bosley, S. L. C., Arnold, J. and Cohen, L. (2009) 'How other people shape our careers: A perspective drawn from career narratives', *Human Relations*, 62: 1487–1520.

Higgins, M. C. and Kram, K. E. (2001) 'Reconceptualizing mentoring at work: A developmental network perspective', *Academy of Management Review*, 26: 264–288.

McLeod, C., O'Donohue, S. and Townley, B. (2011) 'Pot noodles, placement and peer regard: Creative trajectories and communities of practice in the British advertising industry', *British Journal of Management*, 22: 114–131.

Song, L.-J. and Werbel, J. D. (2007) 'Guanxi as impetus: Career exploration in China and the United States', *Career Development International*, 12: 51–67.

Weiss, B. and Feldman, R. S. (2006) 'Looking good and lying to do it: Deception as an impression management strategy in job interviews', *Journal of Applied Social Psychology*, 36: 1070–1086.

Self-Assessment Resources

Assess your networking skills: Forret, M. L. and Dougherty, T. W. (2004) 'Networking behaviors and career outcomes: Differences for men and women?', *Journal of Organizational Behavior*, 25: 419–437.

Assess your social capital: Seibert, S. E., Kraimer, M. L. and Liden, R. C. (2001) 'A social capital theory of career success', *Academy of Management Journal*, 44: 219–237.

Online Resources

How to find a career mentor – see: www.wikihow.com/Find-a-Mentor

Map your network using the LinkedIn InMaps application – see: http://careerhorizons.wordpress.com/2011/01/29/linkedin-tip-visually-map-your-network/

Careers as Resources

10

The objectives of this chapter are:

- to consider the concept of career capital, and how different forms of career capital (human capital, social capital, political capital, cultural capital) are important in the career development process
- to describe and evaluate the theory of the resource-based view of the firm, and how it has influenced human resource management (HRM) practices and careers in organizations
- to identify ways in which organizations are resources to individuals' careers, using concepts such as the boundaryless career, careerism and impression management
- to identify ways in which people can develop different career competencies (knowing why, knowing how and knowing whom), transferable skills and employ-ability resources
- to examine how the exchange relationship between employees and their organiza-tions is continually negotiated in the form of 'psychological contracting'.

235

CASE STUDY

My Career Story, by Adam Lovelock

When I was little, I'd pretend to own my own business. I'd clean cars for family members, sweep the neighbours' driveways – I'd do whatever I could to earn money. My parents taught me at a very young age that I had to earn what I wanted, so I learnt to work hard for the reward. Why did I want to own my own business? I guess it runs in the family. My dad had his own successful company. Although teaming up with him would have been an obvious route for me, I really wanted to have something I could call my own.

After graduating, I traveled the world, acquired some useful life skills and came back re-energized with a desire to run my own company. The only problem: I didn't have a product or service to offer. That's when my friend who worked for Enterprise (a large multinational car rental firm) told me about the company. He said I'd have the chance to run my own business with the backing of a multibillion-dollar brand. To me, that sounded like the golden opportunity.

And that's how I got started. I joined as a management trainee in Chatham, Kent, in southeast England. I worked hard and reaped the rewards. Within a year, I had the keys to my own branch. Within three years of my start date, I received an area manager promotion to run the operations in Essex and Hertfordshire. After that, I had the opportunity to oversee all of the airports in the southeast region and got to hone my skills in a whole new business environment.

I have never found a shortage of opportunities here. I've been able to grow in many roles, and Enterprise has always challenged me to stay at the top of my game. Today, I'm the Group Rental Manager of East Midlands and East Anglia in the UK, and I oversee more than 50 rental branches that have a combined fleet of 8,500 cars. I don't rent cars for a living; I develop people. I help develop great area managers, and, in turn, help them develop great branch managers.

From day one, I've taken pride in seeing like-minded people who want to be successful achieve their personal and professional goals within Enterprise. I have always aspired to be the best at what I do, as opposed to being orientated by money. The great thing I discovered at Enterprise is those two things generally go hand-in-hand.

I love my job and I love my free time, too. I'm a sports enthusiast, and especially love water sports like kite surfing and wake boarding. But I also love trying new sports and activities. Luckily for me, I get to host events each month to reward the top employees in my group, and we always do something fun and adventurous. I see that as one of the perks of the job.

Source: www.enterprisealive.ie/connect-with-us/ive-always-wanted-to-run-my-own-business-my-career-story/ (accessed 2 March 2014).

What do we make of Adam Lovelock's career? First, its basis is his relationship with the Enterprise company: Adam's career is very much an organizational career – a type of career that, as we discuss throughout this book, is no longer the norm. Second, from its very outset (the management traineeship) it has been a managerial career, covering a wide range of management functions – branch manager, area manager, regional manager and group manager. Third, it is characterized by steady upward mobility, with the various jobs Adam held – from the management traineeship to the group management position overseeing 50 branches – carrying increasing responsibility. And fourth, Adam's desire to run his own business seems to be at least partly fulfilled through his senior management position, which allows him to 'do his own thing' within the safe structures of a large, profitable company.

Stop and Consider

Are you attracted to the idea of having an organizational career such as Adam Lovelock's? What do you think are some of the advantages and disadvantages of this type of career?

One way of understanding Adam's career is to think of it as a resource – both to Enterprise and to Adam himself. A resource refers to a means available to achieve an end; a stock or supply that can be drawn on (Barney et al., 2011). Careers are useful – they can be drawn on to achieve other purposes. The notion of employees as human resources to be drawn on for the achievement of organizational goals is now commonplace in business and managerial circles. To Enterprise, Adam is not just a person and an employee: he is a resource to draw on to make profits from car rental operations. To Adam, Enterprise is not just an employer, but also a resource in terms of income, competency development, personal goal fulfilment and valuable work experience – all of which, incidentally, signal his 'employability' to other potential employers.

Lovelock's career can be looked at as a series of investments. Adam invests his time, energy, abilities and skills into Enterprise. Enterprise invests money in Adam's salary, benefits, development and the salaries of those who help him. The investments are therefore mutual. In many cases of this type, the process works well for both parties, and people live out their careers interdependently with, and harmoniously in, the organizations that support them and that they in turn support. In evaluating any employment, it is worthwhile to consider the reciprocities involved, that is, the benefits exchanged between employee and employer and the long-term accrual of those in the employee's career (Rousseau, 2011). Some benefits, such as salary, are immediate, whereas others, such as knowledge or expertise, may pay off over many years. In the same way, the employer may gain instant advantage from some employee inputs, such as work performed before receipt of salary, but will benefit over many years from others, such as ongoing skill development (Ployhart et al., 2011).

The Resource-Based View

The 'resource-based view' (RBV) theory of the firm (Barney, 1991; Barney & Clark, 2007; Kraaijenbrink et al., 2010) has identified three key characteristics of resources that can create competitive advantage for organizations. The theory states that resources need to be:

1. Valuable, meaning that they should enable the organization to outperform their competitors;
2. Rare, meaning that they should be unique in the sense that competitors do not host identical resources; and
3. Inimitable, meaning that competing organizations should not be able to imitate them to the degree that they are able to compete with the organization having the valuable resource.

Organizations naturally seek to maximize their investment by ensuring that the knowledge that employees acquire is maximally relevant to the organization's present and future needs. They seek to protect their investments in their employees by doing all they can to keep them within the organization long term rather than allowing them to leave to work for another organization, especially a competitor. They might, for example, offer long-service rewards, company benefits, stock options and pension arrangements. Conversely, employees often develop extraordinary loyalty and commitment to organizations that look after them in this way and seek to develop and may use their own careers largely for the benefit of the organization (Whitener, 2001).

This is a system of interdependence that can work well for organizations. In fact, it is embodied by what we call their 'human resource' management (HRM) practices. Human resource management tends to define career management as management of employees' careers by the organizations in which they are employed (see Chapter 14). Career management, in this sense, is part of an overall approach to staff management that also includes areas such as personnel selection, training and development, remuneration and performance evaluation, which are integrated with each other and with the general strategic plan of the organization. (For full textbooks about HRM, see Cascio (2012), DeNisi and Griffin (2013) and Dessler (2011).)

The 'resource' view of careers was therefore developed largely by organizations as a way of conceptualizing their ability to combine human inputs with, for example, financial inputs to provide goods and services and make a profit.

But are humans – and their careers – resources? What are the implications of considering them as such? Is there a danger that ready acceptance of this metaphor encourages the appropriation of individuals' personal resources for corporate gain? And what about the other way around? To what extent are organizations resources to individuals' careers, and is this type of 'exploitation' by employees potentially harmful to organizations?

Individuals as Resources to Organizations

The resource-based view is first and foremost a theory of company strategy, which implies that employees' working lives and therefore careers can and should be managed by organizations (Boxall & Purcell, 2003). Other approaches to strategic management suggest that good strategy is based on taking appropriate action in relation to *external* conditions, such as market opportunities and competitors (Homburg et al., 2004; Porter, 1985). In contrast, the resource-based view stresses the *internal* constitution of the company, particularly its human resources – for example, the strategic vision and team dynamics of its managers, and the skills, knowledge, network contacts and other attributes of its staff – as a major basis of its success that enables it to make appropriate responses to external conditions. Although human resources – employees – are not the only resources organizations hold, they are unique in the extent that appropriate investment in them can add value to them and also in that, unlike money or technology, human resources can walk away from the organization if they wish (Lepak & Snell, 2002).

Companies can build and sustain competitive advantage (Campbell et al., 2012) by developing core competencies (Mooney, 2007), such as cutting-edge expertise in a new technology that their competitors cannot rival. Therefore, to succeed in competition, business organizations must have a vision of the core competencies they need to succeed and must either capture these from outside the organization or develop them inside the organization. The competencies of an organization are embodied in the expertise of its employees, which is developed from their career experiences. So, organizations seeking to succeed have a very good reason to intervene actively to influence the careers of their employees. They do this by inducing outsiders with key knowledge to join the organization, inducing insiders with key knowledge to remain within the organization, and developing and deploying these people's expertise as desired by management according to its strategy. Most likely, the intention behind the many transfers of Adam Lovelock within Enterprise was not only to get important jobs done but also to ensure Adam's personal development as an ever-more versatile and valuable company resource, well able to assist its continuing competitiveness.

The competencies involved go beyond the individual skills and capabilities that particular employees may bring, and extend to the integration of these capabilities with others' capabilities and the broader organization – through teamwork, managerial systems and company culture (Bartlett & Ghoshal, 2013). For example, according to Fong (2003), experience in cross-functional (interdisciplinary) teams and the development of interdepartmental careers (like Adam Lovelock's) rather than specialized careers, are among the means of developing an overall human resource with greater long-term value to the company. Sophisticated organizations will therefore try to engineer their employees' careers to have these features.

Organizations as Resources to Individuals

As individuals are 'human resources' to organizations, so are organizations 'career resources' to individuals. Organizations can be used by their employees to build competencies, expertise, networks, reputation and financial reserves, all of which can be transferred to other employment settings (another company, one's own business) if and when a career actor so desires and has the opportunity. Some authors in the HRM field have warned companies about what they call the current-day 'consumerist career mentality' in employees, through which employees treat organizations as tools, merely there to help equip employees with the resources they need to develop their personal projects and individual careers (Dany, 2003; Fournier, 1998).

Reality, however, is likely to be more nuanced. As retirement ages increase around the world and careers are longer than ever, and as economic instabilities are making it harder for companies to promise life-long careers, it makes sense for individuals to work for multiple employers over the course of their career. In order to do so, however, they need to make sure they develop transferable skills that will guarantee their attractiveness to other potential employers, even when they already have secure employment. As a result of these dynamics, young people entering the labor market today are no longer socialized into believing they should find a good employer after graduation and stay there. Rather, they are encouraged to weigh their career decisions against a longer-term vision of the type of career they want, and to assess how each career decision will look on their résumé. Let us consider the case of Dov.

CASE STUDY

Making the Most of It, by Nicky Dries

My friend Dov called me from Rome in 2005, asking for my career advice. Having been an exchange student in Spain and Italy for two years – where he had enjoyed *la dolce vita* – he now faced the decision of where to start his career. He had simultaneously received an offer to go work as a management trainee for Coca-Cola in Madrid, and another offer to become head of the entertainment team of a hotel belonging to the Club Med group in Sicily. 'Which offer should I take?' he asked me. I thought he was joking. 'The Coca-Cola one, of course! That's a real job, at least', I told him. When he took the job in Sicily – thereby extending his dolce far niente lifestyle a bit longer – I couldn't help but wonder how this would affect his further career.

Boy, did he show me. As it turned out, Dov's outgoing attitude and experiences abroad made him a sought-after candidate by international companies who were amazed by both his social skills and fluency in six languages. At the age of 30, he was hired into a senior management position by the Zürich subsidiary of an Italian headhunting company. Up until the global economic crisis hit in 2008, Dov was living the dream: a job that allowed him to do what he does best – charming people into using his company's services – in return for a generous pay check that included variable pay based on his sales numbers. When the crisis hit, all variable pay within the company was cut, but Dov stayed put. He negotiated and received a promotion with a higher salary range.

After three years with the company, his managers informed him of the company's plans to expand its activities to Asia, and told him they wanted him to move to Singapore for at least two years to start up operations over there. Dov hesitated. Although he liked the idea of gaining work experience in Asia – both for the experience itself and for his résumé – he had set his mind on moving to New York for work, as well as enrolling in an executive MBA program (although, technically, he was not yet an executive and too junior to attend such a program). In addition, the Singapore project seemed poorly defined by the company and he feared they underestimated the challenge of setting up a new subsidiary in Asia without any real embeddedness within a local network of business associates and prospective clients. His heart not being completely in it, Dov decided to nevertheless make the most of it. He negotiated for an executive-level salary plus full expatriation benefits; he negotiated for the company to support his application and pay for the executive MBA program worth upwards of 60,000 euros; and he negotiated for a 'no strings attached' clause in his contract (which he did not get). Basically, he negotiated away any doubts he had about the project he would be undertaking in Singapore.

Dov returned home from his stay in Singapore a few months ago. As he had feared all along, the project was a commercial disaster. After a relationship that had lasted five years, he and his employer decided to part: the agreements they had made prior to Dov's departure had been revised too often, and the company had asked him to refund part of his exorbitant expatriate salary back to the company as a sign of his loyalty in times of financial difficulties (which he had been willing to do). Although leaving the company on bad terms has been the biggest disappointment in his career, Dov feels optimistic about his future. Together with an American executive he met through the MBA program, he is now developing a business plan to start his own company, which he plans to run from New York.

A career such as Dov's is typically referred to as a 'boundaryless career' (see also Chapter 7). Boundaryless careers are careers in which individuals accumulate skills and personal reputation as key career resources by moving between employers, as well as in and out of self-employment (Arthur & Rousseau, 1996). Boundaryless career actors aim to reap higher rewards by developing transferable skills rather than organization-specific skills. The boundaryless career model emphasizes the personal rewards people can gain from their careers, through their adaptation of their career paths to their own interests and special abilities (Hopson & Ledger, 2010). A side-effect of this search for personal fulfilment, as we see in Dov's case, is that as boundaryless career actors seek to keep their options open, they tend to reduce their loyalty and commitment to any particular organization. The organizations they work for, therefore, become 'resources' to their careers rather than long-term partners (Stevens, 2001).

In its most extreme form, treating organizations like resources can result in careerism. Careerism is defined as the propensity to pursue career advancement, power and prestige through any positive or negative non-performance-based activity that is deemed necessary (Bratton & Kacmar, 2004). People with a strong careerist orientation believe that personal and organizational goals will always be, in the long run, incompatible. The balance between self-interest and the interests of the organization thus becomes disturbed (Aryee & Chen, 2004). Careerism is often linked to impression management (Chapter 9).

Stop and Consider

Are you a careerist? If you agree with four or more of these seven statements, you might be!

1. It is difficult to advance in organizations through merit alone.
2. It is often necessary to use social relationships with superiors, co-workers and friends to get ahead.
3. It is important to cultivate the appearance of being successful – the appearance of being successful can be as instrumental in terms of advancement as competence.
4. It is sometimes necessary to engage in deceptive behavior to get promotions to which one feels entitled.
5. It is important to recognize that, in the long run, the individual's career goals will be inconsistent with the interests of the organization; therefore, ultimately, it is each person for him or herself.
6. Loyalty to an employer is unlikely to be rewarded.
7. In order to get ahead, it is sometimes necessary to take actions that promote personal advancement rather than those that promote the company's best interests.

Source: Feldman & Weitz (1991).

Although having a careerist attitude and engaging in impression management might lead to objectively positive career outcomes, such as getting promoted, negotiating a higher salary or establishing a strong (possibly intimidating) reputation for yourself – especially when the organization you work for normally rewards careerist behavior – recent research indicates that careerism is ultimately related to low career satisfaction and feelings of personal and social alienation, i.e. the feeling of separation or even estrangement from oneself and from others (Chiaburu et al., 2013). At its most extreme, an organization that rewards careerism might find itself in a position where organizational performance suffers because people are promoted based on their impression management tactics and political 'game-playing', rather than on their competence.

So what to do when you scored highly on the careerism scale above? Your first option is to look for an employer that encourages careerism, as odds are higher that you will be able to navigate the organizational career system to your own advantage. When you do so, beware of the 'Peter principle' – the effect whereby people are promoted until they are found out to be incompetent (Peter & Hull, 1969). Your second option is to have a deeper look into your own careerist beliefs. Where do they come from? From a place of ambition or cynicism? In the former case, have a look at the literature on careerism, impression management and career success. It is important you understand that successful careers are only part political play, and that in an overwhelming number of companies, objectively measured job performance is still the most crucial determinant of promotions and salary. In the latter case, it may be time you re-examine your beliefs about the world of work. Do you really believe that all organizations reward careerist behavior? Which type of organizations do you think are more likely to do so? Take a look at the organizational career management climates described in Chapter 14.

Human Capital Theory

Within the resource-based view of the firm, the focus is not so much on 'humans' but rather on 'human capital' as the currency of career management (Ployhart et al., 2014). Human capital refers to the economic value of an employee's skill set (Campbell et al., 2012; Wright & McMahan, 2011). Individuals can invest in, and develop, their own human capital through education and learning experiences (Ployhart et al., 2011), and such investments are generally highly rewarded in the labor market and can therefore enhance career attainment (Ng et al., 2005). Investments made prior to organizational entry are likely to determine the level at which an individual joins a new employer, which in turn will influence their remuneration level and future advancement opportunities (Bozionelos, 2004).

Farndale et al. (2010) distinguish between four different types of 'career capital' that employees can develop throughout their careers:

- *Human capital*, meaning level of occupation, education and work experience, to the extent that these influence the ability of an individual to perform labor that has economic value. For example: holding an executive position, an MBA degree or 20 years of experience in retail.
- *Social capital* – the sum of the actual and potential resources that can be mobilized through an individual's membership in social networks. For example: belonging to a powerful family, an alumni network of a prestigious school or a group of friends that refer you to potential clients (see Chapter 9).
- *Political capital* – being known in one's network for getting things done – reputational capital; and the capacity to effectively build constituent support and acquire legitimacy by exercising power – representative capital. For example: being known for your expertise, being admired by younger colleagues, being feared.
- *Cultural capital* – characteristics and habits acquired through the process of being socialized into a specific occupation or organization. For example: having access to inside information, knowing the ins and outs of your profession, understanding the unspoken rules within your organization.

Human capital value and uniqueness

In an effort to manage their human resources more efficiently, many organizations have turned to the practice of workforce differentiation, which dictates that employees should be managed differentially based on their level of human capital (Becker et al., 2009). Lepak and Snell (1999, 2002), for instance, argue that the human capital within any given organization can be categorized along two dimensions – value and uniqueness.

- *Value* refers to the potential of the human capital at hand to contribute to its organization's core competence and enhance its competitive advantage. High-value human capital refers to assets that are pivotal to the organization's core business whereas low-value human capital generally refers to 'peripheral' assets. For example, a person with strong research skills is likely to be considered a high-value employee by a research-based organization such as a university, while that same person in a support-level research and development (R&D) role in a commercial organization such as an HR consultancy firm will be considered a peripheral asset compared to those in HR consultancy positions – positions that would be considered peripheral in the context of a university.
- *Uniqueness* refers to the extent to which the organization's human capital would be difficult to replace (high uniqueness) as opposed to being readily available in the labor market and easily copied by competitors (low uniqueness). Although uniqueness can be related to years of experience and expertise in a 'niche' area,

it does not have to be. For example, a young graduate who was raised trilingually and/or comes from a well-respected business family can represent a unique resource to an organization. Alternatively, labor market conditions (see Chapter 2) might dictate who is difficult to replace and who is not: think of the lists of shortage occupations published annually by many countries worldwide.

Based on the conceptual dimensions of value and uniqueness, Lepak and Snell (1999, 2002) distinguish between four human capital quadrants, each possessing different characteristics and carrying different HR implications. In the top right-hand corner of the model (quadrant I), we find human capital that is both valuable and unique. The recommended 'employment mode' for employees falling into this quadrant is internal development, as highly unique skills are not easily 'bought' in the general labor market. The recommended type of employment relationship, then, is organization-focused. Organization-focused exchange relationships encourage significant mutual investment both on the part of employers and employees to achieve long-term competitive advantage. In order to support or create such an employment relationship, organizations will likely rely on a continuity-based HR strategy that encourages employee involvement and optimizes their return on human capital investments. For example, the organization could sponsor career development and mentoring programs aimed specifically at developing organization-specific knowledge in their high-value, high-uniqueness employees (i.e. knowledge that is much more valuable within their specific context than to competitors) (Lepak & Snell, 2002). The other three quadrants are much less likely to be selected for specific organizational career management programs. 'Internal partners' (quadrant II) are employees with skills that are valuable but widely available in the labor market (i.e. high-value, low-uniqueness); 'contract workers' (quadrant III) are those with generic skills of limited strategic value that can be acquired on an ad-hoc basis (i.e. low-value, low-uniqueness); finally, 'external partners' (quadrant IV) possess skills that are unique in some way, but not directly instrumental to the organization's competitive advantage (i.e. low-value, high-uniqueness) (Lepak & Snell, 1999, 2002).

Stop and Consider

Throughout your career, how might you go about developing your human, social, political and cultural capital? Consider formal education as a potential source for development, but also more informal ways of learning and developing (for instance, learning from experience; learning from role models; learning from observation). What can you start doing tomorrow? What would take more time to develop?

Competency and Competence

Boyatzis (1982) wrote the first academic book on competency development. His definition of competency remains, to date, the most cited one: 'an underlying characteristic of a person which results in an effective and/or superior performance of a job [...] it may be a trait, motive, skill, aspect of one's self-image or social role, or body of knowledge that he or she uses' (p. 20). Boyatzis saw competencies as individuals' personal abilities that are closely related to concepts such as needs, motives and traits. His primary focus was on using competencies to separate good from poor performers.

Some authors have criticized Boyatzis' approach to competencies, calling it too broad in the sense that almost everything can be described as a competency. Woodruffe (1993), for instance, proposed a definition of competency that is more behavioral: 'the set of behaviour patterns that the incumbent needs to bring to a position in order to perform its tasks and functions with competence' (p. 17). Interestingly, this definition points to the difference between 'competency' and 'competence'. The term competence is typically used to refer to what needs to be done in a job in order to comply with minimally acceptable performance standards for that job (Whiddett & Hollyforde, 2003). Therefore, competence refers to job- or role-related work tasks, functions or objectives, which can be assessed against certain standards of output. Focusing on the mastery of specified goals or outcomes implies that competence is by definition a retrospective concept (Haase, 2007).

Competencies, on the other hand, focus on the person and not the job. Competencies are not measured directly by their outcomes or objectives, but rather by behaviors observed in effective people (Whiddett & Hollyforde, 2003). They indicate how people work, how they apply their skills and knowledge to their jobs, and what enables them to perform well. Contrary to competence, competency is not retrospective, but rather is used to assess current behavior, as well as to predict further potential. In summary, individuals can demonstrate competence (on the job) by applying their competencies (that they have within them) (Haase, 2007).

Thinking about your competencies allows for realistic assessment of your aspirations and expectations. By studying what type and level of competencies are vital in a desired job, you can make more informed decisions about whether you have the abilities to achieve the required skill level, and plan your career development accordingly. It might also encourage you to evaluate your strengths and weaknesses, which will allow you to identify where your needs for further development lie exactly. Furthermore, reflecting on your unique strengths and weaknesses individualizes the career planning process to make it more personally meaningful to you. If the process is handled well, the output of the above assessments can provide valuable information for creating a realistic and well-timed personal development plan (Craig, 1992).

Career competencies

Some 20 years ago, Quinn (1992) introduced the paradigm of the 'intelligent enterprise', arguing that an organization's success stems from its core competencies, which are a reflection of its internal culture (shared values and beliefs), its overall know-how (accumulation of the performance capabilities embodied in employees' skills, knowledge and expertise) and its business networks (relationships with customers, suppliers, etc.). Subsequently, Arthur et al. (1995) analyzed the potential impact of this new paradigm on work and careers. As a result, they introduced the idea of the 'intelligent career', complementing Quinn's intelligent enterprise. Intelligent careers are defined as any sequence of work roles undertaken at the worker's own discretion, and with personal goals in mind (Amundson et al., 2002). Arthur and his colleagues investigated how individuals can contribute to the competencies of their organization, and concluded that each arena of organizational competency (culture, performance capabilities and business networks – see above) suggests a matching arena of individual competency (DeFillippi & Arthur, 1996).

Arthur et al. (1999) define career competencies as personal competencies that are put at the disposal of the employing organization, but whose benefits often outlast the employment relationship. In individual career management, they are seen as learned capabilities that result in successful performance and are defined as behavioral repertoires and knowledge that are instrumental in the delivery of desired career-related outcomes (Francis-Smythe et al., 2013). Career competencies go far beyond the technical skills and managerial abilities on which company development programs tend to focus (Haase, 2007). They reflect individuals' interpretations of their career situation and are subject to constant change in line with changing circumstances (Amundson et al., 2002).

DeFillippi and Arthur (1996) differentiate between three broad types of career competencies, which they refer to as the 'three ways of knowing':

- *'Knowing-why' competencies* are the individual's motivation and values and the way in which these energize work behavior. Knowing-why competencies influence a person's overall commitment and adaptability to employment situations, and are positively related to career motivation, personal meaning and sense of purpose.
- *'Knowing-how' competencies* are the individual's skills, qualifications, expertise and experience. Knowing-how competencies reflect career-related skills and job-related knowledge.
- *'Knowing-whom' competencies* are the individual's contacts, networks and reputation. Knowing-whom competencies reflect the social contacts, relationships, reputation and attachments that are established within, as well as outside of, the organization while in pursuit of a career.

It is clear from the above that there is a reasonable amount of overlap between these competencies and the different forms of capital (human, social, political and cultural) discussed earlier. The difference between capital and competencies lies in the fact that human capital is considered mostly from the perspective of the employer – what creates value for this organization? – whereas competencies create value at the individual level – what makes me a better employee and enhances my long-term career value?

Knowing-why, knowing-how and knowing-whom are complementary 'ways of knowing'. Each job or project change in our careers typically requires us to invest in at least one way of knowing. For example, in the commitment we make to a new job or project (e.g. Adam Lovelock's realization that he might prefer working for a large company rather than start his own business and his consequent commitment to the organization), we are typically making an investment in our employer from our current motivation or knowing-why. When we offer an employer skills or experience transferred from an earlier job (e.g. Lovelock's all-round experience in Enterprise), we are drawing on knowing-how. When we enhance our work through our network contacts (e.g. Lovelock's organizing of team-building events for his fellow Enterprise-ers), we are drawing largely on knowing-whom. In each case, the fresh investment from one way of knowing has consequences for the other two (Inkson & Arthur, 2001).

As we continue in our careers, our stock of career competencies changes. The organization's investment in us may pay off for us as well as for the organization. Our work may provide new unforeseen opportunities, thus affecting our knowing-why. It may involve us in gaining new knowledge or becoming familiar with a new industry, thus increasing our stock of knowing-how. It may enhance our interactions and reputation among work associates, thus developing our knowing-whom. But the accumulation of competencies over time is far from guaranteed: a dead-end job may reduce our competencies or make them obsolete. To make our competencies work for us, we have to work with our competencies. Here is an example.

CASE STUDY

Building Competencies from Diverse Sources

Marie qualified and practiced briefly as an intensive care nurse, but marriage and childcare intervened. Realizing her work at home was not enough for her, she assisted her businessman husband with his property investment and share portfolios, gradually moving from secretarial assistance to researching and making investment decisions on his behalf. She also learned to do the catering for his business functions. Seeking to extend herself, she trained as a chef and managed a restaurant owned by her husband. Eventually, she bought her own restaurant: she purchased an old warehouse, designed and refurbished it herself and created a high-quality gourmet restaurant that soon had an outstanding reputation.

At this point, Marie's husband suddenly died. When his estate was examined, huge debts were revealed. Marie was forced to sell her successful restaurant and was left with almost nothing. Also, she found that the idea of the restaurant business now seemed trivial and unappealing. Pondering her strengths and weaknesses, she concluded that what she was best at, and liked best, was planning and organizing. As a nurse, she had made a major contribution to the design of a new intensive care facility; as a partner to her husband, she had successfully integrated information from a wide range of sources to plan new real estate developments; as a restaurateur, she had received her main satisfaction from workplace and menu planning. Her restaurant work had also shown her that she had a wide range of management skills, particularly the ability to communicate her plans to others in a way that inspired as well as informed them.

Marie set up shop as a management consultant. Her initial work was done for business friends of her late husband's, who were 'helping her out' as much as trying to improve their businesses. But Marie's single-mindedness and the quality of her work soon led to repeat contracts and new invitations. High fees rolled in. Soon, she was able to take advanced university courses in new planning techniques. For perhaps the first time, she felt her career was truly under way.

Marie's career involved the gradual accumulation of career competencies from a range of experiences. Her knowing-why included the restlessness that impelled her to continually seek new ventures to plan and the sudden recognition of what it was that she was most interested in. Her knowing-how involved a range of skills developed through her work in three different industries – health, finance and hospitality. When her husband died, her knowing-whom resources were thin – his friends – but she quickly used them and her other resources to create a strong network of clients.

Transferable Skills and Employability

Employability refers to the likelihood of obtaining or retaining a job (De Cuyper et al., 2011; Fugate et al., 2004). In times or situations of high unemployment, raid turnover or insecure employment contracts, the argument goes, being able to get employment quickly and easily is even more important than having employment, and that means having skills that can easily be transferred from one job to another.

Originally considered a topic of concern mainly to unemployed people, in today's literature employability is seen as important to the entire working population. It is argued that as most employers can no longer guarantee employment security, they should offer employability security instead, in the form of continuous transferable skills development (Clarke & Patrickson, 2008). Previous work has compared and contrasted employability to movement capital, i.e. the skills, knowledge, competencies and attitudes influencing an individual's career mobility opportunities (Forrier et al., 2009);

ease of movement, i.e. the perception of attractiveness and availability of alternative employment opportunities (Trevor, 2001); career proactivity, i.e. taking initiative in improving current circumstances or creating new ones (Seibert et al., 2001); and job-hopping, i.e. the degree to which employees view their current employment as a stepping stone to better jobs elsewhere (Hamilton & von Treuer, 2012).

As is demonstrated by these related constructs, employability can be conceptualized as both an outcome and an antecedent. Outcome-based measures of employability tend to study objective factors representing the likelihood a person can obtain or retain a job (McArdle et al., 2007). According to this approach, individuals are employable when they can prove that they can find employment, which is measured, for example, by employment status (Mancinelli et al., 2010), or rate their own likelihood of obtaining and retaining employment as high (i.e. 'perceived employability'; e.g. De Cuyper et al., 2011).

In the present chapter, however, we are not so much interested in employability as an outcome, but, rather, in the amount of employability resources people have (as antecedents). Contrary to outcome-based approaches, antecedent-based approaches to employability focus on the resources (i.e. skills, abilities, attitudes and behaviors) that may help people find (new) employment or remain in employment (e.g. Fugate et al., 2004; Van Dam, 2004; Heijde & Van der Heijden, 2006). The opposite of being highly employable, then, is being stuck with a set of highly non-transferable skills. Let us consider the case of Naima.

CASE STUDY

Non-Transferable Skills

Naima, an information technology specialist, acquired early-career expertise working as a programmer and analyst using a software package called Florex. When she moved to a new city to be with her partner, she scanned the help-wanted section of the newspaper until she found an opportunity for a permanent job with a consulting company specializing in Florex applications. During the next five years, Naima was very happy in her position as an analyst and, later, as technical manager for Florex applications. It was a pleasant company to work for, her skills were recognized and her boss sent her to out-of-state training courses and Florex conferences several times to hone her skills.

After three years, it was suggested that she might like to take on new responsibilities, perhaps in sales or client liaison, but Naima regarded herself as a technical person and resisted these opportunities. She then began to feel 'taken for granted' in the company and was offered fewer development opportunities. At the end of her fourth year, she was told her work was satisfactory but was offered no salary increase. The same thing happened at the end of her fifth year. After hearing this, for the first time since joining her company she scanned the help-wanted ads and was concerned to notice that there appeared to be no vacancies in the city for someone with her background. It seemed that interest in Florex was on the wane. With alarm she realized that outside of Florex her marketable skills were slender.

The next day, Naima told her boss she had been upset not to receive a salary increase. She said that if the decision were not changed, she would have to consider looking elsewhere. Her boss was unperturbed. 'Where?', he said.

In this case, Naima has probably developed too much of a specialization in her line of work and too great a dependence on her current employer. What is good for the employer (i.e. keeping Naima on as a relatively low-cost programmer who will not move on because she has no options) is not good for Naima's long-term career. It is good for employees to look for areas of overlap of interests with the employer but wrong to assume that they are there permanently and that the employer will always act to assist their development. Particularly important is any 'knowledge capital' that is in scarce present or future supply. Metaphorically, each of us is, actually or potentially, a knowledge capitalist, a trader and investor of accumulated learning and a joint venture partner of every economic institution within which we work. In the case of Naima the programmer, her knowing-how (expertise in Florex software) has declined in value, her knowing-why (motivation to be a programmer only) is too narrow and her knowing-whom has become confined to one organization.

By contrast, transferable skills are skills you have developed through various jobs, volunteer work, hobbies, sports or other life experiences that might also be applied in other jobs or even in an occupation that is entirely new to you. In addition to being useful to those considering a career change, transferable skills are also of crucial importance to employees threatened by lay-off or those that are chronically dissatisfied with their jobs, as well as to young people entering the labor market or those returning to it after a period of being unemployed. In India – more specifically in the Indian ICT sector – it is even so that if young people do not move around within their industry at least every two years, employers will automatically see this as a signal of skill obsolescence (Cappelli et al., 2010).

How can you identify your transferable skills? They can be deduced from past accomplishments or experiences. For instance, stay-at-home parents or homemakers might find they have skills in budgeting, child development, food services, property management, and so on (McKay, 2013).

The job titles you mention in your résumé (including vacation jobs, internships) likely say very little about the skills you have demonstrated and developed in the jobs you have held so far. Therefore, McKay (2013) recommends that you dissect each job (or even hobby or volunteer activity) you have ever done in order to discover what transferable skills you actually have. If you have limited work experience, you will have to rely on your broader life experiences to get this information. One thing that might help you is to look at job advertisements to see what types of skills, knowledge and traits companies are asking for. Based on these, you then can start compiling your own personal list of the skills you possess, and how you developed each of them (and, possibly, a list of development areas). Remember, if you claim to possess a certain skill throughout a job application procedure, the recruiters are likely to ask for evidence of that skill – so be prepared to answer the question 'can you give a specific example of a situation in the recent past in which you have demonstrated that skill?'.

Just to provide you with some more inspiration, here is a list of skills that are typically considered transferable across occupations, jobs and employers, and that do not necessarily demand work experience (McKay, 2013):

- planning and arranging events and activities
- delegating responsibility
- motivating others
- attending to visual detail
- assessing and evaluating your own work
- assessing and evaluating others' work
- dealing with obstacles and crises
- multi-tasking
- presenting written material
- presenting material orally
- managing time
- repairing equipment or machinery
- coordinating fundraising activities
- coaching
- researching
- building or constructing things
- managing finances
- speaking a foreign language
- utilizing computer software (specify programs)
- training or teaching others.

Stop and Consider

Go through the above bullet-point list and (a) indicate whether each would be highly valuable, moderately valuable or not valuable, in a job or educational course you are currently involved in. Then, (b), go through the list again and note, for each, whether you consider yourself to be good, moderate or poor in that skill. Look for areas where you are poor in skills that would be valuable. What can you do to close the gap?

The Psychological Contract

Throughout this chapter, we have touched upon the relationship between employees and their employers. As we have discussed, if we adopt the metaphor of careers as resources we could say that individual careers are resources to organizations, whilst simultaneously (organizational) careers are resources to individuals. Therefore, a welcome development in our understanding of careers, particularly organizational careers, is the emphasis in the recent careers literature on the notion of the psychological contract as a means of understanding how careers play out in the relationship between employer and employee (Rousseau, 2011). In fact, over the course of the last two decades, the psychological contract has become one of the most influential concepts in the literature due to its ability to explain social exchange relationships and predict employees' attitudes and behaviors (Conway & Briner, 2009).

The psychological contract describes an individual's beliefs regarding reciprocal obligations between them and an organization (Rousseau, 1995). Put differently, it captures what an employee believes to owe the organization and what the employee believes the organization owes him or her in return. In this context, 'contract' is of course a metaphor – there needs to be no written contract, merely a shared understanding by the two parties of reciprocal wants and expectations (e.g. the employer's expectations of standards of work by the employee and the employee's expectation of security and loyalty from the employer). The psychological contract is continually revised and updated in the course of the employment relationship. In fact, a career can be conceptualized as a constantly renegotiated series of psychological contracts (Inkson & King, 2011). This view recognizes the rights of both employees and employers to joint determination of the career and allows for processes of career change, even radical career change, without a change of organization being a necessary precondition.

The recent HRM literature suggests dramatic changes in the relationships between employers and employees (Arnold & Cohen, 2008). The 'old deal' employment relationship in which employee loyalty was rewarded by job security has been said to be partially replaced by a 'new deal' whereby organizations (should) offer their employees ample opportunities for skills development, so that they can uphold both their internal and external employability in the face of today's volatile labor market environment. In fact, several authors now argue that the psychological contract is not so much a contract with a specific employing organization anymore. Instead, they see it as a contract with oneself that in times of frequent changes needs regular re-evaluation (Enache et al., 2013).

Different streams of the literature have adopted very different views of the psychological contract. Where the careers literature promotes a focus on free agency, enthusiastically spelling out the benefits of employability development for employees, employers and labor markets, those in the HRM literature fear that developing employability in employees might cause perverse effects in the form of higher turnover (Dries et al., 2014). The assumption of a negative impact on employee loyalty is problematic for HRM scholars, who advocate the establishment of long-term employment relationships between organizations and their most valuable employees (Lepak & Snell, 2002). In fact, it is likely that organizations will want to retain their highly employable employees the most (Baruch, 2001).

Most of the research on the psychological contract has focused on breach and violation of the psychological contract by employers. Psychological contract breach refers to the extent one party is perceived to have fallen short in fulfilling its obligations, whereas psychological contract violation is defined as the emotional response to what is perceived as a wilful failure to honour one's commitments (Rousseau, 2011). Breach and violation by employers have (from the perspective of employees) proven to have detrimental effects on employees' ensuing attitudes and behaviors.

Have another look at Dov's case above: when his employer violated the agreement that in return for his willingness to move to Singapore for work under adverse business conditions, he would receive ample compensation, he decided to leave the company for good. Where his employer held the unspoken belief that after five years of loyal service Dov would be willing to sacrifice part of his generous salary to help out the company, Dov saw this as a distinct violation of his expectation that the company would understand that moving to Singapore was not his choice in the first place and that he had left 'his life' back home to accommodate the needs of the company – especially since he ended up having to sue the company to receive the severance pay he was legally entitled to. Perceived violation of a psychological contract can cause major trauma to one's career, making the ongoing negotiation and spelling-out of expectations and obligations by both employer and employee vital (Inkson & King, 2011).

Stop and Consider

Have you ever been in a situation (employment-related, educational or personal) where the other party, at least in your opinion, violated an unspoken agreement between you and them? How did that make you feel? Was the violation of the agreement based on a misunderstanding, or of malicious intent? What did you learn from that situation that might help you negotiate with your current employer or with future employers when it comes to your career?

Conclusion

Careers embody the energy, the know-how and the networks that individuals have developed over time. The use of these resources gives every career an economic or societal value that can be used both by the person whose career it is and by other people and institutions, particularly the organizations in which the person is employed. Negotiating how to use this resource for individual and wider benefit may be difficult, but in most cases win-win scenarios can be devised so that the person and the organization both benefit. What is critical is that the career resource should not be allowed to depreciate through lack of development – both individual and organization must constantly seek to invest in its development.

Key Points in this Chapter

- Careers have economic value. To organizations, employees are often seen as resources – as in human resource management – to be used with other resources to achieve organizational goals. The employee's potential is typically built up over a career, making the career a resource as well.
- In the resource-based view of the organization, employees represent major sources of competitive advantage. Organizations often seek to protect this resource by retaining employees in organizational careers through 'psychological contracts'. Large organizations often offer attractive career paths and other rewards to encourage loyalty. They tend to differentiate their investments in employees, however, based on the value and uniqueness of their human capital.
- A good employer can be a major resource to an employee's career. Organizations frequently offer selection and training, human resource development, staffing systems, appraisal and assessment, and organizational career development, providing major potential benefits to their members' careers – and helping them develop employability and transferable skills that they might carry over to another employer. Organizational career management is dealt with in detail in Chapter 14.
- The intelligent career framework provides a model for individuals to develop their own career competencies for their own benefit. Key elements are knowing-why (motivation), knowing-how (expertise) and knowing-whom (networks), all of which can be invested in and grown by the individual.

Questions from this Chapter

General Questions

1. Do you consider yourself to be a resource? If you don't, why not? If so, in what sense? Who does the resource belong to?
2. Think of some organizations you know or have worked in. To what extent do they provide programs with potential career benefits for their staff, such as training,

appraisal and staff development? Would they be good organizations to work for, from a career point of view?

3. Make an assessment of your own career capital, covering knowing-why, knowing-how and knowing-whom. Where did you obtain it, where are you currently investing it and how can you grow it in the future?

'Live Career Case' Study Questions

1. Ask your case person to assess him or herself in terms of the value and uniqueness of their human capital. How valuable is the human, social, political and cultural capital of your case person to their employing organization? And if your case person would choose to leave that organization, how difficult would it be for them to find an adequate replacement?
2. How employable does your case person feel they are? How many alternatives does your case person see beyond their current job, occupation or career type? How broad versus specific are these alternatives in terms of sector and geographic location? Ask your case person to make a list of the non-transferable skills they possess (i.e. skills that are only useful in the current employment situation, and not beyond) versus their transferable skills.
3. Has your case person ever experienced psychological contract breach in their career? If so, ask your case person to tell you the story of how the breach occurred and how the situation was resolved eventually.

Additional Resources

Recommended Further Reading

Campbell, B. A., Coff, R. and Kryscynski, D. (2012) 'Rethinking sustained competitive advantage from human capital', *Academy of Management Review*, 37: 376–395.

Feldman, D. C. and Weitz, B. A. (1991) 'From the invisible hand to the gladhand: Understanding a careerist orientation to work', *Human Resource Management*, 30: 237–257.

Fugate, M., Kinicki, A. J. and Ashforth, B. E. (2004) 'Employability: A psycho-social construct, its dimensions, and applications', *Journal of Vocational Behavior*, 65: 14–38.

Kraaijenbrink, J., Spender, J. C. and Groen, A. J. (2010) 'The resource-based view: A review and assessment of its critiques', *Journal of Management*, 36: 349–372.

Mooney, A. (2007) 'Core competence, distinctive competence, and competitive advantage: What is the difference?', *Journal of Education for Business*, 83: 110–115.

Ployhart, R. E., Nyberg, A. J., Reilly, G. and Maltarich, M. A. (2014) 'Human capital is dead: Long live human capital resources!', *Journal of Management*, 40: 371–398.

Self-assesment resources

Assess your career competencies: Francis-Smythe, J., Haase, S., Thomas, E. and Steele, C. (2013) 'Development and validation of the career competencies indicator (CCI)', *Journal of Career Assessment*, 21(2): 227–248.

Assess your transferable skills: McKay, D. R. (2013) *Transferable skills: Bringing your skills to a new career*. Available at: http://careerplanning.about.com/od/careerchoicechan/a/transferable.htm (accessed 2 March 2014).

Assess your employability: Heijde, C. M. and Van Der Heijden, B. I. (2006) 'A competence-based and multidimensional operationalization and measurement of employability', *Human Resource Management*, 45(3): 449–476.

Online Resources

John Boudreau on human capital – see the YouTube video entitled 'The new science of human capital' posted by Harvard Business Review at: www.youtube.com/watch?v=j3rZSIqZ0pM

Find out which are the shortage occupations in your region – *this knowledge might help you develop a 'unique' profile*: for the UK – www.gov.uk/government/uploads/system/uploads/attachment_data/file/261493/shortageoccupationlistnov11.pdf; for New Zealand – www.immigration.govt.nz/migrant/general/generalinformation/review.htm; for Australia – www.immi.gov.au/Work/Pages/skilled-occupations-lists/skilled-occupations-lists.aspx; for Canada – www.visacenter.org/index.php/page/canadas-shortage--and-priority-occupations-25-and-counting-tick-tock. For other countries, simply look up 'shortage occupations', adding the name of your country in the search string.

More about employability and how to develop it – see the website of the Careers and Employability Service of the University of Kent at: www.kent.ac.uk/careers/sk/skillsdevelop.htm

Careers as Stories

1

Chapter Objectives

The objectives of this chapter are:

- to develop an appreciation of the idea that much of what we know about people's careers is in the form of stories, and that these stories vary according to their context, audience, purpose and other factors
- to understand the role of stories in helping to shape the meanings we ascribe to careers, our identity within them and the framing of stories by career actors to suit personal and career needs
- to see how public stories and rhetoric about careers, for example in the media, reflect and influence some of our career attitudes and behavior
- to read, appreciate and interpret career stories written by others, and to begin to write our own.

CASE STUDY

One Career, Two Stories

Consider this career story from a 1978 pop hit:

Man:

You were working as a waitress in a cocktail bar

When I met you

I picked you out, I shook you up

And turned you around

Turned you into someone new

Now five years later on you've got the world at your feet

Success has been so easy for you

But don't forget it's me who put you where you are now

And I can put you back down too.

Woman:

I was working as a waitress in a cocktail bar

That much is true

But even then I knew I'd find a much better place

Either with or without you

The five years we have had have been such good times

I still love you

But now I think it's time I lived my life on my own

I guess it's just what I must do.

From 'Don't you want me?', performed by The Human League, written by Johann Fransson, Tim Mikael Larsson, John William Callis, Niklas Edgberger and Tobias Lundgen. Copyright: Warner/Chappell Music Scandinavia AB, V2 Music Publishing.

In this case, the same career elicits two totally different stories. The man sees the woman's career as having been dramatically changed by his own actions. His view suggests that powerful people can substantially influence the careers of others. When he says he turned the woman 'into something new', we are reminded of George

Bernard Shaw's play *Pygmalion* (1916), where the powerful and knowledgeable mentor Professor Henry Higgins coached working-class flower-seller Eliza Doolittle to become a great society lady. Such career stories are redolent of myths and legends about sorcerers who can transform ordinary people.

Can other people turn our careers around in this way? Some of the material in Chapter 9 of this book (on careers as relationships) and Chapter 10 (on careers as resources) suggests that sometimes they can. If so, the implied career strategy for those seeking success would be to play a 'political' game, to seek influential and skilful mentors and advisors, and to entrust one's career to their superior knowledge and networks. The career model adopted is that 'it's who you know that counts' and that to get ahead and stay ahead you need to 'oil the wheels'. The story attributes great power to external assistance to the cocktail waitress's career.

In contrast, the woman apparently considers that her career success has been mainly a matter of her own talent, self-belief and personal action. She clearly believes in self-motivation and self-management as a means of career advancement. Moreover, she thinks that she can continue in her success on her own, and that she has reached the stage in her career where her relationship with her mentor/lover may be counter-productive and best severed. In the story she tells about herself, she reminds us of Madonna's career, which we reviewed in Chapter 5 – the loner who succeeds on the basis of raw ability, determination and perseverance, though Madonna also used networks of influential people, manipulating her contacts rather than vice versa. Legends of heroism involve similar individualism and proactive action. The narrative underlying such careers might involve phrases such as 'believe in yourself', 'you can pull yourself up by your own bootstraps', perhaps even 'Look after Number One'.

Who is right about the cocktail waitress's career – the man or the woman? It could be either. It could be both. It could be neither – perhaps her success was a matter of pure luck. What we see in this illustration is a career story – or rather two different stories about the same career, each with its own hero or heroine, plotline and dramatic sequence. With all our understanding of career dynamics, we are unable to say that one of the stories is right and the other one wrong.

Suppose, then, that there is no ultimate truth about any individual career – that careers are no more, or less, than the stories we tell about them, and that every story has its own validity. Perhaps every career story, including all the others in this book, is incomplete, and is not the only account possible of the career in question. Perhaps people tell different versions of their career to their families and friends, to their managers and work colleagues, to the clerks and agency officials they report to in search of work, to the acquaintances they make conversation with in bars or cafés. Perhaps, too, they create and embellish their own career stories in their heads, so that the images of career embodied in these stories change and develop as time goes by.

This chapter, then, starts from the premise that there is no ultimate 'truth' about any individual career, that careers can be considered as no more or less than the stories we tell about them, and that every story has its own validity, and its own usefulness, as well as its own limitations, such as self-justification, self-delusion and distortion, in order to impress others.

Storytelling

Storytelling is a fundamental human activity (Polkinghorne, 1988). Parents read bedtime stories to their children. Children tell their families stories about their football game that day. Shoppers describe to friends the altercations they have with shop assistants. Job applicants recount incidents from their careers to interviewers. And listening to or reading stories and then responding to them is a key part of everyone's life.

When we talk about our careers, we tell stories about ourselves. For example, every time we leave a job, get a new job or experience a career crisis, there is a story to tell (Ibarra & Lineback, 2005). Such incidents are, as it were, paragraphs in a chapter, or chapters in a book, and each book is the story of a life, and it is not finished until the person dies. Any career can be seen as a story or a series of stories.

Social scientists have begun to take an increasing interest in the process of storytelling or narrative. As people experience things, and tell stories about their experiences, they also construct their personal realities and views of the world. We can, for example, gain a rich understanding of organizations by the stories that members tell about their experiences in them (Boje, 1991).

This growing interest in stories as a means of understanding is part of two theoretical movements labeled constructivism and social constructionism (Bassot, 2012; Blustein et al., 2005; Cohen et al., 2004; Hartung, 2010). In both theories, people's actions are considered to be based on their own personal view of the world, and they go through a personal process of constructing knowledge on the basis of their experiences. In constructivism, the emphasis is on the internal processes through which people learn, whereas in social constructionism the creation of individual reality is considered more of a social process, in which views are shaped by shared experiences, such as those presented in the mass media. Thus, a career story can be a unique personal account of a set of events concerning an individual (constructivism). Alternatively, as a social construction it can contain elements of accounts that are shared collectively by different people, or can echo a story-plot, such as 'fast-track to the top' or 'beating the bureaucracy', that is common across society and therefore likely to be understood by many listeners.

The notions of *order of happening* and *connectedness* that are common in stories are important because they provide the essential structuring on which the stories depend for their functions in relation to career: 'When people punctuate their own living into stories, they impose a formal coherence on what would otherwise be a flowing soup' (Weick, 1995: 128). Narrative involves *temporality* (how events are related in time) and *causality* (how events cause each other). But the time involved is subjective rather than measured by the clock, and the causality is subjective and loose rather than rational and precise (Gibson, 2004b).

Characteristics of stories

A story needs a theme, a plot and a way of arranging the characters and events so that the relationships between them are seen. Frequently, a specific story makes a general point. Here is an example.

CASE STUDY

Walking Out

Brenda was a prison officer for 20 years. With limited education and training and having entered the job only because it was secure and better paying than the alternatives available at the time, Brenda had little early ambition. But as time went by and her skills developed, she began to see possibilities for eventual advancement to managerial ranks. The organization was bureaucratic, and there was a prescribed career path laid out in terms of different types of job experience and off-the-job study. Brenda began preparing herself for the job of prison superintendent. This involved many hours of study in addition to her full-time job. Also, because of her interest in her work, she took leave at one point to go to a university in another city, where she earned a degree in criminology. After many years of study, including a major assessment center evaluation that lasted several days, she reached a point where she had only one more course to pass to be able to be considered for superintendent. But at that point, the prison service announced a major restructuring. When that was over, Brenda was called to a one-to-one meeting with a consultant. Calmly, the consultant explained that Brenda's job was unaffected but that the new structure had abolished many superintendent jobs. In addition, the training and development program that Brenda had undertaken had been deemed obsolete and scrapped; hence, if Brenda wanted to be qualified to become a superintendent, she would have to start again, and it would most likely take much longer because of the reduced number of places available. Furious, Brenda glared at the consultant and then said, deliberately, 'I'll tell you what you can do with your job!' Then, she walked out. At that point, she had absolutely no idea what she would do next, but she knew she would never go back, and she felt exultant.

Ibarra and Lineback (2005) suggested that good stories have key characteristics: a protagonist, or main character, that the listener cares about; a background situation requiring the protagonist to take action; trials and tribulations that appear as obstacles in the protagonist's path; a turning point when things must change; and a resolution of triumphant success or tragic failure. These elements are all present in Brenda's career story, told to one of the authors directly by Brenda. The way she presented the story, including the details of the extra efforts she made to gain promotion, and the matter-of-fact, uncaring actions of the consultant, enabled Brenda to dramatize the climax, or punchline, of the story – her walking out. As she told the story, Brenda was flushed with emotion as she recalled her anger. Many people accrue 'I told them what they could do with their ****** job!' stories that contribute to a collective narrative or script, stories that may be driven by emotion and exaggerated for effect.

Career Storytelling in this Book

We, the authors, have asked many people to tell us their career stories. In some cases, our request has been an informal part of a research investigation; some career stories have been specifically gathered for inclusion in this book. In other cases, it has been driven by sociability and curiosity: 'I'm interested in careers – can you tell me about your career?' As we stated in Chapter 1, some people, particularly those in lower-level, temporary or blue-collar jobs, have indignantly insisted they do not have a career, only a job (Dries, 2011). Despite this, most are willing to tell their career stories, and seem to enjoy doing so. Careers are personal and intimate. But whereas many people might want to keep information about, say, their personal relationships, religion, politics or finances private, sharing one's career story with someone else is not usually seen as threatening.

This book is full of career stories, several per chapter. A few are summarized from publicly available sources, such as websites and biographies. But internet writers and biographers have their own point of view. Most of these stories were based on what the career actor said in an interview, and people tend to put their own 'spin' on their own careers. In a few cases, we amalgamated different career stories to make a point or altered details to protect anonymity. All of these stories are therefore authentic, but not every last word in them is true. Every story in the book is included for the purpose of illustrating a career principle, such as inheritance, cycles or the problems of a particular form of career. We massaged the stories to make the point as effectively as we could – not changing the stories, but choosing which parts of them to put in and to emphasize. None of the stories, therefore, is a pure, objective, unembellished account of the career it represents. Perhaps no such thing as a 'pure' career story exists.

In a form of storytelling, as in the 'case study' exercise that runs through this book, we ask students to elicit a career story, or a series of career stories, from an older person, such as a parent, to write it down and to try to analyze it using theoretical frameworks such as those in this book. The stories students write about the career actors they question are frequently inspiring – many stories are told by people who have overcome considerable challenges in their careers and have done amazing things. Some students report that listening to their father's or mother's career story was a great experience for them. Frequently, it was the first time they had heard the story. Frequently, it led them to a new understanding of their parents or of their parents' own childhood (e.g. 'So that's why Dad was always so angry!'). For female students, it is frequently shocking (but enlightening) for them to hear the barriers of gender discrimination that their mothers faced when trying to pursue their early careers: of course, gender discrimination in careers still exists today, but it has probably lessened (Chapter 3). In some cases, students report that understanding their parents' careers by listening to their stories has helped them to get closer to their parents. At the very least, even if you haven't engaged in the formal career case study exercise in the book, it's worth asking your parents or others you know to tell you the story of their careers. You may learn a lot.

Stop and Consider

Ask a parent or other older person to tell you a story from their career. Afterwards, consider the characteristics of the story. What type of story was it – for example, comedy, tragedy, story with a moral? Do you think it was totally true in all respects, or had it been mis-remembered in parts, or exaggerated for effect? Did it have a clear plot, hero or heroine, villain, obstacles to overcome? How far do you think it was representative of the person's whole career? 'Play' with the story and see what you can learn.

Career storytelling and the recording and analysis of stories are also increasingly recognized as a potentially valuable means of research, enabling us to develop career theory (e.g. Young & Valach, 2000), offer informed criticism of conventional career thinking and practice (e.g. El-Sawad, 2005; Severy, 2008) and create new paradigms of career guidance (e.g. Cochran, 1997; McMahon & Watson, 2012; see also Chapter 13).

Career stories can also be an interesting way for career beginners or career actors to find out about careers from those involved in them, particularly if the reader can identify an occupation or field of interest. If you want to browse among career stories, often told in the participants' own words, the web has a multitude of sites – see, for example:

- www.vitae.ac.uk/researchers/200941/Database-of-career-stories.html
- http://icould.com/watch-career-videos/
- http://careerplanning.about.com/od/exploringoccupations/a/real_career_stories.htm
- www.citytowninfo.com/career-stories

(all accessed 23 August 2013).

But why are stories so important to us? What do they do for us? If we think about our careers as stories, how does that help us to understand them or find direction in them?

Finding Meaning Through Stories

According to Polkinghorne (1988), we use narrative to give meaning to our experiences, to join incidents together in coherent wholes, and to understand past events and plan future ones. Because careers are long chains of events, linked by causality, narrative may be particularly appropriate to examining them. Narrative is, says Polkinghorne, 'the primary scheme by means of which human life is made meaningful' (p. 11). Even if we do not verbalize our narratives to others, we rehearse them to ourselves and thereby make sense of our lives. Thus, the stories that people tell 'can illuminate the ways in which individuals make sense of their careers as they unfold through time and space' (Cohen & Mallon, 2001: 48).

A career story is a personal, moving perspective on our working life, including the objective facts and the subjective emotions, attitudes and goals of our careers. We create stories about ourselves retrospectively as a means of remembering day-to-day events, justifying our actions, providing coherence to our lives, projecting ourselves to others ('impression management', see Chapter 9) and sometimes to plan for the future.

In the process of articulating a story, we develop our own meanings and interpretations of events. We reinforce these interpretations by listening to ourselves. Stories are therefore not necessarily told overtly. Their most important functions may be discharged when we tell them internally to ourselves: the story helps us to understand and create or improve, retrospectively, the reasons behind our career decisions.

Consider, for example, this extract from a career story told by Sharon H, a project engineer who, as a student (of sport and recreation), had worked as an unskilled factory operative to pay for her tuition.

CASE STUDY

A Reason for Everything

'I wanted to work in the sports industry. I was always a good all rounder at sports ... I did a qualification in business and finance and then it had bolt-on parts for recreational management. So I basically did that but I came and worked at (Company name) as a kit-cutter because I needed the money.

'I then graduated and still really didn't know what I wanted to do. I thought I still wanted to work in the recreation side of things. Applied for lots of jobs but there wasn't really a lot out there and after doing all the lifeguard training and working in a sports centre, I then decided it really wasn't what I wanted to do. It was a lot of hard work for not a lot of gain back was what I felt at the time. So it didn't give me a challenge.

(Continued)

(Continued)

'I think it was at that point that I found out that I was actually quite good at organising things and I found I was very quick at typing out all of the processes of manufacture for tooling. And it was in 1995, I thought, well, we get new project managers in who have probably been working in different industries, doing a similar job but working doing different things. So I decided to write a project department manual which covered all of the theory of tool making, a glossary of terms, how to choose what particular tool to manufacture for particular components and so on and set it all out.

'And after I wrote that I handed it in to the project managers at the time and they thought it was great. And basically, they offered the position of being a project engineer which I took up with open arms. And I've never looked back since.

'After the birth of my son Jamie in 2001, I was a project engineer before I went away on maternity leave and came back four months later and was offered a different job as a business development manager. Because it was felt by the management at the time that I wouldn't be able to be a project engineer on a four-day week because I wanted to have Fridays off to be able to spend a long weekend with my son.

'I proved the company wrong a year later on that; after being a business development manager for a year we had a change in the management structure. And because through being the business development manager I'd brought on a number of new customers who wanted me to project manage their projects within the industry. And so I did that from 2002 until currently, we've had another new management come into place and they've recognised my skills and have basically promoted me to being the manager of the engineering group.'

Source: http://icould.com/watch-career-videos/ (accessed 23 August 2013), with permission of the career development charity iCould.

Sharon's career is impressive, particularly her proactive action (Chapter 5) in voluntarily writing the project managers' manual which launched her from being a shop-floor worker to being a manager. But the other thing to notice about her story is the way it is told – its (possibly unconscious) emphasis on cause and effect: everything that happens to Sharon in the story, and every action that her company takes, is driven, in her own account, by a *reason*. It appears from this as though Sharon is very rational in her retrospective analysis of her career. Whether, at the time of her writing the manual, that seemed a rational thing to do from the point of view of benefitting her career is another matter. Sharon's story is a good example of *retrospective sensemaking* in a career (Weick, 1995).

Stories help us to impose these patterns. In developing narratives of our lives, we have the benefit of hindsight. We know what we want in the present, and that guides us retrospectively in our search for a plausible story (Weick, 1995). 'Learning occurs as individuals make sense of the experience and come to realise that the stories they previously regarded as discrete and unconnected exhibit coherence through common themes and patterns' (McMahon & Watson, 2012: 215). Our subjective view of careers, say ten years ago, is no longer available to us, so we try to remember it: 'I left university early because…'. But the events and feelings of ten years ago have to fit into a story that is coherent over a long period. Viewed in this way, careers consist of 'improvised work experiences which rise prospectively into fragments and fall retrospectively into patterns' (Weick, 1996: 40). Career stories, in short, help us to make sense of our careers.

Stories and Identity

As indicated in Chapter 8, identity represents a person's sense of individuality and personality – who they are. Identity can be conceptualized as being embodied in the stories we tell about ourselves. The first edition of this book, for example, tells the story of Sara Ford, whose occupation was software tester and whose organization was Microsoft, but whose primary identity was not that of tester or Microsoft employee but as a mathematician, the discipline in which she had been trained (Inkson, 2007: 159). According to narrative theory, Sara would have arrived at that conclusion by observing, narrating and interpreting her own experiences. Identity construction 'implies a telling of the self that synthesizes a number of the elements in a way that shows their coherence and unity' (Bujold, 2004: 473). Identity may be a personal myth (McAdams, 1995), but it is one that we constantly feed through the stories we create and tell about ourselves. Writing one's story is not a statement of the objective truth about oneself but an interpretation of the self based on multiple experiences (Peavy, 1998). And, if variation of identity is needed, we can use stories to reinvent ourselves.

In the confusion of today's flexible, dynamic society, with its contingent work, portfolio careers, improvisation, multiple roles and transactional contracts potentially fragmenting our sense of self (Sennett, 1998), perhaps the narrative process (i.e. storytelling) provides us with the opportunity to find coherence and continuity. Increasingly, career experts advocate the writing, or telling, by career actors, of their personal stories, as a means – possibly with expert assistance – of clarifying their career identities (Meijers & Langelle, 2012). We explore this process further in Chapters 12 and 13.

Creating the Future

The characteristics of narrative include its sequencing over time. Stories also provide an explicit opportunity for career actors to reflect on past events and how they have segued into the present, and to project them ahead into the future. Again, this function can be capitalized on in career advising and counseling processes.

By interpreting the past, we use narrative to make sense of the present and thereby see a way to the future. Career narratives don't end. When we narrate our careers, we must constantly reconfigure the story to take account of new events. The storyline from the past, however, typically provides a strong framework in which present events can be understood and may even give direction for the future. Such narration has been effectively utilized in the practice of narrative career counseling, in which counselor and client move through a series of steps from describing a career problem, to outlining a career story, to developing a narrative about the future and finally acting to make the narrative a reality (McMahon & Watson, 2012), a process we elaborate on in Chapter 13.

Telling Stories to Others

A story also enables listeners, such as spouses, colleagues, employers and counselors, to make their own interpretations and respond. Understanding the overall meaning of a career may thus enable a listener to grasp the issues relevant to a career decision by understanding the meanings of the story of which that decision is part (Bujold, 2004; Cochran, 1991).

A narrative approach enables us to get a sense of how people got to where they are and how they now understand their situation. They are therefore 'less about positions and professions and more about the fashioning of identity over time' (Gibson, 2004b: 178). Stories thus tend to accord the subjective career primacy over the objective, or at least to add the subjective to the objective.

Stories are not static, but evolve and develop as the career moves on and as the career actor struggles to bring coherence, consistency and rationality to what may sometimes be unpredictable and surprising sequences of events. For example, Ibarra & Barbulescu (2010) showed how, during transitions between work roles (Chapter 8), career actors construct 'narrative repertoires' – internal stories – which they continuously revise and refine to justify their actions and explain them to others. For example, an academic developed a story to explain her transition to become an aspiring money manager:

> June's attempts at explaining herself – why she wanted to make such a seemingly crazy career change, why a potential employer should take a chance in her, why she was attracted to a company she never heard of a day before – were at first provisional, sometimes clumsy ways of redefining herself. But ... she experimented with different versions of her story, each time getting feedback on what her audience found plausible and what made her more or less compelling as a job candidate. (Ibarra, 2003: 60–61)

Listening to multiple stories about careers also enables listeners to learn more general lessons about careers, which is why narrative is increasingly used as a (qualitative) research method to study careers. For example, Wallace (2009) noticed specific career tendencies of women accountants as they passed through different career stages. Seeking to account for these, she decided not to ask women accountants direct questions about it, but rather encouraged them to tell their own stories in their own words. Her 13 intensive career interviews enabled her to draw three conclusions that ran contrary to conventional wisdom: (1) that career moves tended to be made for reasons characterized by the word 'opportunity' rather than 'advancement'; (2) that the roles played by women as actors and agents of their own careers (Chapter 5) have been underestimated; and (3) that work–family conflicts did not play a major part in determining the career choices of those in her sample. Listening to the career stories of these women resulted in questions about conventional career scripts and brought home the sheer complexity of careers.

By listening to, or reading, career stories, we can therefore learn about careers. Consider the following stories.

CASE STUDY

Getting into Engineering

How do people decide to become engineers? Here are summaries of four true stories told by four engineers, who all subsequently pursued academic careers, about their choice.

Linda Katehi, living on the Greek island of Salamis in 1966 and 12 years old, had her imagination caught by the sight, on the television in a neighbor's house, of Neil Armstrong, the first man to walk on the moon. But the shots of mission control in Houston, its rows of lights and screens, gripped her even more than those of Armstrong. Although a math teacher helped her, her father told her that if she were an engineer, no one would hire her and no one would marry her. By 1984, she was doctorally qualified.

Wallace Fowler grew up in Greenville, Texas, crazy about airplanes. He knew the specifications of every plane and could tell which engine a B36 had by the sound it made. At that stage, he wanted to be a test pilot. However, health problems prevented that, and he obtained a math degree and became a computer programmer instead. To help him communicate some of his programming analysis to engineers, he took an engineering course. Eventually, he studied engineering at graduate school and later became a top aircraft and aerospace engineering professor.

Janie Foulke grew up on a farm in North Carolina and out of sheer necessity learned to fix things. When she was 9 years old, she received a chemistry set as a Christmas present. When it proved too messy for her bedroom, her father built her a laboratory in an outbuilding. The next year her present was a dissecting kit. Marriage and children interfered with her ambition to go to medical school, but in due course she took a graduate course in medical engineering – a first step to a career in research.

(Continued)

(Continued)

James Melsa's talent for math and science was noticed by his class teacher in Nebraska. The teacher was a science fiction fan and lent him sci-fi books, which caught the boy's imagination and convinced him that he belonged in the laboratory. Afraid that pure science might not bring him the saleable skills of electrical engineering, James enrolled for the latter. Then, in his first job after graduation, he found out that his neighbor was a professor of electrical engineering. James enrolled in his course and so impressed the professor that an academic job quickly followed.

Source: Grose (2005).

Grose (2005), the storyteller who reconfigured the stories told to him by the engineers, did not try to draw lessons. He simply told the stories and allowed the narratives to speak for themselves. Can we conclude anything, from these four cases, about becoming an engineer? There are some common factors that the stories share: all the engineers had built-in interests, relevant childhood experiences, fortunate chances, and parental and/or teacher support that guided their choice. On the other hand, each story is unique, and each might inspire different people in different ways. The stories might be heightened by reading them in full, rather than in the brief summaries above.

We can therefore use career stories to understand individual careers, the careers of specific groups (for example, female doctors) and careers *en masse*. For example, Valkevaara (2002) used stories to try to interpret general features common to the careers of human resource development (HRD) and found that all the stories revealed 'a similar emphasis on the centrality of people, a personal style as a working tool, and understanding of learning as the cornerstones of professional expertise in the practice of HRD' (p. 183). Similarly, Broadbridge (2004) examined stories from male and female retail managers and noted that men were more likely than women to construct career success narratives involving self-promotion. While every story is unique, therefore, hearing many stories may create a basis for generalization.

Stop and Consider

Write down a true story (not more than 200 words) about an incident from your career to date (e.g. getting or losing a job, choosing an educational program, receiving mentorship). Can you identify a protagonist, a need for action, difficulties, a turning point and a resolution? How might you tell the story to meet different circumstances or to tell it to different people? Would others involved in the story tell it the same way? Does the story exemplify any general features of you as a person, your career or the context of careers?

Stories and 'The Truth'

What about the issue of truth? Does it matter that any event, or indeed any career, can yield many different stories to describe it? Which stories are true and which false? Our view is that most career stories are subjective, and important not so much for whether they are true or false, but for how they help us to understand not just the career but also the attitudes of those involved. 'The narrative is not a reproduction of events but a construction that the [story]teller thinks the other should know about' (Young et al., 2002: 219). Consider how the events of a single career can result in quite different career stories.

CASE STUDY

Different Points of View

Wendy: My career? Not much to tell, really. I was a high school dropout. I bummed around for a few years, waitressing work mainly. I had a job in a circus once. I was young, sowing my wild oats. And great experience. When you sleep rough for a few months, you really learn how to look after yourself. I always knew I'd get it right. I planned for it. When I was 20 years old, I started going to night school. Then I went back home for full-time study. By the time I was 25, I had my degree, a business qualification. My grades weren't great, but it's what you can do, what you can talk yourself into that counts. So, I got taken on as a trainee manager by Gracefield Manufacturing. I did a couple of projects for them, organizational development, marketing, lots of fun. I built connections. The company is OK but not very exciting. I've stuck it out for 5 years, but I'm looking around. I can do much, much better.

    Wendy's mother: Wendy's career? You don't want to know! A nightmare. She was trouble in school, expelled for disruptive behavior at 15. We did our best for her, but she walked away from home at 16, never worked much. She got into bad company and was in trouble with the police. There were drugs, thefts, probably worse. We bailed her out all the time, but she still spent time in jail when she was about 19. In the end, the only way we could get her out of her way of life was to buy her the best psychotherapy we could get. It cost us tens of thousands, but it seemed to settle her a bit, and she met her boyfriend, Gary, who was a real stabilizing influence. Even so, she was pretty well unemployable until Jim Gracefield, a family friend, agreed to take her on, as a favor, in low-level accounts work. Gary more or less forced her to go to community college, and eventually she got some kind of diploma. And she's stayed out of trouble and stayed with Gary. But I don't think Jim Gracefield sees much future for her, so I only hope she can hold on to her job. We've looked after her so far, but we can't look after her forever.

One career, two stories. No doubt Jim Gracefield, Gary, Wendy's father and Wendy's friends would tell different stories about Wendy's career. So what is the truth about the career? Is there a single truth? Could the self-confident, ambitious young woman and the anxious, pessimistic mother both be right or both be wrong? Perhaps Wendy's career is no more than the tales people tell about it. And if that is true of Wendy's career, is it not true of all careers?

CASE STUDY

A Tale of Two Cyclists

A dramatic case indicating the unreliability of some career stories concerns the American professional cyclist Lance Armstrong. Up until 2012, the story that Armstrong told, and that was widely believed by many millions of people all over the world, was that after a promising career as a professional road cyclist, he was stricken, at age 25, with testicular cancer that also affected his brain and lungs. His life was threatened, but he was cleared of cancer by a course of chemotherapy. Returning to cycling, Armstrong became the most successful cyclist of all time, winning the world's most prestigious event, the Tour de France, for seven consecutive years from 1999 to 2005, retiring and returning to further cycling success from 2009 to 2011, when he finally retired. To help combat the disease which had nearly terminated his career and perhaps his life, Armstrong also raised many millions of dollars for charity. He wrote the story of his triumph over cancer and his success in an autobiography, *It's Not About the Bike* (Armstrong, 2001). It was a wonderful career story. Armstrong was lauded as a hero worldwide. As Armstrong said himself in 2013, 'This story was so perfect for so long ... You overcome the disease, you win the Tour de France seven times ... I mean, it's just this mythic perfect story' (Lance Armstrong, quoted by Tang, 2013: 1071).

Unfortunately, as Armstrong then admitted, it wasn't true. Or rather, it was true, but not the whole truth. Yes, Armstrong had cancer; yes, he came in first in seven Tours de France, but, as he now admitted, he had been assisted by the systematic and illegal taking, by both himself and many other members of his cycling team, of many performance-enhancing drugs, over the entire period. This was a part of the story that outsiders had persistently rumored over the years, but that Armstrong had emphatically denied in his own accounts. But eventually the evidence for this version of the story became overwhelming and Armstrong was compelled to admit that it was true. Armstrong had been skilled in sophisticated methods of evading the drug-testing regimes imposed by the cycling authorities. An extraordinary aspect of the whole affair was that dozens of other cyclists, team assistants and officials either were involved in the drugs conspiracy or at least knew about it, yet Armstrong's repeated story that he had been hugely successful without using drugs was maintained for years.

There are therefore two stories about Armstrong's career. Even allowing for the illicit drugs, his achievements were remarkable. There is a wonderful heroic, over-coming-the-odds quality about Armstrong's original career story: perhaps people believed it because they *wanted* to believe it. But the factual evidence also revealed him to be a shabby, bullying cheat. Much as we may want 'the simple truth' about careers, the truth is seldom simple and usually impossible to fully determine.

Even where there is no intention, in career stories, to deceive, such stories are always interpretations, and the same events yield different stories that are given different interpretations by different storytellers, who can believe, choose and embellish stories that suit their own purposes. For example, rival stories often circulate at the time of political elections, concerning the birthplace, or military service, or sexual history, or family life of candidates – and listeners can choose which story to believe.

Individual agency or social context?

Career stories again raise the issue of whether careers are perceived to be determined by individual agency (Chapter 5) or social context (see Chapter 1). In Western society, careers tend to be viewed as individualized projects (career as action or agency; see Chapter 5). Individual ego involvement in the career is likely to lead to the career story that each individual tells about him/herself being presented as a personal exercise, either relatively independent of external influences or in overcoming such influences.

A key factor here is what psychologists call 'fundamental attribution error' – the tendency to overestimate the contribution of individuals to events and underestimate the effect of contextual forces (Ross, 1977). In their career stories, career actors are also likely to take credit for achievements in their careers while blaming malign con-textual forces for their failures. For example, many accounts of career include stories about cultural and organizational obstacles encountered and overcome in pursuit of career goals. People tell tales of how they initially failed because they were from 'the wrong side of the tracks', or because they followed advice from teachers which turned out to be wrong, or because they were laid off by an inhumane organization, or because a prejudiced, ignorant interviewer awarded the job to the wrong candidate. Successful individuals will have stories of how they succeeded *despite* such difficulties. Often, a self-justification theme is involved (Mantere et al., 2013).

Writing Résumés

A story which every career actor has to write about their career, probably in different versions, many times during the career, is the *résumé* (French word for 'summary'), sometimes called *curriculum vitae* (Latin term for 'story of a life') or *vita*. A résumé is a document used by job seekers, and normally written by them, to detail their background and skills relevant to the job. It usually includes an account of previous experience in the form of a list of jobs previously held and additional information about them. Job seekers normally send résumés to prospective employers along with a cover letter, and they are likely to be a major tool used by the employer in determining whether it is worthwhile to interview the candidate. Being able to 'tell a good story' in the résumé is therefore a key skill in career self-management and advancement.

A résumé is basically a tool for marketing oneself. Some aspects of a career actor, such as qualifications and jobs previously held, are objective facts and moreover are often checkable by the reader of the résumé. Other features, such as the writer's personal capacities, the precise nature of their experience and the quality of their interpersonal relationships, are more subjective. The résumé writer, obviously keen to present him/herself in the best possible light, may knowingly or unwittingly paint a word picture which others might not agree with. Parts of the résumé are of course likely to be checked later by such means as interviews, referees' reports, checks with previous employers, etc. The writing of one's career story as a résumé therefore raises not just practical but ethical issues, such as whether it is OK to 'embellish' one's résumé by exaggerating on matters that the employer is unlikely to be able to check (Bishop, 2006; Marcoux, 2006).

The form of the résumé can be decided by the writer, and many different formats are possible (chronological or reverse chronological? A standard format for all readers or résumés tailored to specific jobs? Concise or detailed? Modest or 'over the top'? Traditional or novel in presentation?) It lies beyond the scope of this book to offer detailed 'how-to-do-it' advice on résumé writing, but there is much such advice available on the web, as well as professional résumé writers who can (at considerable expense) do it for you, and even some scientific research on employers' responses to different types of résumés (Arnulf et al., 2010: Chen et al., 2011b; Tsai et al., 2011). Randazzo (2012) recommends résumé writing as a basis for increasing the writer's (self)-reflective activity, thus possibly doing productive career-related learning.

Public Stories and Career Scripts

Although one person cannot experience directly what another experiences, the story enables 'its sense, its meaning, to become public' (Ricoeur, 1985: 16). Once a story is told, for example on Facebook pages, it is available for others to listen to or read and make judgments about or learn from. Relatives, friends, co-workers and others tell their own stories and invite imitation. Institutions such as employing organizations and professional associations present us with scripts for our career stories to follow. Social interaction enables us, or even induces us, to develop narratives in sympathy with our social contexts (Young & Valach, 2004).

> Individuals mentally structure the story of their own work life using the social structure provided by society's grand narrative of careers. The narrative frames people's stories of work and its consequences as they think about and take stock of their work lives. In addition to providing a commonsense framework, the grand story of career synchronizes individuals to their culture by telling them in advance how their work lives should proceed and prompting them to stay on schedule. (Savickas, 2005: 49)

The 'grand narrative of careers' that Savickas talks about will be some archetype of how a career ought to work, such as the American Dream story outlined in Chapter 1 (Lucas et al., 2006). The idea of 'career scripts' (Barley, 1989; Dany et al., 2011), which we introduced in Chapter 8, is relevant here. Career scripts are collectively-understood recurrent patterns of career development reflecting common institutional practice (for example, an organizational 'career ladder' script or a competitive 'entrepreneurial breakthrough' script). Such scripts provide cues to action even in apparently 'boundaryless' environments, by providing an amalgam of individual stories and a template against which a career actor can consider and develop their own story, and may thereby contribute to shaping the career (Dany et al., 2011).

Scripts, like some roles (Chapter 8), are a means whereby powerful institutions may predetermine individuals' career stories by writing them in advance, in corporate hype or in reassurances to insecure employees. But such scripts may be untrustworthy. Arthur Miller's (1968) play *Death of a Salesman* catalogues the collapse of the career of the fictional (but all too real) Willy Loman, as, once his productive years in the workforce are over, he is discarded 'like an empty orange peel'. The scripts that Willy knows and built his life around, scripts of individual enterprise and collective loyalty, are exposed in the play as cruel fictions. In keeping with the time-honored role of the rebel in fiction, many career stories (such as Brenda's above) are about people's refusal to allow themselves to be dominated by others' scripts. Zikic and Richardson (2007), for example, show that many individuals who experience involuntary job loss through layoff respond to this potentially catastrophic career event by reframing their own narratives of their careers so that the loss is constructed as a 'blessing in disguise', an opportunity for new career exploration and greater meaning: in effect, new 'scripts' creating new stories for their careers.

Sims (2002) noted that the prospective stories that we imagine into our futures and communicate to prospective employers are often based on role models we have observed and dramas – often fictional – we have seen on television or film. Cultural images in the media and elsewhere impinge on consciousness. *Masterchef* or *American Idol*-style television programs, in which the strong and talented dominate and the weaker are gradually eliminated, may seem to present not just talent-competition entertainment, but plausible, if competitive, career pathways for the ambitious.

At the same time, there is strong interest in learning from existing narratives in the public domain – for example, books, short stories, plays, biographies, autobiographies and television programs – by analyzing their discourse and looking for the underlying messages (Gabriel, 2000; Stead & Bakker, 2010). For example, Cohen and Duberley (2013) have recently used a long-established British radio series, *Desert Island Discs*, in which famous people choose, often as a reflection of their careers, eight pieces of music they would choose to accompany them if shipwrecked on a desert island, and provide a rationale for each. The results, the authors report, provide extensive insights into people's career lifeworlds that are all the more fascinating because they are unsullied by the researcher's own agenda. Such public stories are easily accessible and frequently entertaining.

In many career stories, such as Lance Armstrong's, the storyteller is also the hero and the story takes an epic form. Great epics such as *The Odyssey* present what is considered to be an absolute, objective story in which storyteller and audience share a single view of the world. Osland (1995), in her account of the stories of expatriates living and working far from their home country, used the epic form of the hero's adventure (Campbell, 1968), in which career heroes travel from safe havens to unknown and dangerous places, pursue challenging goals, face great obstacles, receive help from strange sources, fight battles and return home 'the masters of two worlds instead of one' (Osland, 1995: 152). Similarly, ordinary people telling the stories of their careers may find meaning and reassurance by representing themselves as the heroes of their own career epics. Collin (2000) noted, however, that the epic form of story is underpinned by the idea of pattern and destiny and therefore tends to the view that a career should involve progression and destination (or, in the terms of the epic, destiny).

In contrast to the epics of the past, the modern novel focuses on the evolving realities of its characters and the tension between their inner consciousness and outward action. There is no single viewpoint shared by characters or by author and audience – each makes their own interpretation (Collin, 2000). According to Collin, 'the traditional career, loosely interpreted as linear, upward, focused and masculine, [is] like the epic, whereas the increasingly open-ended career of today [is] like the novel' (p. 165). Collin also noted that there is an intermediate category – modern epic – in which the notion of final destiny is replaced by that of perpetual exploration and revitalization, that of linear time by the interweaving of times and places, and that of a single worldview by multiple reflections. That is, she says, 'an even more effective analogy for the fragmented, diverse, open-ended career of today' (p. 165).

Conclusion

As defined in the dictionary, the idea of *story* provides a wide range of ways that narrative can take place: 'an account of imaginary or past events; a narrative, tale or anecdote'; 'the past course of life of a person etc.'; 'the narrative or plot in a novel or play etc.';

'facts or experiences that deserve narration'; 'a fib or lie' (Allen, 1990: 1203). Stories thus extend to selective presentation, imaginative interpretation, creative fiction and deliberate untruths. This chapter has shown that career stories can take all these forms and that the consequences of paying attention to stories – even if they are personal interpretations, means for the storyteller to find meaning, identity or acceptance, pieces of rhetoric, or even self-serving lies – may well be beneficial, because the listener understands more and more about the subjective career or underlying career attitudes of the storyteller. Telling our stories, getting others to tell their stories and seeking to extend career stories into the future may not only be an enjoyable and rewarding activity, but may also provide the basis, as we will show in Chapters 13 and 14, of very useful practice in the fields of career self-management and career counseling.

Key Points in this Chapter

- Storytelling is a universal, fundamental and often very productive human experience. Career stories are plentiful, for example, in this book and on the web.
- Accounts of careers typically contain good stories and *are* good stories. Many stories are worthwhile both in themselves and as a basis for thinking about careers and analyzing them.
- Career stories have value for storytellers. They enable career actors to find meaning in what they do, make retrospective sense of their experience, establish their identity and reflect on the future.
- Career stories have value for listeners. They provide entertainment, empathy and understanding, and enable wider conclusions to be drawn. They can be used by researchers and counselors to achieve their objective.
- Any career story is only one possible version of the career it describes. Stories involve subjectivity, personal interpretation and personal purpose. A story cannot be expected to be a single unembellished truth. Stories strongly represent the subjective career.
- Résumé writing is a key form of career storytelling.
- Career stories sometimes become public. Literature and the mass media often communicate images or archetypes of careers, which can be informative or misleading.

Questions from this Chapter

General Questions

1. Reflect on a story – not necessarily a career story – that someone recently told you about themselves. What did you think of the story? What did you learn about the person from the story?

2. If you had to tell someone a story about your career so far, what story would you tell? Write it down. What can you learn from the story in terms of your identity and the meaning of your career or work experiences?

3. Check whether the story above seems to contain, as Ibarra & Lineback (2005) suggest, a protagonist or main character; a background situation requiring the protagonist to take action; trials and tribulations as obstacles appearing in the protagonist's path; a turning point when things must change; and a resolution of triumphant success or tragic failure. If it doesn't, try to rewrite it or extend it so that it does.

4. In evaluating what we hear about people's careers, is it possible to establish the truth? How?

5. Read a newspaper or magazine story about a celebrity's past career. Also read some job advertisements for high-level jobs. Think about what you have read in terms of the language and discourse used. What impression is the writer trying to make? How much do you believe what you are being told?

6. Choose a celebrity you know about, and write a short account of their career from sources available to you. Show it to friends for comment and consider it in relation to the ideas in this chapter. What do you learn?

'Live Career Case' Study Questions

1. Ask your case person to relate a story about one positive and one negative personal career incident. Invite the case person not to simply identify the incident but to explain exactly what happened in detail. What function do you think the story has for the person?

2. How would you summarize the story that the case person told you, using the various exercises in this book, as it relates to the case person's entire career? Does the story suggest any 'plotlines' running through to the future?

Additional Resources

Recommended Further Reading

Broadbridge, A. (2004) 'It's not what you know, it's who you know', *Journal of Management Development*, 23: 551–562.

Cohen, L. and Mallon, M. (2001) 'My brilliant career? Using stories as a methodological tool in careers research', *International Studies of Management and Organization*, 31: 48–68.

Cohen, L., Duberley, J. and Mallon, M. (2004) 'Social constructionism in the study of career: Accessing the parts that other approaches cannot reach', *Journal of Vocational Behavior*, 64: 407–422.

Ibarra, H. and Barbulescu, R. (2010) 'Identity as narrative: Prevalence, effectiveness, and consequences of narrative identity work in macro work role transitions', *Academy of Management Review*, 35: 135–154.

Young, R. A. and Collin, A. (2004) 'Introduction: Constructivism and social constructionism in the career field', *Journal of Vocational Behavior*, 64: 373–388.

Self-Assessment Resources

Assess your own career story: McMahon, M., Patton, W. and Watson, M. (2004) 'Creating career stories through reflection: An application of the Systems Theory Framework of career development', *Australian Journal of Career Development*, 13(3): 13–17.

Assess others' career stories: Canary, H. E. and Canary, D. J. (2007) 'Making sense of one's career: An analysis and typology of supervisor career stories', *Communication Quarterly*, 55: 225–246.

Online Resources

Hear Steve Jobs' (the founder of Apple who passed away in 2011) career story – see: www.ted.com/talks/steve_jobs_how_to_live_before_you_die

Read 10 empowering career stories – see: www.10careerstories.com/10_career_stories.html

Part 3
Careers in Practice

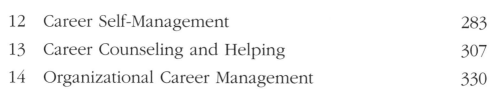

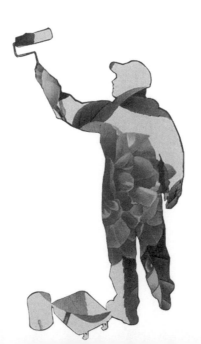

Career Self-Management 12

The objectives of this chapter are:

- to provide a framework for the practice of career self-management (CSM), based on the theories and metaphors covered in this book
- to show that effective CSM is a planned, rational, continuous process including research, goal setting, strategy, feedback and control, but that the career actor also needs the ability to adjust the plan according to contextual forces
- to show how specific skills, particularly self-assessment, information gathering, decision making, adaptability, networking, job hunting and use of social media can assist the CSM process
- to assist you, the reader, to plan and manage your career more effectively, to acquire additional CSM skills and to guide you to appropriate additional sources of information.

CASE STUDY

Getting Started

Nicolas, age 23, has a problem.

On the surface, Nicolas seems to be in a good position to make a start in his career. He is about to graduate from a leading university, with a good degree in sociology. His parents have been supportive of his studies and have helped him financially. During his studies, he has acquired practical experience as well, working part-time in a local fruit and vegetable business. His motor-cycling hobby has given him practical skills in mechanics and enabled him to undertake 'adventure' travel in other countries, improving his self-confidence and language skills. Nicolas is popular and socially skilled, and has good networks in his local community.

So what is the problem? The problem is that Nicolas has no idea what to do next. His professors are encouraging him to do a master's degree, but he's not sure whether he wants more academic study or where it will lead. His father has a friend who he says is willing to offer Nicolas employment in an administrative position in his retail business in town. His mother thinks that option is much too modest for someone of Nicolas's talents: she wants him to look for a management trainee position in a big company, with a view to 'getting to the top'. One of Nicolas's motor-cycling friends wants Nicolas to come with him on a planned three-month odyssey in South America.

And Nicolas? Nicolas just doesn't know. He realizes he wants to develop a career, but he feels hopelessly unprepared. He understands that his social science degree is general rather than specific in application and is unlikely, unless supplemented by postgraduate study, to lead to specialist jobs. He has little real work experience and doesn't really know what sort of work he would like. At university, he developed a somewhat left-wing ideology and he doesn't much like the idea of working in 'big business'. He's not sure what hidden talents he may have, or how to find out.

While at university, he has enjoyed himself but has paid little attention to the labor market or to the necessity, after completion of his degree, of finding paid employment and a career. How does one go about getting a foothold on a career ladder? Which fields of work are growing, which declining? Nicolas suddenly realizes that despite his abilities, motivation and qualifications, and his recognition that his career is critical to his future life satisfaction, he has no idea how to manage that career. Worse, he does not even know how to start.

This book is titled *Understanding Careers*, and its emphasis has indeed been on helping you to increase your understanding. But like Nicolas, you may seek more than understanding: you may have immediate, practical career decisions to make or problems to resolve. Or you may be looking for personal guidelines for career development. This chapter will therefore move from theory to practice. What can you *do* to better plan and manage your career?

In Nicolas's case, a few general propositions can be put forward. Nicolas needs a career plan, or at least a conscious process of career planning: not a rigid plan to the end of his career, but a way to take immediate decisions on a rational basis and move forward from his current situation. He needs to develop a clearer view of himself – for example, his own interests and aptitudes – and about trends in the world of employment and the opportunities available to him. He needs to organize his resources – time, energy and abilities – to provide momentum. He needs to develop good decision-making techniques. He needs to monitor his own progress and, if necessary, modify his goals and actions accordingly. If Nicolas needs all that, you may need the same.

What resources are available to you (and Nicolas) to help you? In this part of the book, we identify three primary sources of assistance: the *career actors* themselves (Nicolas and you), *professional counselors*, and the *organizations* in which career actors work. We conclude this book, therefore, with a chapter on each of these sources. We cover career counseling in Chapter 13, and organizational career management in Chapter 14. In this chapter, we focus on you, the career actor, and strategies you can undertake to optimize your career satisfaction and success. We call this material *career self-management* or CSM for short.

While career actors may receive considerable support from their organizations and from careers counselors, most of their career management will in the end be CSM. Although other sources may be used, in most cultures one's career is ultimately one's own property. It is part of the human task of 'managing oneself' (Drucker, 1999). We must make our own decisions about such matters as what line of work we want to be in, whether we should change jobs, what training and learning we should seek, whether to apply for promotion and how much time and energy to devote to work. We must also learn how to take effective action to implement those decisions, bearing in mind constraints in our environment.

Recapping this Book

First, let's recap what we have already learned about careers in this book, from which to develop a worthwhile practice of CSM.

Chapter 2 emphasized the rapidly changing context of careers, which provides reasons for CSM to be conducted with awareness of 'what is going on out there' in terms of, for example, economic cycles, new technology, the labor market, sunrise and sunset occupations, social networking, etc.

Next, the various metaphors mentioned in Chapters 3–11 offer plenty of insights and guidance about CSM. Here is a brief summary of the CSM implications of each metaphor/chapter:

- The inheritance metaphor (Chapter 3) reminds us that each of us has a unique career starting point. We need to understand what this is and capitalize on it or compensate for it, as appropriate. Our inheritance includes not only our inbuilt personality and abilities, but also our assumptions about work and careers that we learned from our parents and others early in life.

- The cycle metaphor (Chapter 4) reminds us that neither we nor the world around us stay constant: there are rhythms in life that may override predetermined plans or immediate actions. We need to monitor, and anticipate changes in, our learning, motivation, family responsibilities, aging and other cycles. It is likely that different things will matter to us at different stages of our career. Being aware of this adds to our capacity to find work we want and cope with work we have. For example, are we trying to *explore* different possibilities before settling on one or are we trying to *establish* ourselves in a particular line of work and/or sector of the economy? The strategies we adopt will be very different in these two cases.

- The action metaphor (Chapter 5) reminds us that we are able to exercise agency over our careers, express ourselves and take career decisions. There are advantages in doing this rationally rather than impulsively. As we will see later in this chapter, that does not necessarily mean being able to articulate clearly all the factors that have led to a particular decision. But it does mean that we need to consider consciously and carefully what our goals are and how we might achieve them over a given time period (which may be quite short).

- The fit metaphor (Chapter 6) reminds us that finding a good fit between who we are and what we do is often the key to a happy and successful career. Gathering and evaluating information about ourselves and the world of work, and checking the fit between them, are therefore key activities. However, partly because of cycles and stages (see Chapter 4), we may change over time. The nature of our work may also change over time. So experiencing a good fit now does not necessarily mean it will last forever. We also need to be clear what type of fit matters most to us. It is often assumed that fit between person and occupation is the key, but perhaps you might care more about working in a particular location, or industry, or organization, or with a certain kind of people. We can influence the fit we experience both by choosing our jobs carefully and by seeking to 'craft' our roles once we are in them.

- The journey metaphor (Chapter 7) reminds us that careers are whole-of-life experiences, that they take us to new places, that there are issues of destination involved and that there are many different routes and types of travel. We need to consciously monitor and manage the direction of our careers, trying to know where we are trying to get to and how we are going to get there, correcting where necessary. An element of a tourist mentality may be helpful here, so that we are not so focused on our destination that we forget to admire the views on the way and learn from what we see.

- The roles metaphor (Chapter 8) reminds us that different stakeholders (e.g. parents, employers, family) affect how we conduct our careers and that careers involve being clear about both our identity and others' expectations of and entitlements from us. This metaphor also reminds us that most jobs have requirements that we can alter only to a limited extent. Like actors in a play, we will be expected to say and do certain things to fit in with the roles of others and with the overall plot. We need to find out as much as we can about a job, both before our 'audition' (the selection process) and during it. Because at any one time we fulfil various roles in our daily life (e.g. worker, student, parent, leisurite, citizen, child), we also need to be clear how salient each of them is to us, how much we wish to invest in each and how we can maximize their compatibility.

- The relationships metaphor (Chapter 9) reminds us that careers are conducted in social contexts. They have meaning and effect in relation to other people and institutions, and are often expressions of the networks to which we belong. A major part of managing our careers is therefore managing our existing relationships and developing new ones. Relationships enable us to learn from the experience of others, to hear about opportunities, and to develop our sense of who we are (identity). Most lasting relationships are reciprocal, which means that we can be expected to offer the same to other people.

- The resource metaphor (Chapter 10) reminds us that the ultimate societal purpose of most careers is economic and that careers can be viewed as resource components of organizational systems. We should develop our resources with an eye to their value and seek synergies with employing organizations to mutual advantage. For example, our social capital includes the relationships (Chapter 9) we can draw upon to help us achieve our goals. It may well be that some of the people we know are also people who can benefit our employing organization, and vice versa. Our human capital (i.e. qualifications, skills, experiences) is another important resource, but its usefulness may be quite specific to certain contexts: for example, the PhDs possessed by the authors of this book would not help them to get jobs in many sectors other than academia. In building one's resources, goals are important: if you know what you are trying to achieve, you have more chance of finding out what key attributes you are going to need. Because movement between jobs is an important part of most careers, it might be helpful to think about our resources in terms of how mobile they enable us to be. Forrier et al. (2009) call this 'movement capital'.

- The story metaphor (Chapter 11) reminds us that careers are largely subjective phenomena that help us to understand and express our identities and find meaning at work. We can develop different helpful storylines to understand and express our careers and to enhance their future development. Notice the contrast here with the assumption in many of the other metaphors, especially fit, that there is an objectively 'true self' and 'true world of work'. Instead, the story metaphor emphasizes that we have some scope to find our own ways of making sense of our experiences. By developing the stories of our career, we can often develop new understandings of why we might have done the things we did, and what that means for what we might try to do next. Also, to some extent, we may tell differ-ent stories to different audiences – not lying, but emphasizing different aspects of our experience in different circumstances. Our task is to develop stories that are both authentic (that is, they ring true to oneself) and credible (they can be believed and understood by others).

Career Self-Help

There is no shortage of published advice for those seeking to find career satisfaction and success. Since Dale Carnegie (1936) published *How to Win Friends and Influence People*, a practical guide to operationalizing the 'relationships' metaphor, self-help books have offered innumerable guides to getting what you want in careers. You can, for example, *Think and Grow Rich* – a visualization metaphor (Hill, 1960). *Career Warfare: Ten rules for building a personal brand and fighting to keep it* (D'Allessandro, 2004) encourages you to apply military and marketing metaphors to yourself and brand yourself to sell in a tough market. Sher (1994), in *I Could Do Anything, if I Knew What it Was*, offers you the route to 'a richly rewarding career, based on your heart's desire' where you can 'recapture long lost goals, overcome the blocks that inhibit your success, decide what you want to be, and live your dreams forever' (back cover). Hannon (2010) in *What's Next? Follow your passion and find your dream job* offers 16 case studies of people who have successfully made major career changes in mid-life, and draws some conclusions aimed at assisting others. If you want to find out in detail how to use social media to assist your career development, read *Social Networking for Career Success: Using online tools to create a personal brand* (Salpeter, 2011). Hundreds of similar books could be cited.

Some authors provide resources in the form of 'career workbooks' or websites, through which the reader can simultaneously assess their career-relevant attributes, reflect on some of the key factors affecting careers and career decision making and interact with the book by completing questionnaires embedded in the text. For example, Sears and Gordon (2010) provide a book of 140+ pages for the career aspirant to work through, including questionnaires, internet exercises and other activities, enabling readers to dis-cover how their attributes fit with different career alternatives and 'tomorrow's' jobs.

Some people will find that this kind of do-it-yourself career guidance is helpful to them. There are, however, a number of problems with such exercises. Their question-naires and exercises are likely to be unvalidated and unscientific, and the reader may lack the professional skills necessary for proper interpretation of the results. They tend to be simplistic, particularly in their assumptions that 'one-size-fits-all' and their confla-tion of career success and career satisfaction. They often encourage an individualistic success-at-all-costs and/or me-ahead-of-all-other-people philosophy that some would find objectionable. They may focus on the attitudes and interests of readers but ignore or gloss over their likely human limitations of ability and motivation. They tend to underestimate some of the obstacles to career success discussed in this book, such as social structure, labor market realities and variable human energy. Lastly, many of these books are less about the long-term strategic development of a career than about the short-term tactics of finding a job: job finding is an important topic, particularly in times of recession, but not the whole story.

The most popular book in this genre, and probably one of the best, is *What Color is Your Parachute? A practical manual for job hunters and career changers, 2014 edition* (Bolles, 2013). This book is both informative, intensely 'hands-on' and fun to read, and has the advantage that the author prepares a fresh edition every year, enabling him to stay right up to date in terms of changing economic conditions, new websites, etc. It is, however, oriented to the two groups mentioned in the title, i.e. those currently unemployed or in an unsatisfactory job, and those who seek to make a radical career change.

An interesting recent entry to the self-help career literature is *The Start-up of You* (Hoffman & Casnocha, 2012), whose authors take the model (or metaphor) of a business start-up, and advise readers to manage their careers in the manner that entrepreneurs manage Silicon Valley businesses. Thus, you should 'develop a competitive advantage', 'adapt your career plans' as the situation changes, 'build powerful alliances', 'find breakout opportunities', 'become more resilient to industry tsunamis' and 'tap your network for information'. Hoffman and Casnocha provide an interesting and racy account, grounded in relevant practical experience, of practices based on many of the principles we have already outlined in this book, and continue below.

In addition to self-help books about careers, the media – including magazines, newspapers and of course the internet – teem with articles on 'how to build a great career', 'finding the perfect job', 'set career goals and grow rich', 'social networking to the top', etc. Again, these may contain excellent ideas, and reflect extensive experience by the authors, but they tend not to be backed by rigorous research. We encourage readers to surf through such information, but to do so with a critical eye. In the remainder of this chapter, we restrict ourselves to probably duller but more reliable peer-reviewed sources.

Basics of Career Self-Management (CSM)

In today's world, where individuals tend to be held responsible for their own careers, CSM is an essential set of skills and practices which can potentially assist people like Nicolas, and indeed any career actor, to find, and develop, more satisfying and successful careers.

CSM has recently been defined as follows:

> The basic elements of CSM involve the establishment of career goals, the development and implementation of career plans and strategies, and feedback regarding one's progress toward career goals. (Seibert et al., 2013: 169)

CSM is therefore conceptually similar to other forms of management, emphasizing that outcomes result not from chance or inevitability but from personal action based on evidence and reason. Careers, in this view, are not events that happen to us, but events that we actively create and manage by making good, evidence-based decisions.

Consider the classic management formula of PLAN: ORGANIZE: LEAD: CONTROL, a starting-point for any course in organizational management, and apply it to CSM:

- *Planning* means determining goals and deciding how they are to be approached.
- *Organizing* means turning the plan into linked manageable tasks and determining how to accomplish them.
- *Leading* means motivating and influencing key people to get things done.
- *Controlling* is gathering relevant information on progress, comparing it to the plan and taking action to correct any deviation.

In the case of CSM, the idea of *self*-management places responsibility squarely on career actors to manage their own careers. In organizational management, 'planning', 'organizing', 'leading' and 'controlling' are applied to employees and other organizational resources by appointed managers. In CSM, in contrast, career actors take responsibility, possibly with advice and assistance from others, for *self*-planning, *self*-organization *self*-leadership and *self*-control, thus bringing an integrated, rational way of thinking to bear upon their career. Abele and Wiese (2008) have shown, in a large study of professionals, that having career goals and plans, and acting on them, really does enhance both career satisfaction and earnings.

Greenhaus et al. (2010) provide a model of career management that has affinities with these processes of business management (Figure 12.1).

As in business, the process is embedded in, and influenced by, important contextual factors – 'information, opportunities and support from educational, family, work and societal institutions'. In 'career exploration' (Box A), the career actor gathers the kind of information about self and context that has been repeatedly emphasized in this book. This leads to 'awareness of self and environment' (Box B), for example interests, values, talents (self), and opportunities, options and obstacles (environment). This awareness enables a plan to be expressed in terms of goals sought (Box C), such as securing a particular qualification or type of appointment within a specific time frame. The setting of goals enables the career actor to develop and implement a strategy to achieve the goals (Boxes D and E), for instance enrolling on an educational program, acquiring relevant knowledge on the job and/or seeking the ongoing guidance of a wise mentor. The implementation of a strategy will most likely lead to progress of some sort towards the goal, as well as providing feedback to the individual (Boxes F and G). Such developments can then lead to a fresh appraisal of the career (Box H), and then to fresh exploration (Box A), and most likely new awareness, revised goals, changed strategy, etc. Thus, career planning becomes a continuous cycle that potentially lasts as long as the career does. Consider this example:

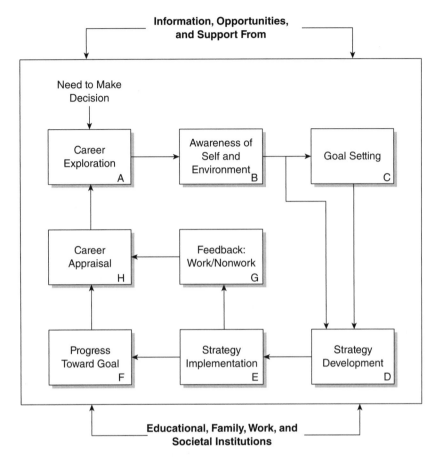

Figure 12.1   Model of Career Management

Source: Reprinted from: J. Greenhaus et al. (2000). *Career Management, 3rd Edition* (p. 24). Dryden Press. Published by permission of Thomson Learning.

CASE STUDY

Creating Her Future

Brought up on a farm, Anneliese thought she might build a career on her love for animals. She deeply admired a local veterinarian, and helped him in his practice in the evenings and at weekends. She set an initial goal of getting into one of her

(Continued)

(Continued)

country's top veterinary colleges and qualifying as a veterinarian. Studying the curricula of veterinary courses, she realized she would have to perform well in biological science, not her best subject academically. Anneliese worked hard to remedy her deficiencies, and, at the second attempt, gained entry to the veterinary science program in a top school.

As her studies continued, she considered what she was enjoying most about her program, assessed the job market in her field and came to the conclusion that her ideal career would be to own and manage her own veterinary practice in a rural area. For this, she would need not only basic qualifications, but practical experience in such a setting, and capital to put down as a deposit on the purchase of a business. To ensure her future, she worked hard to obtain top grades to give her choices in employment, continued to acquire practical experience in her vacation employment as well as on her courses, saved as much as she could and arranged with her parents to lend her money towards the business if necessary. She also took additional courses in small business and in the management of professional practices.

On graduation, Anneliese secured a job as an assistant veterinarian in the kind of practice she wanted to own, and acquired invaluable practical experience, including on the business side. Two years later, with financial assistance from her parents and a bank, she was able to implement her plan and start a business in a small town near the farm she had grown up in. Her career plan now became a business plan, as she sought to maximize the profit from her practice. She was competing with an established practice in the town, and at first business was slow. Anneliese worked hard on her marketing and customer relations, and in the second year business improved markedly. By the third year, she was enjoying her work, the business had grown and she was able to employ an assistant veterinarian.

Then, however, a new career issue emerged. She met, and fell in love with, Jurgen, an aircraft engineer whose career was established in the city, a long way away. Anneliese and Jurgen decided that their first priority must be to find a way of living together and planning a family. Like Anneliese, Jurgen had been successful in his career through a disciplined, step-by-step approach to managing it. Could the two of them now make career planning work for them as life planning, and not for one person but for two?

Note how Anneliese constantly looks ahead, sets goals, implements a planned strategy, uses feedback to make corrections and enacts her career as a deliberate process, but one which can be modified to take account of new information. Further, when her career plan is affected by her wish to develop a personal relationship with Jurgen, the idea of planning and managing the career remains intact, and is likely to be integrated in a life management plan.

Stop and Consider

Make two copies of Figure 12.1. Fill in the empty 'boxes'. Read the case above ('Anneliese') and, on the first copy, complete the boxes by putting in appropriate elements from the case. Then consider some part of your own career, such as choosing and successfully completing your current program of study, and fill in the boxes to show the information, goals, feedback, etc that are relevant in your case.

CSM Strategies and Skills

As indicated earlier, a career strategy can be defined as 'a sequence of activities designed to attain the career goal' (Greenhaus et al., 2010: 54). The word 'strategy' has military origins and is much used in business, signifying that an organization intends to be in charge of its own future and will devise a grand master plan, perhaps looking five or ten years or more ahead. Within such a strategy, shorter term 'tactical' plans and day-to-day operational plans may be fitted. Career strategies, tactics and operations are similarly possible.

Choosing an occupation and seeking a job (both considered in more detail below) are activities that occupy the transitions between education and work, or between different jobs. But careers are continuous and proceed between as well as in transitions. If you want to plan your career, it is important to plan your activities *within* jobs (and within periods of voluntary non-employment) as well as *between* jobs. For example, should you take opportunities to seek new assignments and/or develop new skills in your work? Should you improve your portfolio of career competencies by gaining additional qualifications in your spare time? What kind of relationship should you try to develop with your boss and work associates, and how might that affect your subsequent career? Should you aim to average no more than two years in any new job you take (to cultivate diversity of experience) or stay for at least five (to demonstrate loyalty and build expertise)? Such questions can be answered by reference to a career strategy and by paying attention to your performance and others' feedback.

CSM requires the career actor to have a repertoire of specific skills. We now outline some of these and indicate how they can be developed.

Knowing Oneself

Many experts argue that effective CSM requires career actors to undertake frequent monitoring and review of their own characteristics. External sources of information are available on an ongoing basis, for example academic grades, and feedback from relations, employers, teachers and others. Expert assessments can be obtained, if desired, from career counselors and psychologists. Internally, we observe our own experiences – what we enjoy or don't enjoy, what we seem to be good at, etc. There is good evidence that conscious self-assessments can assist career decision making, especially if professionally guided (Huber, 2013). Gati and Asulin-Perez (2011) note the growing potential of online self-assessments to increase the accuracy of judgments, possibly in advance of visiting a counselor to have more accurate assessments made. But how accurately are we really able to assess ourselves?

Ng and Earl (2008) and Motycka et al. (2010) note that although self-assessment is built into many models and systems of CSM, self-assessments have long been known to have only moderate accuracy. Mabe and West (1982), for example, found only an average correlation of 0.29 between self-assessments of ability and objective test scores. We are however likely to be more accurate in assessing our interests than our abilities (Sitzmann et al., 2010). For example, Miller (2007) demonstrated high congruence between Holland's SDS interests questionnaire (Chapter 6) and simple individual self-ratings.

Chapter 6 provides some insight into such inherent characteristics as values, interests (e.g. the Holland hexagon), career anchors and aptitudes, which influence career satisfaction and success in different occupations. But how can we assess these? Most people have some awareness of the types of activity they find most interesting through, for example, their school work, hobbies and recreation. Formalizing these in written lists, and checking with friends, teachers, etc. may have some value. Writing your vita, keeping a diary of significant events (for example, 'peak' experiences), making a note of ongoing 'hassles' and outlining an ideal job, may help further.

But you may be able to enhance such information by completing validated assessments of interests, values, personality and ability. One way of doing this is to find an online or published set of exercises where you can be guided through the self-assessment process by experts using pre-designed questionnaires, exercises and guidance on how to interpret your results (e.g. Harrington & Hall, 2007). Greenhaus et al. (2010: 70–75) provide background on some particularly popular instruments, as does Chapter 6 of this book.

Understanding the Context

In Chapter 2, we drew attention to the importance of the contexts of careers. If you want to engage in CSM, you need to be knowledgeable about economic, political, occupational, social and other aspects of context likely to affect the present and future 'careerscape' in which you will enact your career in the period ahead. These include:

- government policies affecting education and employment
- technological developments affecting skills requirements
- areas of expertise where there are surpluses or shortages of labor
- 'new' industries and skill requirements
- occupations growing or declining in importance.

There are a number of levels of analysis to consider. Your career will take place in various overlapping and probably shifting contexts: in particular countries or localities; in specific industries and particular organizations within these industries; and in specific occupations and jobs. The internet is brimming with relevant information on all these, for example from government and official sources, professional, industry and trade bodies, educational institutions and employing organizations, though in some cases the information may be biased by the vested interests of its sponsor.

Your contextual assessment must also be projected into the future. Careers last a very long time – 40 years or more in many cases. If you are young, decisions you make now, such as which occupation to enter in 2015–2020, may have consequences for you up to, and indeed beyond, 2055. The occupation or organization you seek to enter now may not even exist in 40 years' time. Even if it does, it may have changed beyond recognition. If you wish to plan your career, you need information not just about the recent past and present, but also about the future.

For example, the continuing moves to a 'new deal at work' – to outsourcing (Davis-Blake & Broschak, 2009), to transactional rather than relational contracts (Cappelli, 1999) and to the increasing adoption of flexible work practices (Leslie et al., 2012), appear to be leading to more and more 'precarious work' (Wilson & Ebert, 2013). Morgan et al. (2013) speculate that this may be causing a growing alienation of young people from structured careers, to a kind of 'vocational restlessness' that can, however, be liberating and adaptive. Are you able to identify personally with this view? Or do you seek the security of a clearer structure for your career?

Extrapolating current trends and the future planning of organizations and institutions, social scientists are able to make predictions that are probably better than guesses on the future of work (e.g. Bergman & Karlsson, 2011; Donkin, 2010). For example, Gratton (2010), drawing on the expertise of a 'think-tank' drawn from multiple major corporations, forecasts significant shifts in the nature of work, towards specialism, connectivity and higher-quality working experiences. She foresees the rapid expansion of virtual teams, more accountability being expected from leadership and the building of ever-more extensive networks and relationships across businesses. How well equipped are you to capitalize on such trends, and how can you manage your career to equip yourself better?

Still, not all predictions about the future are accurate (Margolis, 2001). In the late 1940s, former CEO of IBM Thomas Watson thought that the world market for computers would be about five. In the 1980s, it was widely expected that by the early 21st century there would not be much work to be done, due to technological advances. Instead, it seems that there is plenty of work to be done but it is very unequally distributed. So view predictions about the future with caution. Be aware of what is happening in the specific places and lines of work that matter to you. If you feel that your attributes do not match well with general trends, consider whether niche roles are available where you can be yourself, against the trend.

Choosing an Occupation

Choice of initial occupation is a key decision in many careers, and the focus of much deliberation among students, other young people and their families, and career counselors in the education system and elsewhere. Choice of occupation usually dictates choice of educational program, and making decisions as a teenager which appear to commit one to an irrevocable long-term future can be daunting. Important as these decisions are, however, it is worth remembering that many career actors qualify for one occupation, and later move into a different one (Savickas, 2007). For example, many people, including several career actors whose careers are described in this book, transfer into new occupations or move into management positions (often managing others in their own occupation). So, occupational choices are not necessarily 'forever' choices.

Savickas (2007) relates occupational choice firmly back to the idea of 'fit', discussed in Chapter 6. Again, assessment of self, particularly interests, and matching against characteristics of the occupation, are important. For example, you may want to find the *Fifty Best Jobs for Your* (Holland RIASEC) *Personality* (Farr & Shatkin, 2009a). If you identify particular occupations as being of interest, you need to examine their conditions ('context') in detail. Do you have appropriate abilities and interests? What qualifications are required? How long does training last and how much does it cost? Where can you secure the necessary qualifications? What are the salaries and work conditions like, and will they meet your needs?

Another important question is what are the employment and career prospects in that particular line of work, not only now, but 20 years on? What do some experts consider *The Best Jobs for the 21st Century* (Farr & Shatkin, 2009b)? Reardon et al. (2012) provide a wealth of such information, and Holland RIASEC codes for many occupations. In terms of the Holland system, the categories which appear to characterize growth occupations are S (for 'social') and E (for 'enterprising'), while R (for 'realistic') and C (for 'conventional') appear to be on the decline: the momentum in employment for the moment seems inexorably away from the manual and the routine and towards the interpersonal ('personal services') and the conceptual.

The lived experience of career actors – people who have career experience in the occupations you may be interested in – has special value and is available at a number of websites, for example:

www.vitae.ac.uk/researchers/200941/Database-of-career-stories.html
http://icould.com/watch-career-videos/

http://careerplanning.about.com/od/exploringoccupations/a/real_career_stories.htm
www.phorcast.org.uk/vignettes.php
www.citytowninfo.com/career-stories
www.10careerstories.com/10_career_stories.html

Less formal sources of information include friends and relations who work in the occupation, industry or organization you are interested in, and specialist careers counselors.

> **Stop and Consider**
>
> Think of an occupation that you are slightly interested in from a career point of view, but don't know a lot about. Use the net, including the websites listed above, to gather as much information as you can about the occupation. Give yourself a maximum of an hour on this task, then ask yourself whether what you have learned has increased or decreased your interest. If your interest has increased, spend at least one further hour doing more research.

Developing Career Agility

Some contextual considerations we have highlighted ask demanding questions of the career actor. Would you be comfortable with a life of short-term contracts rather than long-term job security? How do you feel about taking responsibility – including financial responsibility – for your own training and development? Would you enjoy being a semi-autonomous worker in a wide, non-hierarchical network rather than a clear organization structure? How do you feel about a life in a multinational organization, where the only way you can achieve your career goals is to travel and work in foreign cultures? When you ask yourself questions like these, you begin to realize that 'career choice' is a lot more complex than finding an occupation with a good fit to your interests.

Drawing on work on the protean career (Briscoe & Hall, 2006; Hall, 2002; see also Chapter 5), Gubler et al. (2013) suggest that in managing careers we need to display four attributes which collectively achieve a fine balance between knowing ourselves and being able and willing to change in response to new and/or unexpected circumstances:

- Identity: being clear on one's needs, motivation, abilities, values and interests.
- Being values-driven: having personal values that are both the guide to, as well as the measure of, success in one's career.

- Adaptability: being both competent and motivated to learn and to adapt to a changing environment.
- Being self-directed: having a feeling of independence and of being in charge of one's career.

If you lack such characteristics, it does not mean you cannot have a successful and happy career, but you may have to work harder to find the kinds of more structured, secure opportunities and conditions that you may seek. Adaptability (see also Chapter 5) may be partly rooted in personality and therefore not easily changeable (Hamptiaux et al., 2013), though it seems to be possible to increase it through training (Koen et al., 2012) or life experience (Bimrose & Hearne, 2012).

Even excellent, well-prepared career plans can go wrong. Unexpected academic failure, accident, illness and personal crisis can all derail a career, as can economic downturns, layoffs and tight labor markets. Also, many career actors may be ambitious for a degree of success that only a few can actually achieve.

There is not a one-to-one match between the kinds of careers that people want and the jobs that need to be done (and can be paid for) in the outside world. The creative arts, for example painting, music and theater, tend to have far more aspirants seeking to be a prima ballerina or orchestra leader than there are positions available (Dobrow, 2012). But talents and skills acquired with one kind of career in mind can often be adapted to take advantage of other opportunities. Julie's case is an example.

CASE STUDY

Acting It Out

Julie's passion for the theater went back to her childhood. Right through school, she loved acting and played every part she could get. When she went to college, she studied drama, took courses in theatrical improvisation, played parts in regional theater productions and did backstage work at a local professional company. After graduation, she would have loved to make a career in theater, but in this highly competitive industry there were few prospects. To pay her way, she got a part-time job in customer service in an international service company.

Quickly, she learned that customer service was a performance skill like acting, and she acquired an excellent reputation. When it became known in the company that she had theater skills, a salesman asked her to coach him on how to do a presentation. With her assistance, he put on a great performance. Her reputation as a coach grew and she was promoted to a job in the training department. It was through coaching for presentations that she really made her mark.

Julie realized that what she had learned about improvisation could be applied to the corporate world. There were roles to be played, and what made actors believable was their ability to immerse themselves in their roles. She began to apply for senior appointments and treated each interview as a theatrical performance to which her script writing, improvisation and presentation could be applied. For one successful interview, she served breakfast from her briefcase and used the ingredients as a metaphor for how her talents would fit the job. She based another presentation on baseball and ended by throwing a ball to the recruiting manager, who she knew from prior research was a baseball fan, saying, 'Put me in, coach!' It was the beginning of a very successful corporate career.

Source: Inkson & Arthur (2001).

As Julie's story shows, many skills and talents that seem occupation-specific are actually much more general and can be used to advantage in many settings. Julie showed both Adaptability and Identity in her willingness to find how she could contribute in non-theater settings, whilst also staying true to what she loved doing. She was Self-directed in the way she applied for jobs she wanted and found out as much as she could about the key people. She was Values-driven as well, because her belief in the importance of performance skills (for herself and for others) never wavered. Another insight from this story is that, as a parent, you should not get too concerned when your offspring involve themselves in school/college subjects and leisure activities that don't seem likely to lead to a job. Motivation and interest in what they are doing are often more important than being on a track to a readily attainable job.

Right Place, Right Time

When some career actors talk about their careers, they frequently refer to luck. Sometimes this might be modesty or socially acceptable behavior, as in, for example, 'I was lucky enough to be offered the post of chief accountant', when actually the person is very proud of the achievement but does not want to appear boastful. There is no doubt that luck, in the form of unpredictable events the course of which could be neither anticipated nor influenced, does play a part in career (Bright et al., 2009).

However, don't over-estimate the role of luck. It is common to construe luck in career as happening to be in the right place at the right time. However, it seems that some people are better at this than others (Wiseman, 2004). Mitchell et al. (1999) refer to this as 'planned happenstance', by which they mean that through systematic CSM it is possible to maximize one's chances of a 'fortunate' event happening (see also Chapter 9).

We can 'make our own luck' through the way we act: golfer Gary Player, on being told he seemed to be very lucky in the number of long putts he holed, famously replied, 'You know, it's funny – the more I practise the luckier I get.' The more skills we acquire or contacts we make, the higher the chances that we will be 'lucky' enough to have one of them pay off in our career. Being in the right place at the right time is more likely if, for example, a career actor has ensured that they have the right training and qualifications, good contacts in organizations with jobs of the kind they want or up-to-date information about the knowledge and skills expected. It probably also requires some adaptability, because an attractive opportunity may appear unexpectedly, thus requiring a change of one's work and possibly family plans. Self-direction may also be involved, for example where a career actor sees an opportunity that nobody else has, and persuades those with power to create a role for them.

Sometimes the knowledge and insight that lie behind planned happenstance are outside consciousness (Krieshok et al., 2009). This is especially likely for expert career self-managers because experts tend to know their terrain so well that much of their thinking is done automatically and unconsciously, using well-established neural pathways (Arnold, 1997b). That's one reason why they might think their successes are due to luck.

Sternberg et al. (2000) refer to this as tacit knowledge: things we know and can act on but cannot readily articulate. They argue that successful careers depend on knowing the informal social rules of the workplace, and that some people (successful career self-managers) learn these rules much better than others. This learning likely depends on having an open mind, avoiding defensive, self-serving attributions for disappointments and paying close attention to what people in the workplace do and what the consequences are. Of course, this learning does not in itself necessarily mean that a career actor has the skills to take advantage of their knowledge, but it's a good start.

Getting Help

CSM is based on individuals taking responsibility for their own careers. Nevertheless, most career actors have available to them whole networks of associates with the willingness and often some expertise to assist (Chapter 9). Moreover, these people often have a legitimate interest or even a personal 'stake' in the career actor's career, and may have a right to be consulted. In the case at the beginning of this chapter, for example, Nicolas has parents and friends who are interested in his career and seem to have a stake in it. If he wants to, he can probably gain support and help from them and from other relations and friends, his teachers and his part-time employer, not to mention the professional careers service at his university. Public-service or private professional counseling is also available to nearly everyone (see Chapter 13), though sometimes the price may be too high for the career actor to afford. While a CSM approach implies that our final career decisions are our own to take, these stakeholders represent a ('knowing-whom') resource (Chapter 7) that can assist with information, suggestions and further contacts.

Gaining useful help from other people requires that we know people who can give that help, and that we are able to elicit the required help from those people

(Dobrow et al., 2012). These related activities are both covered by the term 'networking' (see also Chapter 9), which is something that we are exhorted to do by most self-help books (e.g. Lindenfield & Lindenfield, 2010). Exactly how to be an effective networker probably varies somewhat between different contexts, because norms about what is acceptable behavior vary. So be observant about things such as the way people address each other and what topics of conversation seem more or less acceptable in your work-related face-to-face or electronic social encounters. Evidence suggests that having a strong set of social contacts does indeed foster a sense of career satisfaction (Ng et al., 2005).

You do not have to be highly extraverted to be an effective networker, but it is important to have enough confidence to believe that people might want to know you. Remember that even eminent people may be less confident than they appear and pleased to make your acquaintance. Be confident that you almost certainly have something to offer other people: specific skills, insights, interests or contacts, or simply being a good conversationalist or a good listener. Even if you are more junior than they are, they may feel they can learn from you about (for example) up-to-date techniques or what people in your generation or echelon of an organization/occupation are thinking.

Career pressures may cause you to try to get to know people who you think can offer you something, such as information, opportunities or access to further contacts. The potential artificiality and exploitative nature of networking relationships may therefore be a concern, but it can be allayed if the benefits are mutual and there is no coercion on either side. Also, it is important to try to enjoy a relationship for its intrinsic interest as well as for what you might get out of it. In real relationships, a lot of the interactions are casual and about fairly peripheral matters, so don't feel you have to trawl for useful information all the time you are interacting with someone.

As discussed in Chapter 9, having an effective mentor can be a significant boost to a career actor's career. Also, the most effective mentoring relationships tend to be informal: that is, occurring spontaneously rather than as part of an organized scheme. Not surprisingly, you are likely to be attractive to a potential mentor if you show willingness to learn, competence, listening skills and (this may be harder to achieve!) remind the mentor of him or herself at an earlier career stage (Allen, 2007). Be clear and open about what you hope the relationship will do for you (again, see Chapter 9 for possibilities) and make sure you know what the potential mentor feels able and willing to give in terms of time and expertise. As with the discussion of networking above, don't neglect the possibility that you may have something to offer the mentor (Ragins & Scandura, 1999).

The principle of reciprocity suggests that if we seek to accept career development assistance from others, we in turn should be willing to assist other career actors, where requested. For example, our role, or potential role, as parents in guiding or facilitating the initial career decisions and choices of our children is particularly important (Kracke, 2002; Marshall et al., 2008), and it may be that you will gain key insights from this book not only about your own career but also about your children's. Acting as an early careers advisor to one's own children can be a critical role and one worth pre-paring for in depth (Carpenter, 2008). Likewise, as managers or future managers, we may play a part in supporting or guiding the careers of our subordinates (Yarnall, 1998). Because we are not just career actors but also relatives, friends and associates of other career actors, we need to be as knowledgeable as we can.

Job Hunting

Job hunting – finding a satisfactory job in line with a career plan – is clearly a funda-mental CSM activity. In the academic literature, the same activity is referred to as 'job search'. The 'hunting' metaphor adopted in many publications conveys the hunter as a skilled professional with an array of modern weapons, operating in a hostile envi-ronment where prey are elusive and there is severe competition from other hunters.

The focus in job hunting should normally be on securing not just any job, but the best job possible given one's career goals. This does not necessarily mean the best-paid or most senior or even the most interesting job available. Sometimes your strategy may be best served by taking a relatively low-level job in a good strategic position: re-read the case of Helga in Chapter 7.

However ambitious your objectives, and however suitable your qualifications are for your long-term goal, you will not get to first base in your career if you are unable to land the job that will set you on your chosen path. It is worthwhile to put consid-erable time and energy into this periodic career task, and to learn the specific skills and drills that have been shown to lead to success. Job hunting, if done in a properly committed way, is itself a full-time job requiring a high level of commitment and the development of specific job-hunting skills (Van Hoye, in press).

It is hardly surprising that research has found job search activity to be related to success in getting a new job (Kanfer et al., 2001). However, there are also more spe-cific findings and insights that can inform your job search in a practical way:

- First, preparatory work is important. Given your career goals, think about what sort(s) of job and employer you are looking for and why. Do some homework about potential opportunities before you start applying for jobs or making it clear on social media sites that you are in the market.
- Second, although preparatory work is important, active job search has to follow. If you lack self-esteem and confidence this can be a challenge. You need to put your-self 'out there' by searching for specific opportunities via formal job advertisements (make sure you know where these are published for the kind of job you want) and informal enquiries to employers and your contacts, making applications, gently enquiring if you hear nothing for a long time and asking for feedback if you are not successful. This can feel risky and threatening. Try to remember that everyone gets rejections, and if possible have friends ready to support you if the worst happens.

- Third, research evidence indicates that, on the whole, informal sources of information about jobs lead to more satisfying jobs than formal sources (Breaugh, 2008; see also Chapter 9). This is where networking is important. Especially if your contacts are well informed about their workplace and in positions of influence, they are likely to be able to give you good information about upcoming opportunities and what the work environment is like (Van Hoye et al., 2009), which may not be quite what the organization's publicity would lead you to believe.

- Fourth, persistence, review and reflection are all important (Van Hooft et al., 2013). Maintaining your efforts in the face of disappointment should go hand in hand with an honest consideration of any feedback you receive from the application/selection process. What does that feedback tell you about the realism of your goal and your strategies for achieving it? Don't rush to negative conclusions after one rejection, but if you start getting a consistent message from employers, such as 'you lack experience in brand management', then your goal may need to change.

- Fifth, it's all very well doing a job search, but you need to do it well. Effective self-presentation on application forms, online and face to face, matter. Researching each opportunity you apply for, and customizing your application to emphasize how you fit that particular role, enable you to show that you have taken the trouble to find out about the role and the organization. Avoid the temptation to just chuck in the same old curriculum vitae/résumé each time. A small amount of editing to customize it can make a big difference to your chances.

- Finally, if you want to be listed by an agency, or are shortlisted for a job, being able to impress in an interview situation will become critical. Being punctual, dressing smartly, making a good first impression, and being articulate and responsive are key skills. Always learn enough about the organization (for example, from its annual reports) to show you have an interest in it and can answer basic questions about it. Read up on interview technique and practice by role playing with friends.

Utilizing Social Media

The mushrooming of personal websites, Facebook, LinkedIn, Twitter and other social network sites is changing career practice dramatically. These have the potential to be a key CSM arena for anyone (Gerard, 2012; Suvankulov et al., 2012).

Social media potentially make your private life public, and enable other stakeholders in your career to learn a lot about you. This carries threats and opportunities. For example, you may think your Facebook story of how you called in sick at work yesterday and spent the day drinking will amuse your friends, but remember that your employer, and/or your prospective employer, may also have access to your pages. You need to be careful what you post and who you make it accessible to. On the other hand, social media, if used well, provide real opportunities to advance your career. Here's one list of suggestions, adapted from Brodock (2012):

- If you haven't already started using social media for your career development, start now. By doing so professionally while you are young, you can appear more mature and forge stronger connections, making you a potentially attractive candidate to future employers.
- Be genuine – this is an opportunity for you to show who you are to potential career contacts. Avoid comments on social media that you would not make face to face.
- If you want to use social media for your career, make your content more career-focused, so that you can connect with people outside your immediate group of friends and add 'weak ties' (Chapter 9).
- Utilize lists, circles and groups, and cultivate them through interaction and conversation.
- Remember that most social networking sites have a section on job opportunities. They also offer the ability to connect directly to people in industries, companies and brands you would love to work for. When such people eventually have jobs to offer, it may help if you have already shown an interest.
- Don't constantly promote yourself – it tends to be frowned on. Keep most of your posts to conversation, general comments and questions, and minimize the sales pitch. Think about what the audience may wish to hear rather than just what you want to say. Show that you want to educate and develop yourself.

Conclusion

Peter Drucker (1999), one of the creators of the management studies discipline, has pointed out that the most important form of management of all is self-management. Certainly, it seems odd that business students, who all have immediate issues relating to the management of their lives and their careers, routinely, and often compulsorily, study courses in the management of organizations but not in self-management or career management, which have direct and immediate relevance to them. Yet, as we have seen, there are some principles of management which seem universal to both self and wider institutions, and others which are specific to careers and which attention to basic theory and research can help aspiring career actors to implement in their own lives. Beyond that, career self-management requires a belief that one can make a difference to one's own career, and a willingness to spend time on it, to explore widely, to be flexible, and to learn on an ongoing basis.

Key Points in this Chapter

- Career self-management (CSM) is about taking the principles elaborated in this book and turning them into personal career actions within a rational management framework involving extensive scanning of oneself and the context, setting

flexible goals, developing a career strategy, making key decisions based on the strategy, implementing these decisions and adjusting the process in the light of experience and feedback.
- Long-term planning tends however to be increasingly disrupted by contextual changes and unexpected events, and the career actor may also need to be adaptable in adjusting to these changes.
- Assistance from others and assessment and counseling from qualified professionals may be used, but the emphasis is on *self*-management, i.e. taking responsibility for one's own career. 'Self-help' publications may assist but should be used with caution.
- Effective CSM is an ongoing process that involves considerable effort and time, and needs to be worked at continuously. Key skills include goal setting, accurate self-assessment, receptiveness to feedback, extensive research on current and future work environments, rational decision making, networking, job hunting, being interviewed and use of the internet and social media.

Questions from this Chapter

General questions

1. Re-read the case at the beginning of the chapter. What further information would you need to begin to help Nicolas? If you were Nicolas, what would you do?
2. Write some notes on the practical application of each of the nine metaphors to your own career as you see it at present.
3. Identify other stakeholders or potential stakeholders in your career. Do you feel they help or hinder you at present in determining and enacting your career? How could they best help you?
4. How applicable do you think the Greenhaus career management model is to your career decision making? What are its main advantages and disadvantages?
5. Outline in your own words some career strategies you think you could follow. Write down some principles that might work for you.
6. What could you do (a) immediately and (b) in the next year, to improve your CSM skills in the following areas?: Decision making, adaptability, building networks, job hunting, using social media.

'Live Career Case' Study Questions

1. Ask you career case person what they think were the key three or four external or internal factors influencing their career. Which metaphors (if any) do their answers appear to represent?

2. Ask your career case person to verbalize: (a) how they have made decisions, particularly choosing occupations and jobs, in their career; (b) whether they have had a career strategy at any time and if so what that strategy was (or is); (c) whether and how their career has involved flexibility and/or improvisation; and (d) how they have gone about looking for jobs, and what advice they can offer on that topic.

Additional Resources

Recommended Further Reading

Bimrose, J. and Hearne, L. (2012) 'Resilience and career adaptability', *Journal of Vocational Behavior*, 81: 338–344.

Drucker, P. (1999) 'Managing oneself', *Harvard Business Review*, 77(2): 64–74, 185.

Gratton, L. R. (2010) 'The future of work', *Business Strategy Review*, 21: 3, 16–23.

Hoffman, R. and Casnocha, B. (2012) '*The Start-up of You*', New York: Crown Business.

Inkson, K. and Arthur, M. B. (2001) 'How to be a successful career capitalist', *Organizational Dynamics*, 30: 1, 48–61.

Reardon, R. C., Lenz, J. G., Sampson, J. P. and Peterson, G. W. (2012) *Career Planning and Development: A comprehensive approach* (4th edn). Dubuque, IA: Kendall Hunt.

Self-Assessment Resources

Assess your career self-management skills: King, Z. (2004) 'Career self-management: Its nature, causes and consequences', *Journal of Vocational Behavior*, 65: 112–133.

Assess your career self-management strategy: King, Z. (2001) 'Career self-management: A framework for guidance of employed adults', *British Journal of Guidance and Counselling*, 29: 65–78.

Assess the importance you attach to career self-management: Stickland, R. (1996) 'Career self-management: Can we live without it?', *European Journal of Work and Organizational Psychology*, 5: 583–596.

Online Resources

The UK's official graduate careers website – see: www.prospects.ac.uk

The career management guide – see: www.cma-canada.org/index.cfm/ci_id/3978/la_id/1/docu ment/1/re_id/0

Career Counseling and Helping

13

The objectives of this chapter are:

- to describe what career counseling is and the forms it can take
- to show how the metaphors of career discussed in this book find expression in career counseling
- to enable readers to understand what they might get and how they might benefit if they seek career counseling
- to show readers some ways of helping others with their career development.

CASE STUDY

Time for a New Start – But How?

Paloma, aged 37, has returned to Spain from Mexico with her young daughter after the breakdown of her marriage to a Mexican man. She has some money saved, and partly because her divorce is quite amicable, she can expect some modest continuing financial support from her ex-husband. Paloma is living with her parents in

(Continued)

(Continued)

Valencia but conditions are cramped and she would rather find a place of her own. To do that she needs a job, but the labor market is tough, with many job seekers.

Paloma didn't enjoy school and left with few qualifications. But she has vocational qualifications in hairdressing and nailcare, and work experience in beauty salons, health clubs and hairdressing. In recent years, however, she has either been a full-time housewife or a beauty salon manager, so has not used these skills for several years. She thinks she has been good at the jobs she has done, but does not feel a particular loyalty to the beauty industry. She has noticed that people tend to see her as a leader but she does not really know why. Sometimes she thinks she should just find a job, any job, but at other times she has a feeling that this is the time in her life to take stock and perhaps take her career in a different direction. There are no obvious sources of advice: she does not have many friends and her parents are out of touch with the world of work. Although she hates to pay money out, perhaps it is time to find a career counselor.

Introducing Career Counseling

Relatively few readers of this book will aspire to be career counselors. However, some will, and we intend that this chapter will provide an initial orientation to the activities and approaches they might undertake. Many other readers will have opportunities to use basic counseling techniques with subordinates or other colleagues as part of managerial work, for example the performance appraisal process or in everyday work activities or interactions. Counseling can also be useful in one's role as parent or friend – indeed, research has repeatedly found that these are the most commonly used sources of career information and advice (e.g. Levine & Hoffner, 2006). If any of this applies to you, we intend that this chapter will give you pointers to how to fulfil this role in an informed and skillful way.

Equally likely, readers of this book will, at some point, like Paloma in the opening case, consider using the services of a career counselor. Indeed, if you are taking a tertiary course, you may already have experienced counseling from a member of your institution's careers center, which probably offers a range of services including counseling. This chapter should help you to understand what you can and cannot expect from counseling. Understanding how the metaphors discussed in this book are reflected in counseling practices may also help you to identify what you might want from counseling.

In most countries, there is no integrated system to provide career counseling for adults not in the education system (Hughes, 2013a, b), and there is no universal system of accreditation of career counselors. Therefore, after school and college/university most people have to find, and pay for, their counseling. In order to find an appropriately qualified career counselor, check for national professional associations and government organizations in your country using terms such as 'career counseling', 'career guidance', 'vocational guidance' and 'career coaching'. These organizations will not usually provide counseling direct, but they will explain the accreditations that are available for career counselors. This will make it easier to evaluate the credentials of the many individuals and businesses offering career counseling.

Definitions and Roles of Career Counseling

In a classic contribution to the field, Crites (1981: 2–15) provided a historical summary of the development of career counseling, especially in the USA. According to Crites, in 1937 the aim of career counseling provided by the (US) National Vocational Guidance Association (NVGA) was as follows: 'to assist the individual to choose, prepare for, enter upon, and progress in an occupation.' This was, at the time, quite a progressive definition. It avoided the assumption that only men have careers. It recognized that people may not only need counseling about which occupation to enter, but also about how to enter it and then how to be successful in it. Despite this, much of the academic literature on career counseling focuses on occupational choice as the key outcome (Sharf, 1992).

More recently, Nathan and Hill (2006: 2) described career counseling as 'a process which enables people to recognize and utilize their resources to make career-related decisions and manage career-related issues'. There is no assumption here that career will be confined to (or framed by) occupation. Further, Nathan and Hill's definition differs from the NVGA one in its emphasis on *empowering* people to do things for themselves rather than 'assisting' them to do things. This definition fits Paloma's situation well: choosing an occupation is relevant to her but this needs to be considered holistically in the light of her resources, constraints and life experiences. And as a mature adult, she needs to be empowered to make her own decisions.

Neither of these definitions is at all specific about how counseling is delivered. Kidd (2007) points out that career counseling is just one of a range of career interventions. Other interventions include career workshops, career information provision, coaching, training in résumé writing and mentoring. In the context of organizational career management (see Chapter 14), additional interventions come into play, such as succession planning, secondments and personal development plans. Career counseling is distinguishable from other interventions in that it usually involves face-to-face interaction between one counselor and one client, over a number of occasions, normally separated by days or weeks (Swanson, 1995).

Finally, it is worth noting the societal functions of career counseling. Its origins in the USA lie in the urbanization of society in the late 19th century and the difficulties this caused, especially for young people, in identifying what work they could do and how they could reach a respected and productive position in society (Savickas &

Baker, 2005). The development of career counseling was therefore a response to potential social problems as well as to individual development, though of course the two are closely linked.

A tension between career counseling for personal versus societal benefit persists to this day. On the one hand, counseling assists individuals to achieve their personal goals. On the other hand, career counseling contributes to society by facilitating a better overall use of the workforce (Watts & Sultana, 2004), for example migrants whose career capital (see Chapter 12) is limited in their new country (Bimrose & McNair, 2011). The personal and societal perspectives are not necessarily in conflict, because if career counseling helps individuals to navigate their careers skillfully, then it should contribute to optimal deployment of labor and therefore to national productivity, health and well-being (Killeen et al., 1992).

Most reviews of career counseling are structured according to different theoretical approaches to career development (e.g. Kidd, 2007; Walsh & Osipow, 1990). These include trait-and-factor, developmental, person-centered, behavioral and psychoanalytic. These different theories make rather different assumptions about what is going on inside a career actor's head and how the counselor should proceed. Even so, there is good evidence that whatever the counselor's theoretical orientation, some core counselor skills are important. These will be discussed later in the chapter.

Given the metaphor-based approach of this book, rather than organizing the discussion around theory, we will instead briefly discuss how the various metaphors find expression in career counseling processes. In some cases, there is a close alignment between metaphor and a specific theory, but in others there is not. Also, some metaphors are more fundamental to career counseling than others, and this is reflected in our commentary.

Career Counseling and Fit

CASE STUDY

A Testing Time

Vittorio is 22 and nearing the end of his university course in geography and environmental science. He is doing well academically in both subject areas, and his academic record before university was also strong in arts, sciences, languages and humanities. He arranges to see a counselor because he cannot make up his mind what to do next. He is very committed to pro-environmental action, but does not know what kind of job he would most like, or what further academic qualifications he might need.

In the first session, the counselor considers Vittorio's educational history and discusses with him what he hopes to gain from counseling, then arranges a time for Vittorio to return and take some online assessments. Because Vittorio clearly has abilities in all areas that might be relevant to jobs he could be interested in, ability tests are unnecessary. Instead, the counselor assigns him assessments of his work values, decision-making difficulties, and interests (see Chapter 6). Before their second meeting, the counselor reviews the results of Vittorio's assessments, and at the meeting goes through them with him.

The results indicate that Vittorio is being torn between attractive possibilities, none of which he feels he knows enough about. He is not a habitually indecisive person and he is not under pressure from parents or others to make a particular choice. His desire to 'save the planet' arises more from social concern for future generations than from a passion for ecology or the beauty of the natural world. His interests are predictably strong in a number of areas, but they are highest in areas related to social action and government rather than (for example) the science of climate change.

The counselor and Vittorio agree that Vittorio will search out information about three kinds of job: town planning, lobbying government and business, and community project organizing. The counselor gives Vittorio suggestions about where to look for this information. At their third meeting a week later, they discuss what Vittorio has found out, and together decide that because community project work seems to be the closest fit with what he would like to do day to day he will pursue this option. The counselor reminds Vittorio that he is free to come back in future if he encounters difficulties or uncertainties.

Vittorio's experience reflects the longest established approach to career counseling – the fit metaphor. It is sometimes referred to as 'trait and factor' counseling (Crites, 1981). Developed in the mid-20th century, it is based on the need to have a true perception of self and of the world of work, and on being able to put the two together (Parsons, 1909; see Chapters 1 and 6). This approach to career counseling focuses mainly on choice of occupation. Its originators assumed that clients would normally, like Vittorio in the case above, be young people in the later stages of education. It positions the counselor as an expert in the field of career with superior knowledge to the client's.

In an extreme form of this kind of counseling, one could imagine the counselor wearing a white coat, like a medical doctor. Indeed, the medical analogy works quite well. The 'patient' lists symptoms. The counselor identifies the general nature of the problem, chooses tests and assessment instruments, diagnoses what is wrong, interprets the results and prescribes the solution (usually entry to an occupation with a good fit). The client is expected to be a passive and grateful recipient of this expertise, and to take the advice, like medicine.

Trait and factor counseling has come under attack for being over-simplified and de-humanizing (McMahon, 2007; Patton & McMahon, 1999). In the extreme form described above, these are accurate criticisms. However, the extreme form is something of a caricature, especially given changes that have occurred since the mid-20th century in the careers landscape and the ways in which professionals are expected to interact with clients. Counselors who place strong reliance on quantitative assessments are often interested in the reasons why a person has not been able to decide on an occupation. Indeed, there are questionnaires to diagnose that, such as Gati's Career Decision-Making Difficulties scale (Gati et al., 1996) and Krumboltz's Career Beliefs Inventory (Krumboltz, 1994b; see Chapter 6). Rather than making an authoritative recommendation, the counselor is also likely to discuss with the client how the client feels about options arising from test results and whether they fit with the client's self-image. We can see this happening in Vittorio's case above.

The influence of this approach to career counseling is strong. Tests and assessments are frequently used in career counseling, even by counselors who do not subscribe to the trait and factor approach. Test results and clients' reactions to taking them form part, but only part, of what the client and counselor discuss. Furthermore, in line with John Holland's approach with the Self Directed Search (Chapter 6), tests and inventories are often completed and scored by the individual for him/herself with the help of printed or online guidance, without the intervention of a counselor (Whiston & Rose, 2013). Most university careers centers offer something of this sort.

Stop and Consider

Have you taken any psychometric tests or questionnaires as part of careers counseling? If so, what did they suggest you should consider for your future? Think about your reactions to the tests. Did they give you a comforting sense of being properly assessed or did they feel dehumanizing and simplistic? How much, if anything, were you told about how the test was developed and what evidence there is that its results are a valid indicator of what occupation to enter?

Career Counseling and Cycles

The cycles metaphor (Chapter 4) reflects a developmental approach to career. Two features of this approach have important implications for career counseling. First, there is a recognition that careers may have distinct phases, each of which is marked by particular concerns and themes which are not confined to choosing an occupation. Even without distinct phases, career actors' concerns and capabilities can change with age. Second, career actors seek to 'implement their self-concept' (Super, 1953), so that our careers reflect our sense of who we are. Given that self-concepts can change over time, it is possible for career actors to outgrow their occupational choices and need to make new ones (Watts & Sultana, 2004).

A counselor who adopts a developmental approach is likely to focus on helping clients – not necessarily young adults seeking to choose an occupation – to clarify and articulate who they are and what they want from work. The counselor will be mindful of likely issues given a person's age and/or career stage, and may use questionnaires such as Super's Adult Career Concerns Inventory to identify what issues are currently most important to the client.

A developmentally oriented counselor is also likely to use *non-directive* counseling techniques. That is, the counselor will construe their role as facilitating the client's decision making and problem solving rather than telling the client what to do (Rogers, 1961). Rather than providing an agenda, the counselor will want to listen to the client, using prompts, silences and empathy to encourage the client to articulate their thoughts and feelings. The counselor will ask questions, but not many, especially at first. The aim is to enable the client to work through issues of personal concern, and in doing so to clarify their self-concept, especially in relation to work. The approach emphasizes that people need to experience congruence between their experience of life and their self-concept.

Sometimes events get in the way of this. We may have been socialized to think of ourself as a certain kind of person, only deserving of approval if we conform to the expectations of others. Or we may have a lot (e.g. training, education) invested in pursuing a certain kind of work, which makes it difficult for us to acknowledge that, deep down, we are not being true to our real self. A non-directive approach by the counselor helps the client to bring any such issues into full consciousness where they can be tackled, albeit sometimes with pain and difficulty. This is seen as key to implementing one's (true) self-concept.

Career counseling reflecting the developmental approach is likely to be relatively lengthy, perhaps occupying between three and ten sessions. It may extend beyond work-related concerns. The focus will be more on the self than on the world of work, which has led some to criticize this type of counseling for being insufficiently engaged with occupational information and the realities of the labor market (Crites, 1981). On the other hand, if done well it can enable career actors to take control of their working lives and develop considerable insight that can be applied in their future.

Many person-centered counseling skills and techniques have gained general acceptance and are seen as normal good practice for counselors in various contexts. These are discussed later in this chapter.

Career Counseling and Stories

In their different ways, both the trait and factor and the developmental approaches to career counseling assume, like Parsons (1909), that there is a true self and a real world, and that an accurate assessment can be made of the relationship between them. As we saw in Chapter 11, the notion of narrative is rather different. A narrative is a story, an *interpretation* of a set of events (Patton & McMahon, 1999). Different observers or participants in a sequence of events may construct different stories about it, so there is no one truth or right answer. Narratives are useful because, much more than test and questionnaire scores, they reflect the way we experience and make sense of our everyday lives. Counselors who listen for clients' life themes and stories can therefore be 'biographers who interpret lives in progress rather than actuaries who count interests and abilities' (Savickas, 1992: 338).

In a narrative approach to counseling, the task for counselor and client is therefore to co-construct a story of past events, the current situation and a way ahead (Hartung, 2013). To be sustained, this story needs to be both authentic (i.e. convincing to oneself) and credible (i.e. convincing to others) (Ibarra & Barbulescu, 2010). Often, it is argued, a client will seek counseling because they have not yet been able to construct a narrative that enables sense making of the past and present, and purposeful action for the future (McMahon & Watson, 2013). The counselor's role is therefore to listen for elements in what the client says that could contribute to a narrative, such as key people, emerging plotlines and cause–effect links. The counselor does not normally single-handedly weave all these elements into a ready-made narrative for the client, but instead works with the client to construct and test out storylines for authenticity and credibility. It is important that the narrative includes clear implications for what to do next, although this may be the last element to fall into place (see the case of Agnes, below).

CASE STUDY

Searching for Excitement

Agnes went to see a career counselor because she had been made redundant and was not sure what to do next. She was an experienced worker in the catering and hospitality sectors, with over 20 years' service in a range of roles. She told the counselor she frequently felt unfulfilled in the hospitality sector, but had never reflected much on her work life and was not sure why she had stayed in some jobs longer than others, and had never sought to try another sector. The counselor invited Agnes to tell the story of her life in detail, including childhood and education as well as work. This took two sessions. The counselor asked a few questions concerning what Agnes remembered about her thoughts and feelings at various moments, to ensure that the account was not simply factual. The counselor also occasionally offered interpretations of what was happening at key moments in Agnes's career and invited Agnes to say whether or not the interpretation made sense. Mainly however, the counselor simply reflected back what Agnes said and used prompts like 'tell me more' to enable Agnes to express fully her thoughts and feelings.

In the third and fourth sessions, the counselor and Agnes worked together to identify storylines and themes in her life and career. One that Agnes found especially helpful was that she had always been looking for something new and exciting, but that in most of the jobs she had held, she had been disappointed, for reasons she could identify. Another theme, which dovetailed well with the first one, was that the various hotels, restaurants and clubs in her home area were constantly competing to be the most exciting, novel venues. Agnes's job choices had been influenced by this. The counselor and Agnes then worked to identify what 'excitement' meant for her and where she might find it. They also discussed how Agnes could explain her emerging narrative and future intentions to her extended family, who valued security and low risk taking above all else.

Patton and McMahon (1999), amongst others, have argued that the increasing attention to narrative in career counseling signals a shift from positivism to constructivism and social constructionism (see Chapters 1 and 11), i.e. that counseling theory and practice are becoming less based on models of cause–effect and an objective reality, and more on individual perception and sense making. A possible implication is that counseling may help a client develop not just one but several stories around their career. That does not mean that one story is true and the others false. Instead, it can mean that different narratives emphasize different elements or themes in the story (Ibarra & Barbulescu, 2010).

Still, the narrative approach to career counseling is not entirely unified. Counselors with a sociological emphasis focus on how a career actor uses language and story to maintain their position in a social world. More psychologically oriented counselors are more likely to work with a client to draw on past experiences, possibly including those from early childhood, to identify consistent themes that reflect what has emerged, or is emerging, as important to the person in their life (Savickas et al., 2009; see also the Agnes case study above). This is framed in terms of narrative, about which Savickas et al. are enthusiastic as the basis for career counseling: 'Today, it is the life story that holds the individual together and provides a biographical bridge with which to cross from one job to the next job' (Savickas et al., 2009: 246). However, this narrative approach to career counseling could also be seen as an in-depth psychological analysis aimed at unearthing the one true self rooted in early childhood experience (Sharf, 1992), albeit expressed as a story rather than a set of scores.

Career Counseling and Other Metaphors

The other core metaphors on which this book is based also point to common issues in career counseling.

Quite often in career counseling, some of the issues the client is wrestling with concern their *inheritance*. As shown in Chapter 3, it is common to face career blockages and difficulties that are caused by characteristics such as one's gender, ethnicity or social class, or by deeply ingrained, perhaps unconscious, beliefs about work and career rooted in our childhood socialization and the personal examples set by our parents. Career counseling sometimes focuses on how to deal with these fixed inherited characteristics (Watkins & Savickas, 1990), for example whether to fight against, or conform with, the sexism that is making it difficult to gain entry to an occupation that is dominated by the other gender; or with deep-rooted assumptions that have been picked up from parents. Being invited to challenge these may create possibilities of seeing one's career in new ways.

The broadening of career counseling from occupational choice to a wide range of career issues has meant a wider focus on *action* (see Chapter 5), so that counselor and client may well work together not only on what the client wants to achieve, but also on the actions needed to achieve it. This may involve structured exercises to increase the client's sense of career self-efficacy (Betz, 2004), and careful use by the counselor of rewards when the client does or says something that represents a step towards achievement of the agreed goals. The reward may simply be verbal encouragement or congratulation. The purpose of the reward is for the client to learn to associate taking appropriate action with good outcomes, thus reinforcing the behavior and making it more likely to recur (Krumboltz, 1965).

Other metaphors can also be used in counseling. The *journey* metaphor (Chapter 7), with implications of destination, alternative routes and progress can help clients to structure their career goals and actions, or to clarify routes to be taken, or organizational, occupational or other boundaries to be crossed. It can also surface feelings and aspirations about the journey. For example, if the career is seen as a roller-coaster ride, what have been the high and low points, and why? The *roles* metaphor (Chapter 8) can be used to focus on the issue of balance between work and other roles in life (see Chapter 8), conflicts between roles, and strategies to deal with the issue (Evans et al., 2013); or to help clients to prepare for transitions between roles (Ebberwein et al., 2004) and respond to transition problems, such as a new occupation or job turning out not to be as good as was hoped. This in turn means developing career adaptability and employability (see Chapters 6, 7 and 12).

Relationships (Chapter 9) and *resources* (Chapter 10) are both relevant to career counseling. The relationship between counselor and client is usually a professional rather than personal one, at least where the counselor officially holds a counseling role rather than doing it informally. The counselor's skills and expert knowledge are a resource for the client – perhaps a very important one, albeit normally for a limited period. Further, much of what is decided on and actioned in career counseling may be about increasing the range and/or depth of relationships in the client's social network. It may also concern how to increase the client's career capital in ways which are well geared to their career goals. Indeed, it can be argued that the best career managers will take advantage of counseling when there is no specific or immediate problem in order to keep reviewing personal strategy and to re-equip self to function effectively in the labor market (Verbruggen et al., 2007).

Using Metaphor in Counseling

Many of us apply metaphor to explain and make sense of our career (Chapter 1; McMahon, 2007). Career actors often use metaphors when talking to counselors, and counselors can use these metaphors to explore their clients' career issues (Inkson & Amundson, 2002). As noted above, the journey metaphor is particularly common, but others also regularly crop up in accounts of career (El-Sawad, 2005). A client might say things like 'I've been swimming with the tide for too long' or 'I have served my time', which respectively relate to what El-Sawad referred to as nautical and disciplinary metaphors. This may simply be a turn of phrase or a cliché (Anderson-Gough et al., 1998). However, it may alternatively be a powerful and economical way of expressing a lot of meaning, and it may contain the seeds of problem resolution as well as depicting the current situation.

A career counselor might invite you to work with your metaphors to help you decide what to do. You can also try to do this for yourself. For example, you might consider just how strong the tide would be if you decided to try to swim against it. What resources might be helpful in swimming against the tide? What might act as metaphorical flippers to increase the strength of your kick? Would the tide eventually turn in your favor, as real tides do? Sometimes the metaphor cannot be extended so far, but even then its use can help to facilitate communication and idea generation (Wickman et al., 1999).

The Career Counseling Process

Some experts on career counseling take a theory-driven approach (e.g. Kidd, 2006; Sharf, 1992), whilst others focus more on the practical dilemmas counselors encounter and their experience of how to deal with them (e.g. Nathan & Hill, 2006; Yost & Corbishley, 1987). These sources are written for counselors, but are nevertheless potentially useful to anyone interested in careers.

As discussed above, the counseling process will vary according to the theoretical approach(es) favored by the counselor. However, most career counselors take an eclectic approach, borrowing ideas and techniques from different theories as they see fit (Whiston & Oliver, 2005). Of course, this has dangers as well as benefits. Unless the counselor has a rationale for using one approach for problem A and another for problem B, there is the risk of incoherence and poor judgment (Crites, 1981, Chapter 8).

Very few counselors will be willing to give you advice or tell you what to do. Instead, they will work with you to help you clarify (i) what the core problem is; (ii) what your preferred outcome is; (iii) what actions to take to try to achieve the preferred outcome; and (iv) the additional skills, motivation or resources you need to take those actions, and how to acquire them. Very occasionally, the counselor may tell you that a particular plan, idea or belief you have is too unrealistic to form a sound basis for action. However, this is rare because although a client's aspirations may be difficult to achieve, difficult is not the same as impossible.

Career counselors' clients are all ages, and the career issues they face are many and varied. Nathan and Hill (2006) say that a common trigger for a person seeking counseling is a sense of actual or likely performance failure, for example being made redundant, feeling that one is not coping with the job, the breakdown of relationships with key people at work or difficulty in balancing work with other parts of life. However, counseling is not – or at least shouldn't be – just about crises and problems. It can also concern opportunity and choice, for example deciding between staying in a job you like versus taking a promotion, or between continuing on a career track where you seem to be successful versus returning to full-time education for a time in order to 'future proof' your skills and knowledge.

There have been academic debates about whether career counseling is a separate endeavor from personal counseling, or indeed from some forms of psychotherapy (Krumboltz, 1993). If you are considering whether to seek career counseling, do not be put off by this. You will almost certainly not be 'psychoanalysed' and receiving counseling is not a sign of weakness or inability to cope. Indeed, some career counseling is similar to coaching, which is trendy and something that many managers and professionals pay for on an ongoing basis (Feldman & Lankau, 2005).

Nevertheless, you may find that the counseling process leads you to redefine the issue you are facing. For example, you may start out by wondering why you cannot settle on a kind of work you like, but then realize that you have moved from job to job because you can never maintain a good relationship with your boss. Counseling may then focus on why that is, and what can be done about it. Alternatively, counseling may take you outside the work sphere, for example if you find that the pressure you feel under due to your career ambitions is interfering with your family life.

Many career counselors structure what they do around Egan's (2013 and many previous editions) *Skilled Helper* model or a variant of it (Kidd, 2007). This scheme for problem solving has three stages:

- In the first stage, the task is to identify what exactly needs to change. As noted above, this may not be what it initially seems to be. At this stage, it is important for the counselor to listen to the client's description of the situation in their own terms, a process which may last for quite a time. Then counselor and client work together to identify the right problem or opportunity to focus on, and in doing so the counselor may explore with the client possible different ways of seeing things.

- In the second stage, the key task is to identify what a good solution might be to the key issues identified in the first stage. This might require some imaginative thinking about what a good outcome might look like, and then some setting of goals that fit the identified key problems and solutions.
- The final stage is mostly about action planning. It concerns what has to be done to accomplish the goals. In particular, given that there is often more than one way of achieving a goal, which way will work best for the client?

Does Career Counseling Benefit the Client?

There is not very much research that evaluates career counseling specifically. Most is about career interventions generally or counseling generally. It is therefore difficult to answer this question conclusively, even though the signs are good (Kidd, 2006, 2007; Whiston & Oliver, 2005). Also, multiple measures of outcomes have been used, so that for any specific potential outcome of career counseling (e.g. career decidedness, career maturity) there is only a very small number of studies, and it is not always clear that the outcome measured is the one that was most important as far as the counselor and client were concerned. With those provisos, the following points can cautiously be made:

- Career counseling has a moderately strong beneficial effect, such that around 70 percent of people who receive it score better on outcome measures than the average person who does not receive it.
- The gains from career counseling seem on the whole to be sustained over the medium to long term (see also Perdrix et al., 2012). There is some suggestion that this is especially the case where counselor and client work on building up support in the client's social networks (see Chapter 9) for the client's plans.
- Compared with 'group' interventions such as career planning workshops, the one-to-one interaction between counselor and client seems to be valuable.
- Clients usually experience career counseling as helpful. This seems to be the case right from the start, and peaks at about four sessions, declining after that.
- Experienced career counselors do not seem to have a greater beneficial effect than novices.

Informal Career Helping

The last bullet point in the previous section may indicate that it is not only experienced career counselors who can provide skilled career help. Career actors seek assistance from many around them – teachers, supervisors, parents, friends – who have no counseling qualifications or experience. If such 'helpers' are frequently used, it is presumably best that they do the job in as skilled a manner as possible.

Basic counseling skills can be, and are, used to good effect by many people working in formal or informal advisory roles. Indeed, the world might be a better place if a counseling style was adopted more often in work conversations (Summerfield & Van Oudtshoorn, 1995). You may well find that learning some basic counseling skills will help your relationships at work and improve the effectiveness of people who work with you or for you. We will distinguish between professional career counseling and this 'amateur' activity by referring to the latter as career *helping*.

Stop and Consider

Imagine that a colleague at work says to you 'I am really annoyed that my application for an internal transfer to the marketing department was rejected. What's wrong with them? What's wrong with me? I feel really down about this.'

How do you think you might respond? Which one of the following responses do you think comes closest to what you might say?

A: 'I'm sure you have a lot to offer but marketing probably have their reasons.'

B: 'It sounds as if you and our marketers really don't see eye to eye.'

C 'What idiots they are in marketing! I'm sure you deserved better. I'm going to tell them as much.'

D: 'What did you say about yourself in your application?'

E: 'You feel angry that your application was not well received by marketing.'

How do we typically respond to what someone says to us in conversations at work? One analysis (Rogers, 1961) suggests five broad types of response which are reflected in the 'Stop and Consider' exercise above, in the same order:

- *Evaluative*: making judgments (positive or negative) about the truth of a statement or about the worth of a person.
- *Interpretive*: reading between the lines of what a person has said; discerning the 'real' meaning behind their statement.
- *Supportive*: agreeing with the person; backing them up; offering your support.
- *Probing*: asking questions to get at more and deeper information.
- *Understanding*: reflecting back what you think you have heard in a way which neither judges nor commands.

In our experience, when managers do a classroom exercise like the one in the 'stop and consider' box above, they have a strong tendency to use evaluative or probing responses (responses A and D). This is understandable, because in managers' work roles decisions have to be made and facts established. However, often the effect of an evaluative response is to close down discussion; if the evaluation is negative, it also tends to make the person feel bad. (If the evaluation is positive, then the response often resembles the supportive style shown in statement C.) Probing responses can be helpful if used sparingly, but they risk shifting the topic of conversation to what the responder cares about, which is not necessarily what the person who made the statement thinks is important.

People often mistakenly think that a counseling style of helping someone means using supportive ('tea and sympathy') and interpretive responses. 'Supportive' implies that the responder is immediately and fully on the person's side, and agrees with their view of things. 'Interpretive' tends to position the responder as an expert who has more insight into other people than they have into themselves. On occasion, both these kinds of response can be appropriate. However, especially in the early stages of a conversation, the most characteristically counseling style response is the 'understanding' one which reflects the person-centered approach to counseling described earlier. Many of the ideas in this approach have been generally adopted and form the basis of much practice in counseling (Nelson-Jones, 2003).

'Understanding' is not a common way of responding in everyday conversations and therefore usually has to be learned. If you see it being used in counseling training videos, it can seem artificial and even embarrassing or irritating, but in a real conversation it feels better. If you are the 'helper' in such conversations, the power of 'understanding' responses is that they (1) enable you to check that you have correctly understood the intended meaning of what has just been said, and (2) leave the way clear for the other person to continue to tell you about their thoughts and feelings.

This may take time, but it is nearly always worth it. Listening carefully to what the person says will give them a chance to hear themselves talk, which can be cathartic and will also help the person reflect on what they just said. It will increase your understanding of their perspective. You will avoid telling the other person they are right or wrong, and getting into the awkward position of having to agree with them from the outset. Even though you show an interest in the other person, you should not take responsibility for their feelings and actions.

A Counseling Style of Career Helping

If it is clear that it would be helpful to adopt a counseling approach in a work-related 'helping' conversation, it is important to manage the ground rules and the setting. This might well involve (1) ensuring you are somewhere you will not be overheard or interrupted; (2) being clear about how much time is available and whether it will be possible to have further sessions if necessary; and (3) establishing that the conversation is confidential (on both sides). The physical setting matters too. It is best to sit at the same level as the other person, facing them but perhaps at a slight angle, and make sure there is no big barrier such as a desk between you.

Throughout the conversation, it is important to show interest in the other person and what they are saying. This is sometimes referred to as 'active listening'. Maintain frequent eye contact with the other person but without constant staring. Avoid distractions such as email alerts, computers and smart phones. Try to ensure you can discreetly see the time without having to look pointedly at your watch. Listen for the person's feelings and attitudes as well as their words. Concentrate on the overall meaning but also the detail of what is being said. This is easier said than done. Make notes if that helps, and if the other person says it's OK. Keep an alert body posture, for example by leaning slightly forward. Use prompts such as 'uh huh', 'right' and 'mmm' to keep the conversation going and to show you are still focused.

Adapting Egan's skilled helper model (see above), you will move through three stages in a counseling conversation: stage 1 is clarifying and exploring the current situation/problem; stage 2 is developing preferred scenarios and possible problem solutions; and stage 3 is formulating strategies and plans. There will not usually be a clear boundary between these stages, and it may well be that only the first two, or even the first one, will be needed. It might all be over in 15 minutes, but don't rush it.

Understanding responses are especially important in stage 1. In effect, you are reflecting back and paraphrasing what the other person just said. It is important to show empathy for the other person, which means understanding the world as the other person sees it. That does not necessarily mean you agree, only that you can see things their way. Also, and this is more an attitude than a skill, it is important to be able to accept the other person for who they are. You do not have to think everything they do is great, but you do need to view them as a person of worth who matters and who has integrity. Towards the end of stage 1, it will often be appropriate to use a few more probing responses in order to complete the clarification and exploration of the current situation. It is often best to make these open: that is, questions that cannot simply be answered yes or no.

In stage 2, there is slightly more emphasis on the role and skills of the counselor. In order to move towards preferred outcomes and solutions, if you can see different and potentially more helpful ways of looking at things, you may gently challenge the other person, but without implying that you know the right answer. Challenge may help the other person re-frame the problem in a way that aids solution. You might use a few interpretive responses to summarize or pick out some common themes you think you can see in what has been said, but again this should be suggested not imposed. Frequent use of understanding responses should continue because this is the best way of encouraging the person to develop their own vision of a good outcome.

A difficulty in informal career helping is that the helper most likely has a broader relationship with the 'helpee', e.g. as parent, friend or boss, and this may cause conflicts in the kind of options identified, for example a parental desire to have one's children close to home versus career opportunities in other cities or countries. If, as a helper, you have managerial responsibilities, it may become clear that there is a preferred solution from an organizational point of view which in your managerial role you would wish to advocate (Nathan & Hill, 2006, Chapter 7). It is important to put that firmly to one side, because you are attempting to enable the person to make effective decisions for him or herself. However, it may also be useful to acknowledge the parental or organizational agenda explicitly to the person, partly because it could be useful information for them.

In stage 3, the emphasis shifts to action planning. Depending on the actions required, the person's existing skills and your own resources, you may adopt a coaching role in order to help them learn new skills or behaviors. You may have specific expertise or knowledge that will be useful to the person in implementing action plans. Now is the time to offer (not impose) it, preferably in a way which imparts your knowledge without telling the person what they should conclude from it or how they should use it. You may be in a position to give feedback on how well the person is doing: for example, in the case of the previous 'Stop and consider' – a colleague whose application was rejected by the marketing department – you might role-play a conversation between the 'helpee' and the marketing manager, and give your views on their performance.

Collectively, the activities in these stages of counseling fit well with Kidd et al.'s (2004) findings about what people value most in those with whom they have career discussions at work. This was interest, commitment and trustworthiness, challenging and facilitative skills, giving honest feedback, and provision of information. Occasionally, you may feel that you are out of your depth and/or that there is some-body else with specific knowledge or expertise that the person might benefit from seeing. With the person's permission, you might refer him or her on.

In the case below, see how many of the features just described you can identify:

What's Wrong with Marketing?

One of Chris's colleagues, Raymond, storms into the office waving an email he has printed off:

> Raymond: 'I am really annoyed that my application for an internal transfer to the marketing department was rejected. What's wrong with them? What's wrong with me? I feel really down about this.'

Raymond looks very agitated. Of course, Chris is busy as usual but can spare a few minutes to talk with him. Chris invites him into a meeting room and changes the

(Continued)

(Continued)

sign on the door to 'Engaged'. There are no laptops, PCs or phones in there. Chris says he can spare 20 minutes for Raymond if he would like to talk about it. Chris has no managerial responsibility for Raymond. They are at the same level of the organization and know each other but are not rivals. They agree that the conversation will be private between the two of them.

Raymond: 'I've had enough of this company, why won't Marketing take me seriously'?

Chris: 'You feel you are not properly appreciated.'

Raymond: 'To say the least. They say they encourage us to move around the company but this is what happens when I try.'

Chris: 'There's a gap between what management say and what happens on the ground.'

Raymond: 'A yawning chasm, more like. Or perhaps it's something about me. Maybe I'm just not good enough at my job, or at least people don't think I am.'

Chris: 'You wonder whether you are seen as a good performer.'

Raymond: 'I do now. On the other hand, I've heard that the marketing department didn't take on anyone from other parts of the company who wanted to move.'

Chris: 'Marketing aren't allowing people to transfer in.'

Raymond: 'It looks that way. But surely they should make an exception for me. I've got relevant experience from my previous company so they could have put me to work almost right away.'

Chris: 'You could have quickly made yourself useful to Marketing.'

Raymond: 'Definitely. And I would have loved to. I'm pretty bored where I am now. Something has to change for me, and soon.'

Chris: 'You feel ready for a move of some kind.'

Raymond: 'Four years is a long time to stay in one job in this company. I'm going to look like a no-hoper. I wish I had taken more time and care over the application to Marketing.'

Chris:	'Your application to Marketing could have been better thought-through.'
Raymond:	'Yes, perhaps I was over-confident. I thought my past experience would make it obvious I was a strong candidate. But given Marketing's reluctance to take anyone, I doubt if it would have made much difference.'
Chris:	'You thought your relevant experience would be self-evident.'
Raymond:	'Yes. I can see that was a mistake now. Also, I don't really know anyone in Marketing that well, so there's no reason to think they would have heard about my past experience.'
Chris:	'People in Marketing aren't very aware of you.'
Raymond:	'I don't think so. I should have made a point of getting to know a few of them and mentioning my past experience in conversation.'
Chris:	'Is it Marketing you want to get into, or is it more a case of needing a change, any change, from your present job'?
Raymond:	'Hmm, good question. Probably more the latter really.'
Chris:	'You are ready for a change.'
Raymond:	'I'd be happy to go into operations management, sales, anything that keeps me busy and not in the office all the time and has plenty of variety.'
Chris:	'You like to stay busy and doing lots of different things.'
Raymond:	'Yes. There are plenty of jobs like that in this company. If Marketing don't rate me then I can try to find someone who does.'
Chris:	'It might be possible to get a transfer to another part of the company.'
Raymond:	'Yes, if they are serious about the internal mobility policy. I can ask HR which parts of the company will be next to offer some opportunities.'
Chris:	'What do you want to do about Marketing?'
Raymond:	'Shoot them?! No. I want them to know I'm disappointed but there's no point in looking like a cry-baby. I can ask them for feedback

(Continued)

(Continued)

> about my application, and what I'd have to do another time to stand a better chance. I'll have to be careful how I do it, and make sure I don't lose my temper with them. Best to write, not talk I think, at least to start with. I'm not very good at wording sensitive things like this though.'

Chris: 'I'd be happy to look at a draft if you think that would be helpful.'

Raymond: 'Oh, would you? Thanks, I'll definitely take you up on that.'

Chris: 'What other aspects of this would you like to talk about right now?'

Raymond: 'None that I can think of. Thanks for listening. There isn't an instant answer but at least I have a plan.'

What did you notice about this case? First, the helper (Chris) makes sure that there will be no interruptions and that the time available for this conversation is clearly understood. Second, notice that most of Chris's contributions to the conversation are 'understanding' type responses. Indeed, the first nine are, and so are some subsequent ones. These give Raymond the chance to expand on his thoughts and feelings, which he does. The three phases of a counseling-style conversation are evident, with the long first phase dominated by helping Raymond articulate his thoughts and feelings, the second phase involving some questions and gentle challenges, and the final phase emphasizing action and how to ensure it is successful. In this case, and in many others, the person being helped has the potential to find their own solution. It just needs a little facilitation.

Although a counseling style is both helpful and under-used in everyday life, it is not always all that a career actor needs to move forward in their career. Bosley and colleagues (Bosley et al., 2007, 2009) have examined the ways in which one person can be an effective career helper for another. An important aspect of this is what Bosley calls credibility: whether the helper has the necessary attributes to indicate to the person being helped that (s)he should take note of what the helper says. Often, the helper requires some expert knowledge to be credible, and also a willingness to accept the worldview of the person being helped, rather than the more neutral stance advocated by most approaches to counseling. It may also be helpful to be clear about what role(s) the helper is adopting. Bosley et al. (2009) suggest five roles, based on in-depth interviews with people in various manual and customer-facing service jobs:

1. *Adviser.* Offers opinions, suggestions and/or recommendations based on their own views of careers.
2. *Informant.* Gives information about jobs, vacancies, occupations without recommending a course of action.

3. *Witness.* Offers general feedback on a person's work, and specific feedback about their skills and personal qualities.
4. *Gatekeeper.* Uses their power to help or hinder access to jobs, promotions and/or development opportunities.
5. *Intermediary.* Uses (or is believed to use) influence to intervene on the person's behalf with gatekeepers.

With the partial exceptions of Informant and Witness, these roles do not sit easily with the first two phases of the counseling process described above. There are therefore many ways of helping another person in their career.

Conclusion

Career counseling performs a vital role in assisting many career actors to make a good career choice, and is of potential value to all. Different approaches, emphasizing for example, fit, adult development and narrative, can be used. Counseling is much wider than assisting with choice of occupation. Assistance can also range from highly professional counseling by expert counselors with extensive training aided by psychometric tests, to informal chats – described here as career 'helping' – in home or work settings. The chances are that a few readers of this book will become involved as professional counselors, but many may find themselves as clients of counselors, or 'helpers' or 'helpees'. Whatever the situation, we have outlined what you can expect from counseling, and some of the practices of counseling and helping which may tend to make it more effective. Whatever role you find yourself in, we hope these principles will work for you.

Key Points in this Chapter

- Career counseling normally involves one-to-one sessions between a person doing the counseling (counselor) and a person seeking counseling (client), concerning various career-related issues, not confined to the traditional focus of choosing an occupation.
- The fit, cycles and stories metaphors outlined in this book are strongly reflected in the different techniques and tools that career counselors use.
- Career counselors don't tell clients what to do: they help clients to make their own decisions.
- Techniques used by counselors include psychometric testing and client narratives encompassing past, present and desired future.

(Continued)

(Continued)

- Most counselors use person-centered ways of communicating which emphasize listening, being non-judgmental, empathy, cautious challenge, interpretation and facilitation of client solutions and action plans.
- Career counseling appears to be effective in improving clients' outcomes.
- The basic techniques of counseling can be used in everyday informal work situations.

Questions from this Chapter

General Questions

1. Would you prefer 'career as fit' or 'career as narrative' type counseling? Why?
2. People often say that the careers help they received at school or college was poor or non-existent. Was this the case for you, and, if so, why? Can you learn anything from this about the kind of career help you will seek in future?
3. Next time someone says something to you that suggests they are concerned about something, try using all or nearly all 'understanding' type responses for at least the first 7 minutes. What happens?
4. Think about the counselor–client interactions reported in this chapter. What do they teach you about counseling that you didn't know before? What, if anything, surprised you?
5. Imagine that you are a career counselor and different clients use the metaphors 'I'm moving along the conveyor belt', 'They want to kick me upstairs' and 'I'm skating on thin ice'. (Invent a few more of your own if you wish). Choose one of these and consider how you as a counselor might use it to help the client move forward.

'Live Career Case' Study Questions

1. Ask your case person to recount any experiences they have had that involved career counseling or professional guidance or advice. Include school, careers, teachers, and the like. Evaluate the experiences in the light of this chapter. What did you learn?
2. Ask your career case person for a metaphor summarizing their current career situation. Think of ways that the metaphor might be used in counseling.

Additional Resources

Recommended Further Reading

Egan, G. (2013) *The Skilled Helper* (10th edn). London: Cengage.

Kidd, J. M. (2006) *Understanding Career Counselling*. London: SAGE.

Kidd, J. M., Hirsh, W. and Jackson, C. (2004) 'Straight talking: The nature of effective career discussion at work', *Journal of Career Development*, 30(4): 231–245.

McMahon, M. (2007) 'Career counseling and metaphor', In K. Inkson (ed.), *Understanding Careers: The metaphors of working lives* (pp. 270–295). Thousand Oaks, CA: SAGE.

McMahon, M. and Watson, M. (2013) 'Story-telling: Crafting identities', *British Journal of Guidance & Counselling*, 41: 277–286.

Verbruggen, M., Sels, L. and Forrier, A. (2007) 'Unraveling the relationship between organizational career management and the need for external career counseling', *Journal of Vocational Behavior*, 71: 69–83.

Self-Assessment Resources

Assess your attitudes towards career counseling: Rochlen, A. B., Mohr, J. J. and Hargrove, B. K. (1999) 'Development of the attitudes toward career counseling scale', *Journal of Counseling Psychology*, 46: 196.

Assess who your career helpers are: Bosley, S. L., Arnold, J. and Cohen, L. (2009) 'How other people shape our careers: A typology drawn from career narratives', *Human Relations*, 62: 1487–1520.

Online Resources

How to find a career counselor – see: www.wikihow.com/Find-a-Good-Career-Counselor

Interested in becoming a career counselor yourself? See: http://psychology.about.com/od/psychologycareerprofiles/p/career-counselor.htm

Organizational Career Management

14

Chapter Objectives

The objectives of this chapter are:

- to examine how organizations play a role in managing the careers of career actors within them
- to describe and examine the Organizational Career Management (OCM) policies and practices that can be implemented in organizations
- to show how the career metaphors explored in this book find expression in OCM
- to show how individual career actors can use OCM to aid their career self-management (CSM)
- to consider, via a case example, things that can go well and badly in OCM
- to assist readers who are (or will be) responsible for OCM to design and manage it effectively.

CASE STUDY

Getting Ahead in the Company

Josie is a recent MBA graduate working in a Boston-based high-tech firm. Identified as a high-potential young manager, she has a passion for sustainability and a strong work identity as a change agent and a socially responsible citizen.

Josie has been a member of the corporate strategic planning group. Although it was not part of her job description, she came up with a business plan for a system of solar panels that could be installed easily on the roofs of the many data warehouses that the company operated. When she mentioned the idea to her boss, he encouraged her to pursue it. Not only was the plan accepted, but as she was discussing her passion for alternative energy work with her CEO, they jointly came up with the idea of creating a new position of Manager for Sustainability, and that part of her identity is now a large part of her formal organizational role.

Josie's organization has a long-standing culture and tradition of providing supportive autonomy for employees' careers, with resources devoted to career planning, and policies that allow employees flexibility to craft jobs that are aligned to their personal values and the organization's business. Part of this culture is the hosting, within the organization, of career communities (see Chapter 9) by the human resource function. These informal career communities meet bi-monthly to discuss shared career interests and exploration. The presence of these communities has a signaling effect through the organization, strengthening the climate and perception of the organization as one that is values-driven and supportive of career exploration.

Josie's career orientation is similarly 'protean' (see Chapter 5), driven by strong values and a self-directed approach to her career. She would probably not stay in any one organization for too long if it did not give her the opportunity to pursue her strong interests. Expressing that part of her career identity is very important to her. In fact, she has had two offers, at much higher salaries, from larger, highly successful technology companies in the last year and she has turned them both down. Because her company has a climate that aligns with her career orientation and encourages employees to use initiative and pursue business ideas sparked by their passion, the firm is able to retain young talent like her. Furthermore, the organization has established a strong reputation as one with a positive climate, distinguishing itself from other organizations and attracting talented people like Josie.

Source: adapted from Hall & Yip (2014), by permission of Oxford University Press, USA.

Josie's experience is just one of many ways that the culture, climate and practices of an organization can influence its external reputation and how employees relate and identify with the organization. Thus, a third strand of careers practice, additional to career self-management (CSM, Chapter 12), counseling by skilled professionals and the help of family, workmates, etc. (Chapter 13) is organizational career management (OCM). Mayo (1991: 75) defined OCM as 'the design and implementation of organizational processes which enable the careers of individuals to be planned and managed in a way that optimizes both the needs of the organization and the preferences and capabilities of individuals'.

Josie's organization uses OCM to support employees' careers. This is expressed through its willingness to create new roles, its crafting of existing ones to fit employee preferences, its tolerance of employees' crafting of their own roles, its openness to career planning discussions, and its support for 'career communities' where people can share their experiences. This is a very enabling approach, where the initiative largely comes from employees and is facilitated by the organization.

However, the balance of power between organization and individual is not always as benign as in Josie's organization. OCM has often operated in a more controlling way, where the organizational agenda is paramount (Hirsh & Jackson, 2004). Here, employees are usually expected to fit in with organizational requirements, and OCM is used to ensure that the internal supply of human resources fits the forecast demand. According to Jeffrey Sonnenfeld (1989: 222), 'a career does not exist in a social vacuum but is in many ways directed by the employer's staffing priorities'.

Indeed, organizations have always had a strong interest in developing, controlling and exploiting the careers of their employees for their advantage. Because it is easier to predict and control what is happening inside the organization than outside it, this gives organizations an interest in developing internal labor markets, that is, filling vacancies from within the organization and developing staff so that they are ready to fill these vacancies. The focus in sophisticated OCM is not so much on individual vacancies and placements as on the development of a career system to process and direct the combined resource embodied in employees' careers toward meeting organizational goals (Duffus, 2004: 144). Still, if we take the last part of Mayo's definition of OCM seriously and seek to 'optimize both the needs of the organization and the preferences and capabilities of individuals', then even this organizationally controlled OCM should take the aspirations of employees into account.

This chapter forms part of the practical section of this book. Our main aims are therefore to help you understand (1) how you might be able to use OCM to your benefit when you are a recipient of it, and (2) how you might design and manage OCM if you are responsible for running it in an organization. We do not aim to offer a wide-ranging analysis of the academic literature on OCM. You can find that in Baruch (2004), Section 3 of Gunz and Peiperl (2007), and Arnold and Cohen (2013).

Organizational Career Systems

Some organizations have official policies about the forms employees' careers should and should not take. For example, some multinational organizations have a policy that nobody can be appointed to a job at a certain level of the organization until they have successfully completed an overseas assignment. Other examples are that employees must have worked for at least three years in a branch before they can be considered for a role in head office; that professional qualifications must be fully completed before a promotion is permitted; and that the organization will pay employees' fees for an approved educational course, but if they leave within two years of completing it, they must pay the fees back.

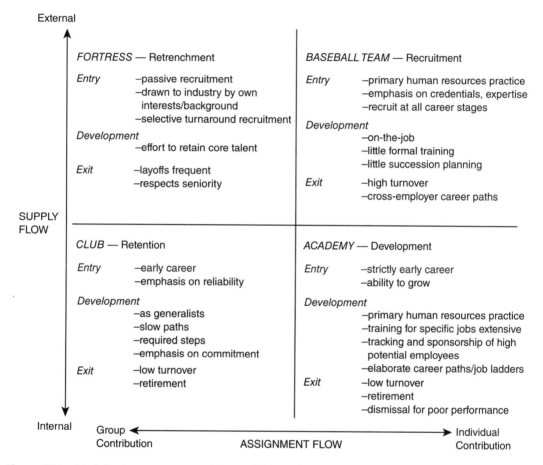

Figure 14.1   Models of career systems (Sonnenfeld & Peiperl, 1988)

OCM policies often arise from the organization's intentional strategy and/or the economic situation it finds itself in. In a nice use of metaphor, Sonnenfeld and Peiperl (1988) and Sonnenfeld (1989) distinguished four organizational career systems (see Figure 14.1):

- A *baseball team* is open to external recruitment at all levels, and assigns and promotes its members on the basis of individual merit.

- By contrast, an *academy* is a more stable institution that strives to develop its members' knowledge, skills and commitment. Academies, although they also reward individual performance, are closed to outside labor markets, preferring to promote from within.
- A *club* or fraternal order focuses on fair treatment for all members and values loyalty proven by seniority (i.e. job tenure). Clubs also use an internal supply of labor, but they pay more attention to group factors when deciding assignments.
- A *fortress* is an institution under siege, and it has low commitment to individuals. It neither limits its labor supply channels nor makes assignments based on individual contributions; the primary goal is institutional survival, even at the cost of individual members.

> ## Stop and Consider
>
> In what type of career system are you most likely to thrive – a baseball team, an academy, a club or a fortress? Why? Assemble a list of questions you might ask in future job interviews to determine which type of career system the recruiting organization uses.

In Sonnenfeld's analysis, there are two fundamental properties of career systems (Figure 14.1). First of all, the degree to which a firm is open to recruiting staff from the external labor market at job levels beyond entry level, which Sonnenfeld refers to as the supply flow, and second, the criteria by which assignment and promotion decisions are made, which he calls the assignment flow. In the early 21st century, we probably need to add to these two dimensions. Organizations differ in the extent to which they seek to develop people (Segers & Inceoglu, 2012) and in which people they seek to develop. Also, as we have already seen, they differ in the extent to which employees have a say in their organizational career.

It is probably worthwhile for career actors to gather such information as they can on the career systems in organizations they work for, or are considering working for, because this helps greatly with career self-management (CSM, see Chapter 12). Unfortunately, it cannot be assumed that the policies in operation are the same as the ones written down. Things may operate rather differently in practice, and/or certain people may be permitted to break the rules, for example where managers give their 'favorites' unwarranted priority in career-enhancing assignments. So it is important to be observant about what happens in practice and to try to understand why (Sternberg, 2000). If you notice this in your own organization, you may even wish to challenge some of what you see, but, if so, take care to consider the possible consequences, good and bad, of doing so.

Managers responsible for OCM need to examine both the stated policies and those operating in practice, if different. Do they fit the organization's current circumstances and needs? Perhaps some of them are a legacy of the past and need to be changed. Some may over-protect the people at the top from competition, or at least be based on a philosophy of 'I had to suffer to get this far, so they have to as well'. You may also be able to see alternative or additional policies that would help both the organization and its staff achieve their goals.

Career Mobility Systems

In general, the careers literature distinguishes between two types of career mobility systems – by which we mean the system of official rules and unofficial norms by which organizations decide for whom, when and how internal upward career mobility is possible. Vinkenburg and Weber (2012) distinguish between contest mobility and sponsored mobility.

Contest mobility refers to a career mobility system in which employees compete for higher-level positions within the framework of an 'open market'. Everyone is welcome to compete for promotion. The basic assumption is that everyone gets a chance, and therefore career outcomes (i.e. being promoted or not being promoted) are attributed to individual effort. According to Turner (1960), in a contest mobility system it is believed that a person of average intelligence who works hard is more deserving of promotion than someone who is more intelligent, but who does not try. In that sense, the idea of contest mobility ties in neatly with the discourse of the American Dream (discussed in Chapter 2), in placing the primary responsibility for career outcomes in the hands of the individual.

Sponsored mobility refers to a career mobility system in which, similarly to the 'officer/other ranks' distinction in the armed forces, there is a 'closed' market for promotion into top-level positions, only accessible to those who since the beginning of their careers have been identified as 'high potentials'. Because speed of advancement accelerates for the chosen few, the selection of candidates for top management positions occurs quite early on in their careers. Sponsors – i.e. the people in charge of the selection of young employees in or out of the elite group of potential successors – are members of the dominant elite (typically top managers themselves), who use their influence to advocate for candidates and actively create career opportunities for them (Ibarra et al., 2010; Turner, 1960).

CASE STUDY

The Golden Boy and the Class Clown

Jack and Jim are brothers with very different personalities, who work in markedly different organizational settings. Jack was always the studious one of the two. After completing his studies at the London School of Economics (LSE), he joined the ranks of a large prestigious consultancy firm. The manager who recruited him into the firm, Richard, was an LSE alumnus himself, who during the job talk found himself looking at young Jack and thinking, approvingly, 'this guy reminds me of a certain someone who was equally ambitious, eager, and impatient at that age' – himself, of course. After Jack was hired, Richard became an unofficial mentor (Chapter 9) to him, providing him with inside information on the politics of the firm, the projects that could further his career and the contacts worth knowing in senior management and among clients. Within a few years, Richard nominated Jack for partnership, saying publicly that if Jack was not made a partner, he (Richard) might be upset enough to veto other board members' favorite candidates. In the meantime, Jack has become somewhat discontented. He feels he has to keep pleasing Richard, and is aware that some people in the company resent the strong-arm tactics Richard is using to get him a partnership.

Jim, on the other hand, having been in the shadows of his brilliant older brother since he was born, has had a very different career path. Always the 'class clown' in high school, he ended up dropping out of three different programs in college before he found his calling – tree surgeon. In addition, and in line with his orientation towards outdoors work, Jim worked part-time as an 'Outward Bound' trainer for a company that organized corporate team building in forests. Having been popular in high school, and helped by 'word of mouth' reputation, he was able to extend his business as a tree surgeon. Then the management team of a national TV network went on an Outward Bound trip with him as a trainer. They were so charmed by his rugged good looks, his smart talk and his love for nature, that they added him to the list of people they were considering for a new survival show, in which candidates were challenged to undertake a three-week trip along the Arctic Circle. After he won the show and the hearts of the overwhelming majority of (female) viewers, another network offered him two shows simultaneously: a gardening show and a survival show for kids. Jim is now a celebrity in his country, and has just finished filming a new show in which he travels around the world in a carbon-neutral way.

Jack's career is a clear case of sponsored mobility. His progress was started and then continued by Richard's support and endorsement. On the face of it, his career is a great success, yet he sometimes feels that it is being 'dictated' by other people, particularly his corporate sponsor. In contrast, Jim's career, after a few false starts, illustrates contest mobility. He had to demonstrate his competence both to the management team to get a chance, and in the survival contest to get further work. His new-found career success is dependent on maintaining his performance and appeal. Even then, especially considering the fickle nature of television programming, it is likely to be finite. It may be only a matter of time before a new up-and-coming person catches the TV production team's eye.

On the other hand, the cases of Jack and Jim also show that contest and sponsored mobility are not as separate as they might seem. Perhaps if Jack had been incompetent relative to others in the company, then even Richard would not have been able or willing to protect him. Jim was sponsored at the start of his television career by the production management team and although he needed to prove himself, he would not have had the opportunity to do that without the sponsorship.

OCM Practices

Many different practices are available to implement OCM. Different academics and practitioners have slightly different ways of describing and categorizing them, but there is broad agreement that the practices (also called interventions, techniques) include those shown in Table 14.1.

Table 14.1 Career Management Practices in Organizations

1. **Internal Vacancy Notification.** Information about jobs available in the organization, normally in advance of any external advertising, and with some details of preferred experience, qualifications and a job description.

2. **Induction and Socialization.** Programmes of instruction, training and work experience that enable a newcomer to become familiar with the organization and prepare them for future roles within it.

3. **Career Paths.** Information about the sequences of jobs that a person can do, or competencies they can acquire, in the organization. This should include details of how high in the organization any path goes, the kinds of moves that are possible and perhaps the skills/experience required.

4. **Career Workbooks.** These consist of questions and exercises designed to help individuals to identify strengths and weaknesses, job and career opportunities, and necessary steps for reaching their goals.

5. **Career Planning Workshops.** Cover some of the same ground as workbooks, but offer more chance for discussion, feedback from others, information about organization-specific opportunities and policies. May include psychometric testing.

6. **Computer Assisted Career Management.** Various packages exist for helping employees to assess their skills, interests and values, and translate these into job options. Sometimes these packages are customized to a particular organization.

7. **Training and Educational Opportunities.** Participation in courses (and/or financial support and information about courses) in the organization or outside it. These can enable employees to update, retrain or deepen their knowledge in particular fields. In keeping with the notion of careers involving sequences, training in this context is not solely to improve performance in a person's present job.

(Continued)

Table 14.1   (Continued)

8. **Secondments.** The opportunity to work in another context, usually in order to gain skills and experience not readily available in the organization.

9. **Personal Development Plans (PDPs).** These often arise from the appraisal process and other sources such as development centres. PDPs are statements of how a person's skills and knowledge might appropriately develop, and how this development could occur, in a given timescale.

10. **Career Action Centers.** Resources such as literature, DVDs and perhaps more personal inputs such as counseling available to employees on a drop-in basis.

11. **Development Centers.** Like assessment centers in that participants are assessed on the basis of their performance in a number of exercises and tests. However, development centers focus more on identifying a person's strengths, weaknesses and styles for the purpose of development, not selection.

12. **Mentoring Programs.** Attaching employees to more senior ones who act as advisors, and perhaps also as advocates, protectors and counselors (see also Chapter 9).

13. **Coaching Programs.** Often similar to and overlapping with mentoring programs, but usually with more of a focus on how an individual can improve his or her performance. The coach is often someone from outside the organization who may 'teach' specific skills and/or use counseling and related techniques to help a person reflect on his/her own behavior at work and find ways to improve.

14. **Individual Counseling.** Can be done by specialists from inside or outside the organization, or by line managers who have received training (see also Chapter 13). May include psychometric testing. This overlaps with mentoring and coaching to some extent. The aim is usually to help a person solve his or her own career problems and/or take career opportunities without imposing a solution.

15. **Job Rotation Schemes.** A group of people swap jobs periodically in order to develop their range of skills and their ability to cover for each other.

16. **Developmental Job Assignments.** Careful use of work tasks can help a person to stay employable for the future, and an organization to benefit from the adaptability of staff. These can also be used as part of succession planning (see below) to get a person ready for a new role.

17. **Succession Planning.** The identification of individuals who are expected to occupy key posts in the future, and who are exposed to experiences which prepare them appropriately. This can be done on a small scale for just one or a small number of senior posts and a small number of individuals, or on a large scale for a whole cohort of people and/or posts at lower levels of the organization. This is sometimes called *talent management*.

18. **Outplacement**. This may involve several interventions listed above. Its purpose is to support people who are leaving the organization to clarify and implement plans for their future.

19. **Retirement and Late Career Programs.** When people approach an age where they are considering withdrawal from full-time work, organizations often provide workshops and training on matters like money management, adjustment to retirement living and considering various bridging or part-time work.

Source: Adapted from Arnold (1997a) and Arnold & Cohen (2013).

Clearly, these practices differ from each other in a number of ways. Baruch and Peiperl (2000) and Baruch (2004) map OCM practices onto two axes: 'level of involvement' (from very low to very high level of organizational involvement needed when dealing with the specific OCM practice) and 'level of sophistication' (from very simple to highly sophisticated and complex). Additional ways of differentiating these practices are in how expensive they are to run, whether they can be done as part of the person's job and whether they require the active participation of line managers (Arnold, 1997a).

Stop and Consider

Have another look at all the different OCM practices listed in Table 14.1. If you were (or indeed are currently) employed by a large organization, which of these would be 'must-haves' for you and which would be 'nice to have', but you could live without? Are there any OCM practices you would rather not see in prospective employers? Make a list of the OCM practices you think you need and why, so that you can ask informed questions about these in future job interviews.

Later in this chapter, we will discuss the use of these practices a little more, particularly from the point of view of employees on the receiving end, and managers responsible for running them. First, however, it is necessary to put OCM into a wider context.

The Rise, Fall and Rise of OCM

In the second half of the 20th century, the development of internal labor markets, particularly for staff in technical, professional and managerial roles, became popular in large companies. To encourage loyalty, companies strove to reinforce attractive arrangements for remuneration, development, security and promotion with strong, appealing organizational cultures (Cappelli, 2008) that encouraged employees to be part of the greater enterprise. The model reached its high point in the great Japanese organizations, such as Honda and Mitsubishi, in which young individuals entering the organization ('salarymen') were offered lifetime employment (Ishida & Spilerman, 2002). They could look forward to a career under paternalistic management, in which their continuing employment, regular promotions and generous pensions were guaranteed; generous assistance in areas such as health, housing and family education was offered; and a 'happy family' metaphor of company life offered further inducements to a company career.

Benefits at Enclos

Enclos, a medium-sized American firm specializing in innovative architectural design, is a good example of a company that seeks to build employee loyalty and

(Continued)

(Continued)

career commitment by offering long-term employee benefits. Just look at their website: the benefits cover the whole life cycle, and the organization appears to be trying to compete in benefits to acquire the best staff and compete commercially.

'At Enclos, we know there is a whole world outside of work, and we endeavor to provide you with programs that help you make the most of it. No matter how your life changes, Enclos offers resources that protect you and your family, help you ease transitions in trying times, or help you grow both professionally and personally. You will find Enclos' benefits to be among the most progressive in the industry.'

The listed benefits include a competitive salary, a companywide bonus plan, medical and dental coverage, short-term and long-term disability insurance, employee life and accidental death and injury insurance, employee voluntary accident insurance, vision insurance, AFLAC (supplemental insurance), paid time off, a generous profit-sharing plan, an employee assistance plan, a college savings plan, education assistance and a flexible spending account.

Why would anyone ever leave?

As discussed in Chapter 2, the fashion for organizational careers peaked in the 1980s, followed in the 1990s by claims – possibly exaggerated (Dany, 2003) – that the (organizational) career was dead (Hall & Associates, 1996). The problem with internal labor markets, clear company hierarchical structures, lifetime employment and even strong organizational cultures had been that their permanence created rigidities that in the long term reduced competitiveness and organizational performance. The globalization process of the latter part of the 20th century created fierce competitive pressures for cost reduction and rationalization in organizations. From the 1980s, in many organizations, staff numbers were reduced (downsizing), whole hierarchical levels of organizations were removed (delayering), work was removed from permanent employees and jobbed out to competitive contractors (outsourcing) and permanent full-time staff were replaced by temporary and part-time 'casual' workers, who could more easily be displaced and rehired (casualization). At the same time, globalization altered international patterns of employment; information technology displaced traditional skills and required new ones; new emphases on multiskilling and teams weakened traditional demarcations around jobs, occupations and professions; and the feminization of the workforce introduced employees who needed new, more flexible patterns of work.

The effect of this organizational restructuring was to destabilize the careers of many workers. Careers that seemed stable and progressive were tarnished by unexpected layoffs. Laid-off employees typically find new jobs eventually and may even experience greater satisfaction than they did in the old job, but it appears their commitment and trust in organizations is reduced by the experience (Pugh et al., 2003).

In addition, restructuring tends to break the ties of loyalty that many employees feel toward their employers, leading to alienation not only by the 'victims' of restructuring but also by those who remain in the restructured organization – the 'survivors' (Devine et al., 2003). The new generation of employment relationships is characterized by psychological contracts (see Chapter 10) that have ceased to be relational. That is, they are no longer based on the expectation of a long-term, mutually rewarding relationship between organization and individual. Instead, they are 'transactional', based on short-term exchanges of work for monetary rewards (Cullinane & Dundon, 2006).

These changes meant that senior managers in many organizations felt that they were no longer able to offer a career to employees. OCM was unaffordable and also an embarrassment because it implied that careers were on offer when in fact they were not (Hirsh & Jackson, 2004). So, when it came to career management, employees were 'on their own', and OCM practices declined. For some, this might have meant more freedom, but for many it meant anxiety and a perceived withdrawal of support by their employer. The organizational changes described above, and the reactions to them, remain very salient today (Hassard et al., 2012).

On the other hand, in recent years, an increasing number of scholars have expressed doubts about the new career literature's claims as concerns the speed and inevitability of the demise of organizational careers (Clarke, 2013; Inkson et al., 2012; Rodrigues & Guest, 2010). In Chapter 7, we showed that even in the current era, boundaryless or inter-organizational careers, while important, lack the universality or even frequency that some of their proponents have claimed, and that many career actors still spend periods of many years working for the same organization. In fact, Hall himself, in a recent piece, proclaimed: 'we were wrong: the organizational career is alive and well' (Hall & Las Heras, 2009: 182).

Even if the career landscape is now less predictable than it once was, it can be argued that in tough economic times career management becomes more important as well as more difficult. Senior managers in organizations need to think harder about future staff requirements, and individuals need to be agile and adaptable. If, in rapidly changing times, careers are seen as necessarily secure, predictable and organized in advance then OCM is probably not viable. However, if careers are seen as an emerging sequence of roles and experiences, then OCM can help to ensure that there is a good match between people and roles in the short-term, and appropriate overall development of staff for the medium term.

An extensive survey in the UK (CIPD, 2011) found that over three quarters of respondents cited retaining key staff and talent as a key aim of OCM. About two thirds saw OCM as identifying and developing talent to meet organizational objectives. De Vos and Dries (2013) conducted a survey of 306 Belgian organizations and found that on average each of 15 OCM practices (a similar list to that shown in Table 14.1) was used for all employees by 50 organizations, and for some employees by 90 organizations. It was notable that coaching, cross-functional training and job rotation were much more commonly used for selected employees only than for all employees. Earlier surveys (Baruch & Peiperl, 2000; Gutteridge et al., 1993; Iles & Mabey, 1993) also showed fairly widespread use of OCM practices in organizations, but perhaps not as extensively as more recently, which supports Hirsh and Jackson's (2004) claim that, especially since the turn of the century, employers have been re-engaging with OCM.

The CIPD survey (2011) and De Vos and Dries (2013) both suggest that those identified as high-fliers receive special attention in OCM, which may explain why some people see it as unfair and biased towards those who already have a lot going for them (Lewis & Arnold, 2012). The possible elitism in OCM practices is also implied by the increasingly popular term 'talent management' (Dries, 2013). The word 'talent' can mean the total human skills and knowledge available to the organization, but more often it seems to mean 'the most talented people, who we least want to lose'. Although some roles are more evidently vital to an organization than others, it seems likely that taking an inclusive approach to talent will pay dividends because it will help to utilize the total human potential of the organization and also contribute to a perception that the organization operates in a fair and just way (Greenberg & Colquitt, 2013).

Career Metaphors and OCM

The 'resource' metaphor (Chapter 10), as embodied in strategic human resource management, suggests that employing organizations can and should endeavor to influence, and even capture, employees' careers for their own as well as the employees' advantage. Is this practical, or desirable?

The cases cited earlier, of large organizations offering major incentives and a good working lifestyle and corporate culture to loyal employees, certainly suggest that powerful organizations can exercise significant control over employees' careers but can also offer them considerable security and opportunity. But the use of the term 'human resource' suggests that the person is part of the company's stock, which can be drawn on and developed for organizational ends (Chapter 10).

Stop and Consider

Ask yourself whether you like being thought of as a resource rather than as a person. What, if any, might be the advantages to you personally of being thought of as a resource? How do you feel about the following quote by Cascio (1995: 310)? 'A career is not something that should be left to each employee: instead it should be managed by the organization to ensure the efficient allocation of human and capital resources.' To what extent should careers be the property (and responsibility) of individuals versus employing organizations? Can you assign an ideal percentage of 'accountability' to both parties in the employment relationship?

The use of the term 'resource' potentially depersonalizes the individuals who make up the resource. It suggests a homogeneous supply of expertise divorced from the individual personalities who provide that expertise. 'Resource' might also disempower, reducing potentially self-determining people to ciphers of the company (Inkson, 2008). However, the author of the above quote (Cascio) changed from his original stance in a subsequent edition of the same book: 'A key feature of the new concept is that the company and the employee are *partners* in career development' (Cascio, 1998: 308, italics added). And yet another few years later, he wrote (Cascio, 2003: 373, italics added): 'A career is not something that should be left to chance. Instead, in the evolving world of work it should be *shaped and managed more by the individual* than by the organization.' This last view makes it much easier for career management to be based on a sense of individual ownership of the career with the support but not control of the organization, as in the case of Josie above. It also recognizes that most careers are inter-organizational, taking place across employers rather than within one organization only (Hall, 2002).

This individualization of career raises major problems for organizations with a 'resources' approach to career as they grapple with the problem of building an organization based on careers that they are not able to 'manage'. People with valuable knowledge and skills are unlikely to tolerate having their careers controlled by their employing organization (Clarke, 2013). Therefore, the way to retain them and maximize their contribution is to facilitate their career development rather than manipulate it. Often, individuals are open to the possibility of meshing their career aspirations with what the organization needs, if their individuality is respected and they are treated as an equal partner in a negotiation (Lips-Wiersma & Hall, 2007). The key is to remember that, unlike material resources, human resources have minds of their own, and can, for example, walk out of the door if they feel their career aspirations are not being met.

The other career metaphors also find expression in OCM, to greater or lesser degrees. The 'inheritance' metaphor (Chapter 3) emphasizes the role of social structure in determining career outcomes. Organizations are social structures, which can mean that only certain career paths are deemed to be the right background to fill top jobs. In this case, your career history in the organization is your inheritance. Intimate knowledge of the organization can give long-service employees a major career advantage over talented newcomers. A broad and varied background is often valued, but equally career histories that are seen as unconventional can be a handicap (CIPD, 2011). Also, some organizations offer OCM for groups with specific 'inheritances'. This has to be done with care in order to avoid discriminatory practices. It can be seen most often in interventions such as career support workshops and mentoring schemes for disadvantaged groups in organizations, as part of an attempt to increase their representation at senior levels (Friedman et al., 1998; Madera et al., 2013).

The cycles metaphor (Chapter 4) comes into play when organizations devise OCM interventions for people at particular career stages. The most obvious manifestations of this are induction and socialization for career starters and retirement planning for finishers (see Table 14.1). However, there are other examples. Some organizations specifically make mentoring opportunities available to career actors in mid-career, as a way of ensuring that their accumulated skills and knowledge are shared, and that their assumed need to be of value to the next generation (generativity) is satisfied (Wang et al., 2012; Chapter 4). The human resource management literature offers guidance about how to incorporate diversity into OCM (e.g. Greer & Virick, 2008).

The action metaphor (Chapter 5) most obviously reflects individual action independent of organizations. However, as the opening case in this chapter illustrates, organizations can facilitate individual action through providing non-directive OCM such as career communities. The fit metaphor (Chapter 6) finds expression in OCM which is designed to ensure that employees are in the right roles for them. So, for example, development centers and succession planning are OCM practices that often use organizational competency models to match people's skills and other attributes to roles available in the organization. Often, this is oriented towards potential future fit after a career actor receives development in readiness for a future role. However, it can also be more immediate and lead to the reassignment of staff to roles that fit them better right now (Froelich et al., 2011).

The journey metaphor (Chapter 7) relates to the role of career paths in OCM. Career actors often want to know what routes through an organization they can pursue, and what are the likely consequences of traveling one route rather than another (Carter et al., 2009). Senior managers in organizations also often like the structure that career paths bring, though especially since the 1990s the pace of change and pressure on organizations sometimes makes it difficult to identify what career paths really are (and are not) available now or in the future. Career workshops and workbooks often include exercises that encourage career actors to consider not just their work career, but the place of this in their life as a whole. The relative importance of different roles (see Chapter 8) as, for example, partner, parent, worker and citizen and how these will be reconciled is an increasingly frequent concern to both individuals and organizations (Beauregard & Henry, 2009).

Most OCM is more about organizational processes and individual careers than it is about relationships. Nevertheless, mentoring, coaching and counseling (see Table 14.1) all involve relationships between the person(s) giving and those receiving. The relationships metaphor is explored in Chapter 9, including mentoring and other developmental relationships. Also, in other forms of OCM, relationships often matter more than might be apparent. In particular, relationships between HR and line managers are frequently important, because line managers are often asked to play a part in implementing OCM practices, for example personal development plans, development centers and developmental job assignments (Gilbert et al., 2011). As we will see below, they do not always perceive this to be an appropriate or high priority task.

OCM's focus on objective aspects of career means that its connections with the stories metaphor are not especially strong or evident. Nevertheless, they do exist. Participation in OCM can itself form a significant part of a career actor's narrative. For example, a secondment to another organization or department might be positioned as a pivotal experience that leads the career actor in a new direction. Also, several OCM practices give senior members of the organization an opportunity to present a narrative about how careers work in the organization. These can have a powerful effect on the attitudes and behavior of organization members, especially when their identities are unclear or fragile and the organization operates in a field that does not have well-worn career tracks (Wright et al., 2012).

Using OCM to Manage Your Career

Rather than the career being the responsibility of either the individual – career self-management (CSM) – or the organization (OCM), the more recent career management literature suggests that these forms of career management are complementary rather than contradictory. As shown in the case of Josie with which we opened this chapter, both types of career management can reinforce one another. Ideally, both the organization (in providing the learning opportunities) and the individual (in seeking learning opportunities) collaborate to maximize positive outcomes for both parties (Lips-Wiersma & Hall, 2007). Research has demonstrated that those who manage their own careers also receive more career management help from the employer. Those with greater CSM skills appear to give themselves a head start in gaining access to organizational sources of career support (De Vos et al., 2009), thereby entering into a virtuous circle of complementary career management activities. There is evidence that organizational career management does indeed increase employees' commitment to continue their careers in that organization (Sturges et al., 2005, 2010; Verbruggen et al., 2007).

As an individual career actor in an organization, it is important for you to make the organization's OCM work for your benefit (King, 2004). This does not mean you are being subversive, though it may mean that the benefit you derive from OCM is not exactly what the organization's senior managers had in mind (Dickmann & Doherty, 2008). You might find it useful to check back to Chapter 12, about CSM, and then consider your current career priorities.

Stop and Consider

Consider the following 12 CSM activities. Try to select some that are important for you right now.

1. Decide what sort of work you want to go into.
2. Define your short- and medium-term career goals.

(Continued)

(Continued)

3. Make influential people aware of your goals.
4. Develop a plan for how to achieve those goals.
5. Decide whether your current organization is a suitable place for you to achieve your goals.
6. Implement your plan to achieve your career goals.
7. Get a clearer sense of your strengths, weaknesses, interests or values.
8. Develop your competencies and experience.
9. Understand better how you and your work are seen by others in your organization.
10. Develop your contacts and social networks.
11. Understand better how careers work in this organization.
12. Develop one or more coherent stories (narratives) about your career.

If you are employed in an organization, does the organization support these in any way? How? If you are not employed, how might an organization support them?

If you are employed in an organization, look again at Table 14.1. If you are a student, consider your educational institution and its career management practices for its staff, as far as you know them. Which of these OCM practices does your organization operate? Probably at least several. Indeed, you may already have experienced some OCM practices in your organization, but you may not know about them all, so have a careful look at your organization's HR information and ask around a bit. Once you know what is potentially on offer, consider whether each OCM practice could help you with your priority CSM activities. For example:

- Looking at the vacancies list (usually available on the organization's website) could give you a good sense of what kinds of job are available in the organization and what they require. That might help you decide whether your career goals can be met in the organization, understand better how careers work in the organization or define your short- and medium-term career goals.
- Secondments, job rotation and developmental job assignments may help you implement your career plans, develop your competencies and experiences or even decide what sort of work you want to go into. Like many OCM practices, these may also, as a side-effect, develop your social contacts and network.

- Personal Development Plans (PDPs) can be a useful way of making a statement about how you wish your career to develop. There is a tendency for them to focus on the next year or so, especially if they are linked with the organization's appraisal or performance management system. You may wish to take a longer-term view, and gain the organization's commitment to, for example, helping you achieve your goals (if they are sufficiently compatible with the organization's) perhaps through training or developmental job moves. The PDP process may also give you a better sense of how you and your work are seen by others, and whether the organization is a suitable place for you to achieve your career goals.
- Career Workshops are usually detached from the performance management process, and therefore give you the chance to reflect on your career with other people who want to do the same in a low-threat environment. As well as expanding your social network, this can help you clarify your career goals and your career-related competencies, interests and values. If there is an organizational input, a workshop can also help you clarify whether or not the organization can provide the kind of opportunities you want.

Being Responsible for OCM

We now examine OCM from the point of view of managers who are responsible for making it work: that may be your position now or in the future. There is no comprehensive taxonomy or list of specific outcomes that OCM should achieve (Kidd & Killeen, 1992). Most OCM practices only serve a small number of purposes (Hirsh et al., 2001), such as:

- filling vacancies
- assessments of potential, competencies, skills or interests
- development of skills and competencies
- identification of viable career options
- actions to implement career plans.

It is important that the goals of any given practice are clear, that they are consistent with the organization's OCM policies and that they contribute to the achievement of both organizational and personal goals. It is not usually helpful to use all of the practices shown in Table 14.1. If they were all used in an organization, most would not add value over and above what the others were achieving. The key is using a small number of OCM practices and knowing what you want them to contribute that is not being achieved by other means (Arnold & Johnson, 1997; Hirsh & Jackson, 2004).

Stop and Consider

If you have either participated in an OCM intervention, or seen one operating, think about what it achieved for the organization, and also whether it had any limitations or even damaging effects. How did the way the OCM was designed and implemented affect these outcomes, do you think? Write down your observations and then compare them with what you read below.

What might be the benefits *for organizations* of using OCM practices to support career policies? Although the benefits of OCM are often hard to prove (in common with many HR practices), many advocates (e.g. Baruch, 2004; Hirsh & Jackson, 2004) would argue that OCM practices can:

- help to attract and retain employees as part of an overall employment package
- lead employees to feel a sense of obligation to the organization to give it something back in return for its support
- improve the overall fit between people and their jobs in the organization
- identify the overall stock of competencies and experience in the organization
- identify training and development needs
- help individuals identify future roles for themselves in the organization, or, if there are none, help them leave the organization on good terms
- encourage employees to take joint responsibility with the organization for their careers
- persuade line managers that they have a key role to play in developing the human resource capacity of the whole organization, not just their team
- ensure that there are people ready to fill key roles when they fall vacant.

If you are involved in running OCM in an organization, it is very important to ensure that you know what the OCM is intended to achieve. For example, which of the benefits above are most important? This will help to define which OCM practices to use and how they can be designed.

In the new, apparently more open-ended career environment, managers often worry that the more they facilitate the personal development of employees within their organization for the benefit of the organization, the more they may simultaneously be increasing the same employees' attractiveness to the external labor market (Ito & Brotheridge, 2005). This is just one of the many organizational issues with delivering effective OCM. Perhaps the key to resolving this dilemma is for managers to retain open communication with each employee so that an employee's interest in making a career move to a new organization is not regarded as disloyalty but as a problem to be openly discussed in the hope of joint resolution (Inkson & King, 2011; Parker & Inkson, 1999). A number of the OCM practices listed in Table 14.1 offer an opportunity for this.

Pitfalls in Managing OCM, and How to Avoid Them

A case study reported by one of the authors (Arnold, 2002) offers a helpful vehicle for illustrating some of the issues in managing OCM.

The author was invited by a large technology company to lead an independent evaluation of the development centers it had been running for a couple of years. Each year there were about 12 development centers, each lasting two days in which about six company employees (henceforth called attendees) were assessed on a range of competencies through a mixture of business simulations, group discussions, presentations, interviews and psychometric tests. Assessors were senior managers in the company who had been trained to assess, plus members of the consultancy company which assisted the company in designing and running the centers. The center attendees were in positions of medium seniority, and had been identified by their bosses and by appraisal ratings in the last three years as having high potential. The performance of each attendee was discussed at length by assessors and they were given a score on each competency and an overall performance rating. A detailed feedback report was prepared, and discussed with attendees two or three weeks later. A development plan was also formulated for each attendee based on their center report and discussion with their supervisor.

This was a resource-intensive piece of OCM in terms of both money and time. From the point of the human resources department which had championed the centers and played a large part in administering them, it was therefore important to show that the large expense was justified. What did the evaluation show, and what lessons can be drawn from it for the effective implementation of OCM? Although this is done in the context of development centers, many of the lessons also apply more widely to other OCM practices.

1. Most attendees, even those who got the lowest scores for their performance at the center, thought that it was well run, and a valid test of their capabilities in the context of this organization. **Lesson:** Investment must be made to ensure that OCM practices are of high technical quality and design. This includes training of those involved – for example, the senior managers who acted as assessors had to do at least two days of training for the role.

2. Nearly all attendees, again including those who were less successful, felt that their report was fair and fed back to them with sensitivity and insight. **Lesson:** be willing

to invest time and care into any feedback element of an OCM activity. The feedback must be justifiable, and time should be taken to explain it.

3. There was concern amongst participants and assessors that some excellent people were not even getting as far as the development center, perhaps because their boss did not want to release them and/or risk losing them from their team. However, it was also recognized that HR had been careful to examine the records of all potential participants, and in some cases query why people had not been nominated to attend. **Lesson:** Ensure that the selection process for participation in an OCM intervention is seen to be thorough and fair.

4. Development plans were nearly always drawn up and agreed by the attendee, their line manager, and a representative of the HR department. **Lesson:** Ensure that actions arising from an OCM practice are clearly defined and agreed by relevant parties.

5. However, the development plans were not always implemented. Attendees said that often, although the plan had been agreed, it was not clear whose responsibility it was to make it happen. Also, their line managers were not always enthusiastic or skilled in playing a role in implementing the plan (see also Dick & Hyde, 2006), especially when it might mean that the attendee left the line manager's team. **Lesson:** Assign responsibilities for making follow-up action happen to named individuals, and when this includes line managers, ensure that they are held accountable for their role, perhaps through their annual performance appraisal.

6. Many of those who got the lowest (and even the middle) overall performance ratings felt like failures after the development center even though they had to be seen as high potential in order to be nominated for participation in it. **Lesson:** As far as possible, keep numerical performance ratings out of OCM. Leave that for the performance management system, which should be separate from OCM.

7. Rumors abounded about the importance of the overall performance rating. Many thought there was a list of top graders kept by HR which senior managers consulted when they wanted to find a high flier for a challenging role. Furthermore, those who got the top rating formed their own exclusive social network and tended to view themselves as the elite of the elite. This caused friction between some employees who had previously been close colleagues and friends. **Lesson:** Be clear about how the information arising from OCM is used in the organization, and discourage rumors.

8. There were disagreements about the role of the performance rating at the center. HR managers had resisted having any rating at all, preferring feedback only. But many senior managers, including some of the assessors, had insisted on it. HR saw the development center as defining the development needs of a cadre of high performers so that they could become even more valuable to the company. In contrast, many senior managers saw it as sorting the best from the also-rans – in effect as a selection device for accelerated development to top positions. **Lesson:** It is sometimes difficult to get general agreement about the exact purposes of an OCM practice. But it matters because if there are different views, then participants

will get mixed messages and the operation of the OCM may be compromised. Senior management support for OCM is likely to be crucial, but more than that, the support needs to be based on a shared perception of what the OCM practice is intended to achieve.

9. Attendees and assessors frequently emphasized how good the centers were for meeting colleagues working in different parts of the business. Attendees felt they had a chance to be noticed by senior people, whilst the assessors said they were able to spot talented managers they might like to have in their team in the future. Both groups said they learned a lot about issues faced by other sections of the company. **Lesson:** Wherever possible, maximize opportunities for people to meet others they would not normally come across.

10. Attendees were assessed using the company's recently revised and rather comprehensive competency framework, which was also used to profile roles in the company. This helped to clarify what the development center feedback meant for attendees' future roles in the company. **Lesson:** Wherever possible, connect OCM with organizational HR initiatives and strategic priorities.

Of course, OCM practices are most obviously applicable to large organizations. Small organizations rarely have the resources, scope or incentives to engage in OCM. Often, they can offer challenging and varied jobs (Arnold et al., 2002) but not longer-term career possibilities. There is scope for small organizations to form informal alliances that would enable them collectively to offer a wider range of OCM, especially training and developmental job assignments (Ahlström-Söderling, 2003).

Conclusion

Organizational career management (OCM) is widely used as a means of meeting organizational staffing needs in a planned way, and providing the career development and support that many employees seek or even expect from their employer. The balance between these two broad goals varies between organizations. It is important that OCM policies reflect the organization's current and future needs, and are not a relic of the past and/or of the prejudices of senior management. There are many different OCM practices that organizations can use to implement their policies, including mentoring schemes, career workshops, succession planning and personal development plans. In general, it is better to do a small number of them thoroughly than a lot of them sketchily. All the metaphors of career are reflected in OCM, but the resource metaphor is most prevalent due to the frequent emphasis in OCM on the optimal deployment of employees to achieve organizational goals. OCM tends to be most effective when it facilitates career self-management (CSM), and individual career actors can help this to happen by thinking carefully about how they can harness an organization's OCM practices to meet their personal goals. OCM practices usually require careful design and implementation, and often have 'ripple effects' through the organization which mean it is important to ensure that all stakeholders are committed to them.

> ## Key Points in this Chapter
>
> - Organizational career management (OCM) is a set of policies and practices designed to influence the career development of employees in such a way that both organizational and personal goals are met.
> - The nature and prevalence of OCM policies and practices in an organization depend partly on the organization's history and current economic position. Important dimensions of OCM include whether recruitment to post-entry positions tends to be internal or external, whether the organization prioritizes medium-term development over immediate productivity, and whether progression in the organization is an open contest or depends on sponsorship by senior members.
> - A wide variety of OCM practices is available (see Table 14.1). It is important that the purposes of those used by an organization are clearly defined and that they support the organization's career policies.
> - Many OCM practices position the employee as a resource (see Chapter 10), and there is a temptation to move them around like chess pieces, regardless of their wishes for themselves. However, this risks alienating employees. Keeping in mind other career metaphors such as fit, relationships and roles helps to ensure that the employee perspective is also reflected in OCM practices.
> - OCM practices are fairly widely used in organizations. However, some of them tend to be reserved for employees identified as high potential. This may make sense in terms of investment of resources, but the demoralizing effects on those who do not have access to the OCM should also be considered.
> - It is often possible for individual career actors to use OCM practices to help meet their own career goals. This may or may not be what the organization's senior managers intend.
> - OCM practices are not automatically successful. They require careful design and planning, and all parties involved need to both understand and feel committed to them.

Questions from this Chapter

General Questions

1. Look again at the opening case study in this chapter. What do you see as the advantages and disadvantages of the facilitative rather than controlling approach to career management taken by Josie's organization?

2. Choose an organization – the one you work for if you have one, or alternatively one you can find information about, for example your university – and discover all you can about its OCM policies and practices. Where does it fit on Sonnenfeld's typology, and does it appear to emphasize contest mobility or sponsored mobility?

3. Consider a hypothetical organization that has employees of a relatively high average age and experience. It plans to continue with its current products but try to expand into new countries. This will require new high level managerial roles, but overall the organization cannot afford to recruit many new senior staff because it has done that over a number of years. Some of those recruits have experience in various parts of the world. Which of the OCM practices in Table 14.1 would you recommend for this organization, and why?

4. If you were responsible for the development centers described in the section 'Pitfalls in Managing OCM, and How to Avoid Them', which of the issues described in points 1 to 10 would you give priority to solving, and why? How might you go about it?

'Live Career Case' Study Questions

1. Ask your career case person what OCM practices (s)he has experienced. What does your case person think were the good and bad features of those practices? Overall, were they beneficial to (i) your case person and (ii) the organization?

2. For which organization did your career case person work the longest? What incentives were there for loyalty to the organization? What were the benefits of the relationship for the case person's career?

Additional Resources

Further Reading

Arnold, J. and Cohen, L. (2013) 'Careers in organizations', in W. B. Walsh, M. L. Savickas & P. J. Hartung (eds.), *Handbook of Vocational Psychology* (4th edn, pp. 273–304). New York: Routledge.

Baruch, Y. (2004) *Managing Careers*. Harlow: Pearson Education.

Baruch, Y. and Peiperl, M. (2000) 'Career management practices: An empirical survey and implications', *Human Resource Management*, 39: 347–366.

Clarke, M. (2013) 'The organizational career: Not dead but in need of redefinition', *The International Journal of Human Resource Management*, 24: 684–703.

Inkson, K. (2008) 'Are humans resources?', *Career Development International*, 13(3): 270–279.

Segers, J. and Inceoglu, I. (2012) 'Exploring supportive and developmental career management through business strategies and coaching', *Human Resource Management*, 51(1): 99–120.

References

Abele, A. E. and Wiese, B. S. (2008) 'The nomological network of self-management strategies and career success', *Journal of Occupational and Organizational Psychology*, 81: 733–749.

Adams, J. D., Hayes, B. and Hopson, B. (1976) *Transition: Understanding and managing personal change*. London: Martin Robertson.

Adler, P. S. and Kwon, S. (2002) 'Social capital: Prospects for a new concept', *Academy of Management Review*, 27: 17–40.

Ahlström-Söderling, R. (2003) 'SME strategic business networks seen as learning organizations', *Journal of Small Business and Enterprise Development*, 10: 444–454.

Aime, F., Van Dyne, L. and Petrenko, O. V. (2011) 'Role innovation through employee social networks: The embedded nature of roles and their effect on job satisfaction and career success', *Organizational Psychology Review*, 1: 339–361.

Alach, P. and Inkson, K. (2004) 'The new office temp: Alternative models of contingent labor', *New Zealand Journal of Employment Relations*, 29: 37–52.

Allen, D. G. and Shanock, L. R. (2013) 'Perceived organizational support and embeddedness as key mechanisms connecting socialization tactics to commitment and turnover among new employees', *Journal of Organizational Behavior*, 34: 350–369.

Allen, N. J. and Meyer, J. P. (1990) 'The measurement and antecedents of affective, continuance and normative commitment to the organization', *Journal of Occupational Psychology*, 63: 1–18.

Allen, R. E. (1990) *The Concise Oxford Dictionary* (8th edn). Oxford: Clarendon Press.

Allen, T. D. (2007) 'Mentoring relationships from the perspective of the mentor', in Ragins, B. R. and Kram, K. E. (eds.) *The Handbook of Mentoring at Work: Theory, research, and practice*, pp. 123–147. New York: SAGE.

Altman, Y. (1997) 'The high-potential fast-flying achiever: Themes from the English literature 1976–1995', *Career Development International*, 2: 324–330.

Altman, Y. and Baruch, Y. (2012) 'Global self-initiated expatriate careers: A new era in international assignments?', *Personnel Review*, 41: 233–255.

Amundson, N. E., Parker, P. and Arthur, M. B. (2002) 'Merging two worlds: Linking occupational and organisational career counselling', *Australian Journal of Career Development*, 11: 26–35.

Anderson-Gough, F., Grey, C. and Robson, K. (1998) '"Work hard, play hard": An analysis of organizational cliché in two accountancy practices', *Organization*, 5: 565–592.

Antcliff, V., Saundry, R. and Stuart, M. (2007) 'Networks and social capital in the UK television industry: The weakness of weak ties', *Human Relations*, 60: 371–393.

Anthoney, S. F. and Armstrong, P. I. (2010) 'Individuals and environments: Linking ability and skill ratings with interests', *Journal of Counseling Psychology*, 57: 36–51.

Armstrong, L. (2001) *It's Not About the Bike*. London: Random House.

Armstrong, P. I., Allison, W. and Rounds, J. (2008) 'Development and initial validation of brief public domain RIASEC marker scales', *Journal of Vocational Behavior*, 73: 287–299.

Armstrong, S. J., Allinson, C. W. and Hayes, J. (2002) 'Formal mentoring systems: An examination of the effects of mentor/protégé cognitive styles on the mentoring process', *Journal of Management Studies*, 39: 1111–1137.

Arnold, J. (1997a) *Managing Careers into the 21st Century*. London: SAGE.

Arnold, J. (1997b) 'Nineteen propositions concerning the nature of effective thinking for career management in a turbulent world', *British Journal of Guidance and Counselling*, 25: 447–462.

Arnold, J. (2002) 'Tensions between assessment, grading and development in development centres: A case study', *International Journal of Human Resource Management*, 13: 975–991.

Arnold, J. (2004) 'The congruence problem in John Holland's theory of vocational decisions', *Journal of Occupational and Organizational Psychology*, 77: 95–113.

Arnold, J. and Cohen, L. (2008) 'The psychology of careers in industrial and organizational settings: A critical but appreciative analysis', *International Review of Industrial and Organizational Psychology*, 23: 1–44.

Arnold, J. and Cohen, L. (2013) 'Careers in organizations', in W. B. Walsh, M. L. Savickas and P.J. Hartung (eds.), *Handbook of Vocational Psychology* (4th edn, pp. 273–304). London: Routledge.

Arnold, J. and Johnson, K. (1997) 'Mentoring in early career', *Human Resource Management Journal*, 7: 61–70.

Arnold, J., Loan-Clarke, J., Coombs, C. R., Wilkinson, A. J., Park, J. and Preston, D. (2006) 'How well can the theory of planned behavior account for occupational intentions?', *Journal of Vocational Behavior*, 69: 374–390.

Arnold, J., Randall, R., Patterson, F., Silvester, J., Robertson, I., Cooper, C., et al. (2010) *Work Psychology: Understanding human behaviour in the workplace* (5th edn). Harlow: Pearson.

Arnold, J., Schalk, R., Bosley, S. and Van Overbeek, S. (2002) 'Graduates' experiences of work in small organizations in the UK and the Netherlands: Better than expected', *International Small Business Journal*, 20: 477–497.

Arnulf, J. K., Tegner, L. and Larssen, O. (2010) 'Impression making by résumé layout: Its impact on the probability of being shortlisted', *European Journal of Work and Organizational Psychology*, 19: 221–230.

Arthur, M. B. (2008) 'Examining contemporary careers: A call for interdisciplinary inquiry', *Human Relations*, 61: 163–186.

Arthur, M. B. and Rousseau, D. (1996) *The Boundaryless Career: A new employment principle for a new organizational era*. New York: Oxford University Press.

Arthur, M. B., Claman, P. H. and DeFillippi, R. J. (1995) 'Intelligent enterprise, intelligent careers', *The Academy of Management Executive*, 9: 7–20.

Arthur, M. B., Hall, D. T. and Lawrence, B. S. (1989) *Handbook of Career Theory*. Cambridge: Cambridge University Press.

Arthur, M. B., Inkson, K. and Pringle, J. K. (1999) *The New Careers: Individual action and economic change*. Thousand Oaks, CA: SAGE.

Aryee, S. and Chay, Y. W. (1994) 'An examination of the impact of career-oriented mentoring on work commitment attitudes and career satisfaction among professional and managerial employees', *British Journal of Management*, 5: 241–249.

Aryee, S. and Chen, Z. X. (2004) 'Countering the trend towards careerist orientation in the age of downsizing: Test of a social exchange model', *Journal of Business Research*, 57: 321–328.

Asaba, E. and Jackson, J. (2011) 'Social ideologies embedded in everyday life: A narrative analysis about disability, identities, and occupation', *Journal of Occupational Science*, 18: 139–152.

Ashby, J. and Schoon, I. (2010) 'Career success: The role of teenage career aspirations, ambition value and gender in predicting adult social status and earnings', *Journal of Vocational Behavior*, 77: 350–360.

Ashforth, B. E. and Saks, A. M. (1996) 'Socialization tactics: Longitudinal effects on newcomer adjustments', *Academy of Management Journal*, 39: 149–178.

Ashforth, B. E., Kreiner, G. E. and Fugate, M. (2000) 'All in a day's work: Boundaries and micro role transitions', *Academy of Management Review*, 25: 472–491.

Athanasou, J. A. and Van Esbroeck, R. (2008) *International Handbook of Career Guidance*. Dordrecht: Springer.

Baber, A. and Waymon, L. (2007) *Make Your Contacts Count: Networking know-how for business and career success*. New York: American Management Association.

Bailyn, L. (1993) *Breaking the Mold: Women, men and time in the new corporate world*. New York: Free Press.

Bakan, D. (1966) *The Duality of Human Existence*. Boston: Beacon.

Baltes, B. B. and Dickson, M. W. (2001) 'Using life-span models in industrial-organizational psychology: The theory of selective optimization with compensation', *Applied Developmental Science*, 5: 51–62.

Banai, M. and Harry, W. (2004) 'Boundaryless global careers: The international itinerants', *International Studies of Management and Organization*, 34: 96–120.

Bandura, A. (1986) *Social Foundations of Thought and Action*. Englewood Cliffs, NJ: Prentice Hall.

Barak, A., Feldman, S. and Noy, A. (1991) 'Traditionality of children's interests as related to their parents' gender stereotypes and traditionality of occupations', *Sex Roles*, 26: 511–524.

Bardick, A. D., Bernes, K. B., Magnusson, K. C. and Witko, K. D. (2005) 'Parents' perceptions of their role in children's career planning', *Guidance & Counselling*, 20: 152–157.

Barley, S. R. (1989) 'Careers, identities and institutions: The legacy of the Chicago school of sociology', in M. B. Arthur, D. T. Hall & B. Lawrence (eds.), *Handbook of Career Theory* (pp. 41–65). Cambridge: Cambridge University Press.

Barney, J. (1991) 'Firm resources and sustained competitive advantage', *Journal of Management*, 17: 99–120.

Barney, J. B. and Clark, D. N. (2007) *Resource-based Theory: Creating and sustaining competitive advantage*. Oxford: Oxford University Press.

Barney, J. B., Ketchen, D. J. and Wright, M. (2011) 'The future of resource-based theory revitalization or decline?', *Journal of Management*, 37: 1299–1315.

Bartlett, C. and Ghoshal, S. (2013) 'Building competitive advantage through people', *Sloan Management Review*, 43: 31–41.

Baruch, Y. (2001) 'Employability: A substitute for loyalty?', *Human Resource Development International*, 4: 543–566.

Baruch, Y. (2004) *Managing Careers: Theory and practice*. Englewood Cliffs, NJ: Prentice Hall.

Baruch, Y. and Peiperl, M. (2000) 'Career management practices: An empirical survey and implications', *Human Resource Management*, 39: 347–366.

Bassot, B. (2012) 'Upholding equality and social justice: A social constructivist perspective on emancipatory career guidance practice', *Australian Journal of Career Development*, 21: 3–13.

Bauer, T. N., Bodner, T., Erdogan, B., Truxillo, D. M. and Tucker, J. S. (2007) 'Newcomer adjustment during organizational socialization: A meta-analytic review of antecedents, outcomes, and methods', *Journal of Applied Psychology*, 92: 707.

Bauman, Z. (1995) *Life in Fragments: Essays in postmodern morality*. Oxford: Blackwell.

Beauregard, T. A. and Henry, L. C. (2009) 'Making the link between work–life balance practices and organizational performance', *Human Resource Management Review*, 19: 9–22.

Becker, B. E., Huselid, M. A. and Beatty, R. W. (2009) *The Differentiated Workforce: Transforming talent into strategic impact*. Boston, MA: Harvard Business School Press.

Beckert, J. and Rossel, J. (2013) 'The price of art: Uncertainty and reputation in the art field', *European Societies*, 15: 178–195.

Beine, M. and Docquier, F. (2001) 'Brain drain and economic growth: Theory and evidence', *Journal of Development Economics*, 64: 275–340.

Bellow, A. (2004) *In Praise of Nepotism*. New York: Anchor.

Bergman, A. and Karlsson, J. C. (2011) 'Three observations on the future of work', *Work, Employment and Society*, 25: 561–568.

Berry, H., Guillén, M. F. and Hendi, A. S. (2014) 'Is there convergence across countries? A spatial approach', *Journal of International Business Studies*, 45: 387–404

Berry, J. W. (2001) 'A psychology of immigration', *Journal of Social Issues*, 57: 615–631.

Bertrand, M. (2013) 'Career, family, and the well-being of college-educated women', *The American Economic Review*, 103: 244–250.

Betz, N. E. (2004) 'Contributions of self-efficacy theory to career counseling: A personal perspective', *The Career Development Quarterly*, 52: 340–353.

Betz, N. E., Fitzgerald, L. F. and Hill, R. E. (1989) 'Trait-factor theories: Traditional cornerstone of career theories', in M. B. Arthur, D. T. Hall & B. S. Lawrence (eds.), *Handbook of Career Theory* (pp. 26–40). Cambridge: Cambridge University Press.

Bimrose, J. and Hearne, L. (2012) 'Resilience and career adaptability', *Journal of Vocational Behavior*, 81: 338–344.

Bimrose, J. and McNair, S. (2011) 'Career support for migrants: Transformation or adaptation?', *Journal of Vocational Behavior*, 78: 325–333.

Binet, A. (1911) 'Nouvelles recherches sur la mesure du niveau intellectuel chez les enfants d'école', [New research on the measurement of the intellectual level of schoolchildren] *L'Année Psychologique*, 17: 145–201.

Bird, A. (1996) 'Careers as repositories of knowledge: Considerations for boundaryless careers', in M. B. Arthur & D. M. Rousseau (eds.), *The Boundaryless Career: A new employment principle for a new organizational era* (pp. 150–168). New York: Oxford University Press.

Bishop, J. D. (2006) 'Moral intuitions versus game theory: A response to Marcus on résumé embellishing', *Journal of Business Ethics*, 67: 181–189.

Bjarnason, T. and Sigurdardottir, T. J. (2003) 'Psychological distress during unemployment and beyond: Social support and material deprivation among youth in six northern European countries', *Social Science & Medicine*, 56: 973–985.

Blair-Loy, M. (2003) *Competing Devotions: Career and family among women executives*. Cambridge, MA: Harvard University Press.

Blanden, J. (2013) 'Cross-country rankings in intergenerational mobility: A comparison of approaches from economics and sociology', *Journal of Economic Surveys*, 27: 38–73.

Blau, P. M. and Duncan, O. D. (1967) *American Occupational Structure*. New York: Wiley.

Blustein, D. L., Kenna, A. C., Murphy, K. A., DeVoy, J. E. and DeWine, D. B. (2005) 'Qualitative research in career development: Exploring the center and margins of discourse about careers and working', *Journal of Career Assessment*, 13: 351–370.

Boje, D. M. (1991) 'The storytelling organization: A study of story performance in an office-supply firm', *Administrative Science Quarterly*, 36: 106–126.

Bolles, R. (2013) *What Color is Your Parachute? A guide for job hunters and career changers*. Berkeley, CA: Tenspeed Press.

Bosley, S., Arnold, J. and Cohen, L. (2007) 'The anatomy of credibility: A conceptual framework of valued career helper attributes', *Journal of Vocational Behavior*, 70: 116–134.

Bosley, S. L., Arnold, J. and Cohen, L. (2009) 'How other people shape our careers: A typology drawn from career narratives', *Human Relations*, 62: 1487–1520.

Bosse, D. A. and Taylor, P. L. (2012) 'The second glass ceiling impedes women entrepreneurs', *Journal of Applied Management and Entrepreneurship,* 17: 52–68.

Bour, N. (2012) *Success at Any Age: The baby boomer's (and Gen Y) guide to becoming an overnight success*. Laguna Niguel, CA: BoomersSuccessGuide.com.

Boxall, P. and Purcell, J. (2003) *Strategy and Human Resource Management*. New York: Palgrave Macmillan.

Boyatzis, R. (1982) *The Competent Manager: A model for effective managers*. New York: John Wiley & Sons.

Boyatzis, R., McKee, A. and Goleman, D. (2002) 'Reawakening your passion for work', *Harvard Business Review*, 80(4): 86–94.

Bozionelos, N. (2003) 'Intra-organizational network resources: Relation to career success and personality', *International Journal of Organizational Analysis*, 11: 41–66.

Bozionelos, N. (2004) 'Mentoring provided: Relation to mentor's career success, personality, and mentoring received', *Journal of Vocational Behavior*, 64: 24–46.

Bradley, H. and Healy, G. (2008) *Ethnicity and Gender at Work: Inequalities, careers and employment relations*. London: Palgrave Macmillan.

Bratton, V. and Kacmar, K. (2004) 'Extreme careerism: The dark side of impression management', in R. W. Griffin & A. M. O'Leary-Kelly (eds.), *The Dark Side of Organizational Behavior* (pp. 291–308). San Francisco: Jossey-Bass.

Breaugh, J. A. (2008) 'Employee recruitment: Current knowledge and important areas for future research', *Human Resource Management Review*, 18: 103–118.

Bridges, W. (1995) *JobShift: How to prosper in a workplace without jobs*. London: Allen & Unwin.

Bright, J. E. and Pryor, R. G. (2005) 'The chaos theory of careers: A user's guide', *The Career Development Quarterly*, 53: 291–305.

Bright, J. E., Pryor, R. G., Chan, E. W. M. and Rijanto, J. (2009) 'Chance events in career development: Influence, control and multiplicity', *Journal of Vocational Behavior*, 75: 14–25.

Brim, O. G. (1976) 'Theories of the male mid-life crisis', *The Counseling Psychologist*, 6: 2–9.

Briscoe, J. P. and Hall, D. T. (2006) 'The interplay of boundaryless and protean careers: Combinations and implications', *Journal of Vocational Behavior*, 69: 4–18.

Briscoe, J.P., Hall, D.T. and DeMuth, R.L.F. (2006) 'Protean and boundaryless careers: An empirical exploration', *Journal of Vocational Behavior,* 69: 30–47.

Broadbridge, A. (2004) 'It's not what you know, it's who you know', *Journal of Management Development*, 23: 551–562.

Brodock, K. (2012) *9 Ways Students Can Use Social Media to Boost Their Careers*. Available at: http://mashable.com/2012/02/10/students-job-search-social-media/

Brookfield GRS (2012) *Global Relocation Trends Survey*. Woodridge, IL: Brookfield Global Relocation Services (GRS).

Brown, D. (2002) 'The role of work values and cultural values in occupational choice, satisfaction, and success', in D. Brown and Associates (eds.), *Career Choice and Development* (4th edn, pp. 465–509). San Francisco: Jossey-Bass.

Brown, J. S. and Duguid, P. (1991) 'Organizational learning and communities-of-practice: Toward a unified view of working, learning, and innovation', *Organization Science*, 2: 40–57.

Brown, S. D. and Rector, C. C. (2008) 'Conceptualizing and diagnosing problems in vocational decision making', in S. D. Brown and R. W. Lent (eds.), *Handbook of Counselling Psychology* (pp. 392–407). New York: Wiley.

Bujold, C. (2004) 'Constructing career through narrative', *Journal of Vocational Behavior*, 64: 470–484.

Bures, A. L., Henderson, D., Mayfield, J., Mayfield, M. and Worley, J. (2011) 'The effects of spousal support and gender on workers' stress and job satisfaction: A cross national investigation of dual career couples', *Journal of Applied Business Research*, 12: 52–58.

Burke, R. (2001) *Advancing Women's Careers: Research and practice*. Malden, MA: Blackwell.

Burt, R. S. (1992) *Structural Holes*. Cambridge, MA: Harvard University Press.

Buzzanell, P. M. and Goldzwig, S. R. (1991) 'Linear and nonlinear career models: Metaphors, paradigms, and ideologies', *Management Communication Quarterly*, 4: 466–505.

Cable, D. M. and Edwards, J. R. (2004) 'Complementary and supplementary fit: A theoretical and empirical integration', *Journal of Applied Psychology*, 89: 822.

Caers, R. and Castelyns, V. (2011) 'LinkedIn and Facebook in Belgium: The influences and biases of social network sites in recruitment and selection procedures', *Social Science Computer Review*, 29: 437–448.

Calo, T. J. (2008) 'Talent management in the era of the aging workforce: The critical role of knowledge transfer', *Public Personnel Management*, 37, 403–416.

Campbell, B. A., Coff, R. and Kryscynski, D. (2012) 'Rethinking sustained competitive advantage from human capital', *Academy of Management Review*, 37: 376–395.

Campbell, J. (1968) *The Hero with a Thousand Faces*. New York: Bollingen Foundation.

Cappelli, P. (1999) *The New Deal at Work: Managing the market-driven workforce*. Boston, MA: Harvard Business Press.

Cappelli, P. (2008) 'Talent management for the twenty-first century', *Harvard Business Review*, 86: 74.

Cappelli, P., Singh, H., Singh, J. and Useem, M. (2010) 'The India way: lessons for the US', *Academy of Management Perspectives*, 24: 6–24.

Carnegie, D. (1936) *How to Win Friends and Influence People*. New York: Simon and Schuster.

Carpenter, H. (2008) *The Career Maze: Guiding your children towards a successful future*. London: New Holland.

Carr, S. C., Inkson, K. and Thorn, K. (2005) 'Talent flow and global careers: Reinterpreting "brain drain"', *Journal of World Business*, 40: 386–398.

Carter, G. W., Cook, K. W. and Dorsey, D. W. (2009) *Career Paths: Charting Courses to Success for Organizations and Their Employees*. New York: John Wiley & Sons.

Cascio, W. (2012) *Managing Human Resources*. New York: McGraw-Hill.

Cascio, W. F. (1995) *Managing Human Resources: Productivity, quality of life, profits* (4th edn). New York: McGraw-Hill.

Cascio, W. F. (1998) *Managing Human Resources: Productivity, quality of life, profits* (5th edn). New York: McGraw-Hill.

Cascio, W. F. (2003) *Managing Human Resources: Productivity, quality of life, profits* (6th edn). New York: McGraw-Hill.

Casey, C. (1999) '"Come, join our family": Discipline and integration in corporate organizational culture', *Human Relations*, 52: 155–178.

Casillas, A. and Robbins, S. B. (2005) 'Test adaptation and cross-cultural assessment from a business perspective: Issues and recommendations', *International Journal of Testing*, 5: 5–21.

Casper, S. and Murray, F. (2005) 'Careers and clusters: Analyzing the career network dynamic of biotechnology clusters', *Journal of Engineering and Technology Management*, 22: 51–74.

Cattell, J. B. (1890) 'Mental tests and measurements', *Mind*, 15: 373–380.

Cerdin, J.-L. and Le Pagneux, M. (2010) 'Career anchors: A comparison between organization-assigned and self-initiated expatriates', *Thunderbird International Business Review*, 52: 287–299.

Chan, T. W. and Boliver, V. (2013) 'The grandparent effect in social mobility evidence from British birth cohort studies', *American Sociological Review*, 78: 662–678.

Chan, W., Suen, W. and Choi, K. F. (2008) 'Investing in reputation: Strategic choices in career-building', *Journal of Economic Behavior & Organization*, 67: 844–854.

Chang, C. L., Chen, V., Klein, G. and Jiang, J. J. (2010) 'Information system personnel career anchor changes leading to career changes', *European Journal of Information Systems*, 20: 103–117.

Chao, G. T., O'Leary-Kelly, A. M., Wolf, S., Klein, H. J and Gardner, P. D. (1994) 'Organizational socialization: Its content and consequences', *Journal of Applied Psychology*, 79: 730.

Chartered Institute for Personnel and Development (CIPD) (2011) *Managing Careers for Organisational Capability*. London: CIPD.

Chen, C., Huang, Y. and Lee, M. (2011) 'Test of a model linking applicant résumé information and hiring recommendations', *International Journal of Selection and Assessment*, 19: 374–387.

Chen, G., Gully, S. M. and Eden, D. (2001) 'Validation of a new general self-efficacy scale', *Organizational Research Methods*, 4: 62–83.

Chen, Z., Veiga, J. F. and Powell, G. N. (2011) 'A survival analysis of the impact of boundary crossings on managerial career advancement up to midcareer', *Journal of Vocational Behavior*, 79: 230–240.

Chia, R. (1996) 'Metaphors and metaphorization in organizational analysis: Thinking beyond the thinkable', in D. Grant & C. Oswick (eds.), *Metaphor and Organizations* (pp. 127–145). Thousand Oaks, CA: SAGE.

Chiaburu, D. S., Diaz, I. and De Vos, A. (2013) 'Employee alienation: Relationships with careerism and career satisfaction', *Journal of Managerial Psychology*, 28: 4–20.

Chou, K. L. and Cheung, K. C. K. (2013) 'Family-friendly policies in the workplace and their effect on work–life conflicts in Hong Kong', *The International Journal of Human Resource Management*, 24: 3872–3885.

Chuai, X., Preece, D. and Iles, P. (2008) 'Is talent management just "old wine in new bottles"? The case of multinational companies in Beijing', *Management Research News*, 31: 901–911.

Chudzikowski, K. (2012) 'Career transitions and career success in the 'new' career era', *Journal of Vocational Behavior*, 81: 298–306.

Chudzikowski, K., Demel, B., Mayrhofer, W., Briscoe, J.P., Unite, J., Milikić, B.B., et al. (2009) 'Career transitions and their causes: A country-comparative perspective', *Journal of Occupational and Organizational Psychology*, 82: 825–849.

Chun, J. U., Sosik, J. J. and Yun, N. L. (2012) 'A longitudinal study of mentors and protégé outcomes in formal mentoring relationships', *Journal of Vocational Behavior*, 33: 1071–1094.

Clark, M. and Arnold, J. (2008) 'The nature, prevalence and correlates of generativity among men in middle career', *Journal of Vocational Behavior*, 73: 473–484.

Clarke, M. (2013) 'The organizational career: Not dead but in need of redefinition', *The International Journal of Human Resource Management*, 24: 684–703.

Clarke, M. and Patrickson, M. (2008) 'The new covenant of employability', *Employee Relations*, 30: 121–141.

Clegg, C. and Spencer, C. (2007) 'A circular and dynamic model of the process of job design', *Journal of Occupational and Organizational Psychology*, 80: 321–339.

Cochran, L. (1991) *Life-shaping Decisions*. New York: Peter Lang.

Cochran, L. (1997) *Career Counseling: A narrative approach*. Thousand Oaks, CA: SAGE.

Coe, S. (2012) *Running my Life*. London: Hodder & Stoughton.

Cohen, L. and Duberley, J. (2013) 'Constructing careers through narrative and music: An analysis of "Desert Island Discs"', *Journal of Vocational Behavior*, 82: 165–175.

Cohen, L. and Mallon, M. (2001) 'My brilliant career? Using stories as a methodological tool in careers research', *International Studies of Management and Organization*, 31: 48–68.

Cohen, L., Duberley, J. and Mallon, M. (2004) 'Social constructionism in the study of career: Accessing the parts that other approaches cannot reach', *Journal of Vocational Behavior*, 64: 407–422.

Collin, A. (2000) 'Epic and novel: The rhetoric of career', *The Future of Career* (pp. 163–177). Cambridge: Cambridge University Press.

Collings, D. G., Doherty, N., Luethy, M. and Osborn, D. (2011) 'Understanding and supporting the career implications of international assignments', *Journal of Vocational Behavior*, 78: 361–371.

Conklin, A. M., Dahling, J. J. and Garcia, P. (2013) 'Linking affective commitment, career self-efficacy and outcome expectations: A test of social cognitive career theory', *Journal of Career Assessment*, 40: 68–83.

Conway, N. and Briner, R. B. (2009) 'Fifty years of psychological contract research: What do we know and what are the main challenges?', *International Review of Industrial and Organizational Psychology*, 24: 71–131.

Correll, S. J. (2001) 'Gender and the career choice process: The role of biased self-assessments', *American Journal of Sociology*, 106: 1691–1730.

Corsun, D. L. and Costen, W. M. (2001) 'Is the glass ceiling unbreakable? Habitus, fields, and the stalling of women and minorities in management', *Journal of Management Inquiry*, 10: 16–25.

Costa, P. T. and McCrae, R. R. (1992) *NEO PI-R Professional Manual*. Odessa, FL: Psychological Assessment Resources.

Cotter, D. A., Hermsen, J. M., Ovadia, S. and Vanneman, R. (2001) 'The glass ceiling effect', *Social Forces*, 80: 655–681.

Craig, S. (1992) 'Using competencies in career development', in R. Boam & P. Sparrow (eds.), *Designing and Achieving Competency: Competency-based approach to developing people and organizations* (pp. 111–127). Maidenhead: McGraw-Hill.

Cranwell-Ward, J., Bossons, P. and Gover, S. (2004) *Mentoring: A Henley review of best practice*. London: Palgrave Macmillan.

Crites, J. O. (1981) *Career Counseling: Models, methods, and materials*. New York: McGraw-Hill.

Crites, J. and Taber, B. (2002) 'Appraising adults' career capabilities: Ability, interests, and personality', in S. G. Niles (ed.), *Adult Career Development: Concepts, issues and practices* (pp. 121–138). Tulsa, OK: National Career Development Association.

Cross, R. and Parker, A. (2004) *The Hidden Power of Social Networks: Understanding how work really gets done in organizations*. Boston: Harvard Business School Press.

Cullinane, N. and Dundon, T. (2006) 'The psychological contract: A critical review', *International Journal of Management Reviews*, 8: 113–129.

Cushman, P. (2005) 'Let's hear it from the males: Issues facing male primary school teachers', *Teaching and Teacher Education*, 21: 227–240.

D'Addio, A. C. (2007) *Intergenerational Transmission of Disadvantage: Mobility or immobility across generations? A review of the evidence for OECD countries*. Social, Employment and Migration Working Papers, No. 52. Paris: OECD.

D'Allessandro, D. F. (2004) *Career Warfare: Ten rules for building a personal brand and fighting to keep it*. New York: McGraw-Hill.

Dany, F. (2003) '"Free actors" and organizations: Critical remarks about the new career literature, based on French insights', *International Journal of Human Resource Management*, 14: 821–838.

Dany, F., Louvel, S. and Valette, A. (2011) 'Academic careers: The limits of the 'boundaryless approach'and the power of promotion scripts', *Human Relations*, 64: 971–996.

Danziger, N., Rachman-Moore, D. and Valency, R. (2008) 'The construct validity of Schein's career anchors orientation inventory', *Career Development International*, 13: 7–19.

Darcy, M. U. and Tracey, T. J. (2007) 'Circumplex structure of Holland's RIASEC interests across gender and time', *Journal of Counseling Psychology*, 54: 17–31.

Darling, D. C. (2003). *The Networking Survival Guide*. New York: McGraw-Hill.

Davidson, J. C. & Caddell, D. P. (1994) 'Religion and the meaning of work', *Journal of the Scientific Study of Religion*, 33: 135–147.

Davis-Blake, A. and Broschak, J. P. (2009) 'Outsourcing and the changing nature of work', *Annual Review of Sociology*, 35: 321–340.

Davison, H. K., Maraist, C. C. and Bing, M. N. (2011) 'Friend or foe? The promise and pitfalls of using social networking sites for HR decisions', *Journal of Business and Psychology*, 26: 153–159.

Dawis, R. V. (1996) 'The theory of work adjustment and person-environment-correspondence counseling', in D. Brown, L. Brooks & Associates (eds.), *Career Development and Choice* (3rd edn, pp. 75–120). San Francisco: Jossey-Bass.

Dawis, R. V. (2002) 'Person-environment-correspondence theory', in D. Brown and Associates (eds.), *Career Choice and Development* (4th edn, pp. 427–464). San Francisco: Jossey-Bass.

Dawis, R. V. and Lofquist, L. H. (1984) *A Psychological Theory of Work Adjustment: An individual-differences model and its applications*. Minneapolis, MN: University of Minnesota Press.

De Angelis, M. (2010) 'The production of commons and the 'explosion' of the middle class', *Antipode*, 42: 954–977.

De Botton, A. (2004) *Status Anxiety*. New York: Pantheon Books.

De Bruin, A. and Dupuis, A. (2004) 'Work–life balance? Insights from non-standard work', *New Zealand Journal of Employment Relations*, 29: 21–37.

Decary-Hetu, D. and Dupont, B. (2013) 'Reputation in a dark network of online criminals', *Global Crime*, 14: 175–196.

De Cooman, R. and Dries, N. (2012) 'Attracting Generation Y: How work values predict organizational attraction in graduating students in Belgium', in S. L. E. Ng and L. Schweitzer (eds.), *Managing the New Workforce: International perspectives on the millennial generation* (pp. 42–63). Northampton, MA: Edward Elgar.

De Cuyper, N., Van der Heijden, B. I. and De Witte, H. (2011) 'Associations between perceived employability, employee well-being, and its contribution to organizational success: A matter of psychological contracts?', *The International Journal of Human Resource Management*, 22: 1486–1503.

De Janasz, S. C., Sullivan, S. E. and Whiting, V. (2003) 'Mentor networks and career success: Lessons for turbulent times', *The Academy of Management Executive*, 17: 78–91.

De Vos, A. and Dries, N. (2013) 'Applying a talent management lens to career management: The role of human capital composition and continuity', *The International Journal of Human Resource Management*, 24: 1816–1831.

De Vos, A., Buyens, D. and Schalk, R. (2003) 'Psychological contract development during organizational socialization: Adaptation to reality and the role of reciprocity', *Journal of Organizational Behavior*, 24: 537–559.

De Vos, A., Dewettinck, K. and Buyens, D. (2009) 'The professional career on the right track: A study on the interaction between career self-management and organizational career management in explaining employee outcomes', *European Journal of Work and Organizational Psychology*, 18: 55–80.

Deckop, J. R., Cirka, C. C. and Andersson, L. M. (2003) 'Doing unto others: The reciprocity of helping behavior in organizations', *Journal of Business Ethics*, 47: 101–113.

DeFillippi, R. J. and Arthur, M. B. (1996) 'Boundaryless contexts and careers: A competency-based perspective', in M. B. Arthur and D. M. Rousseau (eds.), *The Boundaryless Career: A new employment principle for a new organizational era* (pp. 116–131). New York: Oxford University Press.

DeNisi, A. and Griffin, R. (2013) *HR²*. Independence, KY: Cengage Learning.

Dessler, G. (2011) *Fundamentals of Human Resource Management*. Upper Saddle River, NJ: Pearson Higher Education.

Devine, K., Reay, T., Stainton, L. and Collins-Nakai, R. (2003) 'Downsizing outcomes: Better a victim than a survivor?', *Human Resource Management*, 42: 109–124.

Dick, P. and Hyde, R. (2006) 'Line manager involvement in work–life balance and career development: Can't manage, won't manage?', *British Journal of Guidance & Counselling*, 34: 345–364.

Dickmann, M. and Baruch, Y. (2011) *Global Careers*. London: Routledge.

Dickmann, M. and Doherty, N. (2008) 'Exploring the career capital impact of international assignments within distinct organizational contexts', *British Journal of Management*, 19: 145–161.

Dierdorff, E. C. and Morgeson, F. P. (2007) 'Consensus in work role requirements: The influence of discrete occupational context on role expectations', *Journal of Applied Psychology*, 92: 1228.

Dietrich, J. and Salmela-Aro, K. (2013) 'Parental involvement and adolescents' career goal pursuit during the post-school transition', *Journal of Adolescence*, 36: 121–128.

Dik, B. J. and Duffy, R. D. (2009) 'Calling and vocation at work: Definitions and prospects for research and practice', *The Counseling Psychologist*, 37: 424–450.

Dobrow, S. R. (2012) 'Dynamics of calling: A longitudinal study of musicians', *Journal of Organizational Behavior*, 34: 431–452.

Dobrow, S. R., Chandler, D. V., Murphy, W. M. and Kram, K. E. (2012) 'A review of developmental networks: Incorporating a mutuality perspective', *Journal of Management*, 38: 210–242.

Doherty, N., Richardson, J. and Thorn, K. (2013) 'Self-initiated expatriation, career experiences, processes and outcomes', *Career Development International*, 18: 6–11.

Donkin, R. (2010) *The Future of Work*. London: Palgrave Macmillan.

Donnelly, R. (2008) 'Careers and temporal flexibility in the new economy: An Anglo-Dutch comparison of the organisation of consultancy work', *Human Resource Management Journal*, 18: 197–215.

Donohue, R. (2006) 'Person–environment congruence in relation to career change and career persistence', *Journal of Vocational Behavior*, 68: 504–515.

Dougherty, T. W., Dreher, G. F., Arunachalam, V. and Wilbanks, J. E. (2013) 'Mentor status, occupational context, and protégé career outcomes: Differential returns for males and females', *Journal of Vocational Behavior*, 83: 514–527.

Dries, N. (2011) 'The meaning of career success: Avoiding reification through a closer inspection of historical, cultural, and ideological contexts', *Career Development International*, 16: 364–384.

Dries, N. (2013) 'The psychology of talent management: A review and research agenda', *Human Resource Management Review*, 23: 272–285.

Dries, N., Forrier, A., De Vos, A. and Pepermans, R. (2014) 'Self-perceived employability, organization-rated potential, and the psychological contract', *Journal of Managerial Psychology*, 29: 565–581.

Dries, N., Pepermans, R. and Carlier, O. (2008) 'Career success: Constructing a multidimensional model', *Journal of Vocational Behavior*, 73: 254–267.

Dries, N., Pepermans, R. and De Kerpel, E. (2008) 'Exploring four generations' beliefs about career: Is 'satisfied' the new 'successful'?', *Journal of Managerial Psychology*, 23: 907–928.

Driver, M. J. (1979) 'Career concepts and career management in organizations', in C. L. Cooper (ed.), *Behavioral Problems in Organizations*. Englewood Cliffs, NJ: Prentice Hall.

Drucker, P. (1999) 'Managing oneself', *Harvard Business Review*, 77: 64–74, 185.

Duberley, J. and Cohen, L. (2009) 'Gendering career capital: An investigation into scientific careers', *Journal of Vocational Behavior*, 76: 187–197.

Duberley, J., Cohen, L. and Mallon, M. (2006a) 'Constructing scientific careers: Change, continuity and context', *Organization Studies*, 27: 1131–1151.

Duberley, J., Mallon, M. and Cohen, L. (2006b) 'Exploring career transitions: Accounting for structure and agency', *Personnel Review*, 35: 289–296.

Duffus, L. R. (2004) 'The personal strategic plan: A tool for career planning and advancement', *International Journal of Management*, 21: 144–148.

Dupuis, A., Inkson, K. and McLaren, E. (2005) *Pathways to Employment: A study of the employment-related behaviour of young people in New Zealand*. (Labour Market Dynamics Research Program No. 1). Auckland, New Zealand: Massey University.

Durkheim, E. (1893/1964) *The Division of Labor in Society* (G. Simpson, trans.). London: Free Press of Glencoe. (Original work published 1893.)

Dychtwald, K., Erickson, T. and Morison, B. (2004) 'It's time to retire retirement', *Harvard Business Review*, 82: 48–57.

Earley, P. C., and Ang, S. (2003) *Cultural Intelligence: Individual interactions across cultures*. Stanford, CA: Stanford University Press; Thomas, D. C. and Inkson, K. (2009). *Cultural intelligence: Living and working globally* (2nd. Ed.). San Francisco: Berrett-Koehler.

Ebberwein, C. A., Krieshok, T. S., Ulven, J. C. and Prosser, E. C. (2004) 'Voices in transition: Lessons on career adaptability', *The Career Development Quarterly*, 52: 292–308.

Eby, L. T., Butts, M. and Lockwood, A. (2003) 'Predictors of success in the era of the boundaryless career', *Journal of Organizational Behavior*, 24: 689–708.

Eden, D. (1991) 'Applying impression management to create productive self-fulfilling prophecy at work', in R. A. Giacalone & P. Rosenfeld (eds.), *Applied Impression Management: How image-making affects managerial decisions* (pp. 13–40). Newbury Park, CA: SAGE.

Edwards, J. R., Baglioni, A. and Cooper, C. L. (1990) 'Stress, type-a, coping, and psychological and physical symptoms: A multi-sample test of alternative models', *Human Relations*, 43: 919–956.

Egan, G. (2013) *The Skilled Helper* (10th edn). London: Cengage.

Eggerth, D. E. (2008) 'From theory of work adjustment to person–environment correspondence counseling: Vocational psychology as positive psychology', *Journal of Career Assessment*, 16: 60–74.

El-Sawad, A. (2005) 'Becoming a lifer? Unlocking career through metaphor', *Journal of Occupational and Organizational Psychology*, 78: 23–41.

Enache, M., Sallán, J. M., Simo, P. and Fernandez, V. (2013) 'Organizational commitment within a contemporary career context', *International Journal of Manpower*, 34: 880–898.

Ensher, E. A., Murphy, S. E. and Sullivan, S. E. (2002) 'Boundaryless careers in entertainment: Executive women's experiences', in M. A. Peiperl, M. B. Arthur & N. Anand (eds.), *Career Creativity: Explorations in the re-making of work* (pp. 229–254). Oxford: Oxford University Press.

Enterprise (2013) *I've always wanted to run my own business: My career story.* Available at: www.enterprisealive.ie/connect-with-us/ive-always-wanted-to-run-my-own-business-my-career-story/ (accessed 2 March 2014).

Entwistle, D. R. and Alexander, K. L. (1993) 'Entry into school: The beginning school transition and educational stratification in the United States', *Annual Review of Sociology,* 19: 401–423.

Equality Challenge Unit (2011) *Equality in Higher Education: Statistical report 2011, Part 1, Staff.* London: Equality Challenge Unit.

Erikson, E. H. (1959) 'Identity and the life cycle', *Psychological Issues,* 1: 1–171.

Erikson, R. and Goldthorpe, J. H. (1992) *The Constant Flu: A study of class mobility in industrial societies.* Oxford: Clarendon Press.

European Commission (2010) *More Women in Senior Positions: Key to economic stability and growth.* Luxembourg: Publications Office of the European Union.

European Group for Organization Studies (EGOS) (2008) Call for papers, 24th EGOS Colloquium, Sub-theme 26, Organizations and careers: Interactions and their implications.

Eurostat (2013) *Unemployment statistics.* Available at: http://epp.eurostat.ec.europa.eu/statistics_explained/index.php/Unemployment_statistics (accessed 27 February 2013).

Evans, A. M., Carney, J. S. and Wilkinson, M. (2013) 'Work–life balance for men: Counseling implications', *Journal of Counseling & Development,* 91: 436–441.

Evans, D. (1995) *Glamour Blondes: From Mae to Madonna.* London: Britannia Press.

Farndale, E., Scullion, H. and Sparrow, P. (2010) 'The role of the corporate HR function in global talent management', *Journal of World Business,* 45: 161–168.

Farr, M. and Shatkin, L. (2009a) *Fifty Best Jobs for Your Personality.* Indianapolis, IN: JIST Publishing.

Farr, M. and Shatkin, L. (2009b) *Best Jobs for the 21st Century.* Indianapolis, IN: JIST Publishing.

Faulconbridge, J. R., Hall, S. and Beaverstock, J. V. (2008) 'New insights into the internationalization of producer services: Organizational strategies and spatial economies for global headhunting firms', *Environment and Planning A,* 40: 210–234.

Featherman, D. L. and Hauser, R. M. (1978) *Opportunity and Change.* New York: Academic Press.

Feldman, D. C. and Beehr, T. A. (2011) 'A three-phase model of retirement decision making', *American Psychologist,* 66: 193–203.

Feldman, D. C. and Lankau, M. J. (2005) 'Executive coaching: A review and agenda for future research', *Journal of Management,* 31: 829–848.

Feldman, D. C. and Ng, T. W. H. (2007) 'Careers, mobility, embeddedness and success', *Journal of Management,* 33: 350–377.

Feldman, D. C. and Weitz, B. A. (1988) 'Career plateaus reconsidered', *Journal of Management,* 14: 69–80.

Feldman, D. C. and Weitz, B. A. (1991) 'From the invisible hand to the gladhand: Understanding a careerist orientation to work', *Human Resource Management,* 30(2): 237–257.

Ference, T. P., Stoner, J. A. and Warren, E. K. (1977) 'Managing the career plateau', *Academy of Management Review,* 2: 602–612.

Finlay, W. and Coverdill, J. E. (2000) 'Risk, opportunism, and structural holes: How headhunters manage clients and earn fees', *Work and Occupations,* 27: 377–405.

Fong, P. S. (2003) 'Knowledge creation in multidisciplinary project teams: An empirical study of the processes and their dynamic interrelationships', *International Journal of Project Management,* 21: 479–486.

Forbes (2010) Networking is still the best way to find a job, survey says. Available at: www.forbes.com/sites/susanadams/2011/06/07/networking-is-still-the-best-way-to-find-a-job-survey-says/

Forret, M. L. and Dougherty, T. W. (2001) 'Correlates of networking behavior for managerial and professional employees', *Group & Organization Management*, 26: 283–311.

Forret, M. L. and Dougherty, T. W. (2004) 'Networking behaviors and career outcomes: Differences for men and women?', *Journal of Organizational Behavior*, 25: 419–437.

Forret, M. L. and Sullivan, S. E. (2002) 'A balanced scorecard approach to networking: A guide to successfully navigating career changes', *Organizational Dynamics*, 31: 245–258.

Forrier, A., Sels, L. and Stynen, D. (2009) 'Career mobility at the intersection between agent and structure: A conceptual model', *Journal of Occupational and Organizational Psychology*, 82: 739–759.

Fournier, S. (1998) 'Consumers and their brands: Developing relationship theory in consumer research', *Journal of Consumer Research*, 24: 343–353.

Francis-Smythe, J., Haase, S., Thomas, E. and Steele, C. (2013) 'Development and validation of the career competencies indicator (CCI)', *Journal of Career Assessment*, 21: 227–248.

Freedman, M. (2007) *Encore: Finding work that matters in the second half of life*. New York: Public Affairs.

Friedman, R., Kane, M. and Cornfield, D. B. (1998) 'Social support and career optimism: Examining the effectiveness of network groups among black managers', *Human Relations*, 51: 1155–1177.

Friedman, S. D. and Greenhaus, J. H. (2001) *Allies or Enemies? How choices about work and family affect the quality of men's and women's lives*. New York: Oxford University Press.

Froclich, K., McKee, G. and Rathge, R. (2011) 'Succession planning in nonprofit organizations', *Nonprofit Management and Leadership*, 22: 3–20.

Fugate, M., Kinicki, A. J. and Ashforth, B. E. (2004) 'Employability: A psycho-social construct, its dimensions, and applications', *Journal of Vocational Behavior*, 65: 14–38.

Furnham, A. (2010) 'Ethics at work: Money, spirituality and happiness', in R. A. Giacalone & C. L. Jurkiewicz (eds.), *Handbook of Workplace Spirituality and Organizational Performance* (pp. 197–215). Armonk, NY: M. E. Sharpe.

Gabriel, Y. (2000) *Storytelling in Organizations: Facts, fictions, and fantasies*. Oxford: Oxford University Press.

Gallos, J. V. (1989) 'Exploring women's development: Implications for career theory, practice, and research', in M. B. Arthur, D. T. Hall & B. S. Lawrence (eds.), *Handbook of Career Theory* (pp. 110–132). Cambridge: Cambridge University Press.

Gardiner, J., Stuart, M., MacKenzie, M., Forde, C., Greenwood, I. and Perrett, R. (2009) 'Redundancy as a critical life event: Moving on from the Welsh steel industry through career change', *Work, Employment and Society*, 23: 727–745.

Gati, I. and Amir, T. (2010) 'Applying a systemic procedure to locate career decision-making difficulties', *The Career Development Quarterly*, 58: 301–320.

Gati, I. and Asulin-Perez, L. (2011) 'Internet-based self-help career assessments and interventions: Challenges and implications of evidence-based career counseling', *Journal of Career Assessment*, 19: 259–273.

Gati, I., Krausz, M. and Osipow, S. H. (1996) 'A taxonomy of difficulties in career decision making', *Journal of Counseling Psychology*, 43: 510–526.

Gerard, J. G. (2012) 'Linked in with LinkedIn: Three exercises that enhance professional social networking and career building', *Journal of Management Education*, 36: 866–897.

Gerber, M., Grote, G., Gelser, C. and Raedler, S. (2012) 'Managing psychological contracts in the era of the 'new' career', *European Journal of Work and Organizational Psychology*, 21: 195–221.

Ghazi, P. and Jones, J. (2004) *Downshifting: The bestselling guide to happier, healthier living*. London: Hodder & Stoughton.

Ghosh, R. and Reio Jr, T. G. (2013) 'Career benefits associated with mentoring for mentors: A meta-analysis', *Journal of Vocational Behavior*, 83: 106–116.

Gibbons, D. E. (2004) 'Friendship and advice networks in the context of changing professional values', *Administrative Science Quarterly*, 49: 238–262.

Gibson, D. (2012) *You Can Do Anything: Three simple steps to success for graduates*. Lynbrook Landing, VA: Youth Council for Development Alternatives.

Gibson, D. E. (2004a) 'Role models in career development: New directions for theory and research', *Journal of Vocational Behavior*, 65: 134–156.

Gibson, P. (2004b) 'Where to from here? A narrative approach to career counseling', *Career Development International*, 9: 176–189.

Gilbert, C., De Winne, S. and Sels, L. (2011) 'The influence of line managers and HR department on employees' affective commitment', *The International Journal of Human Resource Management*, 22: 1618–1637.

Gilligan, C. (1982) *In a Different Voice: Psychological theory and women's development*. Cambridge, MA: Harvard University Press.

Ginzberg, E., Ginsburg, S., Axelrad, S. and Herma, J. (1951) *Occupational Choice: An approach to a general theory*. New York: Columbia University Press.

Girodo, M., Deck, T. and Morrison, M. (2002) 'Dissociative-type identity disturbances in undercover agents: Socio-cognitive factors behind false-identity appearances and reenactments', *Social Behavior and Personality: An International Journal*, 30: 631–643.

Goffee, R. and Scase, R. (1992) 'Organizational change and the corporate career: The restructuring of managers' job aspirations', *Human Relations*, 45: 363–385.

Goldthorpe, J. H. (2013) 'Understanding – and misunderstanding – social mobility in Britain: The entry of the economists, the confusion of politicians and the limits of educational policy', *Journal of Social Policy*, 42: 431–450.

Goldthorpe, J. H., Lewellyn, C. and Payne, C. (1980) *Social Mobility and Class Structure in Modern Britain*. Oxford: Clarendon Press.

Goodale, J. G. and Hall, D. T. (1976) 'Inheriting a career: The influence of sex, values, and parents', *Journal of Vocational Behavior*, 8: 19–30.

Gottfredson, G. D. (1999) 'John L. Holland's contributions to vocational psychology: A review and an assessment', *Journal of Vocational Behavior*, 55: 74–85.

Gottfredson, G. D. and Holland, J. L. (1991) *The Position Classification Inventory: Professional manual*. Odessa, FL: Psychological Assessment Resources.

Gottfredson, G. D. and Holland, J. L. (eds.). (1996) *Dictionary of Holland Occupational odes*. Odessa, FL: Psychological Assessment Resources.

Gottfredson, L. S. (1981) 'Circumscription and compromise: A developmental theory of occupational aspirations', *Journal of Counseling Psychology*, 28: 545–579.

Gottfredson, L. S. (2002) 'Gottfredson's theory of circumscription, compromise, and self-creation', *Career Choice and Development*, 4: 85–148.

Gottlieb, B. H., Kelloway, E. K. and Barham, E. (1998) *Flexible Work Arrangements*. Chichester: Wiley.

Gouldner, A. W. (1960) 'The norm of reciprocity: A preliminary statement', *American Sociological Review*, 25: 161–178.

Granovetter, M. (1974) *Getting a Job: A study of contacts and careers*. Cambridge, MA: Harvard University Press.

Granovetter, M. (1982) 'The strength of weak ties: A network theory revisited', in P. Marsden & N. Lin (eds.), *Social Structure and Network Analysis* (pp. 105–130). Beverly Hills, CA: SAGE.

Granrose, C. S. and Chua, B. L. (1996) 'Global boundaryless careers: Lessons from Chinese family business', in M. B. Arthur & D. M. Rousseau (eds.), *The Boundaryless Career: A new employment principle for a new organizational era* (pp. 201–217) New York: Oxford University Press.

Grant, A.M. and Wade-Benzoni, K.A. (2009) 'The hot and cool of death awareness at work: Mortality cues, aging, and self-protective and prosocial motivations', *Academy of Management Review,* 34: 600–622.

Gratton, L. R. (2010) 'The future of work', *Business Strategy Review,* 21(3): 16–23.

Greenbank, P. (2011) '"I'd rather talk to someone I know than somebody who knows": The role of networks in undergraduate career decision-making', *Research in Post-Compulsory Education,* 16: 31–45.

Greenberg, J. and Colquitt, J. A. (eds.) (2013) *Handbook of Organizational Justice.* Hove: Psychology Press.

Greenblatt, E. (2002) 'Work-life balance: Wisdom or whining?', *Organizational Dynamics,* 32: 177–193.

Greenhaus, J. H. and Beutell, N. J. (1985) 'Sources of conflict between work and family roles', *Academy of Management Review,* 10: 76–88.

Greenhaus, J. H., Callanan, G. A. and Godschalk, V. M. (2010) *Career Management* (4th edn). Thousand Oaks, CA: Sage.

Greer, C. R. and Virick, M. (2008) 'Diverse succession planning: Lessons from the industry leaders', *Human Resource Management,* 47: 351–367.

Greller, M. M. and Stroh, L. K. (2004) 'Making the most of "late-career" for employers and workers themselves: Becoming elders not relics', *Organizational Dynamics,* 33: 202–214.

Grey, C. (1994) 'Career as a project of the self and labour process discipline', *Sociology,* 28: 479–497.

Grose, T. (2005) The mechanics of a career. *ASEE Prism, 14,* 24–29.

Grote, G. and Hall, D. T. (2013) 'Reference groups: A missing link in career studies', *Journal of Vocational Behavior,* 83: 265–279.

Gubler, M., Arnold, J. and Coombs, C. (2013) 'Reassessing the protean career concept: Empirical findings, conceptual components, and measurement', *Journal of Organizational Behavior,* 35: Supplement 1, S23-S40.

Gunz, H. (1989) 'The dual meaning of managerial careers: Organizational and individual levels of analysis', *Journal of Management Studies,* 26: 225–250.

Gunz, H. P. and Heslin, P. A. (2005) 'Reconceptualizing career success', *Journal of Organizational Behavior,* 26: 105–111.

Gunz, H. and Peiperl, M. (2007) *Handbook of Career Studies.* New York: SAGE.

Gunz, H. P., Evans, M. G. and Jalland, R. M. (2002) 'Chalk lines, open borders, glass walls and frontiers: Careers and creativity', in M. B. Arthur, R. Goffee & N. Anand (eds.), *Career Creativity: Explorations in the re-making of work* (pp. 58–76). Oxford: Oxford University Press.

Guo, C., Porshitz, E. T. and Alves, J. (2013) 'Exploring career agency during self-initiated repatriation: A study of Chinese sea turtles', *Career Development International,* 18: 34–55.

Gutteridge, T. G., Leibowitz, Z. B. and Shore, J. E. (1993) *Organizational Career Development.* San Francisco: Jossey-Bass.

Haase, S. (2007) *Applying career competencies in career management.* Doctoral dissertation. Coventry University, in collaboration with the University of Worcester.

Hadas, M. (2013) 'Up the down staircase: Women's upward mobility and the wage penalty for occupational feminization, 1970–2007', *Social Forces,* 91: 1183–1207.

Hakim, C. (1979) *Occupational Segregation.* London: Department of Labour.

Hall, D. T. (1976) *Careers in Organizations.* Pacific Palisades, CA: Goodyear.

Hall, D. T. (2002) *Careers In and Out of Organizations.* Thousand Oaks, CA: SAGE.

Hall, D. T. (2004) 'The protean career: A quarter-century journey', *Journal of Vocational Behavior*, 65: 1–13.

Hall, D. T. and Associates (1996) *The Career is Dead – Long Live the Career: A relational approach to careers*. San Francisco: Jossey-Bass.

Hall, D. T. and Chandler, D. E. (2005) 'Psychological success: When the career is a calling', *Journal of Organizational Behavior*, 26: 155–176.

Hall, D. T. and Las Heras, M. (2009) 'Long live the organisational career', in A. Collin and W. Patton (eds.), *Vocational, Psychological and Organisational Perspectives on Career: Towards a multidisciplinary dialogue* (pp. 181–196) Rotterdam, the Netherlands: Sense Publishers.

Hall, D. T. and Foster, L. W. (1977) 'Psychological success cycle and goal-setting – goals, performance, and attitudes', *Academy of Management Journal,* 20: 282–290.

Hall, D. T. and Las Heras, M. (2010) 'Reintegrating job design and career theory: Creating not just good jobs but smart jobs', *Journal of Organizational Behavior*, 31: 448–462.

Hall, D. T. and Mirvis, P. H. (1996) 'The new protean career: Psychological success and the path with a heart', in D. T. Hall (ed.), *The Career is Dead–Long Live the Career* (pp. 15–45). San Francisco: Jossey-Bass.

Hall, D. T. and Moss, J. E. (1998) 'The new protean career contract: Helping organizations and individuals adapt', *Organizational Dynamics*, 26 (3): 22–37.

Hall, D. T. and Yip, J. (2014) 'Career cultures and climates in organizations', in B. Schneider and K. Barbera (eds.), *The Oxford Handbook of Organizational Climate and Culture* (pp. 215–234). Oxford: Oxford University Press.

Hall, L. (2010) "The problem that won't go away': Femininity, motherhood and science', *Women's Studies Journal*, 24: 14–30.

Hallberg, U. E., Johansson, G. and Schaufeli, W. B. (2007) 'Type A behavior and work situation: Associations with burnout and work engagement', *Scandinavian Journal of Psychology*, 48:, 135–142.

Hamilton, S. M. and von Treuer, K. (2012) 'An examination of psychological contracts, careerism and ITL', *Career Development International*, 17: 475–494.

Hammond, M. M., Neff, N. L., Farr, J. L., Schwall, A. R. and Zhao, X. (2011) 'Predictors of individual-level innovation at work: A meta-analysis', *Psychology of Aesthetics, Creativity, and the Arts*, 5: 90–105.

Hamptiaux, A., Houssemand, C. and Vrignaud, P. (2013) 'Individual and career adaptability', *Journal of Vocational Behavior*, 83: 130–141.

Handy, C. (1989) *The Age of Unreason*. London: Business Books.

Hannon, K. (2010) *What's Next? Follow your passion and find your dream job*. San Francisco: Chronicle Books.

Hansen, L. S. (2012) 'Integrative life planning (ILP): A holistic theory for career counseling with adults', *Adult Career Development: Concepts, issues and practices* (3rd edn, pp. 59–78). Tulsa, OK: National Career Development Association.

Hantrais, L. and Ackers, P. (2005) 'Women's choices in Europe: Striking the work–life balance', *European Journal of Industrial Relations*, 11: 197–212.

Hardy, D. J. and Walker, R. (2003) 'Temporary but seeking permanence: A study of New Zealand temps', *Leadership and Organizational Development Journal*, 24: 141–152.

Harrington, B. and Hall, D. T. (2007) *Career Management and Work–Life Integration: Using self-assessment to navigate contemporary careers*. Thousand Oaks, CA: SAGE.

Harrison, R. (2006) 'From landlines to cell phones: Negotiating identity positions in new career contexts', *Journal of Employment Counseling*, 43: 18–30.

Hartung, P. J. (2010) 'Practice and research in career counseling and development – 2009', *The Career Development Quarterly*, 59: 98–142.

Hartung, P. J. (2013) 'Careers as story: Making the narrative turn', in W. B. Walsh, M. L. Savickas, & P. J. Hartung (eds.), *Handbook of Vocational Psychology: Theory, research, and practice* (4th edn, pp. 33–52). Mahweh, NJ: Lawrence Erlbaum Associates.

Hartung, P. J., Porfeli, E. J. and Vondracek, F. W. (2005) 'Child vocational development: A review and reconsideration', *Journal of Vocational Behavior*, 66: 385–419.

Hartung, P. J., Porfeli, E. J. and Vondracek, F. W. (2008) 'Career adaptability in childhood', *The Career Development Quarterly*, 57: 63–74.

Hartung, P., Savickas, M. L. and Walsh, B. (2014) *APA Handbook of Career Intervention*. Washington, DC: American Psychological Association.

Hassard, J., Morris, J. and McCann, L. (2012) '"My brilliant career"? New organizational forms and changing managerial careers in Japan, the UK, and USA', *Journal of Management Studies*, 49: 571–599.

Hays, J. C. and Williams, J. R. (2011) 'Testing multiple motives in feedback seeking: The interaction of instrumentality and self-protection motives', *Journal of Vocational Behavior*, 79: 496–504.

Headlam-Wells, J., Gosland, J. and Craig, J. (2006) 'Beyond the organisation: The design and management of e-mentoring systems', *International Journal of Information Management*, 26: 372–385.

Heijde, C. M. and Van Der Heijden, B. I. (2006) 'A competence-based and multidimensional operationalization and measurement of employability', *Human Resource Management*, 45: 449–476.

Hennequin, E. (2007) 'What "career success" means to blue-collar workers', *Career Development International*, 12: 565–561.

Hesketh, B. and Griffin, B. (2005) 'Work adjustment', in W. B. Walsh & M. L. Savickas (eds.), *Handbook of Vocational Psychology* (3rd edn, pp. 245–266). New York: SAGE.

Hesketh, B., Griffin, B. and Loh, V. (2011) 'A future-oriented retirement transition adjustment framework', *Journal of Vocational Behavior*, 79: 303–314.

Heslin, P. A. (2003) 'Self-and-other-referent criteria of career success', *Journal of Career Assessment*, 11: 262–286.

Hicks Stiehm, J. (1996) *It's our Military too! Women and the US military*. Philadelphia, PA: Temple University Press.

Higgins, M. C. (2001) 'Changing careers: The effects of social context', *Journal of Organizational Behavior*, 22: 595–618.

Higgins, M. C. and Kram, K. E. (2001) 'Reconceptualizing mentoring at work: A developmental network perspective', *Academy of Management Review*, 26: 264–288.

Hilbrecht, M., Shaw, S. M., Johnson, L. C. and Andrey, J. (2008) '"I'm home for the kids": Contradictory implications for work–life balance of teleworking mothers', *Gender, Work & Organization*, 15: 454–476.

Hill, N. (1960) *Think and Grow Rich*. New York: Random House.

Hirsh, W. and Jackson, C. (2004) *Managing Careers in Large Organisations*. London: The Work Foundation.

Hirsh, W., Jackson, C. and Kidd, J. M. (2001) *Straight Talking: Effective Career Discussions at Work*. Cambridge: National Institute for Careers Education and Counselling.

Hoffman, R. and Casnocha, B. (2012) *The Start-up of You*. New York: Crown Business.

Hofstede, G. (1980) *Culture's Consequences*. Beverly Hills, CA: SAGE.

Hofstede, G. H. (2001) *Culture's Consequences: Comparing values, behaviors, institutions and organizations across nations*. Thousand Oaks, CA: SAGE.

Hogan, R., Chamorro-Premuzik, T. and Kaiser, R. T. (2013) 'Employability and career success: Bridging the gap between theory and reality', *Industrial and Organizational Psychology*, 6: 3–16.

Holland, J. L. (1959) 'A theory of vocational choice', *Journal of Counseling Psychology*, 6: 35–45.

Holland, J. L. (1973) *Making Vocational Choices*. Englewood Cliffs, NJ: Prentice Hall.

Holland, J. L. (1979) *Professional Manual for the Self-directed Search*. Palo Alto, CA: Consulting Psychologists Press.

Holland, J. L. (1985) *Making Vocational Choices* (2nd edn). Englewood Cliffs, NJ: Prentice Hall.

Holland, J. L. (1997) *Making Vocational Choices: A theory of vocational personalities and work environments* (3rd edn). Odessa, FL: Psychological Assessment Resources.

Holland, J. L. and Messer, M. A. (2013) *Self-Directed Search (SDS) Professional Manual* (5th edn). Lutz, FL: PAR.

Homburg, C., Krohmer, H. and Workman Jr, J. P. (2004) 'A strategy implementation perspective of market orientation', *Journal of Business Research*, 57: 1331–1340.

Hopson, B. and Ledger, K. (2010) *And What Do You Do? 10 steps to creating a portfolio career*. London: A&C Black.

Hu, D., Zhao, J. L. and Cheng, J. (2012) 'Reputation management in an open source developer social network: An empirical study on determinants of positive evaluations', *Decision Support Systems*, 53: 526–533.

Huang, X. (2008) 'Guanxi networks and job searches in China's emerging labour market: A qualitative investigation', *Work, Employment & Society*, 22: 467–484.

Huber, S. G. (2013) 'Multiple learning approaches in the development of school leaders: Theoretical perspectives and empirical findings on self-assessment and feedback', *Educational Management Administration and Leadership*, 41: 527–540.

Hughes, D. (2013a) 'An expanded model of careers professional identity: Time for change?', *British Journal of Guidance & Counselling*, 41: 58–68.

Hughes, D. (2013b) 'The changing UK careers landscape: Tidal waves, turbulence and transformation', *British Journal of Guidance & Counselling*, 41: 226–239.

Hughes, E. C. (1937) 'Institutional office and the person', *American Journal of Sociology*, 43: 404–443.

Hughes, E. C. (1958) *Men and Their Work*. Glencoe, IL: Free Press.

Humphrey, J. C. (1999) 'Organizing sexualities, organized inequalities: Lesbians and gay men in public service occupations', *Gender, Work & Organization*, 6: 134–151.

Hunter, J. E. (1986) 'Cognitive ability, cognitive aptitudes, job knowledge, and job performance', *Journal of Vocational Behavior*, 29: 340–362.

Ibarra, H. (1999) 'Provisional selves: Experimenting with image and identity in professional adaptation', *Administrative Science Quarterly*, 44: 764–791.

Ibarra, H. (2002) 'How to stay stuck in the wrong career', *Harvard Business Review*, 80: 40–48.

Ibarra, H. (2004) *Working Identity: Unconventional strategies for reinventing your career*. Cambridge, MA: Harvard Business Press.

Ibarra, H. and Barbulescu, R. (2010) 'Identity as narrative: Prevalence, effectiveness, and consequences of narrative identity work in macro work role transitions', *Academy of Management Review*, 35: 135–154.

Ibarra, H. and Lineback, K. (2005) 'What's your story?', *Harvard Business Review*, 83: 64–71.

Ibarra, H., Carter, N. M. and Silva, C. (2010) 'Why men still get more promotions than women', *Harvard Business Review*, 88: 80–126.

Iles, P. and Mabey, C. (1993) 'Managerial career development programs: Effectiveness, availability and acceptability', *British Journal of Management*, 4: 103–118.

Inglehart, R. F. (1997) *Modernization and Postmodernization: Cultural, economic and political change in 43 societies*. Princeton, NJ: Princeton University Press.

Inkson, K. (2004) 'Images of career: Nine key metaphors', *Journal of Vocational Behavior*, 65: 96–111.

Inkson, K. (2006) 'Protean and boundaryless careers as metaphors', *Journal of Vocational Behavior,* 67: 48–63.

Inkson, K. (2007) *Understanding Careers: The metaphors of working lives* (1st. ed.). Thousand Oaks, CA.: SAGE

Inkson, K. (2008) 'Are humans resources?', *Career Development International*, 13: 270–279.

Inkson, K. (2014) 'Contemporary conceptualizations of career', in P. J. Hartung, M. L. Savickas and W. B. Walsh (eds). *APA Handbook of Career Intervention*, Vol. 1). Washington, DC: American Psychological Association.

Inkson, K. and Amundson, N. E. (2002) 'Career metaphors and their application in theory and counseling practice', *Journal of Employment Counseling*, 39: 98–108.

Inkson, K. and Arthur, M. B. (2001) 'How to be a successful career capitalist', *Organizational Dynamics*, 31: 48–61.

Inkson, K. and King, Z. (2011) 'Contested terrain in careers: A psychological contract model', *Human Relations*, 64: 37–57.

Inkson K. and Myers, B. (2003) '"The big O.E.": International travel and career development', *Career Development International*, 8: 170–181.

Inkson, K., Arthur, M. B., Pringle, J. and Barry, S. (1997) 'Expatriate assignment versus overseas experience: Contrasting models of human resource development', *Journal of World Business*, 32: 351–368.

Inkson, K., Gunz, H., Ganesh, S. and Roper, J. (2012) 'Boundaryless careers: Bringing back boundaries', *Organization Studies*, 33: 323–340.

Inkson, K., Heising, A. and Rousseau, D. M. (2001) 'The interim manager: Prototype of the twenty-first century worker?', *Human Relations*, 54: 259–284.

Inkson, K., Richardson, M. and Houkamau, C. (2013) 'New patterns of late-career employment', in C. Cooper, R. Burke & J. Field (eds.), *The SAGE Handbook of Aging, Work and Society* (pp. 141–156). London: SAGE.

Ishida, H. and Spilerman, S. (2002) 'Models of career advancement in organizations', *European Sociological Review*, 18: 179–198.

Ito, J. K. and Brotheridge, C. M. (2005) 'Does supporting employees' career adaptability lead to commitment, turnover, or both?', *Human Resource Management*, 44: 5–19.

Ituma, A. and Simpson, R. (2009) 'The "boundaryless" career and career boundaries: Applying an institutionalist perspective to ICT workers in the context of Nigeria', *Human Relations,* 62: 727–761.

Johnson, M. K. (2001) 'Change in job values during the transition to adulthood', *Work and Occupations*, 28: 315–345.

Johnson, M. K. and Mortimer, J. T. (2002) 'Career choice and development from a sociological perspective', in D. Brown & Associates (eds.), *Career Choice and Development* (4th edn, pp. 37–81). San Francisco: Jossey-Bass.

Jones, C. (1996) 'Careers in project networks: The case of the film industry', in M. B. Arthur & D. M. Rousseau (eds.), *The Boundaryless Career: A new employment principle for a new organizational era* (pp. 58–75). New York: Oxford University Press.

Jones, C. (2002) 'Signaling: How signals shape careers in creative industries', in M. A. Peiperl, M. B. Arthur & N. Anand (eds). *Career creativity: Explorations in the re-making of work* (pp. 209–228). Oxford, UK: Oxford University Press.

Joseph, B., Boh, W. F., Ang, S. and Slaughter, S. A. (2012) 'The careerpaths (more or less) travelled: A sequence analysis of IT career histories, mobility patterns and career success', *MIS Quarterly*, 36: 427–452.

Judge, T. A. and Cable, D. M. (2004) 'The effect of physical height on workplace success and income: Preliminary test of a theoretical model', *Journal of Applied Psychology*, 89: 428.

Judge, T. A., Cable, D. M., Boudreau, J. W. and Bretz, R. D. (1995) 'An empirical investigation of the predictors of executive career success', *Personnel Psychology*, 48: 485–519.

Kammeyer-Mueller, J. D. and Judge, T. A. (2008) 'A quantitative review of mentoring research: Test of a model', *Journal of Vocational Behavior*, 72: 269–283.

Kanfer, R. and Ackerman, P. L. (2004) 'Aging, adult development, and work motivation', *Academy of Management Review*, 29: 440–458.

Kanfer, R., Wanberg, C. R. and Kantrowitz, T. M. (2001) 'Job search and employment: A personality–motivational analysis and meta-analytic review', *Journal of Applied Psychology*, 86: 837.

Kanter, R. M. (1977) *Men and Women of the Corporation*. New York: Basic Books.

Kanter, R. M. (1989) 'Careers and the wealth of nations: A macro-perspective on the structure and implications of career forms', in M. B. Arthur, D. T. Hall & B. S. Lawrence (eds.), *Handbook of Career Theory* (pp. 506–521). New York: Cambridge University Press.

Kark, R. & van Dijk, D. (2007) 'Motivation to lead, motivation to follow: The role of the self-regulatory focus in leadership behavior', *Academy of Management Review*, 32: 500–528.

Katz, D. and Kahn, R. L. (1978) *The Social Psychology of Organizations*. New York: Wiley.

Kerckhoff, A. C. (1995) 'Institutional arrangements and stratification processes in industrial societies', *Annual Review of Sociology*, 15: 323–347.

Khapova, S. N. and Korotov, K. (2007) 'Dynamics of western career attributes in the Russian context', *Career Development International*, 12: 68–85.

Khapova, S. N., Vinkenburg, C. J. and Arnold, J. (2009) 'Careers research in Europe: Identity and contribution', *Journal of Occupational and Organizational Psychology*, 82: 709–719.

Kidd, J. M. (2006) *Understanding Career Counselling*. London: SAGE.

Kidd, J. M. (2007) 'Career counselling', in H. Gunz & M. Peiperl (eds.), *Handbook of Career Studies* (pp. 97–113). Thousand Oaks, CA: SAGE.

Kidd, J. M. and Killeen, J. (1992) 'Are the effects of careers guidance worth having? Changes in practice and outcomes', *Journal of Occupational and Organizational Psychology*, 65: 219–234.

Kidd, J. M., Hirsh, W. and Jackson, C. (2004) 'Straight talking: The nature of effective career discussion at work', *Journal of Career Development*, 30: 231–245.

Kiessling, T. S. and Simsek, B. (2011) 'International acquisitions: Retention of a target firm's key top personnel for social capital', *International Journal of Human Resources Development and Management*, 11: 167–178.

Killeen, J., White, M. and Watts, A. G. (1992) *The Economic Value of Careers Guidance* (No. 702). London: Policy Studies Institute.

Kim, S. and Feldman, D. C. (2000) 'Working in retirement: The antecedents of bridge employment and its consequences for quality of life in retirement', *Academy of Management Journal*, 43: 1195–1210.

King, Z. (2004) 'Career self-management: Its nature, causes and consequences', *Journal of Vocational Behavior*, 65: 112–133.

Kittrell, D. (1998) 'A comparison of the evolution of men's and women's dreams in Daniel Levinson's theory of adult development', *Journal of Adult Development*, 5: 105–115.

Klasen, N. and Clutterbuck, D. (2002) *Implementing Mentoring Schemes*. Oxford: Elsevier Butterworth-Heinemann.

Klein, H. J. and Weaver, N. A. (2000) 'The effectiveness of an organizational-level orientation training program in the socialization of new hires', *Personnel Psychology*, 53: 47–66.

Koen, J., Klehe, U.-C. and Van Vianen, A. E. M. (2012) 'Training career adaptability to facilitate a successful school-to-work transition', *Journal of Vocational Behavior*, 81: 395–408.

Kohn, M. L. and Schooler, C. (1983) *Work and personality: An inquiry into the impact of social stratification*. Norwood, NJ: Ablex Publishing.

Kooij, D. T., De Lange, A. H., Jansen, P. G., Kanfer, R. and Dikkers, J. S. (2011) 'Age and work-related motives: Results of a meta-analysis', *Journal of Organizational Behavior*, 32: 197–225.

Korte, R. and Lin, S. (2013) 'Getting on board: Organizational socialization and the contribution of social capital', *Human Relations*, 66: 407–428.

Kossek, E. E., Roberts, K., Fisher, S. and DeMarr, B. (1998) 'Career self-management: A quasi-experimental assessment of a training intervention', *Personnel Psychology,* 51: 935–962.

Kraaijenbrink, J., Spender, J. C. and Groen, A. J. (2010) 'The resource-based view: A review and assessment of its critiques', *Journal of Management*, 36: 349–372.

Kracke, B. (2002) 'The role of personality, parents and peers in adolescents' career exploration', *Journal of Adolescence*, 25: 19–30.

Kragh, S. U. (2012) 'The anthropology of nepotism: Social distance and reciprocity in organizations in developing countries', *International Journal of Cross Cultural Management*, 12: 247–265.

Kram, K. E. (1985) *Mentoring at Work: Developmental relationships in organizational life*. Glenview, IL: Scott Foresman.

Krawiec, K. D. (2000) 'Accounting for greed: Unraveling the rogue trader mystery', *Oregon Law Review*, 79: 301–338

Krieshok, T. S., Black, M. D. and McKay, R. A. (2009) 'Career decision making: The limits of rationality and the abundance of non-conscious processes', *Journal of Vocational Behavior*, 75: 275–290.

Kristof-Brown, A. L., Zimmerman, R. D. and Johnson, E. C. (2005) 'Consequences of individuals' fit at work: A meta-analysis of person–job, person–organization, person–group, and person–supervisor fit', *Personnel Psychology*, 58: 281–342.

Krumboltz, J. D. (1965) 'Behavioral counseling: Rationale and research', *The Personnel and Guidance Journal*, 44: 383–387.

Krumboltz, J. D. (1979) 'A social learning theory of career decision making', in A. M. Mitchell, G. B. Jones and J. D. Krumboltz (eds.), *Social Learning and Career Decision Making* (pp. 19–49). Cranston, RI: Carroll.

Krumboltz, J. D. (1991) *Manual for the Career Beliefs Inventory*. Palo Alto, CA: Consulting Psychologists Press.

Krumboltz, J. D. (1993) 'Integrating career and personal counseling', *The Career Development Quarterly*, 42: 143–148.

Krumboltz, J. D. (1994a) 'Improving career development theory from a social learning perspective', in M. L. Savickas and R. W. Lent (eds.), *Convergence in Career Development Theories* (pp. 9–31). Palo Alto, CA: Consulting Psychologists Press.

Krumboltz, J. D. (1994b) 'The career beliefs inventory', *Journal of Counseling & Development*, 72: 424–428.

Krumboltz, J. D. and Henderson, S. J. (2002) 'A learning theory for career counselors', in S. G. Niles (ed.), *Adult Career Development: Concepts, issues and practices* (3rd ed., pp. 41–57). Tulsa, OK: National Career Development Association.

Krzyzanowska, M. and Mascie-Taylor, C. G. N. (2011) 'Intra- and intergenerational social mobility in relation to height, weight and body mass in a British national cohort', *Journal of Biosocial Science*, 43: 611–618.

Kuder, G. F. and Findley, W. G. (1966) 'The occupational interest survey', *The Personnel and Guidance Journal*, 45: 72–77.

Kupperschmidt, B. (2000) 'Multi-generation employees: Strategies for effective management', *Health Care Manager*, 19: 65–76.

Lambert, S. J. (2000) 'Added benefits: The link between work–life benefits and organizational citizenship behavior', *Academy of Management Journal*, 43: 801–813.

Larson, L. M. (2012) 'Worklife across the lifespan', in E. M. Altmaier & J. Hansen (eds.), *Oxford Handbook of Counseling Psychology* (pp. 128–178). New York: Oxford University Press.

Larwood, L. and Gutek, B. (1987) *Women's Career Development*. Newbury Park, CA: SAGE.

Laurijssen, I. and Glorieux, I. (2013) 'Career trajectories for women after childbirth: Job quality and work–family balance', *European Sociological Review*, 29: 426–436.

Lawrence, B. S. (2011) 'Who is they? Inquiries into how individuals construe social context', *Human Relations*, 64, 749–773

Leach, J. L. and Chakiris, B. J. (1988) 'The future of jobs, work and careers', *Training and Development Journal*, 42(4): 48–54.

Leary, M. & Kowalski, R. (1990) 'Impression management: A literature review and two-component model', *Psychological Bulletin*, 107: 34–47;

Lee, V. E. and Bryk, A. S. (1989) 'A multilevel model of the social distribution of high school achievement', *Sociology of Education*, 62: 172–192.

Lent, R. W., Brown, S. D. and Hackett, G. (2002) 'Social cognitive career theory', in D. Brown & Associates (eds.), *Career Choice and Development* (4th ed., pp. 255–311). San Francisco: Jossey-Bass.

Lepak, D. P. and Snell, S. A. (1999) 'The human resource architecture: Toward a theory of human capital allocation and development', *Academy of Management Review*, 24: 31–48.

Lepak, D. P. and Snell, S. A. (2002) 'Examining the human resource architecture: The relationships among human capital, employment, and human resource configurations', *Journal of Management*, 28: 517–543.

Leslie, L. M., Park, T.-Y. and Mehng, S. A. (2012) 'Flexible work practices: A source of career premiums or penalties?', *Academy of Management Journal*, 55: 1407–1428.

Levine, K. J. and Hoffner, C. A. (2006) 'Adolescents' conceptions of work: What is learned from different sources during anticipatory socialization?', *Journal of Adolescent Research*, 21: 647–669.

Levinson, D. J. (1986) 'A conception of adult development', *American Psychologist*, 46: 3–13.

Levinson, D. J. (1996) *The Seasons of a Woman's Life*. New York: Knopf.

Levinson, D. J., Darrow, C., Klein, E., Levinson, M. and McKee, B. (1978) *The Seasons of a Man's Life*. New York: Knopf.

Lewis, S. and Arnold, J. (2012) 'Organisational career management in the UK retail buying and merchandising community', *International Journal of Retail & Distribution Management*, 40: 451–470.

Lindenfield, G. and Lindenfield, S. (2010) *Confident Networking for Career Success*. London: Little, Brown.

Lips-Wiersma, M. and Hall, D. T. (2007) 'Organizational career development is not dead: A case study on managing the new career during organizational change', *Journal of Organizational Behavior*, 28: 771–792.

Lucas, K., Liu, M. and Buzzanell, P. M. (2006) 'No limits careers: A critical examination of career discourse in the US and China', *International and Intercultural Communication Annual*, 28: 217–242.

Lyons, S. T., Higgins, C. A. and Duxbury, L. (2010) 'Work values: Development of a new three-dimensional structure based on confirmatory smallest space analysis', *Journal of Organizational Behavior*, 31: 969–1002.

Mabe, P. A. and West, S. G. (1982) 'Validity of self-evaluation of ability: A review and meta-analysis', *Journal of Applied Psychology*, 67: 280–296.

Macky, K., Gardner, D. and Forsyth, S. (2008) 'Generational differences at work: Introduction and overview', *Journal of Managerial Psychology*, 23: 857–861.

Madera, J. M., King, E. B. and Hebl, M. R. (2013) 'Enhancing the effects of sexual orientation diversity training: The effects of setting goals and training mentors on attitudes and behaviors', *Journal of Business and Psychology*, 28: 79–91.

Magnus, G. (2008) *The Age of Aging*. London: Wiley.

Maher, J. (2013) 'Women's care/career changes as connection and resilience: Challenging discourses of breakdown and conflict', *Gender, Work & Organization*, 20: 172–183.

Mahroum, S. (2000) 'Highly skilled globetrotter: Mapping the international migration of human capital', *R & D Management*, 30: 23–31.

Mainiero, L. A. and Sullivan, S. E. (2005) 'Kaleidoscope careers: An alternate explanation for the opt-out revolution', *Academy of Management Executive*, 19: 106–123.

Mallon, M. and Cohen, L. (2001) 'Time for a change? Women's accounts of the move from organizational careers to self-employment', *British Journal of Management*, 12: 217–230.

Mancinelli, S., Mazzanti, M., Piva, N. and Ponti, G. (2010) 'Education, reputation or network? Evidence on migrant workers employability', *The Journal of Socio-Economics*, 39: 64–71.

Mantere, S., Aula, P., Schildt, H. and Vaara, E. (2013) 'Narrative attributions of entrepreneurial failure', *Journal of Business Venturing*, 28: 459–473.

Manz, C. C. and Sims, H. P. (1991) 'SuperLeadership: Beyond the myth of heroic leadership', *Organizational Dynamics*, 19: 18–35.

Marcia, J. E. (1966) 'Development and validation of ego-identity status', *Journal of Personality and Social Psychology*, 3: 551.

Marcoux, A. M. (2006). 'A counterintuitive argument for resume embellishment', *Journal of Business Ethics*, 63: 183–194.

Margolis, J. (2001) *A Brief History of Tomorrow: The future, past and present*. London: Bloomsbury.

Markus, H. and Nurius, P. (1986) 'Possible selves', *American Psychologist*, 41: 954–969.

Marshall, J. (1989) 'Re-visioning career concepts: A feminist invitation', in M. B. Arthur, D. T. Hall and B. S. Lawrence (eds.), *Handbook of Career Theory* (pp. 255–311). Cambridge: Cambridge University Press.

Marshall, J. (1995) *Women Managers Moving Along: Exploring life and career choices*. Cambridge: Cambridge University Press.

Marshall, S. K., Young, R.A., Domene, J. F. and Zaidman-Zait, A. (2008) 'Adolescent possible selves as jointly constructed in parent–adolescent conversations and related activities', *Identity: An International Journal of Theory and Research*, 8: 185–204.

Marx, K. and Engels, F. (1848/1967) *The Communist Manifesto*. Harmondsworth: Penguin. (Original work published 1848.)

Mayo, A. (1991) *Managing Careers: Strategies for organizations*. London: Institute of Personnel Management.

Mayrhofer, W., Iallatchitch, A., Meyer, M., Steyerer, J. Schiffinger, M. and Strunk, G. A. (2004) 'Going beyond the individual: Some potential contributions from a career field and habitus perspective for global career research and practice', *Journal of Management Development*, 9: 870–884.

Mayrhofer, W., Meyer, M., Iellatchitch, A. and Schiffinger, M. (2004) 'Careers and human resource management: A European perspective', *Human Resource Management Review*, 14: 473–498.

McAdams, D. P. (1995) 'What do we know when we know a person?', *Journal of Personality*, 63: 365–396.

McAdams, D. P. and De St Aubin, E. (1992) 'A theory of generativity and its assessment through self-report, behavioral acts, and narrative themes in autobiography', *Journal of Personality and Social Psychology*, 62: 1003–1015.

McArdle, S., Waters, L., Briscoe, J. P. and Hall, D. T. T. (2007) 'Employability during unemployment: Adaptability, career identity and human and social capital', *Journal of Vocational Behavior*, 71: 247–264.

McCann, L., Hassard, J. and Morris, J (2010) 'Restructuring managerial labour in the USA, the UK and Japan: Challenging the salience of 'varieties of capitalism', *British Journal of Industrial Relations*, 48: 347–374.

McCrae, R. R. and Costa Jr, P. T. (2003) *Personality in Adulthood: A five-factor theory perspective*. New York: Guilford Press.

McKay, D. R. (2013) *Transferable Skills: Bringing your skills to a new career*. Available at: http://careerplanning.about.com/od/careerchoicechan/a/transferable.htm (accessed 2 March 2014).

McLeod, C., O'Donohoe, S. and Townley, B. (2009) 'The elephant in the room? Class and creative careers in British advertising agencies', *Human Relations*, 62: 1011–1039.

McLeod, C., O'Donohue, S. and Townley, B. (2011) 'Pot noodles, placement and peer regard: Creative trajectories and communities of practice in the British advertising industry', *British Journal of Management*, 22: 114–131.

McMahon, M. (2007) 'Career counseling and metaphor', in K. Inkson (ed.), *Understanding Careers: The metaphors of working life* (pp. 15–27). Thousand Oaks, CA: SAGE.

McMahon, M. and Patton, W. (2002) 'Using qualitative assessment in career counselling', *International Journal for Educational and Vocational Guidance*, 2: 51–66.

McMahon, M. and Watson, M. (2012) 'Story crafting: Strategies for facilitating narrative career counselling', *International Journal for Educational and Vocational Guidance*, 12: 211–224.

McMahon, M. and Watson, M. (2013) 'Story-telling: Crafting identities', *British Journal of Guidance & Counselling*, 41: 277–286.

McMillan, L. H. W. and O'Driscoll, M. P. (2004) 'Workaholism and health: Implications for organizations', *Journal of Organizational Change Management*, 17: 509–519.

McNulty, Y. and Inkson, K. (2013) 'Managing expatriates: An RoI approach', New York: Business Expert Press.

Meijers, F. and Langelle, R. (2012) 'Narratives at work: The development of career identity', *British Journal of Guidance & Counselling*, 40: 157–176.

Michaels, E. Handfield-Jones, H. and Axelrod, B. (2001) *The War for Talent*. Boston, MA: Harvard Business School Press.

Mignot, P. (2004) 'Metaphor and "career"', *Journal of Vocational Behavior*, 64: 455–469.

Milkie, M. A. and Peltola, P. (1999) 'Playing all the roles: Gender and the work–family balancing act', *Journal of Marriage and the Family*, 476–490.

Miller, A. (1968) *Death of a Salesman*. London: Heinemann Educational.

Miller, M. J. (2007) 'Examining the degree of congruency between a traditional career instrument and an online self-assessment exercise', *Journal of Employment Counseling*, 44: 11–16.

Mirvis, P. H. and Hall, D. T. (1994) 'Psychological success and the boundaryless career', *Journal of Organizational Behavior*, 15: 365–380.

Mitchell, K. (1979) 'A social learning theory of career decision making', in A. M. Mitchell, G. B. Jones and J. D. Krumboltz (eds.), *Social Learning and Career Decision Making* (pp. 19–49). Cranston, RI: Carroll.

Mitchell, K., Levin, S. and Krumboltz, J. D. (1999) 'Planned happenstance: Constructing unexpected career opportunities', *Journal of Counseling & Development*, 77: 115–124.

Mitchell, K. and Krumboltz, J. D. (1996) 'Krumboltz's learning theory of career choice and counseling', in D. Brown and L. Brooks (eds.), *Career Choice and Development* (pp. 233–280). San Francisco: Jossey-Bass.

Money magazine (2013) 'Women CEOs of Fortune 500 companies', Available at: http://money.cnn.com/magazines/fortune/fortune500/womenceos/ (accessed 8 February 2006). Updated statistics available at http://en.wikipedia.org.wiki/List_of_women_CEOs_of_Fortune_500_companies (accessed 19 August 2014).

Mooney, A. (2007) 'Core competence, distinctive competence, and competitive advantage: What is the difference?', *Journal of Education for Business*, 83: 110–115.

Moore, C., Gunz, H. and Hall, D. T. (2007) 'Tracing the historical roots of career theory in management and organization studies', in H. Gunz, and M. Peiperl (eds.), *Handbook of Career Studies* (pp. 39–54). Los Angeles, CA: SAGE.

Morgan, G. (1986) *Images of Organization*. Beverley Hills, CA: SAGE.

Morgan, G., Wood, J. and Nelligan, P. (2013) 'Beyond the vocational fragments: Creative work, precarious labour and the idea of "flexploitation"', *The Economic and Labour Relations Review*, 24: 397–415.

Morgan, R. (2003) *Sisterhood is Forever: The women's anthology for a new millennium*. New York: Washington Square Press.

Motycka, C. A., Rose, R. L., Ried, L. D. and Brazeau, G. (2010) 'Self-assessment in pharmacy and health science education and professional practice', *American Journal of Pharmaceutical Education*, 74(5): 1–7.

Mouw, T. (2003) 'Social capital and finding a job: Do contacts matter?', *American Sociological Review*, 68: 868–898.

Mudrack, P. E. and Naughton, T. J. (2001) 'The assessment of workaholism as behavioral tendencies: Scale development and preliminary empirical testing', *International Journal of Stress Management*, 8: 93–111.

Mulholland, K. (2003) *Class, Gender and the Family Business*. New York: Palgrave Macmillan.

Myers, I. B., McCaulley, M. H. and Most, R. (1985) *Manual: A guide to the development and use of the Myers-Briggs type indicator*. Palo Alto, CA: Consulting Psychologists Press.

Nachbagauer, A. G. and Riedl, G. (2002) 'Effects of concepts of career plateaus on performance, work satisfaction and commitment', *International Journal of Manpower*, 23: 716–733.

Nath, V. (2011) 'Aesthetic and emotional labour through stigma: National identity management and racial abuse in offshored Indian call centres', *Work, Employment & Society*, 25: 709–725.

Nathan, R. and Hill, L. (2006) *Career Counselling*, 2nd edn. London: SAGE.

Nauta, M. M. (2010) 'The development, evolution, and status of Holland's theory of vocational personalities: Reflections and future directions for counseling psychology', *Journal of Counseling Psychology*, 57: 11.

Neapolitan, J. (1980) 'Occupational change in mid-career: An exploratory investigation', *Journal of Vocational Behavior*, 16: 212–225.

Nelson-Jones, R. (2003) *Basic Counselling Skills*. London: SAGE.

Newton, P. M. (1994) 'Daniel Levinson and his theory of adult development: A reminiscence and some clarifications', *Journal of Adult Development*, 1: 135–147.

Ng, J. R. and Earl, J. K. (2008) 'Accuracy in self-assessment: The role of feedback, self-efficacy and goal orientation', *Australian Journal of Career Development*, 17(3): 39–50.

Ng, T. W. and Feldman, D. C. (2008) 'The relationship of age to ten dimensions of job performance', *Journal of Applied Psychology*, 93: 392.

Ng, T. W., Eby, L. T., Sorensen, K. L. and Feldman, D. C. (2005) 'Predictors of objective and subjective career success: A meta-analysis', *Personnel Psychology*, 58: 367–408.

Nicholson, N. (1984) 'A theory of work-role transitions', *Administrative Science Quarterly*, 29: 172–191.

Nicholson, N. and West, M. A. (1988) *Managerial Job Change: Men and women in transition*. Cambridge: Cambridge University Press.

Niesche, R. (2003) 'Power and homosexuality in the teaching workplace', *Social Alternatives*, 22: 43–47.

Nilsson, K. (2012) 'Why work beyond 65? Discourse on the decision to continue working or retire early', *Nordic Journal of Working Life Studies*, 2: 7–28.

Noor, N. M. (2004) 'Work–family conflict, work- and family-role salience, and women's well-being', *The Journal of Social Psychology*, 144: 389–406.

Obodaru, O. (2012) 'The self not taken: How alternative selves develop and how they influence our professional lives', *Academy of Management Review*, 37: 34–57.

O'Brien, D., Zong, L. and Dickinson, H. (2011) 'The reach and influence of social capital for career advancement and firm development: Elite managers and Russia's exit from socialism', *Management and Organization Review*, 7: 303–327.

OECD (2013) *Employment Outlook*. Paris, France: OECD.

Ogbor, J. O. (2000) 'Mythicizing and reification in entrepreneurial discourse: Ideology-critique of entrepreneurial studies', *Journal of Management Studies*, 37: 605–635.

O'Neil, D. A. and Bilimoria, D. (2005) 'Women's career development phases: Idealism, endurance, and reinvention', *Career Development International*, 10: 168–189.

Orbe, M. P., Allen, B. J. and Flores, L. A. (eds.), *International and Intercultural Communication Annual*, Vol. 28 (pp. 217–242). Thousand Oaks, CA: SAGE.

Organization for Economic Co-operation and Development (OECD) (2006) *Live Longer, Work Longer*. Paris: OECD.

Organization for Economic Co-operation and Development (OECD) (2007) *Pensions at a Glance: Public policies across OECD countries*. Paris: OECD.

Ornstein, S. and Isabella, L. (1990) 'Age vs stage models of career attitudes of women: A partial replication and extension', *Journal of Vocational Behavior*, 36: 1–19.

Ortony, A. (1993) *Metaphor and Thought* (2nd edn). Cambridge: Cambridge University Press.

Osland, J. S. (1995) *The Adventure of Working Abroad*. San Francisco: Jossey-Bass.

Owen, J. (2012) *How to Influence and Persuade*. London: Pearson.

Parker, P. and Inkson, K. (1999) 'New forms of career: The challenge to human resource management', *Asia-Pacific Journal of Human Resources*, 37: 67–76.

Parker, P., Arthur, M. B. and Inkson, K. (2004) 'Career communities: A preliminary exploration of member-defined career support structures', *Journal of Organizational Behavior*, 25: 489–514.

Parker, S. C. and Rougier, J. C. (2007) 'The retirement behaviour of the self-employed in Britain', *Applied Economics*, 39: 697–713.

Parsons, F. (1909) *Choosing a Vocation*. Boston: Houghton Mifflin.

Patton, W. and McMahon, M. (1999) *Career Development and Systems Theory: A new relationship*. Pacific Grove, CA: Brooks/Cole.

Patton, W. and McMahon, M. (2006) *Career Development and Systems Theory* (2nd edn). Rotterdam: Sense Publishers.

Peavy, R. V. (1998) *Sociodynamic Counseling: A constructivist perspective*. Victoria, BC, Canada: Trafford.

Peel, S. and Inkson, K. (2004) 'Contracting careers: Choosing between self- and organizational management', *Career Development International*, 9: 542–558.

Peiperl, M. A., Arthur, M. B., Goffee, R. and Morris, T. (2000) *Career Frontiers: New conceptions of working lives*. Oxford: Oxford University Press.

Peplau, L. A. and Fingerhut, A. (2004) 'The paradox of the lesbian worker', *Journal of Social Issues*, 60: 719–735.

Perdrix, S., Stauffer, S., Masdonati, J., Massoudi, K. and Rossier, J. (2012) 'Effectiveness of career counseling: A one-year follow-up', *Journal of Vocational Behavior*, 80: 565–578.

Perlmutter, M. and Hall, E. (1992) *Adult Development and Aging*. New York: Wiley.

Perrewé, P. L., Zellars, K. L., Ferris, G. R., Rossi, A. M., Kacmar, C. J. and Ralston, D. A. (2004) 'Neutralizing job stressors: Political skill as an antidote to the dysfunctional consequences of role conflict', *Academy of Management Journal*, 47: 141–152.

Perrone, K. M., Wright, S. L. and Jackson, V. Z. (2009) 'Traditional and nontraditional gender roles and work–family interface for men and women', *Journal of Career Development*, 36: 8–24.

Perry-Smith, J. E. and Blum, T. C. (2000) 'Work–family human resource bundles and perceived organizational performance', *Academy of Management Journal*, 43: 1107–1117.

Peter, L. J. and Hull, R. (1969) *The Peter Principle: Why things always go wrong*. New York: William Morrow and Co.

Peterson, G. W., Sampson Jr, J. P. and Reardon, R. C. (1991) *Career Development and Services: A cognitive approach*. Pacific Grove, CA: Brooks/Cole Publishing.

Pezzoni, M., Sterzi, V. and Lissone, F. (2012) 'Career progress in centralized academic systems: Social capital and institutions in France and Italy', *Research Policy*, 41: 704–719.

Phillips, S. D. (1997) 'Toward an expanded definition of adaptive decision making', *The Career Development Quarterly*, 45: 275–287.

Plimmer, G. and Schmidt, A. (2007) 'Possible selves and career transition: It's who you want to be, not what you want to do', *New Directions for Adult and Continuing Education*, 61–74.

Ployhart, R. E., Nyberg, A. J., Reilly, G. and Maltarich, M. A. (2014) 'Human capital is dead; Long live human capital resources!', *Journal of Management*, 40: 371–398.

Ployhart, R. E., Van Iddekinge, C. H. and MacKenzie, W. I. (2011) 'Acquiring and developing human capital in service contexts: The interconnectedness of human capital resources', *Academy of Management Journal*, 54: 353–368.

Poehnell, G. and Amundson, N. (2002) 'CareerCraft: Engaging with, energizing, and empowering career creativity', in M. A. Peiperl, M. B. Arthur and N. Anand (eds.), *Career Creativity: Explorations in the re-making of work* (pp. 105–122). New York: Oxford University Press.

Polanyi, M. (1966) *The Tacit Dimension*. London: Routledge and Kegan Paul.

Polkinghorne, D. E. (1988) *Narrative Knowing and the Human Sciences*. Albany, NY: State University of New York Press.

Porfeli, E. J. and Lee, B. (2012) 'Career development during childhood and adolescence', *New Directions for Youth Development*, 2012(134): 11–22.

Porter, M. E. (1985) *Competitive Advantage: Creating and sustaining superior performance*. New York: Free Press.

Posthuma, R. A. and Campion, M. A. (2009) 'Age stereotypes in the workplace: Common stereotypes, moderators, and future research directions', *Journal of Management*, 35: 158–188.

Powell, G. N. and Graves, L. M. (2003) *Women and Men in Management* (3rd edn). Thousand Oaks, CA: SAGE.

Pringle, J. and Mallon, M. (2003) 'Challenges for the boundaryless career odyssey', *International Journal of Human Resource Management*, 14: 839–853.

Proctor & Gamble (2012) 'Diversity and inclusion', P & G annual report. Available at: www.pg.com/en_US/downloads/company/purpose_people/PG_DiversityInclusion_AR_2012.pdf (accessed 18 February 2014).

Pryor, R. G. L. and Bright, J. E. (2009) 'Game as a career metaphor: A chaos theory career counselling application', *British Journal of Guidance & Counselling*, 37: 39–50.

Pugh, S. D., Skarlicki, D. P. and Passell, B. S. (2003) 'After the fall: Layoff victims' trust and cynicism in re-employment', *Journal of Occupational and Organizational Psychology*, 76: 201–212.

Quinn, J. B. (1992) 'The intelligent enterprise a new paradigm', *The Executive*, 6: 48–63.

Ragins, B. R., Cotton, J. L. and Miller, J. S. (2000) 'Marginal mentoring: The effects of type of mentoring, quality of relationship, and program design on work and career attitudes', *Academy of Management Journal*, 43: 1177–1194.

Ragins, B. R. and Kram, K. E. (2007) *The Handbook of Mentoring at Work: Theory, research, and practice*. Thousand Oaks, CA: SAGE.

Ragins, B. R. and Scandura, T. A. (1999) 'Burden or blessing? Expected costs and benefits of being a mentor', *Journal of Organizational Behavior*, 20: 493–509.

Raider, H. J. and Burt, R. S. (1996) 'Boundaryless careers and social capital', in M. B. Arthur and D. M. Rousseau (eds.), *The Boundaryless Career: A new employment principle for a new organizational era* (pp. 187–200). New York: Oxford University Press.

Randazzo, C. (2012) 'Positioning résumés and cover letters as reflective-reflexive process', *Business Communication Quarterly*, 75: 377–391.

Rastetter, D. and Cornelis, D. (2012) 'Networking: Career promoting strategies for women in executive positions', *Gruppendynamik und Organisations Beratung*, 44: 1–4.

Raz, A. E. (2007) 'Communities of practice or communities of coping? Employee compliance among CSRs in Israeli call centres', *The Learning Organization*, 14: 375–387.

Reardon, R. C., Lenz, J., Sampson, J. and Peterson, G. (2012) *Career Development and Planning: A comprehensive approach* (4th edn). Dunuque, IA: Kendall-Hunt.

Rholes, W. S. and Simpson, J. A. (2004) *Adult Attachment: Theory, research and clinical implications*. New York: Guilford.

Ricoeur, P. (1985) *Interpretation Theory: Discourse and the surplus of meaning*. Fort Worth, TX: Texas Christian University Press.

Roberts, L. M., Dutton, J. E., Spreitzer, G., Heaphy, E. D. and Quinn, R. E. (2005) 'Composing the reflected best-self portrait: Building pathways for becoming extraordinary in work organizations', *Academy of Management Review*, 30: 712–736.

Roberts, P. and Newton, P. M. (1987) 'Levinsonian studies of women's adult development', *Psychology and Aging*, 2: 154.

Roborgh, P. and Stacey, B. G. (1987) 'Happiness and radical career change among New Zealanders. *The Journal of Psychology*, 121: 501–514.

Rodrigues, R. A. and Guest, D. (2010) 'Have careers become boundaryless?', *Human Relations*, 63: 1157–1175.

Rodrigues, R., Guest, D. and Budjanovcanin, A. (2013) 'From anchors to orientations: Towards a contemporary theory of career preferences', *Journal of Vocational Behavior*, 82: 142–152.

Roe, A. (1956) *The Psychology of Occupations*. New York: Wiley.

Roese, N. J. and Summerville, A. (2005) 'What we regret most ... and why', *Personality & Social Psychology Bulletin*, 31: 1273–1285.

Rogers, C. R. (1961) *On Becoming a Person*. Boston: Houghton Mifflin.

Roper, J., Ganesh, S. and Inkson, K. (2010) 'Neoliberalism and knowledge interests in boundaryless careers discourse', *Work, Employment and Society*, 24: 661–679.

Rose, D. and Harrison, E. (2007) 'The European Socio-Economic Classification: A new social class schema for comparative European research', *European Societies*, 9: 459–490.

Rosenbaum, J. E. (1989) 'Organizational career systems and employee misperceptions', in M. Arthur, D.T. Hall & B. S. Lawrence (eds.), *Handbook of Career Theory*. Cambridge: Cambridge University Press.

Rosenbaum, J. E. and Miller, S. R. (1996) 'Moving in, up, or out: Tournaments and other institutional signals of career attainments', in M. B. Arthur and D. M. Rousseau (eds.), *The Boundaryless Career: A new employment principle for a new organizational era* (pp. 350–369). New York: Oxford University Press.

Ross, L. (1977) 'The intuitive psychologist and his shortcomings: Distortions in the attribution process', *Advances in Experimental Social Psychology*, 10: 173–220.

Roth, J. A. (1963) *Timetables: Structuring the passage of time in hospital treatment and other careers*. Indianapolis, IN: Bobbs-Merrill.

Rotondo, D. M. and Perrewé, P. L. (2000) 'Coping with a career plateau: An empirical examination of what works and what doesn't', *Journal of Applied Social Psychology*, 30: 2622–2646.

Rounds, J. B. Dawis, R. and Lofquist, L. H. (1987) 'Measurement of person–environment fit and prediction of satisfaction in the theory of work adjustment', *Journal of Vocational Behavior*, 31: 297–318.

Rousseau, D. M. (1995) *Psychological Contracts in Organizations: Understanding written and unwritten agreements*. Thousand Oaks, CA: SAGE.

Rousseau, D. M. (2011) The individual–organization relationship: The psychological contract', in S. Zedeck (ed.), *APA Handbook of Industrial and Organizational Psychology, Vol 3: Maintaining, expanding, and contracting the organization* (pp. 191–220). Washington, DC: American Psychological Association.

Salpeter. M. (2011) *Social Networking for Career Success: Using online tools to create a personal brand*. New York: Learning Express.

Salthouse, T. A. (2010) 'Selective review of cognitive aging', *Journal of the International Neuropsychological Society*, 16: 754–760.

Samuel, L. R. (2012) *The American Dream: A cultural history*. Syracuse, NY: Syracuse University Press.

Sargent, M. (1994) *The New Sociology for Australians*. Melbourne, Australia: Longman Cheshire.

Savickas, M. L. (1992) 'New directions in career assessment', in D. H. Montross and C. J. Shinkman (eds.), *Career Development: Theory and practice* (pp. 336–355) Springfield, IL: Thomas.

Savickas, M. L. (1997) 'Career adaptability: An integrative construct for Life-Span, Life-Space theory', *The Career Development Quarterly*, 45: 247–259.

Savickas, M. L. (2000) 'Renovating the psychology of careers for the twenty-first century', in A. Collin and R. Young (eds.), *The Future of Career* (pp. 53–68). New York: Cambridge University Press.

Savickas, M. L. (2002) 'Career construction: A developmental theory of vocational behavior', *Career Choice and Development* (4th edn, pp. 149–205). San Francisco: Jossey-Bass.

Savickas, M. L. (2004) 'Vocational psychology, overview', in C. Spielberger (ed.), *Encyclopedia of Applied Psychology* (pp. 655–667). Amsterdam: Elsevier.

Savickas, M. L. (2005) 'The theory and practice of career construction', in S. D. Brown and R. W. Lent (eds.), *Career Development and Counseling: Putting theory and research to work* (pp. 42–70). Hoboken, NJ: Wiley.

Savickas, M. L. (2007) 'Occupational choice' in H. Gunz and M. Peiperl (eds.), *Handbook of Career Studies* (pp. 79–96). Thousand Oaks, CA: SAGE.

Savickas, M. L. (2008) 'Helping people choose jobs: A history of the guidance profession', in J. A. Athanasous and R. Van Esbroeck (eds.), *International Handbook of Career Guidance* (pp. 97–113). Dordrecht: Springer.

Savickas, M. L. (2012a) 'Life design: A paradigm for career intervention in the 21st century', *Journal of Counseling and Development*, 90: 13–19.

Savickas, M. L. (2012b) 'Career construction: A developmental theory of vocational behavior', in D. Brown and Associates (eds.), *Career Choice and Development* (4th edn, pp. 149–205). San Francisco: Jossey-Bass.

Savickas, M. L. and Baker, D. B. (2005) 'The history of vocational psychology: Antecedents, origin, and early development', in W. B. Walsh and M. L. Savickas (eds.), *Handbook of Vocational Psychology* (3rd edn, pp. 15–49). Mahwah, NJ: Erlbaum.

Savickas, M. L. and Porfeli, E. J. (2011) 'Revision of the career maturity inventory: The adaptability form', *Journal of Career Assessment*, 19: 355–374.

Savickas, M. L. and Porfeli, E. J. (2012) 'Career adapt-abilities scale: Construction, reliability, and measurement equivalence across 13 countries', *Journal of Vocational Behavior*, 60: 661–673.

Savickas, M. L., Nota, L., Rossier, J., Dauwalder, J., Duarte, M. E. and Guichard, J., et al. (2009) 'Life designing: A paradigm for career construction in the 21st century', *Journal of Vocational Behavior*, 75: 239–250.

Saxenian, A.-L. (1996) 'Beyond boundaries: Open labor markets and learning in Silicon Valley', in M. B. Arthur and D. M. Rousseau (eds.), *The Boundaryless Career: A new employment principle for a new organizational era* (pp. 23–39). New York: Oxford University Press.

Schein, E. H. (1971) 'The individual, the organization and the career: A conceptual scheme', *Journal of Applied Behavioral Science*, 7: 401–426.

Schein, E. H. (1978) *Career Dynamics: Matching individual and organizational needs.* Reading, MA: Addison-Wesley.

Schein, E. H. (1985) *Career Anchors: Discovering your real values.* San Francisco: University Associates.

Schein, E. H. (1993) *Career Anchors: Discovering your real values* (revised edn). London: Pfeiffer.

Schein, E. H. (1996) 'Career anchors revisited: Implications for career development in the 21st century', *Academy of Management Executive*, 10: 80–88.

Schlenker, B. R. (1980) *Impression Management: The self-concept, social identity, and interpersonal relations.* Pacific Grove, CA: Brooks/Cole.

Schmidt, F. L. (2002) 'The role of general cognitive ability and job performance: Why there cannot be a debate', *Human Performance*, 15: 187–210.

Schneider, B. (1987) 'The people make the place', *Personnel Psychology*, 40: 437–453.

Schultheiss, D. E. P. (2008) 'Current status and future agenda for the theory, research, and practice of childhood career development', *The Career Development Quarterly*, 57: 7–24.

Sears, S. J., and Gordon, V. N. (2010) *Building Your Career: A guide to your future* (4th edn). Upper Saddle River, NJ: Pearson Higher Education.

Seeck, H. and Parzefall, M. (2008) 'Employee agency: Challenges and opportunities for psychological contract theory', *Personnel Review*, 37: 473–489.

Segers, J. and Inceoglu, I. (2012) 'Exploring supportive and developmental career management through business strategies and coaching', *Human Resource Management*, 51: 99–120.

Seibert, S. E., Kraimer, M. L., Holtom, B. C. and Pierotti, A. J. (2013) 'Even the best laid plans sometimes go askew: CSM processes, career shocks, and the decision to pursue graduate education', *Journal of Applied Psychology*, 98: 169–182.

Seibert, S. E., Kraimer, M. L. and Crant, J. M. (2001) 'What do proactive people do? A longitudinal model linking proactive personality and career success', *Personnel Psychology*, 54: 845–874.

Sels, L., Van Woensel, A. and Herremans, W. (2008) 'Over rode, oranje en groene lichten in het eindeloopbaanbeleid [about red, orange and green lights in the 'career ending policies']', *Over.Werk. Tijdschrift Van Het Steunpunt WSE*, 1: 8–33.

Senge, P. (1990) *The Fifth Discipline: The art and practice of the learning organization.* New York, NY: Doubleday.

Sennet, R. (1998) *The Corrosion of Character: The personal consequences of work in the new capitalism.* New York: W. W. Norton.

Severy, L. E. (2008) 'Analysis of an online career narrative intervention: "What's my story?"', *The Career Development Quarterly*, 56: 268–273.

Sharf, R. (1992) *Applying Career Development Theory to Counseling,* Pacific Grove, CA: Brooks/Cole.

Shaw, G. B. (1916) *Pygmalion.* New York: Brentano.

Shepard, H. A. (1984) 'On the realization of human potential: The path with a heart', in M. B. Arthur, L. Bailyn, D. J. Levinson, and H. A. Shephard (eds.), *Working with Careers* (pp. 25–46). New York: Graduate School of Business, Columbia University.

Sher, B. (1994) *I Could Do Anything, if I Knew What It Was.* New York: Dell.

Sheridan, A. (2002) 'What you know and who you know: "Successful" women's experiences of accessing board positions', *Career Development International*, 7: 203–210.

Shultz, K. S. and Wang, M. (2011) 'Psychological perspectives on the changing nature of retirement', *American Psychologist*, 66: 170.

Sidani, Y. M. and Thornberry, J. (2013) 'Nepotism in the Arab world: An institutional theory perspective', *Business Ethics Quarterly*, 5: 91–112.

Sims, D. (2002) 'Careers as prospective story telling: A narrative understanding', Paper presented at Sub-Theme 14, the Colloquium of the European Group for Organization Studies. Barcelona, Spain, July.

Sitzmann, T., Ely, K., Brown, K. G. and Bauer, K. (2010) 'Self-assessment of knowledge: A cognitive learning or affective measure', *Academy of Management Learning and Education*, 9: 169–191.

Smart, R. and Peterson, C. (1994) 'Stability versus transition in women's career development: A test of Levinson's theory', *Journal of Vocational Behavior*, 45: 241–260.

Smeeding, T. M., Erikson, R. and Janti, M. (2011) *Persistence, Privilege and Parenting: The comparative study of intergenerational mobility.* New York: Russell SAGE Foundation.

Smith, J. (2011) 'Agency and female teachers' career decisions: A life history study of 40 women', *Educational Management Administration & Leadership*, 39: 7–24.

Snir, R. and Harpaz, I. (2012) 'Beyond workaholism: Towards a general model of heavy work investment', *Human Resource Management Review*, 22: 232–243.

Sommerlund, J. & Boutaiba, S. (2007) 'Borders of "the boundaryless career"', *Journal of Organizational Change Management*, 20: 525–538.

Song, L. J. and Werbel, J. D. (2007) 'Guanxi as impetus? Career exploration in China and the United States', *Career Development International*, 12: 51–67.

Sonnenfeld, J. A. (1989) 'Career system profiles and strategic staffing', in M. B. Arthur, D. T. Hall and B. S. Lawrence (eds.), *Handbook of Career Theory* (pp. 202–224). Cambridge: Cambridge University Press.

Sonnenfeld, J. A. and Peiperl, M. A. (1988) 'Staffing policy as a strategic response: A typology of career systems', *Academy of Management Review*, 13: 588–600.

Sosik, J. J. and Jung, D. I. (2003) 'Impression management strategies and performance in information technology consulting: The role of self-other rating agreement on charismatic leadership', *Management Communication Quarterly*, 17: 233–268.

Spearman, C. (1923) *The Nature of 'Intelligence' and the Principles of Cognition.* London: Macmillan.

Spokane, A. R. and Cruza-Guet, M. C. (2005) 'Holland's theory of vocational personalities in work environments', in S. D. Brown, and R. W. Lent (eds.), *Career Development and Counseling: Putting theory and research to work* (pp. 24–41). New York: Wiley.

Spokane, A. R., Meir, E. I. and Catalano, M. (2000) 'Person–environment congruence and Holland's theory: A review and reconsideration', *Journal of Vocational Behavior*, 57: 137–187.

Stead, G. B. and Bakker, T. M. (2010) 'Discourse analysis in career counseling and development', *The Career Development Quarterly*, 59: 72–86.

Sternberg, R. J. (2000) *Practical Intelligence in Everyday Life*. Cambridge: Cambridge University Press.

Sternberg, R. J., Forsythe, G. B., Hedlund, J., Horvath, J. A., Wagner, R. K., Williams, W. M., et al. (eds.). (2000) *Practical Intelligence in Everyday Life*. Cambridge: Cambridge University Press.

Stevens, A. H. (2005) 'The more things change, the more they remain the same: Trends in long-term employment in the United States, 1969–2002', Working Paper No. 11878. Cambridge, MA: National Bureau of Economic Research.

Stevens, P. (2001) *Portfolio Careerism: Are you ready?* Sydney: Center for Worklife Counseling.

Stevenson, A. and Waite, M. (eds.) (2011) *Concise Oxford English Dictionary*. Book & CD-ROM set. Oxford: Oxford University Press.

Stevenson, R. L. (1907) *Travels with a Donkey in the Cevennes*. London: Chatto & Windus.

Stevenson, S. (2012) 'What your klout score really means', Available at: www.wired.com/business/2012/04/ff_klout/ (accessed 27 February 2014).

Stewart, N. (1947) 'AGTC scores for army personnel grouped by occupation', *Occupations*, 26: 5–41.

Sturges, J. and Guest, D. (2004) 'Working to live or living to work? Work/life balance early in the career', *Human Resource Management Journal*, 14: 5–20.

Sturges, J., Conway, N. and Liefooghe, A. (2010) 'Organizational support, individual attributes, and the practice of career self-management behavior', *Group & Organization Management*, 35: 108–141.

Sturges, J., Conway, N., Guest, D. and Liefooghe, A. (2005) 'Managing the career deal: The psychological contract as a framework for understanding career management, organizational commitment and work behavior', *Journal of Organizational Behavior*, 26: 821–838.

Sullivan, S. E. (1999) 'The changing nature of careers: A review and research agenda', *Journal of Management,* 25: 457–484.

Sullivan, S.E. and Baruch, Y. (2009) 'Advances in career theory and research: A critical review and agenda for future exploration', *Journal of Management*, 35: 1542–1571.

Summerfield, J. and Van Oudtshoorn, L. (1995) *Counselling in the Workplace*. London: Institute of Personnel and Development.

Super, D. E. (1953) 'A theory of vocational development', *American Psychologist*, 8: 185–190.

Super, D. E. (1957) *The Psychology of Careers*. New York: Harper & Row.

Super, D. E. (1980) 'A life-span, life-space approach to career development', *Journal of Vocational Behavior*, 16: 282–298.

Super, D. E. (1985) 'Coming of age in Middletown', *American Psychologist*, 40: 405–414.

Super, D. E. (1990) 'A life-span, life-space approach to career development', in D. Brown, L. Brooks & Associates, *Career Choice and Development* (2nd. ed.), pp. 197–261. San Francisco: Jossey-Bass.

Super, D. E. (1992) 'Toward a comprehensive theory of career development', in D. H. Montross and C. J. Shinkman (eds.), *Career Development: Theory and practice* (pp. 35–64). Springfield, IL: Charles C. Thomas.

Super, D. E. and Nevill, D. D. (eds.). (1985) *The Values Scale*. Palo Alto, CA: Consulting Psychologists Press.

Super, D. E., Savickas, M. L. and Super, C. M. (1996) 'The life-span, life-space approach to careers', in D. Brown, L. Brooks, & Associates (eds.), *Career Choice and Development* (3rd edn, pp. 121–178). San Francisco: Jossey-Bass.

Super, D. E., Thompson, A. S. and Lindeman, R. H. (1988) *Adult Career Concerns Inventory: Manual for research and exploratory use in counseling*. Paul Alto, CA: Consulting Psychologists Press.

Suutari, V. and Brewster, C. (2000) 'Making their own way: International experience through self-initiated foreign assignments', *Journal of World Business*, 35: 417–436.

Suutari, V. and Taka, M. (2004) 'Career anchors of managers with global careers', *Journal of Management Development*, 23: 833–847.

Suvankulov, F., Lau, M. C. K. and Chau, F. H. C. (2012) 'Job search on the internet and its outcome', *Internet Research*, 22: 298–317.

Svejenova, S., Vives, L. and Alvarez, J. L. (2010) 'At the crossroads of agency and communion: Defining the shared career', *Journal of Organizational Behavior*, 31: 707–725.

Swanson, J. L. (1995) 'The process and outcome of career counseling', in W. B. Walsh and S. H. Osipow (eds.), *Handbook of Vocational Psychology: Theory, research, and practice* (pp. 217–259). Mahweh, NJ: Lawrence Erlbaum Associates.

Swanson, J. L. and Fouad, N. A. (1999) *Career Theory and Practice: Learning through case studies*. Thousand Oaks, CA: SAGE.

Tang, M. H. (2013) 'The Lance Armstrong story: Should we find another hero?', *Pediatric Blood & Cancer*, 60: 1071–1072.

Taylor, K. M. and Betz, N. E. (1983) 'Applications of self-efficacy theory to the understanding and treatment of career indecision', *Journal of Vocational Behavior*, 22: 63–81.

Tempest, S., McKinlay, A. and Starkey, K. (2004) 'Careering alone: Careers and social capital in the financial services and television industries', *Human Relations*, 57: 1523–1545.

Tharenou, P. (2005) 'Does mentor support increase women's career advancement more than men's? The differential effects of career and psychosocial support', *Australian Journal of Management*, 30: 77–109.

The *Telegraph* (2013) 'Self-employment hits 20-year high as people try to avoid unemployment, ONS says', Available at: www.telegraph.co.uk/news/uknews/9344366/Self-employment-hits-20-year-high-as-people-try-to-avoid-unemployment-ONS-says.html (accessed 20 July 2013).

Thomas, D. C. (2002) *Essentials of International Management: A cross-cultural perspective*. Thousand Oaks, CA: SAGE.

Thomas, D. C. and Inkson, K. (2007) 'Careers across cultures', in M. Peiperl, & H. Gunz (eds.), *Handbook of Career Studies* (pp. 451–470). Thousand Oaks, CA: SAGE.

Thomas, D. C. and Inkson, K. (2009) *Cultural intelligence: Living and working globally* (2nd. ed.). San Francisco: Berrett-Koehler.

Thomas, D. C., Lazarova, M. B. and Inkson, K. (eds.) (2005) 'Global careers: New phenomenon or new perspectives?', *Journal of World Business*, 40: 349–440.

Tomlinson, J., Muzio, D., Sommerlad, H., Webley, L. and Duff, L. (2013) 'Structure, agency and career strategies of white women and black and minority ethnic individuals in the legal profession', *Human Relations*, 66: 245–269.

Tracey, T. J. and Hopkins, N. (2003) 'Correspondence of interests and abilities with occupational choice', *Journal of Counseling Psychology*, 48: 178–189.

Tracey, T. J. and Rounds, J. (1996) 'The spherical representation of vocational interests', *Journal of Vocational Behavior*, 48: 3–41.

Tranberg, M., Slane, S. and Ekeberg, S. E. (1993) 'The relation between interest congruence and satisfaction: A meta-analysis', *Journal of Vocational Behavior*, 42: 253–264.

Treiman, D. J. (1977) *Occupational Prestige in Comparative Perspective.* New York: Academic Press.

Trevor, C. O. (2001) 'Interactions among actual ease-of-movement determinants and job satisfaction in the prediction of voluntary turnover', *Academy of Management Journal*, 44: 621–638.

Truxillo, D. M., Cadiz, D. M., Rineer, J. R., Zaniboni, S. and Fraccaroli, F. (2012) 'A lifespan perspective on job design: Fitting the job and the worker to promote job satisfaction, engagement, and performance', *Organizational Psychology Review*, 2: 340–360.

Tsabari, O., Tziner, A. and Meir, E. I. (2005) 'Updated meta-analysis on the relationship between congruence and satisfaction', *Journal of Career Assessment*, 13: 216–232.

Tsai, W., Chi, N., Huang, T. and Hsu, A. (2011) 'The effects of applicant resume contents on recruiters' hiring recommendations: The mediating roles of recruiter fit perceptions', *Applied Psychology*, 60: 231–254.

Turner, R. H. (1960) 'Sponsored and contest mobility and the school system', *American Sociological Review*, 855–867.

Tykocinski, O. E., Pittman, T. S. and Tuttle, E. E. (1995) 'Inaction inertia: Foregoing future benefits as a result of an initial failure to act', *Journal of Personality and Social Psychology*, 68: 793–803.

Valcour, M. (2010) 'Career success in times of economic crisis', Paper presented at the Third International Conference on New Work, New Employment, New Careers. Bordeaux, France, May 21.

Valkevaara, T. (2002) 'Exploring the construction of professional expertise in HRD: Analysis of four HR developers' work histories and career stories', *Journal of European Industrial Training*, 26: 183–195.

Van Buren, H. J. (2003) 'Boundaryless careers and employability obligations', *Business Ethics Quarterly*, 13: 131–149.

Van Dam, K. (2004) 'Antecedents and consequences of employability orientation', *European Journal of Work and Organizational Psychology*, 13: 29–51.

Van den Born, A. and Van Witteloostuijn, A. (2013) 'Drivers of freelance career success', *Journal of Organizational Behavior*, 34: 24–46.

Van Emmerik, H., Baugh, S. G. and Euwema, M. C. (2005) 'Who wants to be a mentor? An examination of attitudinal, instrumental, and social motivational components', *Career Development International*, 10: 310–324.

Van Hooft, E. A., Wanberg, C. R. and Van Hoye, G. (2013) 'Moving beyond job search quantity: Towards a conceptualization and self-regulatory framework of job search quality', *Organizational Psychology Review*, 3: 3–40.

Van Hoye, G. (in press) 'Job search behavior as a multidimensional construct: A review of different job search behaviors and sources', In U. C. Klehe and E. A. J. Van Hooft (eds.), *Oxford Handbook of Job Loss and Job Search*. Oxford: Oxford University Press.

Van Hoye, G., Van Hooft, E. A. and Lievens, F. (2009) 'Networking as a job search behaviour: A social network perspective', *Journal of Occupational and Organizational Psychology*, 82: 661–682.

Van Maanen, J. and Schein, E. H. (1979) 'Toward a theory of organizational socialization', *Research in Organizational Behavior*, 1: 209–264.

Van Vianen, A. E., Klehe, U., Koen, J. and Dries, N. (2012) 'Career adapt-abilities scale – Netherlands form: Psychometric properties and relationships to ability, personality, and regulatory focus', *Journal of Vocational Behavior*, 80: 716–724.

Vance, C. M. (2005) 'The quest for building global competence: A taxonomy of self-initiating career path strategies for gaining business experience abroad', *Journal of World Business*, 40: 374–385.

Varma, A., Pichler, S. and Toh, S. M. (2011) 'A performance theory perspective on expatriate success: The role of self-efficacy and motivation', *International Journal of Human Resources Development and Management*, 11: 38–50.

Verbruggen, M. (2013) 'When people don't realize their career decisions: Towards a theory of career inaction', Paper presented at the 29th EGOS Colloquium. Montreal, Canada, July.

Verbruggen, M. and Sels, L. (2010) 'Social-cognitive factors affecting clients' career and life satisfaction after counseling', *Journal of Career Assessment*, 18: 3–15.

Verbruggen, M., Sels, L. and Forrier, A. (2007) 'Unraveling the relationship between organizational career management and the need for external career counseling', *Journal of Vocational Behavior*, 71: 69–83.

Vinkenburg, C. J. and Weber, T. (2012) 'Managerial career patterns: A review of the empirical evidence', *Journal of Vocational Behavior*, 80: 592–607.

Von Cranach M. and Valach L. (1983) 'The social dimension of goal directed action', in H. Tajfel (ed.), *The Social Dimension of Social Psychology* (pp. 285–299). Cambridge: Cambridge University Press.

Wallace, P. (2009) 'Career stories of women professional accountants: Examining the personal narratives of career using Simone de Beauvoir's feminist existentialist philosophy as a theoretical framework', *Qualitative Research in Organizations and Management: An International Journal*, 4: 62–84.

Walsh, W. and Osipow, S. H. (1990) *Career Counseling: Contemporary topics in vocational psychology*. Mahweh, NJ: Lawrence Erlbaum.

Wanberg, C. R., Hough, L. M. and Song, Z. (2002) 'Predictive validity of a multidisciplinary model of reemployment success', *Journal of Applied Psychology*, 87: 1100.

Wang, M. and Shultz, K. S. (2010) 'Employee retirement: A review and recommendations for future investigation', *Journal of Management*, 36: 172–206.

Wang, M., Henkens, K. and Van Solinge, H. (2011) 'Retirement adjustment', *American Psychologist*, 66: 204–213.

Wang, M., Olson, D. A. and Shultz, K. S. (2012) *Mid and Late Career Issues: An Integrative Perspective*. London: Routledge.

Watkins, C. E. and Savickas, M. L. (1990) 'Psychodynamic career counseling', in W. B. Walsh, and S. H. Osipow (eds.), *Career Counseling: Contemporary topics in vocational psychology* (pp. 79–116). Mahweh, NJ: Lawrence Erlbaum.

Watson, M. and McMahon, M. (2005) 'Children's career development: A research review from a learning perspective', *Journal of Vocational Behavior*, 67: 119–132.

Watts, A. G. and Sultana, R. G. (2004) 'Career guidance policies in 37 countries: Contrasts and common themes', *International Journal for Educational and Vocational Guidance*, 4: 105–122.

Weber, M. (1920/1947) *The Theory of Social and Economic Organization* (trans. A. M. Henderson and T. Parsons). New York: Oxford University Press. (Original work published 1920.)

Weber, M. (1922/1978) *Economy and Society: An outline of interpretive sociology* Berkeley: University of California Press. (Original work published 1922.)

Wegge, J., Van Dick, R. and Von Bernstorff, C. (2010) 'Emotional dissonance in call centre work', *Journal of Managerial Psychology*, 25: 596–619.

Wei, L., Liu, J., Chen, Y. and Wu, L. (2010) 'Political skill, supervisor–subordinate guanxi and career prospects in chinese firms', *Journal of Management Studies*, 47: 437–454.

Weick, K. E. (1995) *Sensemaking in Organizations*. Thousand Oaks, CA: SAGE.

Weick, K. E. (1996) Enactment and the boundaryless career: Organizing as we work', in M. B. Arthur and D. M. Rousseau (eds.), *The Boundaryless Career: A new employment principle for a new economic era* (pp. 40–57). New York: Oxford University Press.

Weigl, M., Müller, A., Hornung, S., Zacher, H. and Angerer, P. (2013) 'The moderating effects of job control and selection, optimization, and compensation strategies on the age–work ability relationship', *Journal of Organizational Behavior*, 34: 607–628.

Weiler, S. and Bernasek, A. (2001) 'Dodging the glass ceiling? Networks and the new wave of women entrepreneurs', *The Social Science Journal*, 38: 85–103.

Weiss, B. and Feldman, R. S. (2006) 'Looking good and lying to do it: Deception as an impression management strategy in job interviews', *Journal of Applied Social Psychology*, 36: 1070–1086.

Weiten, W. (2001) *Psychology: Themes and variations* (5th edn). Belmont, CA: Wadsworth/Thomson Learning.

Weldon, E. (2010) 'Managing talent in China', in R. Silzer and B.E. Dowell (eds.), *Strategy-driven Talent Management: A leadership imperative* (pp. 559–614). San Francisco: Jossey-Bass.

Wenger, E. (1998) *Communities of Practice: Learning, meaning, and identity*. New York: Cambridge University Press.

Whiddett, S. and Hollyforde, S. (2003) *A Practical Guide to Competencies: How to enhance individual and organisational performance*. London: CIPD Publishing.

Whiston, S. C. and Oliver, L. W. (2005) 'Career counseling process and outcome', in W. B. Walsh and M. L. Savickas (eds.), *Handbook of Vocational Psychology: Theory, research, and practice* (3rd edn, pp. 155–194). Mahweh, NJ: Lawrence Erlbaum.

Whiston, S. C. and Rose, C. S. (2013) 'Career counseling with emerging adults', in W. B. Walsh, M. L. Savickas and P. J. Hartung (eds.), *Handbook of Vocational Psychology: Theory, research, and practice* (4th edn, pp. 249–272). Mahweh, NJ: Lawrence Erlbaum.

White, M., Hill, S., McGovern, P., Mills, C. and Smeaton, D. (2003) 'High-performance management practices, working hours and work–life balance', *British Journal of Industrial Relations*, 41: 175–195.

Whitener, E. M. (2001) 'Do "high commitment" human resources practices affect employee commitment? A cross-level analysis using hierarchical linear modeling', *Journal of Management*, 27: 515–535.

Wickman, S. A., Daniels, M. H., White, L. J. and Fesmire, S. A. (1999) 'A "primer" in conceptual metaphor for counselors', *Journal of Counseling and Development*, 77: 389–394.

Williams, C. (2003) 'Sky service: The demands of emotional labor in the airline industry', *Gender, Work and Organization*, 10: 513–550.

Wills, J. B. and Brauer, J. R. (2012) 'Have children adapted to their mothers working, or was adaptation unnecessary? Cohort effects and the relationship between maternal employment and child well-being', *Social Science Research*, 41: 425–443.

Wils, L., Wils, T. and Tremblay, M. (2010) 'Toward a career anchor structure: An empirical investigation of engineers', *Relations industrielles/Industrial Relations*, 65: 236–256.

Wilson, F. (1999) 'Genderquake? Did you feel the earth move?', *Organization*, 6: 529–541.

Wilson, S. and Ebert, N. (2013) 'Precarious work: Economic, sociological and political perspectives', *The Economic and Labour Relations Review*, 24: 263–278.

Wilson, W. J. (1981) 'Race, class and public policy', *American Sociologist*, 16: 125–134.

Winter, D. (2010) *Non-stop action*. Available at: http://careersintheory.wordpress.com/2010/10/07/non-stop-action/

Wiseman, R. (2004) *The Luck Factor: The scientific study of the lucky mind*. New York: Random House.

Wolf, N. (1993) *Fire with Fire: New female power and how it will change the twenty-first century*. New York: Random House.

Wong, C., Wong, P. and Peng, K. Z. (2011) 'An exploratory study on the relationship between parents' career interests and the career interests of young adults', *International Journal for Educational and Vocational Guidance*, 11: 39–53.

Wong, J. Y. and Earl, J. K. (2009) 'Towards an integrated model of individual, psychosocial, and organizational predictors of retirement adjustment', *Journal of Vocational Behavior*, 75: 1–13.

Woodruffe, C. (1993) 'What is meant by a competency?', *Leadership & Organization Development Journal*, 14: 29–36.

Wright, C., Nyberg, D. and Grant, D. (2012) '"Hippies on the third floor": Climate change, narrative identity and the micro-politics of corporate environmentalism', *Organization Studies*, 33: 1451–1475.

Wright, P. M. and McMahan, G. C. (2011) 'Exploring human capital: Putting "human" back into strategic human resource management', *Human Resource Management Journal*, 21: 93–104.

Wright, R. (1997) 'Occupational gender in women's and men's occupations', *Qualitative Sociology*, 20: 437–442.

Wrzesniewski, A. and Dutton, J. E. (2001) 'Crafting a job: Revisioning employees as active crafters of their work', *Academy of Management Review*, 26: 179–201.

Yang, S. and Guy, M. E. (2006) 'GenXers versus boomers: Work motivators and management implications', *Public Performance & Management Review*, 29: 267–284.

Yang, W., Stokes, G. S. and Hui, C. H. (2005) 'Cross-cultural validation of Holland's interest structure in Chinese population', *Journal of Vocational Behavior*, 67: 379–396.

Yarnall, J. (1998) 'Line manages as career developers: Rhetoric or reality?', *Personnel Review*, 27: 378–395.

Yost, E. B. and Corbishley, M. A. (1987) *Career Counseling: A psychological approach*. San Francisco: Jossey-Bass.

Young, R. A. and Collin, A. (2004) 'Introduction: Constructivism and social constructionism in the career field', *Journal of Vocational Behavior*, 64: 373–388.

Young, R. A. and Friesen, J. D. (1992) 'The intentions of parents in influencing the career development of their children', *Career Development Quarterly*, 40: 198–207.

Young, R. A. and Valach. L. (2000) 'Reconceptualising career theory and research', in A. Collin, and R. A. Young, *The Future of Career* (pp. 181–196). Cambridge, UK; Cambridge University Press.

Young, R. A. and Valach, L. (2004) 'The construction of career through goal-directed action', *Journal of Vocational Behavior*, 64: 499–514.

Young, R. A. and Valach, L. (2008) 'Action theory: An integrative paradigm for research and evaluation in career', in J. Athanasou and R. Van Esbroeck (eds.), *International Handbook of Career Guidance* (pp. 643–658). Amsterdam: Springer-Science.

Young, R. A., Valach, A. and Collin, A. (2002) 'A contextualist explanation of career', in D. Brown and Associates (ed.), *Career Choice and Development* (4th edn, pp. 206–252). San Francisco: Jossey-Bass.

Young, R. A., Marshall, S. K., Valach, L., Domene, J. F, Graham, M. D. and Zaidman-Zait, A. (2005) 'Transition to adulthood: Action, projects, and counseling', *Journal of Counseling Psychology*, 52: 215–223.

Young, R. A., Marshall, S. K., Valach, L., Domene, J. F., Graham, M. D. and Zaidman-Zait, A. (2011) *Transition to Adulthood: Action, projects, and counseling*. New York: Springer.

Zeitz, G., Blau, G. and Fertig, J. (2008) 'Boundaryless careers and institutional resources', *International Journal of Human Resource Management*, 20: 372–398.

Zhan, Y., Wang, M., Liu, S. and Shultz, K. S. (2009) 'Bridge employment and retirees' health: A longitudinal investigation', *Journal of Occupational Health Psychology*, 14: 374–389.

Zhang, L., Liu, J., Loi, R., Lau, V. P. and Ngo, H. (2010) 'Social capital and career outcomes: A study of Chinese employees', *The International Journal of Human Resource Management*, 21: 1323–1336.

Zikic, J. and Richardson, J. (2007) 'Unlocking the careers of business professionals following job loss: Sensemaking and career exploration of older workers', *Canadian Journal of Administrative Science*, 24: 58–73.

Zytowski, D. G. (1994) 'A super contribution to vocational theory: Work values', *The Career Development Quarterly*, 43: 25–31.

Subject Index

Abilities, 140, 142–143
  tests of, 143
Adult Career Concerns Inventory, 101, 313
Age-stage theories, 89–101
Agency, 68, 114–115, 273
Aging, 11, 102
Aging population, 102
Agricultural economy, 40
Alger, Horatio, 52
American Dream, 52, 54, 66
Armstrong, Lance, 272–273
Attraction-Selection-Attrition (ASA) model, 140
Autonomy at work, 101
Azoff, Donnie, 220

Baby boomers, 47
Belfort, Jason, 220
'Big Five' personality factors, 143
Becoming one's own man (BOOM, Levinson), 95
Blue-collar workers, 55
Boundaries, 174
Boundaryless careers, 18, 43, 174–177, 181, 242
  critique of, 175–177
Bourdieu, Pierre, 38–39
Brain drain, 179
Bridge employment, 108
Bureaucratic careers, 170
Business schools, 18

Calendar cycles, 101–102
Career
  balance, 12
  contexts, see context
  definition of, 12–13, 14–15
  evolving sequence, 15
  focus on employment, 15
  history of, 12–14
  importance, 2, 11
  longevity, 15

Career cont.
  objective versus subjective, 15
  occupations connected with, 2
Career actors, 10
Career adaptability, 91, 122
Career agility, 297
Career anchors, 155–158, 167–168, 178
Career capital, 243–245, 247–248
Career case studies (in this book), 3–4, 4–5, 263–264
Career communities, 226–227
Career competencies, 247–249
Career construction theory, 122–123
Career counseling, 307–318
  accreditation, 308–309
  'cycles' approach, 312–313
  effects, 319
  'fit' approach, 310–312
  history of, 309–310
  metaphor, use of, 315–316
  narrative approach, 313–315
  objectives, 309
  other approaches, 316–318
  process, 317–319
  theories of, 309
Career decision-making, 11–12, 17–18, 115–121, 312
Career development, 17, 19
Career helping, 300–301, 319–327
  counseling style, 321–327
  example, 323–327
  forms of, 320–321
  listening, 321
  roles of, 326–327
Career ideology, 54–56
Career inaction, 131–132
Career interventions, 309
Career management, 19
Career maturity, 124

Name Index